A Village Wedding.

—·:·—

The Vicar of Aylesford & Mrs. Thorndike
wish to invite you to the marriage
of their eldest daughter

Sybil,

with Mr. Lewis Casson,

which will be solemized
in the quaint Old Parish Church of Aylesford,
on December 22nd, at a quarter before 2 o'clock,
and will you come to the Vicarage
directly after the service to meet the
Bride and Bridegroom.

Aylesford Vicarage,
      December, 1908.

Lewis & Sybil

A MEMOIR

John Casson

COLLINS
ST JAMES'S PLACE, LONDON
1972

William Collins Sons & Co Ltd
London · Glasgow · Sydney · Auckland
Toronto · Johannesburg

First published 1972
Reprinted 1974
© John Casson 1972
ISBN 0 00 211488 7
Set in Monotype Perpetua
Made and Printed in Great Britain by
William Collins Sons & Co Ltd Glasgow

CONTENTS

ILLUSTRATIONS

For Patricia
and all old friends
round Walla Burra Crag

PROLOGUE

ON Sunday 22nd December, 1968, we gave a party to celebrate their Diamond Wedding. It was quite a big party as our parties go, for there were something like ninety people in the Holland Park flat that we had been lent by some very dear friends. And on that evening sixty years of marriage, a whole lifetime of theatre, of families and friendships, of travel, of hardships, of holidays, of fun and worry, of joy and frustration, of heaven and hell, of all the whirling kaleidoscope of happenings that make up our lives, seemed to come together into focus for a brief couple of hours between six and eight o'clock. But on this special evening the vividness and contrasts of the patterns had to be multiplied by a hundred because it was the Diamond Wedding Day of Sybil and Lewis. Everybody had very special and personal memories of them, and we all shared what we had with everybody else.

'Don't let's do anything elaborate,' Patricia had said. 'We'll give them champagne to drink, and mince pies to eat because it's Christmas.' And so she made two or three hundred mince pies and I ordered four dozen bottles of champagne, which by all the caterers' guidebooks should have been more than enough for ninety people. In the event we had two bottles left after the party and not a single mince pie. But there were a lot of happy people, happy to be there, proud to know each other and all thrilled to have the chance of giving their love and affection to Sybil and Lewis.

It had been a frantic business deciding whom we would ask to the party. Almost at the beginning we had to arrange for a second party on the following Sunday for relations only. After all we do love our relations but we do like our friends as well, and the relations alone came to nearly a hundred. And so for the day itself we made a rule that only close relations would be asked, children and grandchildren with respective husbands and wives (there were two great-grandchildren, our grandsons, but they and their parents were in Australia). But even so the problem of how to avoid offending anyone, always the greatest and most time-consuming of Casson problems was enormous. We probably did offend a few, but nobody has ever said anything, so they are probably much too nice to bear a grudge and have allowed us to get away with it.

On the day, Sybil and Lewis arrived from their flat in Chelsea at half past five. They were thrilled with the arrangements. We Cassons are nearly always thrilled rather than delighted by what we approve and especially Sybil who held up her hands and said, 'Darlings, you've been splendid. It all looks marvellous, doesn't it Lewis? And are those two gorgeous looking chairs over there for us? Just like thrones and royalty.'

'We thought you'd be better sitting down and let them come to you. After all you've got to say "Hallo" to ninety of them.'

'We don't mind standing, do we Lewis? Oh, and look at the lovely Christmas tree. And Lewis, look what they've rigged up over our chairs. The number 60 in tinsel! And are those comic little doll things sitting on the figures meant to be us? Crumbs!'

As always she enveloped the whole room and everybody in it with her warmth and her energy, while Lewis stood happily beaming behind her. He had been rather dreading the party, feeling that he wouldn't measure up to the image that he thought we had made of him. He never could understand that we loved him as he actually was, rather than as he felt he ought to be. But when we did manage to get them seated, while the rest of us bustled round them putting finishing touches to the room, he forgot to worry about it and changed from a slightly fussed old gentleman into what he really was, the head of the Casson family.

They looked gorgeous sitting there together, joyfully holding hands. 'We went to early service this morning,' said Sybil. 'We wanted to say how thankful we are for our wonderful sixty years, and how lucky we are to have all you darlings round us. Wouldn't it be lovely if everybody forgot to come and we could have a party all to ourselves! Oh, but then we wouldn't see all the other darlings who are coming. Are we having champagne? How delicious. I adore champagne, but don't give me too much or I shall get squiffy. John, we've been absolutely inundated with telegrams. Your dear Anthony and his Janneke and the two darling babies sent us one from Melbourne. I do wish they were here. And, my dears, the flowers! Pat, you'll have to come over and take some of them.

We haven't room to breathe in the flat and Lewis couldn't have a bath this morning. How lovely yours are looking here, darling. I wish I could arrange flowers like you. You must give me lessons some time.'

For a little time before the party began the family did actually have the party to ourselves. This is what Sybil always adores, what I suppose every mother adores, having as many of her family as possible gathered together, as it were, playing at her feet.

But then suddenly the front door bell rang and we all went to action stations. The guests had begun to arrive. Their hats and coats were whipped away from them as they came in and they were asked to sign a vellum scroll specially prepared by Jane so that we could have a complete record of everybody who came. Then we steered them into the throne room and heard the recognition of 'Darling' from Sybil as she made each one feel that he or she was the one above all she had been waiting to see – which in every case was I am sure, absolutely true at the moment of greeting. Soon there was a jostling throng of people, most of whom knew each other, all of whom were lifelong friends of Sybil and Lewis and most of whom brought into my mind pictures of happenings in the life of our family as long as I had known it.

Athene and Beau Hannen were among the first to greet them. They, with Basil Dean, had probably known them longest. Basil Dean knew them even before I did in the Manchester Repertory days before the First World War. Athene and Beau always make me think of Dymchurch on the Kent coast where we all used to go for those long summer holidays of sand castles, picnics and kites.

There was Gladys Cooper into whose dressing-room at the Playhouse I had been taken by Sybil when I was a young naval cadet, overjoyed because I just happened to have a long-since forgotten autograph book in my pocket. Now here she was as beautiful as ever stooping down to pin an enormous diamanté brooch on to Sybil's frock. She had been brought by her daughter and son-in-law, Joan and Robert Morley, and only a few days earlier we had been asked, with Sybil and Lewis, to the party Robert was giving for her eightieth birthday. He had secretly bought up all the seats at St Martin's Theatre, where she was playing in *Out of the Question* with Dulcie Gray and Michael Dennison, and invited about seventy of her and his friends to meet at the Ivy at 8.15 on the night. After a glass or two of champagne we were all led across the road into the theatre and took our places in the stalls. It was all a perfectly normal performance of the play until after about seven minutes, just after Gladys's first appearance, the front door bell rang and Gladys said her line, 'That's probably my grandson, will you let him in?' But when the door opened in walked Robert bearing a huge tray of champagne and wishing her a happy birthday. At first Gladys thought that a normal audience was out front and desperately, as an old pro, could only think of how she was going to get the play going again. Then the lights went up and she saw us laughing and cheering from the stalls, where a few minutes later she joined us and sat down with Sybil and Lewis while photographers went to town. It was then that Patricia overheard a little quiet snatch of dialogue. 'Well, Sybil darling, what about this?' said Gladys. 'Wonderful, darling,' said Sybil, 'but not *entirely* professional, is it?' 'Oh, I know,' answered Gladys, 'but Robert always was an amateur.' And now here they all were again, Sybil, Lewis, Gladys, Robert, Joan and the Dennisons.

Tony Quayle I had known since we were teenagers, when I, as a midshipman, had felt rather superior to a mere actor. I hope I didn't show it, but if I did Tony never seems to have held it against me. His wife Dorothy Hyson, had been the first love of my brother's life when he was 14 and she was 12. In fact it was the first time I had ever seen my brother in the rôle of a rival. But I wasn't in the running, I fear. Jack Hawkins had been the page to the Bastard of Orleans in the first and wonderful production of *Saint Joan* in 1924. It was still playing, then at the Lyceum, at the time of the General Strike in 1926. Jack and my brother and I used to climb up on to the roof of the theatre between shows and watch the blacklegs unloading rolls of paper outside the offices of the old *Morning Post* in the street below us.

In 1941 Patricia had been asked by Lewis to go at once to Cambridge where a small touring repertory company run by Sybil's sister Eileen had come to grief. People hadn't come to see the show, and finally they were all stranded with little or no money and no prospects of getting any. Patricia arrived with Lewis's power of attorney in her pocket. She saw the last performance of the show on the night she arrived – it was Obey's *Noah* – and next morning paid off the company and took the now very sick Eileen off with her to Wales.

She then reported to Lewis. At the end of it he said, 'Were any of them any good?'

'Not really,' Patricia answered, 'except for one quite brilliant young

man who played Noah. I think his name was Paul Scofield.' Lewis
sent for him and offered him a job with his company touring South
Wales. Paul joined them and immediately got mumps! But through
this meeting he got his first West End job a little later with Lewis in
John Steinbeck's *The Moon is Down*. Years later when Patricia was in
London on a visit from Australia she went with Sybil to see Paul in
A Dead Secret. Afterwards they went round to see him, and Patricia
was rather put out to find that she was the only non-star in the
crowded room and so she let Sybil take the floor, which she would have
done anyway. But Paul walked straight across the room to Patricia
flung his arms round her and said to the others, 'Ladies and gentlemen,
this is the lady who discovered me!'

Oh, the memories that came crowding in! I remembered meeting
Emlyn Williams for the first time at the end of August, 1939, when
he and Sybil were both playing in *The Corn is Green* at the Piccadilly. I
went to see Sybil in her dressing-room before catching the night train
at Euston to join the cruiser *Southampton* at Scapa Flow. We saw a lot
of him again in 1955 when he was captivating Australian audiences with
his readings of Dickens and Dylan Thomas. One night after his show he
and Robert Helpmann came for supper to our house in Melbourne. The
party went on till five the next morning while each of them capped the
stories of the other. After he and his wife had greeted Sybil and Lewis
for their diamond wedding he looked round at the gathering and said
'My God, if a bomb fell on this lot there'd be no London theatre left!'

Patricia had briefed my niece Diana and her American husband Bill
Graham, to collect people's hats and coats as they came in. They were
on a sort of extended honeymoon from their job of teaching drama at
the university of Minnesota. They were both, therefore, theatre-
minded. Bill, however, hadn't ever met many of the top actors. He
never really recovered from the moment when he opened the door of
our flat to be confronted by his hero John Gielgud dressed in a hat and
coat of black sable. He took the garments like a somnambulist and was
seen carrying them off to the cloakroom rather like a neophyte taking
part in some esoteric ceremony. Dear John Gielgud, who had been
Prospero in *The Tempest* with Lewis as Gonzalo on the night in 1940
when Sybil came to the theatre with the news that I had not returned
from a raid over Norway. He too had come to our home in Australia
and we had one of those lovely long rambling lunches that you hope

are never going to end. We had all told stories of Sybil and Lewis and they were warm friendly and witty stories so that the afternoon had a sort of glow to it that came from the words rather than the wine.

The guests continued to pour in. The Liveseys, Roger and Ursula, who are almost part of every part of the family, the Redgraves, the Attenboroughs, Tarquin Olivier, Sybil's godson, with his wife and his mother, Jill Esmond (who had sent me lovely parcels from U.S.A. when I was a prisoner in Germany). Larry Olivier, to his and our sorrow, wasn't well that day and couldn't be there. We had played together in Carlyle Square and at his father's vicarage when we were children and we had all been firmly and gently taken charge of by his elder sister Sybille. Larry is a couple of years my senior and when he joined the Fleet Air Arm at the beginning of the war I had rather hoped that I might perhaps find myself as his squadron commander. But it was not to be and I had to content myself with being called 'Sir' by Lieutenant Ralph Richardson when, as a strange Lieutenant-Commander, I offered him a gin one night in the mess at an R.N. Air Station near Southampton.

One of the happier sights on this afternoon was that of Sir Bronson Albery standing in the middle of our drawing-room greeting each actor like a long-lost child. There could have been only very few there that day who had not at some time been under his management. He and his wife and family were very much bound up with our childhood because Lewis and he were together in management in the twenties and of course it was during this period that *Saint Joan* was produced. It is impossible to imagine the extent to which Joan affected all our lives. Almost overnight we suddenly seemed to become 'well off' and although later we weren't always that 'well off' we never again felt that we were hard up. It was in a way a sort of confidence-builder for us all, and because it was tangible we believed in it and so believed in ourselves just that bit more. 'Bronnie and Una' used to come and see us at Carlyle Square. I remember once I was sitting under our grand piano making something out of Meccano. From where I sat I watched Lewis and Bronnie standing with their backs to the fire while Sybil played Chopin over my head both physically and mentally. They were very patient, my parents, and very seldom sent us away when grown-ups were talking. I suppose this was because a bit earlier our houses had never been big enough for there to be anywhere to send us, and the habit had stuck. Neither the Alberys nor any of our other friends seemed to mind, or if they did they were too nice to say so.

There was Marjorie Forsyth, who is very close to us because she and her husband Matthew, who died in an accident in 1954, have worked with Sybil and Lewis off and on since the first *Saint Joan*. They both acted, but Lewis always said that Matthew was the best stage-manager he ever had. It was during a rehearsal of *Macbeth* in 1926 that Matthew as stage-manager was courageous enough to interrupt Lewis when he was riding the crest of a creative wave like a demon possessed, to suggest that Marjorie, as Third Witch, might be allowed to rest. 'Rest? Whatever for?' snapped Lewis – both he and Sybil feel that there is something immoral about having a rest – and Matthew said quietly, 'Well you see Marjorie is going to have a baby.' Whereupon Lewis's demoniac drive turned at once to gentle solicitude and Marjorie was allowed to rest. Years later, when I was Commander of a naval air station on the west coast of Scotland just after the war, Matthew was directing the Citizens' Theatre in Glasgow. Just before Christmas I took a trip to Glasgow and saw the theatre and the show. I was feeling pretty restless and out of touch with the navy after five years in a prison camp. A week after seeing Matthew I telephoned him and asked, 'If I leave the navy will you give me a job in your theatre?' Matthew, bless him, didn't seem surprised. But he was rightly a little cautious. 'I hope you'll think very carefully, John, before you chuck the navy for the theatre. The navy's nice and secure for a married man with a family, and God knows, you know what the theatre's like. But I'll always be delighted to have a Casson in my company and if you want a job I'll take you on as an assistant stage-manager and small part actor at £9 a week.' Two months later I joined him at the Citizens'. But that is another part of the story.

The list of guests goes on and on and the endless stream of memories is deluging my mind. There were so many more, each with vivid pictures surrounding them. Joyce and Reggie Grenfell, whom we always seem to be meeting in different parts of the world. Peggy Ashcroft whom I first remember with Sybil in the memorable Paul Robeson *Othello*, at the Savoy. Margaret Rutherford and Stringer Davis, Carlton Hobbs (Hobbo) and his wife. The Michael MacOwans and, bless her, the oldest lady of the theatre, Ellaline Terris, at 98 well aware that she was the grande-dame over them all moving through the room like an empress. When I was sixteen there was a charity matinee of *Quality Street* played by the children of actors and actresses. I was lucky enough to be playing Valentine Brown and after it was over Ellaline Terris and her husband, Sir Seymour Hicks, came to see us. 'My boy,' said Sir Seymour, 'I played this part twenty years ago.' And he then told me at some length how he played it, and then said, 'But you were splendid, my boy, splendid.' I wish I had seen him play it. Who has ever played comedy with his style and flourish? Two days later I received a parcel with a book inside it. It was called *Difficulties* and was written and indeed signed by Sir Seymour. It was about the problems that a young man faces in coping with the 'facts of life'. I have often wondered whether the book was meant to help me as an actor or as a sailor. He had seen me attempting to be the former and had been told that my calling was the latter.

One of the most memorable moments was when we opened the door to Cardinal Heenan, Archbishop of Westminster. Sybil had very specially asked for 'Father John', as she calls him, to be invited. I had written the letter of invitation telling him this and adding that although a Sunday was a good day for actors to attend a party I realised that it was not the most convenient for a priest. He had replied that of course he would be there to offer his congratulations and 'to give Sybil a kiss'. When he swept into the room in crimson cap and black soutane with crimson piping, Ursula Livesey whispered to me 'My goodness, how we'd all adore to make an entrance like that!'

For two invigorating and lovely hours the flat was a bedlam of joyful sound as we all drank champagne, munched mince pies, talked our heads off and shouted greetings at each other across the room. At one point Sybil and Lewis moved out into the dining-room where we hoped the party would spread to ease the crush. 'Well I'm going into the other room,' Sybil had shouted. 'Come on Lewis. They've got someone hidden in there.' As she moved off the train of her skirt caught on the leg of a chair. Lewis, ever attentive to her, saw it first and stooped to free it. And then without letting go followed her through into the next room – her faithful retainer and her protector. Later on I jumped up on to a chair and made a sort of speech proposing their health. I don't remember much of what I said except that I didn't think any of us really believed, by the look of them, that they had been married for sixty years, but I hoped they had because if they hadn't I was, at my age, in a rather embarrassing position. Then we all waved our glasses and drank to many happy returns. But eventually it had to come to an end. Sybil and Lewis were beginning to wilt while assuring us individually that they were good for another couple of hours. But Sybil said quietly to me, 'I must get Lewis home. He's getting very tired.' And Lewis said to Patricia, 'It's time Sybil gave her voice a rest. She must be exhausted.' And so at last we took them to their car.

'Aren't they marvellous,' said Penny as we all turned to go indoors. Suddenly the hilarity, and euphoria almost, that we had all been caught up in at the party, changed quite smoothly and quickly into a feeling of quiet, unquestioning affection. When we got back into the flat the last of the guests had gone and the three ladies who had waited on us so well had by now just as competently cleared away the glasses and had nearly finished the washing-up.

Patricia was the first to speak. 'Don't know about anybody else, but I've had a ball. Is there any champagne left?'

'Praise be, yes, there is,' I answered. 'Two bottles.'

'Shall we just give them a quick ring first?' said I, and without waiting for the general approval I picked up the telephone and dialled their number. Sybil's voice answered with her very distinctive 'Hallo?' on a rising, questioning inflection, which seems to say 'I don't know who you are, but it's nice of you to ring, though I'm not sure yet whether I can say "Yes" to whatever it is you're going to ask.' In other words it is a sort of welcome with caution. 'Hallo, me love' I said.

'Oh John! Darling! (It's John, Lewis.) What a lovely, lovely party. We did so enjoy it. (Didn't we, Lewis.) What angel people. My dear, *everyone* was there. Where were all our relations? Oh, I know, you told me. They're next week, aren't they. Wasn't Father John a love to come. And Ellaline! 98! Isn't she wonderful, dear old thing. How wonderfully Pat did it all. Aren't you all *dead* after it?'

'You both must be very tired now,' I chipped agilely in.

'Well we *are* a bit tired, darling. I've made us a scrambled egg and we're in our dressing gowns by the fire. We shall go straight to bed when we've finished. Good night, John dear, and let me have a quick word with Pat.' Patricia said a few words of good night and then put down the phone.

'Sybil sends her love and good night to everyone and says she's sorry they're so **tired**!'

'They're incredible!' said Bill Graham who was meeting the Casson family *en masse* for the first time. And according to Patricia, who had faced it in 1935, it's a fairly alarming experience.

'What were they like as parents?' Dirk Campbell, my nephew, turned to Kiff, who turned to me.

'Marvellous I would say, wouldn't you John?'

'Ye-es. But saying they were marvellous doesn't really say anything does it? Most parents are marvellous as their children see it, though it doesn't always last. What I mean is, they were marvellous as we saw it while we were children and marvellous in different ways at our different ages. But after all that was a fairly uncritical judgement. I *thought* they were marvellous people then. I think they are marvellous people now in quite a different way.'

'Daddy's right,' said Jane. 'After all you two haven't been the same people to us all the time. But you're not bad as parents.'

'Well, Daddy, what *do* you think Granny and Granddaddy were like as parents?' asked Penny. 'What do you mean by "marvellous"?'

This is what always seems to happen to me, my arguments boomerang! What *were* they like as parents? How did they look to a small boy of two, of six, of ten? What did the cocky young cadet think of them or the slightly lunatic fighter pilot? What did his fiancée think of them and they of her? And what sort of things had happened that were the raw material of the thoughts? I should have to think about this because here was I in my sixtieth year, and Sybil and Lewis had been around for all this time.

We finished the last of the champagne and the marvellous party was over. 'Aren't they marvellous?' went on echoing in my mind. I must think about it, think back on my years with them. They certainly have been marvellous and we have all had a lot of fun together in one way and another – and a few fights too in a not very unfriendly way. What is the magic? What's the secret? What have the two of them got in greater abundance than the rest of us? As a first approximation I should think it is a passionate enthusiasm for living and an almost total dedication to exploring and practising the art of living in terms of acting. Marvellous! I must think about it.

Chapter 2

BEFORE 1914

THE first time that I remember meeting them was obviously not the first time they met me. Nor did either of them figure at all in my very first recollection. This was concerned with Sybil's parents, the Rev. Arthur Thorndike and his wife Agnes Macdonald Thorndike, known to all as 'Donnie'. Granpapa at this time was vicar of St James the Less in Pimlico, and I was born at the vicarage at 75 St George's Square on 28th October, 1909, two days after Lewis's birthday and four days after Sybil's. This makes all three of us Scorpions – indeed four of us because my youngest sister Ann was born on 6th November – though it is doubtful if this interesting fact has had much effect on our lives other than our having the fun of a bunch of birthdays close together.

Shortly after I was born, when I was about six months old they tell me, Sybil and Lewis were offered jobs by an American gentleman called John Drew to tour American towns for a year with a repertoire of plays. I'm glad to know that the reason why they were very against accepting the invitation was because it meant leaving me. When I was told this some years later I remember it greatly increased in me an already high respect for my parents. However, they were very hard up at the time and, in the event, economics prevailed over parental responsibility and I was left in the excellent care of my grandparents. Whether this had any serious psychological effect on me, I shall never know, but I do know, because I've been told, that when they returned I wouldn't have a bar of either of them, and yelled for my nurse. Just before or just after this time came my first actual conscious recollection. It was of sitting between my grandparents on the seat of a horse-carriage drawing up outside a small red-brick house which I later discovered was called Pear Tree Cottage. It must have been after they returned from America because I was only 18 months old when they got back and we never went to the cottage after I was 2. But I do know Sybil and Lewis weren't there, and I can only hope I hadn't been 'taken off to the country' in an infantile huff. The cottage was at Dymchurch on Romney Marsh and when Granny bought a cottage there under the sea wall and within jumping distance of the long, hard, yellow sands, it became our holiday home till we were nearly grown up. Even now the word 'Dym' conjures up smells and tastes and sights all tinged with that magical adventure of childhood. And so Dymchurch was what I first remember. Then there is a gap of about a year, during which, like in H. G. Wells's *Time Machine*, the events just skipped by and never came into focus. There is a brief moment when Sybil and Lewis took me out into the dark one night and showed me the stars. I don't remember my parents at all at that moment but I do remember the multitude of sparkling lights. My reaction so impressed them that this occasion has always been known as 'The night John saw the stars', and it perhaps accounts for my continuing interest in astronomy.

The first very clear memory of both of them is of a day in a comic little semi-detached house in Heaton Park, a suburb of Manchester, which Sybil and Lewis had taken when they joined Miss Horniman's Repertory at the Gaiety Theatre. It was at 106 King's Road (unadopted). On this day I went up the stairs holding Lewis's hand. 'We're going to see Christopher,' he said. I had no idea what this meant, but it sounded very exciting. We went into the room, and there was a lady in white starchy clothes over by the chest-of-drawers (I am also vividly aware of a bottle of stout on the chest-of-drawers, but this can't have been true). I didn't like the look of her. She had that grown-up look of disapproval. But there in the big double bed was Sybil, long hair down over her shoulders, smiling at me. She helped me up onto the bed and apparently I then shouted in a loud voice, 'Where's Kiffer?' She helped me to lean over her and peer into the cradle by her side. This was my introduction to my brother Christopher, and because 'Kiffer' was the nearest I could get to his name, Kiffer or Kiff he has been to us ever since.

Like everybody else's early memories, however, these days in Manchester are pretty vague to me. Sybil and Lewis took me for walks in Heaton Park and there was a great collection of rocks there, which they helped me to climb. In fact we call them 'Wales' after the mountains in Lewis's childhood home in Denbigh. I remember crawling about backstage at the theatre, and seeing a new and rather frightening Lewis, conducting rehearsals, so very different from the wonderful, kindly, twinkly sort of person with whom I had fascinating conversations and who used to tell me marvellous stories.

Sybil at this time was to me a tall, warm, utterly comfy person, with whom I felt completely safe and secure. I seem to remember her mostly in an ankle-length close-fitting tweed skirt and white blouse of the period. Even to-day when I hear the word 'lap' used, I at once see a picture of Sybil's grey skirt in front of my eyes. She always seemed to be smiling, not the sort of sugary, 'nice to meet you' sort of smile, but the deeper, wiser, confident sort of smile that made me know for certain that it was a jolly nice world to be alive in.

Lewis gave me quite another feeling. There was awe in it and a certain pleasurable sensation of strength. When he was doing anything in a determined way, and that's the way he did most things, he had a concentrated frown, an intense earnestness, that seemed to say, 'Not just now, I'm busy.' You felt you could break in only if your ideas were completely to the point, otherwise they would probably be dismissed as trivial. I still have a picture of him fixing hooks under the lintel of the bedroom door in Manchester on which to hang a swing for me. And it was just the same look that I saw later when he drove his old Tin Lizzie Ford or was coping with recalcitrant actors at rehearsal. It was a fairly clear signal to 'keep off the grass' and as children we kept off the grass when this signal was flying. Moreover it applied to Sybil just as much as to the rest of us. She could be very forthright at rehearsals and very much one to have her own way. Many are the verbal battles my brother and I have watched, sitting quiet as mice at the back of the stalls while 'Daddy and Mummy' fought it out. But in the end Lewis's 'Look' would appear, and Sybil would pipe down to become the humble actress quietly taking her orders from the producer.

This was not, however, by any means the only Lewis I knew. The other was the exciting person who used to take me out before breakfast round the neighbourhood of King's Road (unadopted). Sometimes we took a football to kick along and at others we got out my little pedal motor-car which had been given to me by Uncle Morny, the fine actor Morton Selten. I was too small to propel it unaided and so Lewis used to fasten a piece of string on to the front and tow me along while I steered. This Lewis was almost God himself. There was absolutely nothing he did not know and nothing he could not do. 'Ask Daddy' was the answer to any apparently insoluble problem, and 'Daddy', I'm bound to say, always seemed to produce an answer. And of course it was the right answer, for even to think that it might not be was a kind of blasphemy that was unthinkable.

I don't think this was an unusual way of seeing one's father in those days. Indeed it is probably universal even to-day, although to-day disillusion probably sets in at a much earlier age. At school I can remember the feeling of bewildered astonishment on finding that the clinching argument of 'My pater says so' was unacceptable to the ignorant masses.

This attitude to Lewis, however, did not have the awe in it that was conjured up by the 'Look'. He had so much humour in him, and no one has ever had eyes that twinkled so much with fun. I think his greatest asset was his very strong powers of suggestion. When he told you something in that deep, Welsh-musical voice, carrying in its tones all the sincerity and integrity which was so much part of him, it never occurred to me to doubt what he was saying. This was probably the secret of his success as a producer. If you could survive the 'Look' you found you had a friend who was entirely on your side, and so there was no point in not believing what he said. I think he would have been a very successful hypnotist if his mind had turned that way.

Two examples from the Manchester days underline this astonishing depth of penetration into people's minds which was verging on the psycho-analytical. When I was about 2 or 3 I had one of those little toy boats to play with in the bath. How it started I don't know, perhaps some careless remark by a nurse, but I conceived the idea that the boat might disappear down into the gurgling whirlpool of the plug. I'm told that this fear rapidly developed into a kind of phobia so that I even had fears of being sucked into the maelstrom myself. It got to the point where even a mention of the bath brought on a paroxysm of fear. Then Lewis took a hand. He suggested to me that it would surely be better to burn the boat in a huge bonfire rather than risk its going down the drain. Apparently I thought this a splendid idea. And so that evening Lewis and Sybil and I went solemnly into the tiny back garden. The faggots had already been suitably laid, and the sacrificial fire was lit. With all the dramatic flourish and style of which he was so capable, Lewis took the little wooden boat and laid it on top of the blaze (part of the miracle to me was that Lewis didn't burn himself). The three of us stood ceremonially silent and still as the little boat was consumed.

Then we gave a cheer, the Reveille after the Last Post, and we went indoors. From that moment all fear of the whirlpool completely disappeared.

The second example of suggestion was less drastic but nonetheless effective. It was a story called 'The Twelve Trees' and it was designed as a lullaby or possibly a soporific. Lewis first told it to me in Manchester and it could only be told if two conditions were fulfilled. The listener had to be in bed and his or her eyes had to be shut. The story is a very simple one, but it had its own precise and regular rhythm and its own unvarying 'tune'.

'Once upon a time there was an old man who on his long walk home from work had to pass twelve trees, and then he would be home, and he'd go to bed and he'd go to sleep, 'cos he was *so* tired and *so-oo* sleepy that he didn't know what to do. So he went walking and walking up the hill and down the hill and at last he came to the first tree. And he said "I've only got eleven more trees to go and then I shall be home and I'll go to bed and I'll go to sleep because I'm *so-o* tired and *so-oo* sleepy that I don't know what to do." So he went walking and walking up the hill and down the hill and at last he came to the second tree . . .' and so on until the listener was in a deep, deep sleep. I can even find myself beginning to feel sleepy as I write it. However, if for some reason I was very wide awake and when in the early days I was the only listener, it was found that I could outrun the twelve trees fairly easily. And so in later editions for my brother and sisters the number was increased to thirty trees and no one was ever known to survive more than twenty.

This little lullaby has a sequel. In 1944 Patricia and Mary, who during most of the war had set up house together, bought a house in Ashstead, Surrey, to have as a base at which to receive their respective returning husbands. It was called 'Balbedie', which, with apologies to whoever named it, they thought was an awful name. It had a jolly garden and a lot of trees numbering near enough thirty. And so the house was re-christened 'Thirty-Trees'. We sold it a year or two later but now after twenty-five years we see that it is still 'Thirty-Trees', and I've no doubt the present inhabitants still have the same trouble on the telephone convincing tradesmen that it is not Thirty-Three!

There were lots more stories, all most unusual and very far from the usual run of 'happy-ever-after', but in an odd sort of way most of them had some kind of a moral in them. It is an interesting exercise when one is in what is called the 'elderly bracket' to speculate on where someone's pet ideas came from. I am quite sure that the outlooks of my brother, sisters and me have been considerably influenced by Lewis's stories.

For instance there is the strange story of the glass mountain on top of which was a priceless jade elephant to be obtained simply for the taking. The hero of the tale began to climb up the smooth glass mountainside on which there were minute and precarious holds. He always began well and always eventually realised what excellent progress he was making. He would then look up at the jade elephant and become ambitious. And, like Julius Caesar, his ambition was always his downfall. 'Then he got ambitious and slid right to the bottom again.' There could be few better ways of teaching the lesson of 'Keep your mind on what you're doing, and never mind the reward,' 'Give no thought for the things of to-morrow,' or even Browning's 'Image the whole, then execute the parts.' It certainly made us all feel very suspicious of ambition even before we saw Sybil and Lewis in *Julius Caesar* or *Henry VIII*, but we were very pleased to discover that Shakespeare agreed with us.

They were at the Gaiety, Manchester, for not quite two years, and as I was only 2 or 3 years old I'm afraid I don't remember much about it or the people there. The owner of the company, the redoubtable Miss Horniman, is to me a shadowy, angular and rather forbidding figure in a plain beige coat and skirt of severe cut. Milton Rosmer once gave me a penny for some sweets and Edith Goodall served me a plateful of sliced oranges which made me feel sick.

But I do remember Sybil playing Romp in Lawrence Housman's *Prunella*. Romp, as her name suggests, was a rowdy, untidy girl, and Sybil must have played it with unusual gusto. For some reason I was allowed to see it and it scared the living daylights out of me. I used to have nightmares about it for years, that sort of nightmare in which all the familiar and friendly faces become hostile and evil. Sybil's Romp showed me that my goddess of a mother could also be a hearty harridan, who was to me both hostile and frighteningly evil, and it took me quite a time to get over it.

Since then I've often wondered whether it is wise to let very young children go to the theatre. Naturally we all did almost before we could talk, but an imaginative child does not learn at once to distinguish between the real and the imaginary. It is surely only in the unconscious knowledge that at the end of a play we can come back to reality that allows us to keep our sanity when we witness high drama. If we don't know that 'it's all right, they're only actors', and I don't think small children do always know, then the effect of a play or a film can be unpleasantly traumatic. We have seen this with our own youngest daughter, Jane, who wouldn't go to the cinema for years after seeing *The Wizard of Oz* at the age of 4 or 5. She was panic-stricken by the horror of what were to her real happenings. I wonder if we grow -ups take our children to *Peter Pan*, *Where the Rainbow Ends*, *Bambi*, *Snow White* and so on because we want to see them ourselves and so take the children as an excuse. Certainly I was given the willies by Sybil reading all of Alice's various adventures to me. The Red Queen, the Caterpillar and the Ugly Duchess still give me a feeling of disquiet, which probably explains why only a few years ago I failed to reach an understanding with a managing director who reminded me of the Jabberwock! Lewis, too, told me, when Mary was playing Wendy, that he had always thought Peter Pan to be a psychologically most unhealthy play and ought to be given an X certificate!

Anyway it's much too late now for the Cassons. We seem to have survived our respective traumas, and we must have had a lot of them in one way or another. They were probably offset by our being allowed to act ourselves, and so learning that the whole business was something of an entertaining game. I shall go into all this later in some detail because I have a feeling that we children never took the theatre quite as seriously as our parents and so perhaps didn't go so far as they did. At this time all I knew was that the theatre was not only a way of life, it was the only way of life. This was what the 'right' sort of people did. The rest were 'audience', provided by God for the benefit of actors.

In 1913 Sybil took Christopher and me off to London while Lewis went off to produce in Glasgow for a year. The indefatigable Granny had found a house for us at 40 Bessborough Street, just round the corner from St George's Square. It was one of the thousands of London terrace houses with two rooms on each floor and front doors arranged in pairs under pillared portios. The top floor was let to Auntie Maud, Donnie's widowed sister-in-law, a gorgeous black-haired lady with a sparkling eye and a voice like Vox Humana on a cathedral organ. Her laugh, and she laughed often, shook the house to its foundations.

Maud had married Donnie's brother, the Rev. William Bowers, our Great-Uncle Willie, when she was only seventeen and he a middle-aged bachelor. When he died suddenly in 1915 Auntie Maud was heart-broken, but it didn't stop her from being gay and jolly with us children and it was a great treat to be taken upstairs to her flat where she kept a supply of exotic confectionery.

On 22nd May, 1914, my sister Mary was born in Bessborough Street while Christopher and I were in the throes of whooping cough. I remember being allowed in to see Sybil, and not being allowed to kiss her except on the hand. This seemed to be the most frightful imposi-tion at the time because we had missed her very much during the few days of her travail, when we, for obvious reasons, had been kept out of her way. It is almost impossible to describe how utterly indispensable Sybil's presence was to us. She had a way of talking about things and of listening that somehow made our problems and worries disappear. Nothing could be really black as long as Sybil was with us. And so, fond as we were of Alice and Nelly, the two young sisters who had been brought from Granpapa's early parish in Kent to look after us, we felt deeply aggrieved when we were whisked away to Dymchurch immediately after seeing Sybil and our new sister.

We were packed into the Tin Lizzie, whooping cough and all, and set off down the Folkstone Road to the coast. I can remember at some point in the journey being very sick all over the back of the car. Lewis put on the 'Look' and proceeded to mop up the mess with his tweed cap. What eventually happened to the cap we shall now never know, but it was my first experience of a facet of Lewis's personality, which I have noticed all my life. When a crisis occurred, of any sort, he at once put on the 'Look' and took some very quick and decisive action. That the action might be the wrong one, or one that caused a bigger crisis than the first, was quite irrelevant. Action was all and had to be taken. Lewis was never one to wring his hands.

Despite this crisis, and one more when the engine boiled, and we were all ordered to take action at once by jumping out of the car, we arrived at Dymchurch none the worse for the journey. There we proceeded to get rid of the whoops in salty, sunny air, and there a few weeks later we were joined by Sybil and the baby Mary. Lewis

The author with his
maternal grandfather

The Thorndike family in 1914
Left to right: Russell, Frank, Sybil, Eileen

Lewis (about 20) and his father

went off somewhere to earn the money to keep us. From time to time he would suddenly appear, stay a day or two and like a whirlwind disappear again.

In those long, warm, sunny days of the summer of 1914 Sybil had at last a chance of getting to know her eldest son as a person. I was by now four years old and could talk and listen if not intelligently at least coherently, and so I too began to know her as a person rather than as a guardian goddess. Day after day we used to go out on to the wonderful sandy beach and build exciting castles and elaborate irrigation systems. Or, best of all, we would sit together on the shingle under the sea-wall, while we played a game, which she had invented, called 'Making Plans'. It consisted solely of making plans for a ship of which she and I were to be the owners. We would talk for hours about it and I wish I could remember what we said. But I do remember that it was to have been a wonderful ship, and that, though it never got beyond the planning stage and the plans didn't even last beyond that summer, it was a catalyst that gave Sybil and me a respect and affection for each other that goes way beyond filial love. We each then began to learn to enjoy the other's talk and to know that in the other we were each of us sure of an appreciative audience. It also implanted in me an as yet unconscious, but later unswerving, desire to be a sailor, which carried me off nine years later to a training ship and on into the Royal Navy.

When I got tired of planning the ship I used to say to Sybil, 'Tell me about when you were a little girl.' Most small children seem to enjoy hearing about their parents' childhood. I suppose it breaks down the barrier of the years. The grown-up has to become temporarily a child, and the child enjoys seeing the important and perhaps awe-inspiring grown-up as somebody like himself. For a moment or two old and young really speak the same language.

'Well,' Sybil would begin. 'Where shall we start?'

'Rochester,' I'd say.

'Granpapa and Grannie took me there when I was a very little girl. You know he's called a Canon now, Canon Thorndike, which is a sort of special clergyman. Well, in those days he was a Minor Canon, which isn't so important as a Canon and we lived in a funny little street called Minor Canon Row, right beside Rochester Cathedral, where all the other minor canons lived.''

I at once got a picture of a veritable army of minor canons who were in some way mixed up with pictures I had seen of coal mines. I didn't understand how canons could also be miners, but perhaps it was something they all had to do before they were thought to be good enough to become full-blown canons. But then my mind used to wander, because it was just as nice merely to listen to the sound of her voice as it was to listen to what she was saying. It was not only as nice, it was much easier too. Gradually the pieces of the family jig-saw began to fall into place, though on the whole at this time it was mostly Thorndike family. In fact there were a lot of Thorndikes in Dymchurch that summer. We had two little houses next door to each other in the middle of 'Marine Terrace' just behind the sea-wall, one of which was to be our holiday home right through till 1930. Sybil with the help of Alice and Nelly was looking after us in No. 4. In No. 3 were the grandparents Arthur and Donnie and Sybil's younger brothers and sister. In order of age there was Russell, who I think about this time was writing the original *Dr Syn*, the now famous eighteenth century smuggling parson of Dymchurch-under-the-Wall, whom he invented. Russell is my Godfather and was always a great favourite with us. He had such wonderful stories to tell us of his own Münchhausian adventures. A year or two earlier he had been a member of Matheson Lang's world touring company and so had been to places like India and China. This in itself would have been exciting enough in all conscience, but to Russell happenings were never enough on their own. Being a writer as well as an actor he turned, and still turns, every event in his and other people's lives into a romantic adventure. I remember sitting openmouthed while he told me all about the Indian Rajahs, the Chinese Mandarins and, of course, thrilling stories of diabolical Chinese tortures. He brought home to me a box of tin soldiers on horseback, who, now I come to think of it, were perfectly dressed in the uniform of the Household Cavalry and had probably been bought at a toy shop near Victoria Station. But this wouldn't do for Russell. He told me that they had come from a collection in the Emperor's Palace at Peking and that, and here came the final touch of realism, on the passage home they had all been seasick in the Bay of Bengal. Russell is the real actor of the family. He lives and breathes in a world not of make-believe but of a reality wildly and often madly intensified by his own bounding imagination. I defy anyone ever to be bored in Russell's company. There's no telling what sort of emotion he will conjure up in you, but it certainly won't be boredom.

Next came Eileen, then I suppose in her middle-twenties. She went about all day with her hair hanging down below her shoulders and she was a model of Sybil in the way she plunged into everything with a sort of ravenous enthusiasm. It was all rather overwhelming for a small boy, but where Russell was always good for a laugh, Eileen was always good for a lark. And whereas we were never bored with Russell, Eileen never seemed to get bored with us. She was a gorgeous person and had completely enchanted Tom, the one-eyed fisherman, who was always coming round to the door with gifts of fresh mackerel on the off chance of a word with 'Miss Eileen'.

And last of all there was Frank, then about twenty, and the gay, urbane member of the family. Frank had run away from school and had got a job with a famous theatrical manager by inviting him to lunch at the manager's favourite restaurant. Frank had done his homework and found out not only where his man lunched and what were his favourite dishes, but also the route the great man followed from his office to the restaurant. Frank gave ten bob each to half a dozen commissionaires, called for his guest at the office and sauntered with him to the restaurant. Each commissionaire as they passed tipped his hat and said, 'Good morning, Mr Thorndike. Nice to see you back in London.' The two of them enjoyed their lunch and Frank got the job. Frank was killed in France in August, 1917, as a pilot in the R.F.C. From what I have heard he got his plane into a cloud and quite simply spun in. As he had gone to France with about four hours solo flying to his credit, it isn't perhaps surprising. Sybil always believes that Frank would have been the biggest star of them all. He had looks, he had style, and he had an air of sophistication about him, which in some way his brother and sisters always lacked.

I wish I had known Frank for longer because I think we would have got on well together. After this Dymchurch holiday, he came rushing in to Bessborough Street a few times, first in the uniform of a private in the Westminster Dragoons, which he joined that year with Russell, and then later as the dashing young pilot of the R.F.C. The pictures of him are very vivid, but there are too few of them.

But because of the plethora of Thorndikes at this time, it is not really surprising that it was this side of the family that I got to know about rather than the Cassons. None of the mysterious Welsh uncles, aunts and cousins had appeared and I plied Sybil with further questions about her past.

It must have been on another day when I said:

'Didn't they keep you awake?'

'What, the minor canons, darling?'

'No, the bells. Didn't they make an awful noise?'

'Oh, the cathedral bells. Oh no! We loved them. They made us feel we belonged to the cathedral. Father belonged, of course, Grandpapa, I mean. But it was nice that we were all in it too. Grannie used to have tea-parties with lots of lovely cakes and buns. Uncle Russell and I used to recite and sing songs and do plays for everybody. It was great fun. And then I learnt to play the piano, and when I was ten I used to give piano lessons.'

This didn't seem to me in the least unusual. After all when a girl was ten she was getting on a bit.

'But one day,' she went on, 'I hurt my wrist and had to stop playing the piano so hard. I had been getting up every morning at five o'clock and practising till breakfast time. And so then I became an actress.'

Whenever she told me this I always had that feeling of relief that comes from knowing that the story has a happy ending. To be an actress was so obviously the only aim for any woman worthy of the name and I sometimes held my breath with agony at the thought that Sybil might have become so ordinary a thing as a pianist.

'And when did you meet Daddy?'

'I met him in Dublin, at the zoo, and he was talking to the lions.'

'What! Right in the cage with them?'

'No, he was outside. And I thought "What a nice man" and some-one said, "That's Lewis Casson." He liked me and I liked him and so we got married.'

'And what did he do when he was a little boy?'

'You must ask him, darling. He must tell you his story.'

But he wasn't there that day and somehow he never told us much about himself as a boy. We had to fill in the gaps years later. I don't know quite why he never talked about it himself. He certainly wasn't at all the extrovert that Sybil has always been. Not that he was hard to talk to – far from it. He just had to be wheedled into talking about himself and as a child I never seemed to get into the wheedling situation with him. He always had so many other fascinating things to talk about and to do. For instance, he used to help me climb right round the drawing-room without touching the floor, over sideboards, up on to shelves, across the mantelpiece (and part of the game was not to touch the clock or the ornaments) and over to the piano. The scene had to be set first, of course, by the judicious positioning of chairs and occasional tables between what were otherwise impassable precipices. There was also the 'aeroplane game' in which I sat on a wooden frame (I fancy it was a small easel) and was whirled about round the room until the climactic moment when I was dropped on to a pile of cushions. In those days aeroplanes crashed as often as not and so the drama would have been incomplete without an accident.

And so there never seemed to be time to hear his biographical history. We gradually found out some of the details of his early days, but because he didn't tell us much of it as a story, I for one have never been able to form the clear pictures that I have of Sybil and her sister and brothers.

I can see, as clearly as if I had been there, Sybil and Russell putting on plays of murderous drama in the attic at Minor Canon Row, Sybil being taken to London by Donnie to interview teachers and impresarios, and Russell going to Windsor and becoming Queen Victoria's boy soloist, and all the other adventures that they seemed to have had. But I only saw Lewis's childhood as a few sparsely scattered and not altogether accurate historical facts. Most of them came to us from Sybil anyway and so Lewis's early life never seemed to come alive to us as much as hers. And it was a long time yet to go before he would be telling us of it himself.

In the meantime we frolicked in the sun with the Thorndikes and everybody talked their heads off. We bathed in the sea and afterwards stuffed ourselves with huge, fresh, sticky 'penny buns' from Smith's the baker shop. Everyone was gay, energetic and intoxicated by the smell of Romney Marsh mingled with the salty air; while across the Channel, Europe was gathering itself to plunge into war – the Great War – now only a few weeks away.

Chapter 3

THE FIRST WAR

THE 4th August, 1914, did not signify the beginning of a war to me. It was nevertheless a very significant and dramatic day. Sybil, I think, had already left Dymchurch for London taking with her the baby Mary, and Nelly to help her. At Dymchurch she had received a letter from Ben Greet asking her to join a theatre in the Waterloo Road, which was putting on Shakespeare plays at popular prices. It was being run by a remarkable woman and Ben Greet had said to Sybil: 'You'll enjoy it, Syb, because you're as mad as she is.' The remarkable woman was Lilian Baylis and the theatre was the Old Vic. So Sybil was in London, while Kiff and I were left at Dymchurch in the care of Alice.

One fine evening just before we went to bed we were thrilled to hear a 'honk honk' outside the window. There was Lewis with his peaked cloth cap on back to front, at the wheel of the Tin Lizzie, just arrived from London.

'Hallo,' he shouted as we rushed out, 'I've come to take you all back to London. We'll leave in the morning if Alice can be ready.'

Naturally we didn't ask why. It was enough that we were going off by car to London, and that 'Daddy' had come for us. But, of course, with the declaration of war, Lewis and Sybil felt it would be safer to have us children away from the coast. We were after all only thirty miles from France and no one knew quite what the Germans might be up to.

Next morning, with the sun shining, off we went in the car. Alice had Kiff in the back while I sat in the front beside Lewis who, every now and then, let me 'drive' — that is, hold on to the steering wheel. In those days in that car it would have been a good run to do the seventy-five miles to London in three or four hours. But we didn't, I fear, have a 'good run'. Half-way up Maidstone Hill Lewis swerved rather too violently to avoid a dog, and the tie-rod connecting the two front wheels snapped. The car ran into a high wall, rolled over on its right side and tumbled us all on to the road. By a miracle no one was badly hurt. Lewis had swung himself out by the steering wheel and I had slid down on to the upholstery at the side. Alice, holding Christopher in her arms, had given her elbow a nasty crack, and had shielded Christopher completely. I had a cut on the side of my knee from a piece of the glass windscreen and was immensely proud of the blood streaming down my leg. This time Lewis's actions were not only swift but very effective. The 'Look' appeared, we were all taken into a nearby house, given tea and buns and I, to my delight, had my leg bandaged. The last I remember of that day is Lewis pushing us all into a train and handing Kiff and me comics to read. But I think we all went to the vicarage in St George's Square to be cosseted by Grannie Donnie for a few days before going back to 40 Bessborough Street. And that was the outbreak of war!

At all events, for quite a time 'The War' didn't mean nearly so much to us as 'The Accident'. We talked about it incessantly and re-enacted it with unlimited variations on the floor of the nursery. People round us talked more and more about the War and one evening I was wheeled in a pushchair by Sybil and Lewis down Bessborough Street to Vauxhall Bridge Road. There was a long column of soldiers in khaki marching towards Vauxhall Bridge and on to France, while the brass band in front played 'It's a long way to Tipperary'. I was fascinated and couldn't understand why Sybil and Lewis were looking so solemn in the face of such excitement. I wanted to shout with joy and probably did, but they stood silently beside the pushchair holding hands and staring at all those marching men. Then Lewis said suddenly, 'I must be in this' and we turned away and went home.

Within a matter of days Lewis presented himself at the recruiting office at the Duke of York's Barracks in Chelsea and joined a unit of the Army Service Corps. He was at once sent off to a camp at St Albans where the contrast between the vigorous life of an imaginative and energetic actor and producer on the one hand and the required thoughtless existence of a private soldier under training on the other, was too much for Lewis. He wrote to his colonel saying that he wasn't used to loafing and that so far this was all that seemed to be required of him in the army. Could he be given some work to do? The colonel was happy to oblige and arranged for him to become a camp cook. He performed his culinary tasks apparently with skill if not distinction until he was put on to driving lorries.

One day about this time, I was standing by the window in Bess-borough Street when an army lorry pulled up outside the door. Out of it sprang what appeared to me to be a horde of soldiers led by Lewis, who ran up our front steps and thundered on the door. Soon the house seemed to be full of laughing loud-talking men being introduced to Sybil, lighting cigarettes and flopping into chairs round the room. Sybil went off to the kitchen and with Alice and Nelly made a vast dish of bacon and eggs. I can still see the soldiers tucking into it as though they hadn't eaten anything for days. Sybil was bustling around pouring tea and giving a superb but somewhat 'ham' performance of a capable middle-class housewife overjoyed at having a huge crowd of vigorous men in her home, to whom she could show off the prodigality of her larder and her skill in using it. The fact that the war limited the first and that Alice and Nelly had more or less taken over the other in no way diminished the panache with which she played her rôle.

In the middle of September I went down with a mild attack of scarlet fever. Lewis was at St Albans and so Granny swept Alice and Nelly, Christopher and Mary off to the Vicarage to keep them out of harm's way, while Sybil and I were left on our own in two rooms at Bessborough Street to get through the six weeks quarantine. We had a very frequent visitor called Mrs Walks. She was a Christian Scientist, which has always been one of Sybil's sidelines, and always called Sybil 'Sadie dear' because they met while Sybil was playing Sadie in some play. I always thought she said 'Seedy dear' and got it all mixed with feeling 'seedy' and so I didn't think much of Mrs Walks. She was forever telling Sybil that doctors were no good to anybody and that prayer was the only remedy, even for scarlet fever. One evening, however, while she was in the bedroom with Sybil and me, the front door bell rang. We heard Mrs Heaton answer it and then the voice of old Dr Halley, our family doctor, who had come on one of his regular visits to me. He had the deepest voice of anybody I've ever known and a rather thin lugubrious face. He did everything very slowly, as if to demonstrate that nothing or nobody gets any better by hurrying. But Sybil and Mrs Walks did hurry. 'Quick!' said Sybil. 'Hide in the next room. He mustn't find you here!' And there was a great to-do and whispering as they went off together. From the landing Sybil archly called out, 'Just *one* minute, Dr Halley. We are just putting things straight.' The feeling of high drama was in the air and I remember being in agony that the villain (Dr Halley) would catch the heroine (Sybil) in the very act of duplicity. It seemed that despite the fortification provided by prayer, the champions of Faith and Medical Science could not be allowed to meet for fear of some unnamable cataclysm. I don't think it occurred to Sybil that Mrs Walks could just say, 'Good evening Doctor. I'll wait in the next room.' Why throw away a good bit of drama when it was available? And so we went straight into the second act of a melodramatic French farce with me as the five-year-old audience of one. All the time Sybil was gaily talking to the doctor, I could see the cowering Mrs Walks 'behind the arras' in the next room hardly daring to breathe. Oh, let her not cough or sneeze! The feeling of joyful relief when the doctor finally departed and Mrs Walks could come out of her hiding place was indescribable! Life could never be dull with Sybil in charge of the scenario!

I still remember my scarlet fever time as a tremendous skylark. After that summer when Sybil and I had got to know each other so well at Dymchurch, this six weeks of being closeted together, and seeing no one but Dr Halley, the redoubtable Mrs Heaton, who cooked and housekept, and the conspiratorial Mrs Walks, put the seal on a very special relationship between Sybil and me. I was the only one of the children who, as a child, lived with her free of nannies and servants. After this she could never again be only the gorgeous mother who swept in with love and high spirits and then swept out and off to the theatre. I certainly thought she was gorgeous but I also knew that she got depressed or huffy or self-concerned and even at 5 years old I knew that for all her high spirits and bounding energy she still needed cheering up from time to time. Furthermore I used to watch her scrubbing the floors with carbolic every morning, dusting the room and doing all the other household chores. Again, I'm sure that she coped with this as she has coped with any other tiresome problem all through her life, by treating it as a part in a play that must be played well. I'm not sure that I don't even do a lot of this myself and if so I probably began to learn the technique when I had scarlet fever.

Sybil had already begun rehearsals for her Old Vic engagement before I went sick but, of course, we were both contagious and so she couldn't rehearse during the six weeks quarantine. But that didn't stop her working on her parts. She acted them all to me over and over again and I used to ask her questions about it. She has told me since that making sense of your words to a small boy of 5 is not a bad test for an actress's ability to make her words meaningful. In between times she played on our old Bluthner grand piano and when she stopped playing 'grown-up' music she would play songs, dances and marches for me to sing and mime – it was glorious!

Then on 28th October, my fifth birthday, we were released from captivity. We celebrated the joyful day by riding on the top of a horse-bus all the way to St Paul's Cathedral and back and Sybil kept me enthralled by telling me about everything we passed. This wasn't just the world of Pimlico. This was London. And it was from this day I'm sure that London became what it has been ever since for me – Home! But on my fifth birthday I only remember the fun of being with Sybil on the top of the bus talking our heads off and laughing at everything. Within days the whole family was ensconced in Bessborough Street again, Alice and Nelly were once more in charge of Christopher, Mary and me, while Sybil could begin work in earnest at the Old Vic.

I suppose it is impossible for any of us to be certain about the chronology of the events of our childhood. Our memories don't always agree with the historical evidence, which is apt to be so much the worse for the historical evidence. What I remember is much more real to me than what I have later on been told as the facts. And so in those early days of the war there was a whole string of things that I know happened in a certain order, but which I simply cannot fit into the recorded events of the time. Looking at them now makes me think of a whole crowd of film shots strung together by someone who has no idea of montage.

There was old Mrs Tichball who kept the toy shop along Tatchbrook Street where Sybil used to take us to buy toys. Sybil's logic in explaining that a tuppeny tin fire engine was a better one than the extravagant two and threepenny one, gave me, even then, one or two doubts about either her truthfulness or her sanity. She used to have long conversations with Mr Gifford the chemist about the relative merits of tooth-powder and the new-fangled toothpaste, and they both roared with laughter one day when he gave me a tiny cake of blue soap and told me it would make my hair grow. I couldn't think what was funny about it. I also remember very well that when Alice and Nelly took us for a walk round Warwick Street, they didn't talk or let me talk to the old harridans who kept the stalls. 'Don't talk to them. They're nasty old things,' said Alice. And so I was very surprised next time I was there with Sybil to find that she talked to them all as long lost friends. 'Aren't they darlings!' she often said to my complete bewilderment.

It was in the Belgrave Road branch of Lloyds Bank at the corner of Warwick Way that Sybil fainted one day. It was the first time that my sister Ann, to be born at the end of 1915, had made herself felt, but it was many years before I knew that this was the cause. Christopher and I with Mary in the pushchair, were all taken into the manager's resplendent office where Sybil was lying back on a rather uncomfortable-looking chaise-longue sipping a glass of water.

Now I come to think of it and if my arithmetic is right, this must have happened in the spring of 1915. Late in February, Lewis, now a sergeant, was sent to the front with a unit of the Army Service Corps. Some twenty years later just after my own marriage, I rather tactlessly asked Sybil why, when they were so hard-up, they had allowed themselves the luxury of a fourth child. But Sybil was equal to it and without even pausing for breath answered, 'Well darling, you see it was his last night before going to France!' So this must have been in the late spring!

We certainly had a family Christmas at Bessborough Street at the end of 1914 or at least it began there early in the morning when we awoke at 6 a.m. to see the great white mountains of pillow cases stuffed with presents on the ends of our beds. But we had Christmas dinner at the vicarage with Granpapa and Grannie and sang carols at the children's service that afternoon at St James the Less where Granpapa in his white surplice told us the story of Bethlehem.

Granpapa Thorndike was a very handsome, well set up man of about sixty at this time. He gave the fine bone structure of his face to Sybil and with it an undaunted relish for the sheer delight of being alive. Sybil adored him with an almost religious devotion though he was by no means one of those other-worldly clerics who terrify us by the majesty of their holiness. Sybil told me that when she was about 16 she was watching him at evensong one night as he stood arms raised in prayer, his beautiful voice intoning the litany and raptly gazing up into the darkness of the roof. After the service Sybil had said to him, 'Father what were your thoughts at that wonderful moment when you were looking up just before the Blessing?' Granpapa answered with all the forthrightness of the Thorndike family's love of emphasis: 'My dear! I was thinking how *splendid* it would have been if I had been on a *trapeze* swinging across the *aisle*!' But he believed absolutely in the truth of the Book of Genesis, read prayers in a voice that dared one on pain of apocalyptic disaster not to believe him and saw the Pope and all his works as the Beast of the Revelations. He had been something of an athlete and mountaineer in his youth, took a cold bath every morning, wore a little gold half-moon pince-nez when he was reading and smelt slightly of fresh soap.

Grannie Donnie was anything but awe-inspiring. She always had something exciting for us to do and an infinite variety of sweetmeats stowed in little boxes in her underclothes drawer and in various parts of the house. She had what is called an ample figure, which she nearly always seemed to cover with rather shapeless pale grey silky materials. On her bosom she wore a plain silver cross on a silver chain. It clinked on the button of her blouse, which had the same effect as a Swiss cow-bell in that we could always hear her coming. It was she who arranged the jollifications for the family, and to go round to the vicarage 'to see Grannie' turned any day into a delight. Sybil must have inherited her energy from Donnie. Those people, and they are legion, who think Sybil the most energetic of all, never knew Donnie Thorndike. Her mothers' meetings were legendary, not for bringing mothers closer into the bosom of the Church but for their sheer entertainment value. Talking was her delight and she had a fund of stories that would have made the Arabian Nights look dusty. That they were not always the most suitable stories for mothers' meetings or indeed for a vicar's wife, worried her not at all. Once, in my hearing, Granpapa mildly protested that she was not bringing enough religion into the meetings: 'Fiddlesticks!' she cried. 'Don't be so stuffy, Arthur! They all love it, and it does them just as much good as the Bible. You mustn't be pompous and holy-bob.' And I can only suppose that she went on as imperturbably as ever making the mothers roar with laughter. When they'd had enough of the stories she played the piano for them and made them all sing sentimental ballads which she led in an unashamedly strident soprano. But interwoven with all this jollity was an incredible ability to imagine every conceivable disaster. She devoured all the sensational items in the newspapers and then foresaw that almost all of the disasters would somehow happen to all of us. This went on even to the day she died in 1933. None of us was safe from dangers that ranged from earthquakes to seduction, from ship-wrecks to financial ruin, from hell-fire to sinister gentlemen in macin-toshes who lurked at every street corner. When as a fairly well-built young midshipman of 18, I brought another midshipman of the same age on leave with me, we spent a few weeks at Dymchurch, where Grannie at that time was the châtelaine in charge of the household. We hired a boat one day to go fishing and casually told her of our intentions over lunch. To our astonishment Grannie burst into a flood of terrify-ing warning of the dangers of boating! 'I don't know what Sybil will say when you're both washed up drowned. I've been told all the boats on this coast are leaky and dangerous. Oh, my! What am I going to do? I won't have it. I'll just have to go away and sell the cottage if this sort of thing goes on – you ungrateful boys!'

It was useless to try to explain that we'd been at sea for two years, that our duties put us in charge of large sailing launches and small dinghies, that we had sailed in the calm of the Mediterranean and in the fury of Atlantic gales. She was adamant. No boating! And that was that!

But in 1915 she was warm, comfy, welcoming Grannie, for whom nothing was too much trouble, who was a bit of a fusspot and whom we all adored. She was always bustling around looking after some-one.

That Christmas of 1914, and in the months that followed, we were sometimes in Bessborough Street and sometimes at the vicarage. We used to be taken over Waterloo Bridge to the Old Vic. We called it 'The Theatre' because we knew that was where Sybil went at night. 'I'm off to the theatre' she said as a man says 'I'm off to the office' and gradually this place became part of our lives. I know 'The Theatre' seemed to be a very tiresomely demanding thing that often kept Sybil away when we knew she would be much happier with us.

One evening I had been put to bed and Sybil was getting ready to go off to the theatre. She was running rather late and seemed to me to be getting rather desperate about it. I remember asking: 'Why does it matter if you're late?'

'Mr Ben Greet would be furious.'

'What would he do?'

'Oh, he'd tell me he didn't want me to go to the theatre any more.'

'That would be lovely, because then you could stay at home every night.'

'Ah, but then I wouldn't get any money and we'd all starve. Oh dear look at the time. It's later than ever. I must fly!'

And she flew down the stairs and out through the front door leaving a very anxious little boy behind, who now saw all sorts of threatening dangers in the world of grown-ups, and worst of all one special rascally man who could even hold Sybil in his power! After this it was years before I could think of poor old Ben Greet as anything less than the villain of a melodrama.

Lord knows the money wasn't much. Sybil got ten shillings a performance at the Old Vic and Lewis was sending home twenty-five shillings a week from his by no means princely pay as a sergeant in France. It must have been a pretty grim struggle for them both to keep the family going. But I never remember feeling that we were poorly off. We were shown the 'poor children' in the streets as if we were rich, and Sybil gave us pennies to give them. And, of course, in those days the poor were very poor. To see barefooted children in the streets of London even in winter was rarely thought to be unusual or worthy of remark. But it was very much worthy of remark for Sybil, whose heart embraced them all.

When the Zeppelins came over London we had the excitement of being woken up in the middle of the night and of being taken down into the basement and fed on milk and biscuits which was after all a splendid way of passing the night. Sybil saw to it that we were never frightened by the bangs and the booms. She made us think of it as some sort of grown-up skylark and we were only furious that we weren't allowed out in the street to watch it all. We had seen the searchlights from our bedroom window and had been reassured by Sybil's 'Don't they look lovely those lights. Come on darlings, we're going down into the basement to get something to eat.' I did hear someone telling Sybil about the bomb that fell just round the corner in Lupus Street, 'The hole was so big you could put a horse and cart in it,' and I kept wondering why anyone would want to put a horse and cart in a hole in the ground. But as it didn't seem to surprise Sybil I knew it was all right and stopped worrying about it.

In the spring, the Zeps became more threatening and the three of us were once more dispatched to Dymchurch. By now the threat of air raids was thought to be worse than German submarines and as no one seemed to be likely to come across the Channel, we would all be much better going to Dym. It was the beginning of a long period when Alice and Nelly ruled our lives. For the next two years it was 'week-end Sybil' we were to know and in this particular summer we hardly saw her at all. But we saw three waterspouts in a thunderstorm over the Channel that everyone thought were the ubiquitous submarines. And we were hauled out of bed early one morning to gallop over the fields and dikes of Romney Marsh to be able to stare with the whole population of the village at a naval blimp – a two-seater gas-filled airship – that had force-landed a mile in-shore. However, these things were merely part of the astonishing and adventure-filled world of any child. The War, as a war, didn't really touch us at all. Kiff and I knew vaguely that Lewis was doing something dangerous. We saw men in blue uniforms called 'wounded soldiers' and wondered if Lewis would ever be one of them. Sybil had told us a little about people called Germans, who were 'against us'. But her deeply held pacifistic views even then would not allow her to tell us to hate the enemy. Alice and Nelly, however, had no such inhibitions, and thus are the teachings of our well-intentioned parents so often frustrated. They told us blood-curdling stories of the atrocities committed by 'those awful Germans' so that when, later on in the war, we came across a group of German prisoners working in a field we knew we had come face to face with the legions of Lucifer.

And so we played on the beach through all the months of the summer. When Sybil managed to get a couple of days off in August she found she was the mother of three children all burnt dark brown and with hair bleached flaxen by the sun. She says she hardly knew us; but we certainly knew her. Fond as we were of Alice and Nelly, and they really were darlings, they never seemed to think of the exciting things to do that we always did with Sybil.

With Sybil everything became ten times more wonderful and the best of everything was always about to happen. If it didn't, well who cared? She always had lots more things for us to do. We were, however, an awful long way from London. As the summer faded and the leaves turned brown, it became nearly impossible for Sybil to visit us at all, especially as the time of Ann's arrival was getting to be very near. And as always in those days when there was a problem to be solved, it was Grannie who solved it. She found us a cottage only twenty miles from London at Kingsdown on the road to Folkestone. It had two tiny rooms on the ground floor with a kitchen at the back and a loo at the bottom of the garden. Upstairs there were two small bedrooms. We had our baths in an old battered tin tub in front of the sitting-room fire. The rent was half a crown a week, which even Sybil and Lewis could afford.

Once more were we all brought up from Dymchurch to the Pimlico vicarage for a week or two and then in early October we moved into Grey Cottage under the watchful eye of Mr and Mrs Hopperton, the farmer and his wife on whose farm the cottage stood. Mr Hopperton was one of those people for whom nobody seemed to have thought of finding a Christian name. He may have had one but no one ever heard it. His wife called him 'Mr Hopperton' and the squire called him 'Hopperton'. He had a bald head and a thick brown moustache which Mary, now eighteen months old, found irresistible. Mrs Hopperton was a waspish lady who scared the daylights out of us all. She had a biting tongue and a voice that made sure that most of the village knew what she was thinking when she was on the warpath – and she must have had a lot of wars. But they gave us the free run of their farm and so the doors of the country people's world began to open up for us little 'townies'.

The nearest stations were Fawkham, four miles away down the lane, or Eynsford, three miles away over the fields. Sometimes when she could afford it and certainly before Ann was born, Sybil would hire the services of a Mr Swanscombe, who ran a very rattletrap motor-bike and sidecar as a sort of taxi. And so we now saw her nearly every week-end. She came down early on Sunday and went back after lunch on Monday to be in time for the evening show at the Old Vic.

Ann was born in London on 6th November, 1915, just after my own sixth birthday. The news came to us on a wet morning while Kiff and I were standing up on a bench playing with toys on the window-sill. 'You've got a new baby sister,' said Nelly. 'And she's called Ann.' But we went on with our playing unmoved by the momentous news. However, two or three weeks later Sybil came to Kingsdown and brought Ann with her.

Sybil was with us for Christmas and we had a lovely time in the little front room of Grey Cottage. After tea Sybil invited old Bob the farm-hand to come and join us. He used to sleep in the hayloft and eat in the farmhouse scullery and so didn't have much fun. Sybil played the piano for us and we danced and sang till long after our proper bedtime with old Bob, his bearded face grinning at us, beating the time with a huge mugful of cocoa that Alice had been asked to give him though she disapproved of 'asking farmhands into the house'.

All the next year we were at Kingsdown. Sybil used to give a 'View-Halloo' when she came across the fields into sight of the cottage and we would rush out of the back door to go tearing across the grass to her. 'Don't get so excited the pair of you,' Nelly would say to Kiff and me. 'You don't want to knock your mother down.' But what did she know about it? 'Mummy' had arrived and so the sun was shining and everybody became doubly alive.

Kingsdown was a new world for us. Up till now we had never lived with fields at the back door and woods on the other side of the lane. At Dymchurch there had been no garden but only the sea and the miles of golden sands. At Kingsdown in the spring of 1916 we first knew the loveliness of the English countryside. And we saw it through the eyes of Sybil. On those all too short Sundays and the occasional longer breaks between Old Vic productions, she took us into the woods and fields and made us see it all with that intensity of focus that only the great artists seem to be able to manage.

As the snow left the land we saw our first snowdrops in the garden. We watched the crocuses come up with that impudent gaiety that tells us that the winter is nearly gone. In April, Sybil took us for walks along the lanes and we watched the multitude of primroses bursting out under the hedgerows. In May, we all shouted for joy as the huge carpets of bluebells spread through the woods. And so on through the summer of wild roses, lilac, gooseberries, honeysuckle, raspberries, wild strawberries, hollyhocks and green beech trees. We skylarked our days in a sort of open-eyed delight with Sybil's visits injecting us each time with new and lively enthusiasms. We weren't surprised that Sybil knew all about this world, though many people even now might wonder how she came to be at home in it. The fact, of course, is that this was the world into which she was born. Although her actual birthplace was Gainsborough in Lincolnshire, she spent nearly all of her childhood, first at Rochester, where her father was a minor canon, and later at Aylesford where he was the vicar. At all events she is a country girl at heart, and she loves the country – as long as there are plenty of people around who will keep it in order for her! She has always loved the idea of being a farmer's wife, and it would only last half an hour if she were, just as she wants to be a nurse or a doctor or St Teresa or Madame Curie. To talk to her in a garden you would think the only thing that interests her is to get away from the rush and bustle of the town, put on a floppy old hat and to start rooting out weeds or coax a host of horticultural wonders into colourful fecundity in an old-world corner of Tudor England. And it's quite true for the moment, as long as there is someone around to sort it all out later. But that is exactly what it means to be an actor. You can have all the emotional excitement of being whatever you want to be without the bother of doing the tiresome chores that have to accompany it in real life. It's wonderful to think of oneself as proud Cortez standing on a peak in Darien as long as one can have that moment on its own and not have to bother with all the tiresomeness of sixteenth century travel. As an actor you spend your life doing just this. It's the stage manager's job to prepare the scene for you, to provide you with your props at the right time and to clear up the mess afterwards. But it makes you tremendously sensitive to what is significant in a collection of happenings. You are for instance instantly aware of a whole complicated set of relationships between people in a crowd. You can feel their pains and their delights. You can know what it means to be rich, and why you aren't happy with your riches, without ever having had any money. You can know what it feels like to be destitute with an intensity of feeling that is like a deluge, while being quite hopeless at doing anything practical about the problems of poverty. Actors 'see' so much more clearly and quickly than others but they need those others to take action about what they, the actors, have seen.

And while we are about it, this power of vision, this intense awareness, and hence tremendous feeling and emotion, causes the really good actors to develop what is, in effect, their greatest contribution to society – the communicating of their clearer vision to those who have to take the actions that keep the world running. They not only 'see' and feel more than the rest of us, they use more feeling when they express what they 'see'. This means that they learn not to be afraid of the power of their own emotions, and at the same time they learn how to control and use them.

Some time during the thirties Sybil was engaged in some public argument about disarmament, which she was advocating as powerfully as she advocates all the host of causes which she so vigorously espouses. Her ideas very much annoyed a well-known writer of thrillers. He wrote to her: 'Your views are both ridiculous and unpatriotic. They are the kind of emotional rubbish one might expect from an actress.' Sybil replied: 'Dear Mr So-and-so, thank you so much for your letter. Yes, I am emotional and I am an actress. But being an actress I have had to learn to control my emotions . . .' Her reply captivated the writer, who wrote back: 'Dear Dame Sybil, you are a lady and on this occasion I regret that I was not a gentleman. . . .'

This control and fearless use of emotion in communicating their vision does, however, mean that nearly everything that actors do and say is part of a performance. Sybil has really never stopped performing and it is always a superb performance on the largest scale. But this doesn't mean for a moment that she is insincere. In fact, it means just the opposite. Her intellectual honesty is without peer. But she abstracts from a situation only what is to her effectively dramatic and projects it with enormous power to whomsoever is within range. To be with Sybil is to see everything through an enormous emotional magnifying glass. It is wildly exciting. But if you're not used to it you find yourself a couple of hours later wondering why you feel so tired. As children we were lucky enough to be brought up with it and so can control the doses of our own stimulation. And it is always immensely stimulating.

And so at Kingsdown we were carried along both willingly and willy-nilly by Sybil's enthusiasm. We did a bit of digging in the garden, and it was good dramatic digging. It made us lovers of flowers but poor gardeners. We had a rabbit in a hutch but it died of poor animal husbandry. We had adventures and games in the woods with Sybil for ever suggesting new things to do which she made us believe were our ideas. We played with the village children and had serious talks from Sybil on their ways of talking. 'They're very nice children, darlings, but you mustn't talk like they do or I shan't let you play with them.' So we learnt about good speech too.

I was even taught by Sybil to recite the 'Romans, countryman and lovers' speech of Brutus in what I imagine was a high piping soprano voice. It had to be 'acted', of course, and we made a 'pulpit' out of a kitchen chair. I stood on the seat and harangued the crowd in the forum leaning over the back. She even made me perform it one afternoon to the assembled children of the village school. Old Mr Palfryman, the lame headmaster, was wildly enthusiastic, but I was very disgusted by the cool reception given to it by the children. The poor little things couldn't have had the faintest idea what it was about, but it was my first experience of philistinism.

We were also persuaded by Sybil to dress up as elves and fairies and she wound us up in all sorts of wispy veils and scarves. She explained the rudiments of classical dancing to us so that we could float and glide among the woodland trees casting magic spells on moles and rabbits. We rather enjoyed this game until one day Kiff and I rashly glided accidentally into the middle of a Boy Scouts' camp to the astonishment of the scouts and to our own utter confusion.

We stayed at Kingsdown off and on until early in 1918, and in June of 1917 I saw my first piece of real life serious drama without any acting. We were in the little sitting-room one afternoon and Sybil was kneeling on the floor helping us with some game. Suddenly there was a loud knocking. 'Open the front door, John darling,' said Sybil and I reached up and undid the latch. A tall fat girl stood outside who thrust into my hand an orange envelope saying as she did so, 'Telegram for yer mum.' Never as long as I live shall I forget the look of abject terror on Sybil's face as she tore open the telegram. In those days of long casualty lists telegrams were frequent and horrifying, and Sybil fully expected to read that Lewis had been killed in action. But as she read she gave a great sigh of relief and said: 'Thank God, he's wounded.' At 7 years old I was astonished that she should be so pleased to know that Lewis was wounded until she told me that this would probably mean he would be coming home soon. And some weeks later when she came on her next visit, she brought Lewis with her.

He came wearing the uniform of a captain in the Royal Engineers, for he had been commissioned in 1916. It was found then that he had a half-completed chemistry degree and so he was thought to be just the fellow who would know about gas. One night he had been ordered to lay a large number of cylinders of phosgene out in No Man's Land. There was himself, a sergeant and a dozen privates from the R.E.s and he was to have had a large carrying party of a hundred Australians. The Australians, for some reason, failed to turn up and so Lewis took his baker's dozen engineers and they did the job on their own. Lewis got a Military Cross for the night's work and a wound in his shoulder from a piece of shrapnel. One night, forty years later, he told the story of it at a dinner in Melbourne. He never understood why the Australians were not very enthusiastic when he thanked them for his M.C.!

After tea on the evening he arrived Lewis put his soldier's knapsack on the table and began to unpack it. Almost everything in it was for us children. 'Here is something for John' he said in a solemn ritualistic voice, and pulled out a huge bar of chocolate. 'Isn't that lovely, darling' Sybil applauded from the other end of the table. And then came 'Here is something for Christopher' and an identical bar came forth, with another to follow for Mary. But there were old candle ends, an identification disc, a bit of copper wire, and the greatest thrill of all, a pair of blood-stained braces. It was a nice mid-summer's Christmas. We hadn't had a father in the house for over two years but if this was what a father was like then the longer he stayed around the better.

He had three weeks leave which was spent almost entirely walking with Sybil along the footpaths of the Kent countryside. Kiff and I were allowed to go with them sometimes on the strict understanding that it was a 'grown-up walk' on which there was to be no dawdling and no being carried if we got tired. We walked miles and miles over fields of grass and round the edges of cornfields. We strode through the woods and Lewis cut us off long straight hazel sticks so that we could better look the part of walkers. Only once did we ever ride and that was when we were picked up three miles from home by our 'rich' friends, Captain and Mrs Lance, who lived in one of the 'big houses', and actually owned a motor-car. The motor-car in question broke down still a mile and a half from home when Captain Lance demonstrated that the car would actually reach forty-five miles an hour. Something made a nasty noise under the bonnet and it refused to go any farther. Sybil, Kiff and I set off once more on the long trudge home leaving Lewis with the Lances and his 'Look' to cope with the car. He returned home soaked in sweat some hours later having pushed the car for a mile and a half. Thus did we learn that cars were things that broke down and that Lewis could usually cope when they did. In the coming years there was going to be a line of Lewis's so-called motor-cars that were going to break down in every part of the country, and Lewis's ability to cope was to be tested under many and varying conditions.

At this time, however, motor-cars were only owned by the rich, among whom we definitely did not belong. Lewis and Sybil always seemed to be on familiar terms with the gentry of the district but we were never 'of them', and never got asked to their houses. Alice and Nelly spoke of Squire and Mrs Sugden rather as though they were about to genuflect, and Mrs Hamlin, a widow living in the next property, was charmingly patronising to us all. The vicar and his wife, Mr and Mrs Warland, were warm hearted and hospitable and we got on like a house on fire with all the villagers. I suppose that the 'stage' was still not yet an altogether respectable profession, especially if you were not at the top of the tree. One old villager had heard that Sybil was an actress and one day in a burst of enthusiasm said to her: 'Oim a-comin' to see yer a-jumpin' through the 'oops!' The circus and the stage were all one to him, and after all, none of us would have thought it entirely out of the question to imagine Sybil standing up in a tinsel tu-tu balanced on the broad rump of a circus horse! But it would hardly have given us an entry into the Kent county society of 1917.

In August, Lewis took Sybil back to London at the end of his leave, and towards the end of the month Nelly gently told us the news of Frank's death in France. It didn't seem to us to be a very terrible thing because Sybil had always said that when people died they went off to a place where everybody was happy. But it was a fearful blow to the Thorndikes. Frank had always been one of those people for whom death seemed impossible. Russell felt it very deeply because he and Frank had done so much together and had always revelled in each other's company.

Russell told me that he and Frank had made an agreement. If either of them were killed he would appear to the other at once in some sort of disguise. On the night of Frank's death Russell swears that a mouse came and sat on his pillow and wouldn't be frightened away. He has always been sure it was Frank, and perhaps it was. Russell has such wonderful fancies and fantasies and somehow one always believes him when he describes them.

In the early autumn Lewis was given a job at the War Office and so Grey Cottage was abandoned and we all went back to London. By now the house in Bessborough Street had been let and in the event we were

Sybil about 26

Lewis as *Dante*, one of his earliest performances *c.* 1905
From a pencil drawing by Ernest Jackson

never to live there again. The vicarage in St George's Square was large and we took over two of the rooms upstairs. But of course, we took over the whole household as well. Granny was thrilled to have the four children to look after and cosset but Granpapa must have found our rumbustiousness very trying at times. I don't think we gave him an awful lot of peace, but he was never bad-tempered with us. We saw lots of Sybil and began to know more and more of Lewis. I was even taken by Sybil one day to visit him in a dingy room at the War Office and I was enchanted to be told by Sybil that it was a very secret room where they made 'plans'.

The 9th December was a Sunday that year. At about 6.30 in the evening Kiff and I were playing with bricks sprawled all over the drawing-room carpet. Granny had gone off early to evensong because she was the organist, and had taken Sybil with her. I think Lewis must have been away. Granpapa was upstairs writing his sermon. Then we heard him running down the stairs. I called out: 'Look what we've built, Granpapa,' and he shouted back, 'Not to-night dears. I'm very late. Good night,' and off he went. Those were the last words any of us in the family were to hear him speak. He was late and so he hurried all the way to church, and he hurried too much. Twenty minutes later the choir moved out from the vestry into the back of the church and Granpapa gave out the number of the first hymn. As the choir began to sing he had a heart attack and fell back. By the time his beloved Donnie, hastily summoned from the organ loft, had reached his side he was dead.

An hour later Sybil came home from the church and found me in pyjamas cleaning my teeth in Granpapa's bathroom. Her face was puffed and red and she was still crying. She sat on a chair and I went over to her.

'What's the matter Mummy?'

'Granpapa has gone, darling. He died in church. We've all got to be very brave and help Granny.'

And soon afterwards when I had run upstairs to the bedroom and told Kiff we heard Granny coming up the stairs almost out of her mind with grief, while the voice of warm-hearted Auntie Maud tried in vain to comfort her.

For some weeks they feared that she really would go insane. She and her Arthur had been married for thirty-six years and in all that time they had not spent one day apart. She just could not even begin to think of life without him. It was a very sad Christmas for us all, although even Granny tried not to let her grief spoil the celebrations for us children. It was Russell who had the brainwave to cheer everybody up. He wrote a short play for himself, Christopher and me to act to the entire household in the drawing-room on Boxing Day. I don't remember what it was all about except that Russell played the part of some horrifying Arabian spirit and that Christopher forgot his lines, while I felt very superior about it. All the servants were thrilled to see 'Mr Russell' acting for them and applauded loudly. We beamed delightedly, quite certain that the applause was for us. It was a splendid evening and we all enjoyed ourselves hugely.

Eventually Granny pulled herself together, but she was unable to go to the funeral. And so Lewis, Sybil, Russell and Eileen all went down together to Aylesford. Granpapa was buried beside the church where he had been the vicar, and in which Lewis and Sybil had been married exactly nine years before.

The family now faced a very big problem. After Granpapa's death we had to leave the vicarage and find somewhere else to live. It must have been a very trying time for Lewis and Sybil. They had to find a house within reasonable distance of both the War Office and the Old Vic. It had to be big enough for a family and it had to be cheap. This would have been quite a problem at any time, but with the war on, they must have been in despair.

Kiff and I went off down to Kingsdown directly after Christmas and investigated the new Holly Tree Cottage. It was a tiny semi-detached labourer's cottage owned by Squire Sugden. Our next door neighbours were Mr and Mrs Gamus Mills. It was he who thought Sybil was a trick rider, and his wife gave us toffees for collecting dandelions from which she made a most unpleasant wine. We had first come to the cottage on my eighth birthday, when Sybil, Kiff and I spent a cold but magical week-end trying the place out. We had woken up on my birthday to a miraculously blue sky and a dazzling white frost that crunched under our feet and sparkled like some sort of breathless beatific vision. After breakfast we had rushed out into the woods and chased each other through the trees. Early on Monday morning Gamus Mills had harnessed up the squire's horse and cart and we had been driven in the dark, and I think in a fog, to Kemsing Station five miles away to catch the milk train to London.

We had a blissful summer at Kingsdown while our parents searched and searched for somewhere in London to house the family. At last some time in July we heard that they had found the very place in Westminster. In those days if you turned off the embankment by Millbank Gardens into Wood Street you came almost at once into a real slum which ran right through to Vauxhall Bridge Road behind the Army and Navy Stores. Just beyond Smith Square was one of those little archways which ran through into a very narrow court with tiny, scruffy little houses on either side. Lewis and Sybil had found and rented the house over the archway. The front door was actually in the tunnel and led into a room that had once been a shop. It had three floors, and on each side the house extended down the courtyard by the length of one very small room. Thus on the top floor Kiff and I had a cabin-like room each and were able to run a string across the yard from one window to the other on which we could send secret messages. During July they had spent a disquieting time getting rid of every conceivable variety of house and bed bugs and in clearing them out Lewis found his experiences in the trenches unexpectedly useful. In August we moved in. The shop became the drawing-room and the familiar family furniture from Bessborough Street soon made us all feel at home. We had yet to learn about our neighbours, who were poor in the real terrifying sense of the word, and the unmistakable smell of their poverty was never absent when we opened the back windows.

Number 35 Wood Street, now buried beneath vast steel and concrete office blocks, was to be our home for the next two years. In September Kiff and I were sent to Albert Bridge School, or 'Mrs Spencer's' as we called it, to which we travelled by No. 11 bus every morning from Westminster Abbey to Chelsea Town Hall.

One morning there was a great shouting in the street outside the school and all the sirens started blowing. 'That means the war's over' said our form-mistress. It was eleven o'clock on the 11th November, 1918.

An hour later 'the Casson boys' were called downstairs to find Lewis in uniform waiting to take us home. He and Sybil had felt that two small boys of 9 and 7 should not be left to come home alone on a day when London was obviously going to go wild. And how right they were. But Lewis made sure that we remembered the day by insisting that all three of us walked home from Chelsea to Westminster. In the King's Road he bought each of us a large Union Jack, which we waved like mad all along the streets crammed with cheering excited people, and the old open buses packed with soldiers and girls singing at the top of their voices.

That night into the waste patch at the back of the 'Court' people dragged the very mattresses from their beds, piled them high with old bits of furniture and made a gigantic bonfire. They burnt almost everything they owned and spent what little savings they had on bottles of whatever alcohol they could get.

At the edge of the patch we all stood and watched, Lewis, Sybil and the four children. Lewis and Sybil had tears rolling down their cheeks and we four gazed in wonder as the fire blazed red and everybody sang lugubrious sentimental songs. Here we were with the family intact and about to begin to live together in a real family life.

And it was here that some months later Lewis walked into the dining-room at breakfast in a speckly tweed suit. Now the war was really over. Lewis was a civilian again. We all cheered and celebrated by having a whole half-pound of the butter ration for breakfast.

Chapter 4

BEGINNING TO BE KNOWN

THE Christmas attraction at the Old Vic in 1917 was an entirely idiotic revue performed by the same actors who, for three years, had been playing almost nothing but Shakespeare. Russell, now invalided out of the army and a leading man in the company, wrote the 'book' and Sybil the music. However, Sybil firmly maintains that she was not very inventive as a composer, and that is why most of the tunes could be recognised by the musically astute as deriving from Hymns Ancient and Modern and even the Messiah. All the bubbling and energetic foolery of the days of the Rochester attic-acting went into the show and it was a riot. The whole company of skilful professional actors jumped at the chance, as most actors do, of playing charades. Sybil was Columbine in a harlequinade and she played a part in an Ibsen burlesque called *Spooks*. It so happened that Charles Cochran's manager visited the show and took a fancy to Sybil. By now she had played at the Old Vic every woman's part that Shakespeare ever wrote and quite a few of the men's as well (I remember her as Touchstone when I was 6, which horrified me, and her Prince Hal, which would have reminded me of a principal boy except that I had not yet seen a pantomime!). It is therefore an odd turn of fate that her first break into the West End was given her by Cochran as a support for the French comedian Leon Morton in a short farcical sketch in a variety bill at the London Pavilion. It was followed by the part of a French woman in an odd sentimental tear-jerking sketch called *The Kiddies in the Ruins*, which came in the middle of a show about Bruce Bairnsfather's 'Old Bill' called *The Better 'Ole*. What Cochran was up to we shall now never know. It has been suggested that he was perspicacious enough to see not only the fine actress in her but also a certain primness, and that he felt a large dose of the rough-and-tumble down-to-earth blunt vulgarity of the variety artists would do her a lot of good. Personally I don't believe it, but the fact remains that it almost certainly did do her acting a lot of good, and she certainly enjoyed the experience with the same enthusiasm as she has enjoyed every experience that has come her way.

All four of us children were taken to see *The Kiddies in the Ruins*, though what Ann, at the age of 2½, could have made of it Heaven knows. I do know that when she caught sight of Sybil on the stage amid the ruins of a French village she shouted 'Mummy' at the top of her voice to the considerable astonishment of the audience and the utter dismayed embarrassment of her elder brothers aged 8 and 6.

This led to the job of understudying Madge Titheridge in a war thriller called *Night Watch*, which opened just after the Armistice, and to a second-lead under Lilian Braithwaite in *The Chinese Puzzle* in April 1919. Kiff and I adored this play, which I remember as my first real appreciation of 'the drama'. Sybil was the young wife of a diplomat who was negotiating with a distinguished Chinese gentleman the terms of a desperately secret treaty. Sybil's mother in the play was something of a crook and could only avoid going to gaol if Sybil would photograph the treaty for her. I shall never forget the thrilling moment when the young diplomat questioned his wife about the document and Sybil fell in a dead faint as the noble Chinese gentleman, played by Leon M. Lion, took full responsibility for the 'leak' to save the young wife's honour and her marriage. And backstage we both got to know and adore Lilian Braithwaite, who was the first 'star' we ever met. And so our move to Wood Street coincided almost exactly with Sybil's first move in the direction of fame. It was still little more than a nudge but the move had begun.

In the meanwhile we had had our first Christmas at Wood Street. Rations were just beginning to be enlarged and there was a gorgeous feeling of 'family' in the house. We had huge pillow cases of toys on our beds in the early hours of the morning and a turkey and plum pudding, both of tremendous proportions, in the middle of the day. During the morning, however, Sybil took on what was for us a new rôle, that of the 'Bountiful Lady of the Vicarage'. She had laid in a great pile of jolly little toys and at eleven o'clock the mothers from the court at the back came one by one with their children into our sitting-room to receive such Christmas cheer as Lewis and Sybil could afford to give them – a toy for each child and a shilling for the mothers. All four of us Casson children had to be there to give our greetings and to learn that if we were going to enjoy ourselves we had to see that others had something too. God knows it wasn't much, but our neighbours were as poor as their hearts were warm and from this day on they became our friends, though, it must be added, rather to the astonishment of our other friends who came to visit us.

At the beginning of the New Year, Lewis had been demobbed and was playing in *Cyrano de Bergerac* at the Garrick under Robert Loraine whom he had met long before the war in the Vedrenne-Barker season at the Court Theatre. He had not entirely shut himself off from acting and production while he had been in the army. In France he had organised amateur concerts and persuaded his officers and men to contribute their party pieces. Only the other day I was shown a concert programme in which I saw that Major L. T. Casson had recited 'If' and 'Once more into the breach . . .'. And in 1915 or '16 when he was on leave he played Fortinbras in *Hamlet* at the Old Vic. It was of course strictly against the King's Regulations for an enlisted soldier to appear on the stage of the theatre, and so on the programme of that production there appeared the name of a most promising actor called 'Christopher Holland'. Holland was the maiden name of Lewis's mother and I've often wondered if anyone remembered this name. I remember the Fortinbras though, for at the age of six I was allowed to see this *Hamlet*; Russell's Hamlet and Sybil's Ophelia, all four and a half hours of uncut *Hamlet*, with an interval for food in the middle. I sat on the steps in the circle, for the house was packed, and refused to leave even in the interval in case someone stole my 'place', and old Ben Greet brought me a bag of Bath buns to eat during the second half.

The extraordinary thing about my early recollections of Lewis's acting is that he always seemed to have the 'Look' on his face. It had been there all the time in Manchester and here it was again as Fortinbras. In fact one of the earliest portraits of him as an actor, before he became a professional, shows him as a rather stern Dante. The picture has always hung on the wall of Sybil's bedroom and so perhaps gave me my first awareness of the 'Look'. It epitomises the Welsh rebel in him. It is not that he was 'anti' but rather that he seemed impatiently indignant whenever he was working at anything. There was a fierce energy in it that prohibited any sort of 'slackness' when you were in his presence. It could, of course, be very alarming and especially so to a small boy, who wasn't able entirely to dissociate the play from real life, and as we shall see it certainly intimidated the timid among his players when he was producing.

When we were taken to see *Cyrano*, Lewis's 'Look' seemed to be sterner than ever as Cyrano's friend who interrupts Cyrano's love scene with Roxane to say 'He has brought his death by coming here.' Lewis seemed not only to be reprimanding everyone in the cast but the whole audience as well for bringing about the death of his friend.

After the show Lewis took us to meet Robert Loraine, who to our enormous delight was just taking off the huge false Cyrano nose. It wasn't until I became a midshipman and began to read everything I could lay my hands on about flying, that I discovered that Robert Loraine was one of the early pioneers in aviation. He had been among the intrepid few who had competed with Bleriot for the *Daily Mail* prize for the first man to fly the Channel. He certainly made a wonderful Cyrano. It made such an impression on me that I have used it ever since in conversations with Lewis as an example of what I think good dramatic theatre ought to be. It has everything for the actor, swashbuckling sword-play, good comedy, an exciting battle-scene and last minute rescue, and a heart-rending story of unrequited love. I suppose this sort of drama has now been taken over by the movies, and I must say José Ferrer's Cyrano was superb. But plays now seem to be much more the concern of literature or vehicles for the evangelising of ideas that never seem to be stated. Lewis and Sybil managed mostly to find a combination of both drama and evangelising, if not proselytizing, in their acting, but as probably the lowest-brow member of the family I have always preferred the show to the message. *Cyrano* was for me the first experience of a play to revel in and enjoy as entertainment, rather than to take part in as an esoteric ceremony that would somehow do one good.

Cyrano, however, was significant for Lewis and Sybil in a much more important way than for me. In the company playing a small part was a man called Bruce Winston in whom Lewis found a kindred spirit. He was not only an actor but a man of great talent in theatrical design and costume. He was also immensely fat and when he appeared at Wood Street for the first time, we were fascinated by this enormous bulk. Ordinary chairs seemed to disappear when he sat on them. Like many fat men, however, he was very light on his feet and an excellent dancer, so that when he moved through a room it was like watching some vast bubble floating across the surface of a pond. He was well-read, artistic, Jewish and extravagant in ideas, voice, gestures and tastes. I believe he and Lewis shared a dressing-room and both of them had a lot of long waits during the show. And so they talked and talked and they began to plan productions they would do when they had more time, and, above all, more money. What they talked most about, as their ideas began to focus, was Gilbert Murray's translation of *The Trojan Women*, with Sybil as Hecuba. They would do it with unadorned simplicity in scenery and costume which Bruce would design, so that the scenery would be no more than the background of a portrait, a kind of framework on which the audience could fill in the details from their own imaginations while concentrating entirely on the sound and the movement of the actors.

Bruce used to come to Wood Street on Sundays and after a huge family lunch, Sybil would take the four of us off for a walk in St James's Park, leaving Lewis and Bruce to 'talk about their plans, darling'. We'd all come together again for family tea, at the centre of which was usually a large Fuller's chocolate cake. In fact even now if anyone talks of a family tea I always see this chocolate cake in my mind. We must have polished one off regularly every Sunday for the next ten or twelve years. We never knew then what Lewis and Bruce had been talking about while we had been having fun in the park with Sybil, but it didn't really matter because they gave their full attention to the four of us as soon as we got home and we played games and heard stories till bedtime.

When it became warmer Sybil used to read to us under the trees by the St James's Park lake. Of course she reads superbly suiting her performance to her audience, which on these afternoons was the four of us sprawled on the grass around her. We weren't just listening to a story. We were completely transported into another world. I can still quite vividly see every character in *The Secret Garden* as though we had spent large parts of our summer in that strange household on the Yorkshire moors. There was for me always a sudden jolt back into the park as Sybil banged the book shut and said: 'Time to go home to tea. I'm ravenous.'

With both Sybil and Lewis in work the family finances were beginning to look up. We weren't becoming 'rich' or anything as unrespectable as that, but there were more comforts in the house, more toys and more 'treats'. And one day when Kiff and I got home from school we found just inside the front door a rather battered lady's bicycle, which Lewis had acquired at the old Caledonian Market for the enormous sum of five pounds. He never had the slightest sense of embarrassment or shame in what he looked like in public in either his clothes or his behaviour. He always did what he had to do and what he wanted to do in the way he wanted. And as he couldn't afford a car he got a bicycle and a lady's bicycle at that, on which he trundled round the London streets.

But for us it meant that in the spring evenings he would take Kiff and me round Smith Square and 'teach us to ride'. In those days one did have to learn to ride a bicycle. I don't know why this was so. Nowadays one gives a child a small bicycle and lets him get on with it himself. We used to clamber on to the saddle, which could be put just low enough for Kiff (and which incidentally used to make Lewis look even more incongruous when he couldn't be bothered to put it up again for himself). Lewis would then trot along holding the bike by the saddle and occasionally letting go while each of us in turn wobbled round the back streets. It was a great day when I first went solo and was sent off round the square while Lewis waited for me at the corner. Once we had mastered the art and could get on and off with a reasonable chance of not running into a lamp-post, Lewis was saved a lot of evening exercise, but it meant he had to find two more bicycles. Fortunately the leading man, the hero of *The Chinese Puzzle*, Roger Kenyon, came to the rescue and gave us a proper child's bicycle, which Lewis collected somewhere in the north of London and rode through the traffic all the way home. He must have looked very odd indeed doing this because he had to stick his knees out almost at right angles to avoid fouling the handlebars.

With this little machine and a slightly bigger bright green one which he acquired for me, we used to set off, Lewis, Kiff and I, on an occasional Sunday expedition to the City, or perhaps the South Bank or Regent's Park. We kept in strict single file in order of seniority with Lewis in the lead, occasionally making a sweeping circle round to chivy up one of us who might be straggling. It was on these jaunts that I first became aware of Lewis's almost complete intolerance of any action that he considered to be careless or incompetent.

I went off into a bit of a dream on one of these jaunts while crossing Ludgate Circus. The traffic wasn't very heavy in those days, especially on a Sunday, but I was weaving vaguely around in front of a prowling taxi. Lewis leapt off his bike and we all pulled into the kerb where he tore the tripes out of me for not keeping my mind on the job. Letting one's mind wander while on a job was about the worst crime in Lewis's book and I've seen him use the same withering blast on some unfortunate actor who during rehearsal had let his mind drift away from what he was doing. But though his scorn was searing he was never known to bear a grudge. On this Sunday he told Sybil all about it in such a jolly way that we all roared with laughter at 'Old John going to sleep in front of a taxi.'

There was of course a carrier on the back of the bicycle on to which Lewis would strap a cushion for one of us to use as a passenger seat. Sometimes we would travel the five miles from Westminster to Putney on a Sunday morning to call on the Reeds and be back in time for lunch. Uncle Arthur Reed was a quiet gentle man, who talked to us in a highish voice with the slow and pedantic precision of the scholar. And he was a considerable scholar, who during his life built up a very great reputation at King's College London for his work in the field of Tudor drama.

During these Sunday morning visits while Tom and Owen and I played complicated games in the back garden Lewis would be asking Arthur's advice about *The Trojan Women*, the project which was now growing fast in the minds of him and Bruce Winston. All we could see through the window of Uncle Arthur's study was their two faces in earnest conversation, Lewis dynamic and thrusting and Uncle Arthur sitting back with a slight smile on his face nodding or shaking his head at whatever it was that Lewis was saying. Then suddenly Lewis would jump to his feet and shout to me that it was time for us to be off on the trundle home to Wood Street.

On one of these journeys home Lewis called on Elsie Fogerty somewhere in Kensington. I was left in the street for half an hour to guard the precious bicycle. At the end of this time a short, round and formidable battleship of a lady descended to the front door firing all her guns in rage at Lewis for having left me outside. She swept me off to her upstairs flat while I protested that someone would steal the bicycle.

'What! That old thing?' she cried. 'It's just like your father to go round on an old derelict like that.'

She sat me down at a little table and put a gigantic apricot tart in front of me while she and Lewis continued with their discussion. He had come to consult her on some problem of his or Sybil's voice and they plunged into deep technicalities. He regarded her as the greatest living expert on anything to do with the technique of human speech and the mechanics of the voice. Lewis had known her before he met Sybil and he was one of 'Fogey's' heroes. In fact she was probably in love with him. She was the first of Lewis's friends to whom Sybil was introduced after they became engaged. Apparently Fogey looked her up and down and in a not altogether friendly voice said: 'Well I hope you're worthy of him.' She was bossy, motherly, at times coy to the point of kittenishness and always on the vocal warpath. Nearly fifteen years later Kiff was to study under her guidance at her Central School of Drama at the Albert Hall where she preached, until her death in 1945, the gospel of using words and speech with the precision and skill that a musician applies to his instrument.

On 19th June, 1919, all Europe celebrated the signing of the Peace of Versailles and London went gloriously raving mad. Kiff, Mary and Ann had gone off to Dymchurch but for some reason my education was thought to be more important than theirs and I stayed on at Wood Street with Lewis and Sybil. He was still playing in *Cyrano* at the Garrick but Sybil had just finished *The Chinese Puzzle* and so was free at night. As soon as it was dark she and I set off together to see the sights, and see them we certainly did. We must have walked for miles through the dancing, singing, laughing, drinking crowds. We went through Parliament Square, past Whitehall to Trafalgar Square down to the Mall to the huge throng outside Buckingham Palace and across Green Park to Piccadilly. But just before we got to the Ritz the whole sky over Hyde Park exploded into a blazing ballet of fireworks. I had never seen anything like it and nor had Sybil. We stood together 'oo-ing' and 'oh-ing' for half an hour and she was jumping about with excitement as much as I. Then she said: 'Come on, darling. We must go or we shall miss your father. Aren't fireworks glorious? We ought to have them every night to cheer people up.'

But no one needed cheering up that night. As we went along Piccadilly there were paper hats, squeakers, whistles and streamers to be bought and Sybil bought them all. We wore the hats, blew on the squeakers and whistles and threw the streamers. And to my delight she bought me a gadget called a tickler. It consisted of a bunch of soft bristles on the end of a short wire and one used it to tickle the face of any unwary member of the crowd. I remember getting into a fencing match with a man who got a 'veritable touch' on Sybil's nose with his tickler, which I thought was going much too far. But I was thrilled at the 'honour' when Sybil was accosted and propositioned by an Australian soldier. He moved off when I strongly expressed my approval of the encounter feeling no doubt that a small boy was a not altogether welcome companion under the circumstances.

Soon after half past eleven we reported to the stage door of the Garrick and collected Lewis, but not before Robert Loraine had given me a bar of chocolate with instructions never to forget this evening of celebration. Lewis, Sybil and I wandered down past St Martin's into Northumberland Avenue and along the embankment to Wood Street where once again the inhabitants of the Court had been having a tremendous bonfire in the waste patch at the back. We stood with them for a little while and then went indoors for the habitual and almost ritualistic Casson after-theatre supper – cocoa and bread and marmalade.

In the late summer Sybil was given what must have been her first lead in the West End. She was cast as the heroine of a tremendous Drury Lane melodrama, playing opposite Stanley Logan as the hero. It was one of the last of the realistic dramas that included every possible ingenious and spectacular effect to draw the crowd before the cinema took over completely.

Sybil as always held us enthralled by her accounts of the play when she came home every evening from rehearsals. 'I'm a secretary to someone at the Embassy in Paris,' she told us, 'and engaged to Stanley Logan who is an R.A.F. officer and the son of a big steelworks owner. There's a strike at the steel works and Stanley has to pour the molten steel himself and I make a speech to the crowd to tell them how dangerous it is and how quiet they must be while he does it.'

'Why must they be quiet?'

'Because if he was disturbed he would fall into the molten steel and be shrivelled to nothing in a flash.'

We revelled in the thought of this exquisite horror and Sybil has never hesitated to pile it on whenever she has the chance.

'That's the first part,' she went on. 'And then I go back to the Embassy in Paris and get kidnapped by the villain and his gang, who want to find out about a treaty, and I know about it and they take me to an awful dungeon just below the water level, and they are just going to torture me to make me tell them about the treaty when dear Stanley breaks down the door and rescues me. Then, my *dears*, an awful thing happens. The walls of the dungeon collapse and the river rushes in and we're all nearly drowned. But it's all right because we can both swim and the villains can't.'

We listened open-mouthed as she strode round the tiny sitting-room at Wood Street telling us all the details and using her lines from the play to make it seem more real. And it was, of course, entirely real both to her and to us. When the show opened and we were allowed to see it for ourselves we found that the producer had left nothing to the imagination and had put in the lot. A great stream of white hot molten steel thundered and hissed down into the huge cauldron in a shower of magnificent sparks, a real taxi with the villain inside came on to the stage into which Sybil innocently climbed on her way home from the embassy and whisked her off at high speed into the wings and away to a gruesome dive on the Left Bank.

But it was the scene in the dive that really hit the high spot. There was Sybil in the middle of the stage held firmly in a chair by two ruffians while the villain stood behind her (after all we had to see his face too) uttering appalling threats, when in rushed Stanley Logan taking a huge flight of steps in one heroic leap. As he touched the floor, and just as the enemy rushed at him down came the back wall with a crash and there displayed for us were the twinkling lights of Paris and what was apparently a huge cascade of water pouring on to the stage. It certainly looked real and they certainly seemed to be swimming around as the huge Drury Lane movable stage slowly sank down to give the effect of the water rising. It was all done not with mirrors but with lights and it was magnificent.

In those days actors took curtain calls after each act and I do remember we were all breathlessly amazed, when Sybil and Stanley took their call, to see that they were bone dry.

The show was so topical and up to the minute that it ended with a scene of the fireworks display of Peace Celebration Night in Hyde Park, and as the rockets sparked their way up the cyclorama at the back Sybil and Stanley fell into each other's arms.

She very nearly fell good and proper into Stanley's arms, and certainly fell heavily for Stanley, or so I have been told. Apparently the realism of the drama became realistic in life and there must have been some fireworks around Wood Street as well as on the stage of the Lane. But of course we never heard anything of it except that there were odd moments of mysterious tension, which we thought were part of some new play. It all blew over when Sybil's vicarage upbringing asserted itself and I for one didn't know anything about it till I was well into my forties. It is always astonishing in adult life to discover what one's parents have been up to. After all they have never been anything but 'pretty old'.

The realism of *The Great Day* had another overwhelming effect on our Wood Street neighbours. Sybil got seats in the gallery for half a dozen very tough barrow-ladies and when Sybil got into the taxi they nearly jumped down into the stalls in their eagerness to save the day. 'Don't you get in there Mrs Cassin! 'E's going to do yer in!' one of them cried. This must have not only disturbed but completely baffled the audience for 'Mrs Cassin' couldn't be connected with the unknown name of 'Sybil Thorndike' on the programme. And late that night when Sybil came out of the stage door to go home there stood a phalanx of avenging harpies, hatpins drawn and ready, waiting 'to cop that bloody villain if we wait all night'. Sybil had to go back into the theatre and come out again arm-in-arm with Gerald Lawrence to show them that he was really 'an absolute darling'.

Meanwhile Lewis and Bruce went on planning for their own production of 'The Greeks'. In the last months of 1919 Lilian Baylis told Lewis he could have the Old Vic for a few matinées. He and Bruce jumped at the chance and on the 14th October, they produced Sybil as Hecuba in *The Trojan Women*. All the matinées were packed full and the critics raved about her.

About ten years later I remember asking Sybil rather naïvely why they hadn't transferred the play to another theatre right away.

'We hadn't got a bean, darling,' she told me. 'I don't think we had more than a couple of hundred pounds between us. But Lewis managed to persuade Charles Gulliver to let us do some more matinées at the Holborn Empire. You remember don't you? I played *The Great Day* at night at Drury Lane and *The Trojan Women* in the afternoon all among the props of the variety theatre. It was fun. But we had a bit of luck. Lewis had to speak at a big Drama League dinner. Lord Howard de

Walden was in the chair and they all got up and made speeches about how marvellous the English theatre was. Then Lewis was asked to say something and the devil got into him. You know what he's like when people make polite speeches patting each other on the back. Well he was awful. He told them that the theatre had never been worse, that none of them cared tuppence for good plays or good acting, that managers could spend thousands on trash and not a ha'penny on anything serious and what the deuce were they going to do about it. My dear, it was terribly hot-making. He was so *rude*! When he sat down again, breathing fire like a dragon, hardly anybody applauded and none of us knew where to look. But it did the trick you know. Lord Howard de Walden thought it was marvellous of him to speak out like that, and lent us a thousand pounds, which was a *fortune*. And somehow we borrowed another five hundred and rented the Holborn Empire for a season of matinées.'

There were other consequences of that first *Trojan Women*. Of course Sybil gave some seats once more to the tough old harridans in the back court. They met Sybil next morning and bearing in mind that Greek tragedy is not everybody's cup of tea, asked them in some trepidation how they had enjoyed the show. The tallest and grimmest of them beamed at her and in a hoarse whisper that could be heard across the river said, 'Ducks, it was luvly. We had a nice walk across Westminster Bridge; saw yer play, 'ad a good cry, and then come 'ome and 'ad shrimps and winkles for tea.'

'Oh,' thought Sybil. 'That's that. So much for the appreciation of drama among the working classes.'

But then the old gorgon went on, 'That play dearie is just like us ain't it? Ain't we bin in the bloody war? Ain't we lost our bloody sons and 'usbands?' Could there ever have been a more heart-warming comment on an actress's ability to play Hecuba?

At this time Sybil and Lewis, while coping with the excitement of *The Trojan Women*, were getting increasingly worried about the suitability of Wood Street as a place to bring up children. Sybil tells me that I came home from school one day and shouted up the stairs: 'Mummy, what's a bugger?' This brought Sybil downstairs very sharply asking, 'Darling, where on earth did you hear that dreadful word?'

'It's chalked up on the wall by the front door, Mummy.' And indeed it was, along with other graffiti of unrepeatable vulgarity!

Sybil approaching stardom *c.* 1920

Medea performed outside the Christ Church Library

Furthermore, Kiff and I used to lean out of the window of our tiny little bedrooms and have long and extraordinary conversations with our neighbours down in the court below. We learnt a great deal that we probably shouldn't have, but our knowledge of the bawdier side of the cockney tongue was vastly increased. Obviously this couldn't go on, especially as the headmaster of my school at Wimbledon, to which I had been sent that autumn, had reported to Lewis that I was 'a bright boy but given on occasions to using epithets most unsuitable in a school such as King's!' But what could they do? They had to be in London, the family was large and rents were high. It seemed as if we would all have to be sent to boarding school, which they couldn't afford, or grow up with a vocabulary of which a bargee might have been proud. The Fates, however, were equal to the occasion.

The Trojan Women had been seen by George Booth, the scholarly and artistic head of the Booth shipping line. He and his wife had been thrilled by Hecuba and wrote to Sybil: 'We hear that you are looking for a house. Our whole family is leaving London for a year. Would you like to have our house on Camden Hill while you look around?'

'We would love it,' replied Sybil. 'But what sort of rent are you asking?'

'You can have the house as it stands for a thousand pounds a week or for nothing,' was George Booth's proposition. Sybil and Lewis still didn't have a bob between them and so they took it for nothing, blessing the name not only of George Booth and his wife but of his whole family.

In the early spring of 1920 the headmaster of King's, Wimbledon, sent for me and said, 'Casson, I have a note from your mother asking me to remind you to go home to Kensington to-night and not to Westminster.' But we weren't likely to forget the move to this enormous and exciting house. It was called 'The New House' and still stands on the north corner of Camden Hill Road and Duchess of Bedford Walk. It is no longer 'The New House' but 'High Veldt', and is the London home of the High Commissioner for South Africa. When we got there on that evening in 1920 after flogging up the hill from High Street, Kensington, we were thrilled more than anything by the apparent vastness of the place and, after Wood Street, the amount of space. Before we went to bed that night we explored everything and forgot to do our homework. We counted forty-two rooms altogether, counting everything. It had one huge semi-circular main staircase to the first floor with a banister absolutely designed for sliding down and equally absolutely forbidden. There were two more staircases, one at each end leading to the vast second floor where lived the servants at one end, and the children with all their appendages in a flat at the other. What a place it was and what times we had there!

Sybil for the first and only time in her life became a châtelaine and revelled in it. There was hardly a relation, and they are legion, who didn't come to stay. Daniel Thorndike, Russell and Rosemary's eldest son was very nearly born there on the 10th March of that year. Eileen with her eldest on the way had one of the best of the servants' rooms on the top floor – after all we didn't have many servants. Grannie Donnie came and beamed all over everything. This was the way her Sybil should be living. Hadn't she been sought after by all the most eligible young men of the Kentish aristocracy before she married Lewis? 'I'm very fond of Lewis' she used to say, 'but the Cassons are a very odd lot. You should have seen them all at the wedding! I didn't know where to look. And anyway Lewis ought to be taller for Sybil. She needs a big man.' She got over her disappointment about Lewis, though never the awe in which she held him, and never the feeling that somehow Sybil should be the mistress of a large and suitable family mansion, a country estate if possible, but failing that a splendid London 'establishment'. And here we all were in an establishment suitable and splendid enough for everyone.

It was from The New House that Lewis and Sybil and Bruce went forth to battle in their own season of matinées at the Holborn Empire. They began with an encore of *The Trojan Women* and followed it with a production of Shaw's *Candida*, the play Shaw had seen her in before she married. He had laughingly applauded her energetic and uninhibited playing and had said: 'Capital! Capital young lady! Now go away, get married, have three or four children, wash the nappies and cook the meals. And then come back and I'll let you play Candida!' Now she was married and had four children. She had not washed all the nappies nor cooked all the meals thanks mostly to Alice and Nelly, but she had 'acted through' the operations and that is enough always for Sybil to 'get the picture'.

Then came another Gilbert Murray Euripides, the *Medea*, probably one of Sybil's greatest and most exciting performances, and a produc-

tion in which Lewis brought to the highest pitch his skill in verbal and
vocal orchestration. This was great theatre and great drama and the
critics were not slow to discover it. Lewis and Sybil were, as it were,
off, though their family did not at that time notice any change in the
routine at home. We all had our evening meal around six, at which
Lewis and Sybil discussed their work in terms that were miles above
our heads. Then off they went to the theatre when they had a play on,
or to the drawing-room to 'do their parts' for the next one when they
had not. Actors may as a general rule speak of being unemployed as
'resting' but it is a word that would never have been used by the
Cassons. Even now Sybil cannot sit and relax in an armchair without
feeling guilty.

The growth of their reputations, if not their fortunes, began about
now but was slow to show itself to us. They had to put on evening
dress from time to time and go off to what became known as 'gorgeous
dinners' which were described in every detail to us over the breakfast
table next morning. New faces appeared more and more frequently as
visitors to the New House. One of them was a rabid Roman Catholic
Irishman called Tom Kealy, who decided that Sybil had to be 'taken
up' and he was the man to do it. So he became her press agent and tore
in and out of the offices and pubs of Fleet Street singing her praises to
all who would listen and to many who would not. Sybil virtually
replaced Catholicism as his religion. He was a dear man with one false
hand permanently clothed in a shiny brown glove, and with a face like a
disappointed eagle. Thanks to his buttonholings of the feature writers
in Fleet Street, at breakfast one morning Sybil said to the four of us
with a self-deprecating laugh, 'Did you know your father and mother
are becoming quite famous? Isn't it fun!' I did know because she had
become 'famous' at my prep school on Wimbledon Common. One day
when I was returning a book to the library I saw a cutting from a newspaper on the school literary society noticeboard. At the head of it was
a picture of Sybil as Medea with underneath an article on the production. It didn't cut much ice, however, for when, hoping to obtain a
little vicarious notoriety myself, I airily said to one of the prefects
standing near, 'That's my mater,' he replied, 'Rot! If your mater was
an actress your people couldn't afford to send you to a proper school
like this!'

But in the spring holidays I was able to earn my first theatrical salary of two pounds a week as one of the sons of Medea. Tom Kealy's daughter Doris was the other and senior one and we were duly slaughtered off-stage at each performance. I did, however, absolutely decline to do the screaming which of course accompanied the slaughter, as it would have been far too unmasculine. And so it was left to Doris and one of the ladies of the Greek chorus to curdle the blood of the audience.

I don't remember as much as I should of this production of *Medea*, which must have been from all accounts a tremendous experience for anyone who saw it and was old enough to appreciate it. But I can still see as a very clear 'mental film' the appalling end of Jason's bride when she adorned herself with the poisoned robes sent by the abandoned Medea. This story was told by Lewis as the Messenger in a performance which, for sheer dramatic impact, few others can have equalled. He also performed the speech that summer at our school prize-giving, which I didn't appreciate nearly so much. On the stage it was magnificent but at school – well, dash it all, a fellow's pater ought to be more dignified. Sybil's final speech in the play, before Medea ascends to the Sun-god in a chariot of fire from the top of the walls of Corinth, still rings in my ears, as also does the lovely rich voice of Nicholas Hannen as the heroically splendid Jason.

It wasn't really 'the drama' for us. It was much more an exciting way of living denied to less fortunate mortals who were clearly very envious, and indeed jealous, of our good fortune. Kiff and I took it in turns to play the second son – after all there was the two pounds a week to be considered – and so we both soon knew the whole play by heart and had seen it from out front, from on stage, back stage and indeed 'over' stage, when we had climbed up into the 'flies' with the stage-hands to have a bird's eye view of it all.

I remember very clearly one night after the show when Lewis, Sybil and I were all having supper in the vast kitchen at New House, Lewis was reading his mail and I noticed with some concern that my school report was among the letters. I knew already, but had not mentioned to them, that at the end of term in a class of twenty-three I had come twenty-third. Lewis opened the letter while I watched with growing anxiety for the 'Look' to appear. But instead a most wicked twinkle appeared in his eye. He merely passed me the report to look at saying, 'Oh dear, that's not very good is it?' as though we were together considering with great tolerance the recalcitrance of a third party. I blushed and Lewis went on twinkling. Then Sybil said, 'Well, anyway, he's a nice boy so what difference does it make?' All three of us went on with our supper and the subject was never mentioned again. It so happened that I had by mistake been put into a grade above my own age group, which was corrected the next term, but it must have been rather a dilemma for Sybil. There is no relation, or relation of relation of Sybil's who is not for her a genius in some way. There was one rather distant cousin who really was a bit of a pill, who had very little humour and a pretty low I.Q., of whom Sybil said, 'I know he's awful but he is absolutely brilliant at tying parcels.' Sybil has a genius for seeing genius where most of us see suet pudding. Lewis, on the other hand, seldom saw genius but was marvellous at ferreting out potential ability. When he saw something wrong he could never let it pass – never, even if it had nothing to do with him like telling a bad car driver his faults. But his criticism was more against the action than the person and he was often genuinely astonished when his criticism was taken personally. He assumed that everyone would want to know where he was going wrong, as on the whole he did himself.

In May of 1920, they were both engaged to play parts in an almost entirely incomprehensible and unbelievable thriller called *The Mystery of the Yellow Room*. There was no yellow room that I can remember but there was a great deal of insoluble mystery. Sybil was the heroine, Franklin Dyall the villain, Lewis a sort of unheroic hero whose name was Darsai and Nicholas Hannen Sybil's father in a vast white wig and a beard of Santa Claus proportions. There was a splendidly dramatic scene when Old Dad, beard and all, sat down in a high-backed wing armchair before the fire with his back to the audience ostensibly to have a snooze. His daughter, Sybil, bustled about the stage in a heroine-like manner until the moment when she said something to Dad. Then – oh the horrific ecstasy – out of the chair bounded the villain. Hence of course, the large white beard that could so easily in gloomy, sinister lighting transform Dyall into Hannen and back to Dyall. There was also a trial scene in which I'm fairly sure that Lewis was tried. I know he snarled and 'Looked' at everyone throughout the scene. It was certainly incomprehensible to me at the age of 9, but as Lewis and Sybil have always maintained it was incomprehensible to them, I imagine it must have been so to the audience of the not very long run of the play. But it was from this play that their next exciting venture was to come.

In the middle of that summer we were all brought into the vast and sumptuous New House drawing-room to meet a dapper rotund little man called José Levy. We said our dutiful how-d'you-dos and went off giggling about our visitor not knowing that having seen *The Yellow Room* José Levy had proposed that the three of them should go into management together to put on Grand Guignol in London. In company with a lot of other Londoners we wouldn't have known what Grand Guignol was. But we were very soon to learn.

That evening after tea Sybil told the four of us what Grand Guignol meant by telling us about the thriller-cum-horror one-act plays put on in France and named after a French marionette called Guignol. 'There'll be lots of exciting murders and crimes and all sorts of other terribly quirky things and everyone will be terrified. Then we'll do one or two funny ones in the middle to let them get their breaths back and then more horrors. Uncle Russell's going to come too and he can frighten anyone! It'll be just like the plays he and I used to do in the attic when we were children. Lots of blood and agony! I'm not sure if we'll be able to let you see them all because you'll all have awful nightmares. But you like being frightened a bit, don't you? It's such fun!'

And fun it was! We weren't allowed to see them all but quite enough to give us the nightmares we weren't supposed to have.

Each 'bill' lasted for a season of seven or eight weeks and consisted of five or six one-act plays, of which at least two were real heart-stopping horrors. The worst, which we did not see, was *The Old Women*, set in a convent that cared for the mentally sick. Sybil played the part of a girl who had her eyes put out with a bodkin by three apparently harmless old ducks (one of whom was played by Russell!). During one performance a gentleman stood up in the stalls and shouted: 'This is monstrous.' He then rushed out and was sick on the mat in the foyer. The actors were all delighted at the effect of their artistry and of course the indignation of many other intrepid theatre-goers was excellent publicity.

They had a certain amount of trouble with the censor with some of the plays which the Lord Chamberlain thought too horrifying for the London audiences. When they came to do *The Old Women* they realised that they would be going well over the Lord Chamberlain's sensibilities. And so they devised a cunning plan to dish the worthy censor. Russell at that time had a week-end cottage at Wrotham in Kent. Lewis then announced that they would stage a theatrical performance in the Parish Hall for the benefit of the Wrotham villagers and duly submitted the script to the censor. Apparently the psychological balance of the villagers of Wrotham was of no great concern to the Lord Chamberlain's office and the script was passed for their edification. And of course once a licence had been granted it was valid and legal for any other performance anywhere else.

Lewis produced nearly all the plays and at last he was able to exercise not only his skill as an actor, producer and artist but also his practical ingenuity which had enabled him to manage his father's organ business before he entered the theatre. To have six different settings and sometimes more on the tiny stage of the Little Theatre in the Adelphi, was not only a problem but a series of problems. Not only did he act in many of the plays as well as produce them but he burnt a large quantity of midnight oil with José Levy translating many of the plays from the French. José was the more knowledgeable in the language but Lewis's French was pretty good and so he was able to make the translations of José more actable on the English stage.

There were some marvellous productions. Kiff and I, at the tender ages of 10 and 8, were allowed to see Russell frightened to death in a darkened wax-work exhibition, Sybil strangling a lecherous old colonel, being strangled herself as a cocotte, being crushed to death in a room with a hydraulic press for a ceiling, Russell as Sybil's lover being thrown to a pack of wolfhounds by an irate and hirsute husband, Sybil as a corpse brought back to life by an electrical machine, and being made into a corpse on one end of a telephone while Lewis, as her husband, listened to it on the other. In this last one I am bound to say Kiff and I lost our nerve, and half-way through it the audience were probably amazed to see two sheepish and frightened little boys creep towards the pass door where they could view the proceedings less realistically. It was during *The Kill* (Russell to the dogs) that they received a visit from the R.S.P.C.A. Earlier in the play two real magnificent wolfhounds were brought on to the stage. Later during the 'kill' off stage the howling of the dogs was demoniacal. The R.S.P.C.A. inspector saw the show and demanded to be allowed back stage at the next performance. 'Nothing could make the dogs howl in this way,' he declared, 'except the most vicious cruelty.' I was there that night and I well remember his discomfiture. When the moment came he was shown Lewis dressed only in his underclothes (he was also making up for the next play) and the stage manager standing in the wings baying like the hounds of hell into lamp glasses!

There was another play called *Eight o' Clock* about the last half-hour of a man's life before he was hanged at eight in the morning. Russell was the condemned man and Lewis the prison chaplain. Their dialogue not unnaturally made frequent references to the time, gradually increasing the tension as the minutes ticked by. One night after the show a retired prison governor came round to say that although he had enjoyed the play there was one bad mistake that he had to point out to them. There would never have been a clock on the wall of a condemned cell, and in any case how on earth did they manage to make the dialogue keep so accurately in time with it. Lewis at once took him on to the stage where the cell set was still standing. There was no clock on the wall. The governor had been so aware of the time by the playing of the scene that he had actually 'seen' a clock on the wall.

In *Changing Guard* a charming little fantasy in which Death was turned away from a child's sick bed, the part of Death was played by Lewis with another actor, Ralph Neale, sitting on his shoulders and wearing a ghastly papier-mâché mask. To our great delight Lewis made the mask himself at home at the place where, as long as I knew him, he did any sort of work that called for the use of his hands – the grand piano. Whether he was writing, mending china, tinkering with an old clock, he would lean his powerful diaphragm against the broad curve of the piano-top and get down to the job. I suppose it fitted his height and as long as he didn't mind standing, in fact he preferred it, he had a splendid work-bench. Sybil did lodge a token protest every now and then and called forth irritated growls when she tried to spread a protective covering of newspaper. But it wasn't the same thing for him and after all he had absolute confidence, misplaced as it happened, that he would not mark or mar the fine dark polished surface. If he had ever been able to have his own workshop, one of his dearest unfulfilled wishes, we were all certain that he would have had a gorgeous bench made in exactly the shape of a concert grand!

They all played every sort of part and sometimes the audience found it hard to believe that, for example, the hideously moronic sixteen-year-old slut in a farce called *The Chemist* was the same actress they had seen half an hour earlier as a soignée aristocratic countess, or they were unable to associate the happy, sleek, blackhaired French woman about to be murdered with a flashy and vulgar tart from the East End. In this latter play *De Mortuis* by Stanley Logan, Sybil visited some of the second-hand dress shops in the Mile End Road so that she could look the part. She explained to the lady in the shop as she thought, that she wanted the clothes for a play and then went on to explain the sort of woman she was playing. 'I'm a woman of not very good taste, who would dress vulgarly and flashily and is no better than she should be.' The shop lady sniffed very loudly and answered, 'Oh well, we have to serve everybody.'

We had all grown so used to the New House and had had such a gay summer pretending to be the rich gentry that we had almost forgotten that our time would soon be over. One day Sybil said, 'Would you mind if we have to go back to Wood Street, darlings? Your father and I simply can't find a house that we can afford. They're all terribly expensive.' We didn't think much of a return to Wood Street after our taste of the delights of Kensington and we were immensely thrilled and relieved when Lewis announced a few weeks later that he had bought the lease of a house in Chelsea. It was an eleven year lease and it cost £700. They were given the chance of buying the freehold, but they felt that the price was beyond them and it was too expensive anyway. £1,300 was a lot of money to the Cassons in those days. They hadn't even got the money to buy the lease and so had to borrow it from Aunt Lucy, the rich dowager head of the Casson family, a rather terrifying old lady who lived in Portmadoc in North Wales and who constituted herself as the keeper of the morals, class awareness and general social behaviour of the entire Casson family – distaffs and all. Lewis was later to inherit her estate and the house at Portmadoc called Bron-y-Garth where he and Sybil had spent part of their honeymoon, and where much later Patricia and I were to do the very same thing.

At this time none of us children knew Aunt Lucy except as a star visitor to tea about once a year. But tea or no tea she coughed up the seven hundred pounds and at the end of October, a few days before my eleventh birthday, we said good-bye to the opulent magnificence of the New House and moved to No. 6 Carlyle Square. Most of the family cash had been spent in the nine or ten months of high living in Kensington. It had been tremendous fun and the unlimited space had done us all a lot of good. It had given Sybil the chance to give a marvellous performance of the 'Duchess of Dillwater', and the part had suited her well, even though she had perhaps overplayed it at times. But Lewis's upper-middle-class socialism had not really suited the part of the 'Duke'. He told me that he had always felt that he was an intruder in the house and that at any moment a gigantic and formidable butler might come in through the door and say, 'And what might you be wanting, my man?' To the four children another move was a great excitement anyway, though we didn't know for many, many years that No. 6 was to become the real home of the family. Lewis used to say that of all the many houses that we lived in, it was No. 6 that was really home to him. And it was here that the four of us passed from childhood to adulthood and where we really knew ourselves as a tightly knit family.

But before we establish ourselves in this magical part of London, I must fill in some details about Lewis. I never filled them in myself till I was in my thirties and then only because Patricia found them out. Lewis never talked about his early life until he was an old man and then I wished I had known it all much sooner. The details of Sybil's early years have been widely known for many years but without some knowledge of Lewis's background much of our family life together seems out of balance or even incomprehensible.

Chapter 5

INTERLUDE FOR LEWIS

IN the village of Seathwaite in the Duddon Valley there stands a very small church surrounded by one of the smallest churchyards I have ever seen. The gravestones seem to be divided almost entirely among two names, Walker and Casson. It was here throughout most of the latter part of the eighteenth century the Rev. Robert Walker was the rector, until his death at the age of 92, in 1802. He was an astonishing man. He was rector, schoolmaster, doctor and wise counsellor to the whole district, ran a small farm, sheared his own sheep on a slab of stone that is still just outside the door of his church (and to which we have all made our pilgrimage), married, loved, honoured and cherished a wife and brought up a family of fifteen children on a stipend of four pounds per annum rising to fifteen. He was also an expert on plants, fossils and astronomy. His grandfather clock now stands in our dining-room in Chelsea. Before Lewis gave it to me to take to Australia he pasted a typewritten sheet on the inside of the door of the clock. It reads:

This clock was the property of 'Wonderful Walker' (The Rev. Robert Walker) Vicar of Seathwaite in the Duddon Valley, North Lancashire, for 67 years until his death in 1802 at the age of 92. In 'The Old Church Clock' (Parkinson) there is a full account of him by Wordsworth. In 1745 he hid this clock in a slate quarry when the Young Pretender was marching South from Scotland. The face, is, I believe, original, but the works were new about 1830.

and then follows the direct line of descendants from Parson Walker to our present family in the person of my grandson Randal.

His daughter became a Mrs Wilson and her daughter Esther Wilson so bewitched a certain young Thomas Casson that he married her. She was made of sterling stuff for she rode pillion, on a horse of course, behind her Thomas from Cumberland to North Wales where the slate quarries at Festiniog were just beginning. They prospered with their slates and it was Mrs Esther Casson who opened soup kitchens for the quarriers and their families when the Napoleonic wars reduced the demand for slates to almost nothing, and made the quarriers go on with their quarrying until all the way down from the quarries to the little port of Madoc there were piles of slates ready to be shipped when times were better. And, of course, her charity tempered with foresight made her and her husband a great deal of money.

Thomas and Esther had two sons, William, who was Lewis's grand-father, and John, and as they were both born in Wales the Cassons thereafter regarded themselves as Welsh. They kept one link with Seathwaite, which is still intact. Just above the village rises the hill of Wallow Barrow Crag. On Christmas Day wherever Cassons are gathered together we drink a toast 'To all old friends round Wallow Barrow Crag'. We still do it to-day, but we spell it 'Walla Burra'. The tradi-tion must have begun when Thomas and Esther left Seathwaite for Wales. Thomas was a great adventurer and speculator. He bought a schooner to transport his slates from Portmadoc and he even bought land on the harbour of San Francisco on which he built a kind of fore-runner of a housing estate consisting of wooden huts known as Thomas's Lots, which were all lost in the great earthquake.

His son William married a very wealthy lady from Cheshire, and the ceremony we were always told, took place at Gretna Green. John founded 'Casson's Bank' which operated at Festiniog, Pwllheli and Portmadoc. Three sons were born to William, who were William the second, Thomas the second and Randal. Lewis was the son of Thomas II, who died just after I was born.

My grandfather, Taed, as we called him, being Welsh for grand-father, was put into his Uncle John's bank and, I suppose, he and his father intended that he should become a banker. He would certainly have made more money if he had, but his life and the lives of his seven offspring would probably have been the poorer. Banking to Taed could never have been more than a means of obtaining the bread and butter for his family. His passion in life was music, and especially organ music, which meant mostly ecclesiastical music. And he married a wife who was deeply, devoutly and Welshly religious, who also died soon after I was born, and whom we were taught to call Naen, the Welsh for grandmother.

In 1841 a certain Captain Lewis Holland-Thomas, part owner of a schooner plying between Liverpool and Valparaiso, took as his bride the daughter of a Cheshire parson. The poor girl was taken out to the schooner in Liverpool harbour in a small open dinghy one very wet Sunday afternoon. A day or two later the schooner, *Laura Ann*, sailed down the Irish Channel bound for the Southern Seas and the Horn. The worthy Captain kept a fairly close diary of this voyage, which lasted four years, and there is still a copy of it in our possession. He records that his dear wife was not a very good sailor, but though he was clearly very sorry for her he doesn't seem to have felt particularly responsible for what must have been a miserable voyage for her, as this extract shows:

. . . It was settled that my intended would accompany me on the voyage. At this time of excitement and bustle my beloved Winny was looking rather worn and exhausted, but was in pretty good spirits, tho' the thought of leaving her beloved friends (and she had many who loved her sincerely) must have weighed upon her spirits. I could not help thinking that I was about to act rather selfishly in taking her from her home and friends and all the comforts of life to traverse the wild and stormy ocean.

Wild and stormy the ocean undoubtedly proved to be after they were married and had embarked in the tiny schooner. The worthy young captain wrote in his diary some months later tossing somewhere in the South Atlantic:

Sunday, 12th September 1842. Latitude 40° South. Blowing a heavy gale from West South West and high rough sea running, breaking on board of the vessel and carrying away some of our bulwarks. My dear wife after this had many frights, and much disagreeable rolling and pitching to put up with and was much to be pitied. Still, she was uncommonly cheerful and in much better health than when we sailed. She used to feel much alarmed when a heavy sea struck the ship with a stunning noise.

Poor dear, she must have had a frightful time! But she stuck it out and at the end of the year Holland-Thomas left her ashore with friends in Valparaiso for the arrival of their first-born, while he sailed on with a cargo for Honolulu. While he was away his daughter, my grand-mother, was born and christened Laura Ann after the schooner in which she had been conceived. Her father not only sailed schooners, but he preached from the Bible and started Sunday schools wherever he went, which meant that his daughter was brought up on strictly, and very strictly, low church lines, and she passed on her upbringing to Lewis and her other six children after she met and married Thomas Casson.

When Casson's Bank was taken over by the Bank of North and South Wales, William and Thomas were sent to Liverpool to continue to learn more about banking while their younger brother Randal became a solicitor, and incidentally later on employed Lloyd George as an articled clerk. Thus it was that in 1875, Lewis was born in Birkenhead. There were two other children at this time; Frances, the elder, who died of cancer in 1914 and William (our 'Uncle Will') who was killed at the Battle of Loos in 1915. Soon after Lewis's birth Thomas was made manager of the Denbigh Branch of the North and South Wales Bank and he brought Laura Ann (Naen) and the family back to Wales with him.

Eventually there were seven children. After Lewis came Esther, then Randal, Elsie and Annie, who died in London of scarlet fever at the age of seven. Taed's knowledge and skill as a banker, however, was outweighed by his passion for singing, reciting, amateur acting and his beloved organ. They had great jollifications, sing-songs and soirées at the house in Denbigh, but otherwise lived the life of a sensible and pleasant upper-middle-class family.

To begin with William was sent to the local school and Lewis was to follow him later, but an incident occurred which Lewis told me about with great glee when I was old enough to appreciate it. It appears that Will and Lewis shared a bedroom and one night Will explained the 'facts of life' in some detail as he had learnt them at this local school. But their conference had been overheard by their astonished and dismayed parents. Will and Lewis were at once brought downstairs and made to kneel down by their mother and pray for chastity and purity of heart. Will was taken away from, and Lewis never went to, the local school and they were both sent to Ruthin, where the pupils to-day revere Lewis's name as a distinguished Old Boy of the school.

In the meanwhile Taed spent more and more of his time working on his undoubtedly brilliant inventions for the improvement of church organs, at which he was something of a genius, and less and less on working at banking at which he was not. He was enthusiastic, artistic, guileless and ingenuous and so although many of his inventions are still being used in organs throughout the world, he hardly ever remembered to patent any of them and most of them were pirated.

In 1891 Lewis, having in his own words 'slacked his way through Ruthin Grammar School' and having got little out of it but two rather dubious certificates for electricity and chemistry issued in South Kensington, was apprenticed to a local iron foundry where he worked on a lathe as a preparatory course before having a go at organs. At the end of this time he was transferred to an organ-building firm in Shepherd's Bush in which Taed had bought a kind of wispy but by no means sleeping partnership. He spent so much of his time travelling to and fro between Denbigh and Shepherd's Bush that at last the patience of the people at the bank ran out and he was asked to resign.

To say he was delighted would be pitching it a bit high, but it seems he didn't mind as much as a man with a large family ought to have minded and he moved his family to London in 1892.

Unfortunately the move to London was almost simultaneous with the collapse of the organ firm at Shepherd's Bush, and from then on the fortunes of the Thomas Cassons never really recovered. They lived first at Gunter Grove where Annie died, and when their finances deteriorated even more they moved to Kilburn, where they were very hard up indeed.

Taed's younger brother, Randal, had in the meantime become a solicitor and a very successful solicitor. After a very long engagement of about ten years he had married Miss Lucy Nesbit, the daughter of a noble house in Staffordshire, one of whose forebears had been surgeon to Nelson. They had decided very sensibly, but not perhaps so romantically, that they would not marry till, as it were, Randal had made his pile, or at any rate enough of a pile for them to buy Bron-y-Garth and live in a style which they both felt they could enjoy, and to which they aspired. They must have found the financial difficulties of my grandfather extremely trying but there is no record of their having complained. Randal with elder brother William had already saved Thomas once from bankruptcy. He now came to the rescue again and helped him to start a small company called 'The Positive Organ Company', in which a number of friends also invested. Lewis, who had been training at the Central Technical School at South Kensington, and walking there and back every day from Kilburn to save the train fares, now abandoned his course and joined his father making Positive Organs. This invention of Taed's really should have brought success to the Cassons. It was a small compact machine on castors and self-blown like a harmonium but with pipes like a proper organ and altogether an admirable instrument for small churches, chapels or parish halls. And, in fact, it sold well. Lewis found one in an outback Australian church only a few years ago, some went to darkest Africa, and once, when he was in America a man came up to him and said: 'Are you by any chance any relation to *the* Thomas Casson who invented the Positive Organ?'

But alas, whenever Taed made any money he put it not only into his small organ for which there was a market but also into further inventions for bigger organs. They were equally ingenious but being bigger they were much more expensive. They sold quite a few but as Lewis said, 'The clergy never paid the bills.' And so the family were never really out of dire financial straits. Fortunately for the younger children Naen had a little private income of her own which she resolutely refused to contribute to the organ-building ventures. The money was spent, so Lewis said, on educating the children who had not yet grown up.

At Kilburn the family were parishioners at the very High Anglican Church of St Augustine's. Lewis helped with parish work and organised boys' clubs and social gatherings. He and his father sang in the choir and so the gatherings involved sing-songs, recitations and indeed amateur theatricals. As a result of one of these performances in which Lewis played a part, he met Charles Fry the teacher of elocution at the London Organ School for which Taed had built organs. Lewis was persuaded by Fry to take part in his shortened and simplified versions of Shakespeare's plays. They were really recitals with costumes, and they gave Lewis his first chance of learning something about the art of speech and acting.

Lewis thoroughly enjoyed these performances the more so as it was clear that he had some talent for acting. He got more experience still in the classes of a drama teacher who was delighted to find a spare man to bring some heavy bass into her choruses of female sopranos. She was a wildly energetic, gypsy-like and exciting actress called Rosina Philippi, who later and coincidentally became Russell's mother-in-law.

Lewis was, of course, still earning his very meagre living at the organ workshop and had little thought at this time of becoming a professional actor. On the contrary his church activities convinced him that he had a vocation as a priest. The family was a deeply religious one, at first on the basis of the puritanical rather Calvinistic variety of certain parts of Wales. Then in London they swung to the far more dramatic and colourful fervour of the Anglican High Church, first at St Cuthbert's, Earl's Court, and then at the even higher St Augustine's, Kilburn. His parents accepted his choice with at least equanimity if not whole-hearted enthusiasm, and so he joined the teaching staff at St Augustine's both to absorb and to disseminate the gospel of the Church. There was as always no money for his training or anything else and so there was no hope of his studying theology at a university.

He showed such promise at St Augustine's that he was sent as a pupil for two years to St Mark's College for Teachers in Chelsea and was then put on their staff. Among other things, he taught, somewhat incongruously, chemistry and drawing. I found out about the latter when I asked him what had brought about the bright blue spot on the inside of his left wrist.

'I got cross with one of my drawing pupils at St Mark's,' he said, 'and I banged my hand down on his desk – and he was holding a very sharp pencil point upwards on the desk, which went into my wrist.'

All this time on a low salary at the organ works, on miserable pocket money at St Augustine's and St Mark's, he continued to act with various amateur and semi-amateur theatrical groups. While working with Charles Fry he had met William Poel, whose devoted disciple and evangelist he remained for the rest of his life. Poel was a man whose passion in life was presenting the plays of Shakespeare as they would have been done in the Tudor and Stuart days. He had developed a form of theatrical speech that was devoted entirely to making the thoughts of the writer significant to an audience and projecting them on a scale commensurate with the size of the building or the audience. It was a highly stylised speech, and the art of the actor in Poel's view consisted of making the stylised speech appear to be natural. Thus there would be realism of speech and action without the audience's losing any of the significance. This doctrine and the skill became Lewis's theatrical religion. He maintained that present-day actors had lost sight of this principle and that acting had become a kind of psychological self-indulgence. Actors, he insisted, were now mostly having a splendid time giving superb performances to themselves inside their heads or at most to each other. It is considered 'ham' even to consider the presence of an audience and that unless you are in the front few rows of the stalls the words cannot even be heard, let alone understood and appreciated.

And so Poel became Lewis's god. In later years those actors who worked under his direction, and had the sheer endurance to stand up under his continual hammering at the tunes, the rhythms and phrasing of the speech, have grown not only in fame but in stature. Perhaps I had better remember the warning of 'no names, no pack-drill' and only mention that it is mostly his pupils who are blessed by the audiences, because they can be heard. Moreover, they could thank William Poel for teaching what he knew to a fiery young evangelical, socialistic, religious, energetic actor and producer to be called Lewis Casson.

If he learnt his craft of speech from William Poel he learnt his early socialism from a certain Rev. J. R. Thomas under whom he studied at St Augustine's, who not only opened the door to Fabian thought, but also and ironically turned him away from the priesthood. His fiery Welsh-blooded evangelism, the adventurousness of Holland-Thomas, the austere dedicated devotion to whatever was conceived as duty from the daughter of Holland-Thomas, his mother, and the intuition and imagination of the artist combined with the warm humour and humanity of his father, Thomas Casson, seemed suddenly to come to a point of focus in the profession of acting. He could pursue every one of his goals, artistic, religious, political and social, in the theatre, and so make some attempt to harmonise the conflicting furies within him and put the tremendous energy to work.

Lewis's first job as a professional was a small part in a play called *The Duke of Killiekrankie*, but it was not long before he was invited by Harley Granville Barker to join the Vedrenne-Barker company at the Court Theatre in Sloane Square. Next to Poel, Granville Barker was Lewis's greatest mentor and whenever his name was mentioned in our household, one always felt one should genuflect. He was younger than Lewis, but had already established himself as a scholar and a director. And when years later he gave up the theatre, Lewis felt like Browning when he wrote *The Lost Leader*. Lewis oscillated between two theories about the cause of his retreat. One was that he had been eaten alive by his second wife and the other that he had become an agent in the British Secret Service, which later became Lewis's standard explanation when people he knew began behaving with any degree of eccentricity.

In 1907, when the Court season closed, Miss Horniman was just starting up in Manchester and Lewis joined the company as an actor. From all accounts he set few Thameses on fire with his acting, while his socialism and his pacifism made him appear rather grumpy, and I believe he barked out his lines in a kind of machine-gun rattle. Even

Sybil, describing to Russell her first meeting with him a year later, wrote: 'Nigel and May Playfair introduced us, but he only barked out a sort of huffy "How-d'ye-do" to me and didn't speak another word. He wore a very shabby overcoat and a hat drawn over his eyes like a tramp – he looks as if he would fight you if you gave him a chance, but quite suddenly something Nigel said made him laugh and he looked quite different, and he's got a really lovely voice, very direct. . . .'

As the letter shows Sybil was able to see beyond the 'Look' of the dedicated world-improver to the warm-hearted and good-humoured human being. And naturally I am very glad she did! But the austerity of his upbringing had an effect on him which lasted all his life. He could never again be lighthearted about anything to do with money. Any talk on financial matters brought the 'Look' to his face. Just after the World War II, I had occasion to travel on a No. 19 bus with him from Chelsea Town Hall to Piccadilly Circus in order to visit our bank at the bottom of Lower Regent Street. In those days it was a fourpenny fare, but if you got off at the Ritz it was only $2\frac{1}{2}$d. As we were a little short of time I said, 'Two fourpennies please' to the conductor and it really upset him. Quite crossly he said, 'We could have got off at the Ritz and walked.' And yet in the mid-fifties when I had to put down a two thousand pound deposit to purchase a house in Melbourne (Australia), I cabled him for a loan of this large sum and he sent me a cheque almost by return of post without a question being asked.

His mother said to Sybil when they became engaged: 'I'm so glad you're going to marry Lewis. He has always been such a help and so kind. He used to be so good with the younger children and mended all their toys for them.'

He was always enchanting with small children, who seemed never to have any fear of him. He could talk to them in their own language and when he was with them they always knew he was more interested in them and their problems than anything else in the world. That he could also be frightening to any man, woman or child whom he believed to be guilty of a misdemeanour, no one would deny. But the fear was a fear of moral opprobrium rather than of any physical threat. It was paradoxical that a man of such violence in personality could abhor any form of physical violence with an equally violent passion, and that such a convinced pacifist could make himself fight as a soldier in the coming war with such a dedicated concentration.

This was the man who, in 1908, met Sybil in the Dublin Zoo. Two violent natures came together and produced a fire that was to carry them through over sixty years of creative artistry together. Lewis's violent nature was kept under rigid control by his immensely strong willpower and on the whole only showed itself in what can only be described as the ferocity of his attack on his work. Sybil's violence, on the other hand, has its sources deeply within her and whatever the consequences, it explodes all over the place in a blazing enthusiasm for everything she encounters. This explosiveness, which on its own could be destructive, and indeed sometimes has been, is controlled and tempered by an uncanny intuitive ability to adapt her own strong personality to that of whomsoever is with her at the moment. When someone talks with Sybil that person feels that he is the one person that Sybil wants to meet and that her enthusiasm for him and what he does, is above all other. The result is that he feels completely at home with her and so much the more significant as a person for being able to sustain her obvious delighted interest. I think it was Noel Coward who said: 'No one likes anyone as much as Sybil loves everyone.' And it's not very far from the truth, though this unflagging enthusiasm can, at times, be as exhausting as a prolonged exposure to the sun. When you work or live with Sybil you must develop a kind of 'enthusiasm tan'. You won't outshine her. You can only find a lotion so that you can absorb the rays without being frizzled up.

Lewis used the theatre as a tool in his struggle to convert the world to his own belief in, and devotion to, something very like Shaw's Life Force. Sybil uses it much more as a kind of self-indulgence in unselfishness. She would really like to turn the world into a kind of gigantic school treat where everyone was not so much happy as jolly, and spent their time in never-ending junketings, which would be prevented from becoming orgies by the universal high principles not of a Church Militant, but a Church Enthusiastic or a Church Joyful.

Now at the end of 1920, they had been married for twelve stormy and exciting years. They had four children, who were now 11, 9, 7½ and 6. And I at 11 was just saying good-bye, obviously not to my childhood, but certainly to my infancy. I was about to become a kind of acolyte to Lewis, following his ways, trying to imitate his habits, learning a lot and enjoying a lot.

As a family we were about to begin eleven years of reasonably stable family life. Up till now, thanks mainly to the war and lack of money, there had been something rather makeshift about it all. We had, as it were, been campers at our various dwelling houses. It had been by no means unpleasant but it had lacked continuity and so had had an air of uncertainty. That these eleven years were also going to be the period of Lewis and Sybil's greatest theatrical success may, or may not, have been coincidental.

Great-Uncle Randal had died of pneumonia in Taormina in Sicily in 1912. His widow, Aunt Lucy, had lived ever since in her mansion at Portmadoc. They had had one son, Alec, who had been turned down physically for the army in 1916. Aunt Lucy had badgered everyone of influence that she knew in the army, until Alec was finally accepted. He was reported missing in the spring of 1918. In 1920 a skeleton was found in Polygon Wood and on one of the fingers was a silver ring engraved with the crest of the Casson family. Thus Lewis had become Aunt Lucy's heir and I became the possessor of the silver ring.

And so the family, which had come from the imaginative and artistic, but impecunious, Thomas Casson moved into their home in Chelsea financed by the money earned by his less exciting but much more stable brother Randal. What a happy home it proved to be, and I would like to be able to say how grateful we all were to Great-Uncle Randal and his diligence, but I don't remember our gratitude being mentioned! But we were grateful to Aunt Lucy, who with his wealth enabled not only ourselves, but many other uncles and cousins, to have a little more fun than they might have done.

And so we moved to No. 6, Carlyle Square.

Chapter 6

COMINGS AND GOINGS AT CARLYLE SQUARE

CARLYLE SQUARE runs off the north side of King's Road and the rather bigger houses on the west side back on to Old Church Street. It is a typical London square, with a garden surrounded by spiked iron railings, to enter which one requires a key purchased with one's subscription to the Gardens Committee. Lewis and Sybil soon found it an admirable place in which to say over their lines, much to the astonishment of the other residents until they got used to it.

Just before we left Kensington a new member joined the staff. The 'sporty' Madge had left us to be married and it was thought that someone with a bit more class should be found to be a kind of nursery-governess for Mary and Ann, while at the same time keeping 'an eye on the boys'. Sybil found her in Kingsdown and her name was Violet Ings, or 'Vi' as she was always called. She was 23 (I know that because it was the first question I asked her and she told me straight out). She had a pleasant face, very firm ideas about discipline and a fine old temper when 'the boys' got up to mischief. She was to be with us for the next 16 years, at the end graduating to housekeeper before disappearing back into Kent. Thus there were six Cassons, Grannie, who now came to live with us, Vi, Old Cook and a house-parlour maid. How we all fitted in, Lord knows, but fit in we did and liked it. I don't remember any of us getting in each other's hair. The exceptions, of course, were Lewis and Grannie, who somehow never quite seemed to hit it off. Donnie was terrified of Lewis when he was in 'one of his moods', which meant that he was trying to think, and he used to get awfully impatient with her when she wanted to have 'cosy little chats', which was with anyone in sight. Kiff and I used to play a game of arranging to get Lewis and Grannie in a room together and then going out and listening at the door while they sparred with each other.

But it is rather incredible that somehow Lewis could do his production planning on the dining-room table, and Sybil could go through her parts with her usual gusto without apparently being put off by the rest of the household. Of course they were never at home in the evenings. Dinner was at 6.15 p.m. and at seven they were off to the theatre. Kiff and I left the house every morning at about 8.15 a.m. to travel by bus to Wimbledon Common and we got home at five. This meant that if we wanted any help with our homework from Lewis, and I for one very often did, then it had to be done in the hour before dinner. Being actors, and therefore not getting to bed till late, they rarely rose before nine and usually had breakfast in their dressing gowns. But just after eight we would go into their bedroom to say 'Good morning' and to collect our bus fares for the day. This time was also a sort of reserve time in case homework had proved to be more difficult than had been thought. There was many a morning during the first two years at Carlyle Square when poor Lewis was called by me at seven o'clock and asked to wrestle with the problems of ablative absolutes in Latin or of running water into plugless baths in mathematics. He used to struggle up to the surface cursing, not me, but the school for not teaching me the things for which he thought he was paying the fees. Sybil with long hair down her back would sit up and make soothing noises to us both to keep the peace and avoid 'waking Grannie' in the next room.

For a while after Granpapa died Grannie had lived in a flat near us at the other end of Wood Street. Then an old friend of them both, a High Anglican priest whose name was Father John Olivier, and his wife asked her to go and be the organist at his parish church in Letchworth. There were three children, Sybille, the eldest, Dickie and Larry. And that was how we got to know Larry, and how Sybille Olivier took on the job of baby-sitting for us from time to time in Wood Street. At any rate the job had now come to an end; Grannie was ensconced at Carlyle Square, and once more became part of our lives. It worked really very well because she could entertain her friends on the ground floor after Lewis and Sybil had gone to the theatre and could keep out of their hair when they had work to do. And she could and would always play the piano for us whenever we wanted it, which was often. Thanks to this and to her I can still sing my way through most of the English Hymnal and Hymns Ancient and Modern. This sort of singing had very little to do with religion. It was just fun. But, of course, the fun brought us into a certain amount of religious thinking. We got on to familiar terms with the Trinity, the angels and archangels, the troops of Midian, the cohorts of the saints and band after happy band of pilgrims.

Not until we came to Carlyle Square, however, did we as a family go to church as a matter of routine. This is not to say, of course, that Lewis and Sybil were not religious. Lewis, as I hope I've shown, came from a most devout family and was himself deeply religious. But the onslaught of his socialism, combined with his engineering and scientific education, brought him to an intensely rationalistic philosophy overlaid with, or possibly underpinned by, a kind of poetic pantheism. It was a struggle that plagued him for the rest of his life.

Sybil, on the other hand, has never swerved from being an enthusiastic orthodox vicar's daughter. Her orthodoxy has affected her life, but never controlled it. She has an almost infinite capacity to rationalise what she wants to do and intends to do into terms that for her do not contradict the doctrines of the Anglican Church. I really believe if, for some reason, she had to steal the Crown Jewels she would do it without a qualm of conscience if she could find a way of making it a crusade to lighten the Gentiles and bring them to a state of Grace. Religion has always been another of those areas in which Lewis and Sybil's differing views and approaches complemented each other and so enriched them both.

Their four children grew up therefore with religious beliefs that were taken seriously but not earnestly. It was a religion that had as much room for laughter as for tears, and we could make family jokes about Church or even the Almighty Himself without becoming impious or blasphemous. We certainly couldn't be doing with what in the family we have always called a 'holy-bob', that is someone who clearly feels superior to other people because he believes that the 'Happy Land' is not as far, far away from him as it is from others, and is very earnest about his superiority.

The point is that, thanks to Lewis and Sybil, we all grew up knowing that religion matters and we have been arguing about it ever since we could talk. But despite our having a clerical grandfather, we were not regular church-goers in our early years and I don't ever remember being urged in any way to become one. We never went to church at Dymchurch and only very occasionally at Kingsdown. We went twice to Sunday school there with the vicar's daughter and were bored to death. And we occasionally went to the afternoon children's service at St James the Less. At Wood Street we had our first taste of really High Anglican at St Matthews in Great Peter Street, Westminster. We liked it but somehow never caught on. We went for bike rides with Lewis in the mornings on Sunday and for walks with either him or Sybil, or both, in the afternoons and this was to us much more important. But if we didn't go to church we did all stand round the piano in the evening, Lewis, Sybil, Grannie and the four of us, and sing hymns at the tops of our not inconsiderable voices while Sybil, or sometimes Grannie, played the accompaniment.

When we got to Carlyle Square, however, the pattern changed. We discovered St Mary's, Graham Street, near Sloane Square. It was an Anglican church where the services were so 'High' that, apart from their being conducted in English, and that they were under the Archbishop of Canterbury, they were as near Roman as makes no difference. We learnt to call services 'mass'. The priests were in rich and colourful vestments. There were candles, incense, sanctuary bells. And above all there was continuous movement by priests and servers, who knew how to walk superbly with formalised ritual and ceremony. We were enthralled by it all and 'Church' took on an entirely new meaning for us. There was now drama in it, there was a 'plot' and there was something to be caught up in.

Lewis didn't always come – Sybil used to say that he 'needed his rest'. But he came often enough for us to think of him as part of it, and Sybil came nearly always. For the first time we really felt we belonged to a church and were carried away by it all.

The vicar was Father Whitby, whom Sybil adored with a slightly more than spiritual devotion. His second-in-command was Father Laing, who always preached the sermon for the Family Mass at ten on Sundays. Kiff and I idolised him and in fact he got us worked up into a fine old religious fervour, which, among other things, caused us to build a wall shrine for our bedroom out of Meccano. We never understood why Lewis and Sybil chortled with delight when they first saw it, because their chortles were clearly not of spiritual joy but earthly laughter.

When, in the autumn of 1922, Kiff and I were sent to be prepared for confirmation by Father Laing, Lewis and Sybil had to face a barrage of theological conundrums at the evening meal and the arguments were unending. Whether it did anyone any spiritual good, I don't know. I have certainly forgotten most of Father Laing's teaching. But what we did gather unconsciously and slowly was the knowledge of our parents' sense of tolerance. We could talk to them about God and Heaven and hell and eternity, and all the rest of these so difficult concepts, with a matter-of-factness that I am sure laid a much firmer religious foundation for us than any strict disciplines of orthodoxy would have done.

But it was not all as reverent as perhaps it should have been. For example, to this day the family has accepted as part of its language two concepts about people's behaviour at church. They would have been considered profane if not blasphemous by many parents, I feel sure, but with us they merely emphasised that we could feel religious without being scared of religion – like Granpapa and his trapeze over the aisle. We called one such form of behaviour the 'Holy Conceit', which described what we thought of as an over-holy and sanctimonious look some people have on their faces as they walk back to their seats after taking Holy Communion. It is an expression which says, as Kiff put it at the age of ten, 'I mustn't *show* you how much better I am than the rest of you, but I *am*.' The other was a kind of competition which we called the 'Holy Rush'. In our church, people knelt rather than stood in the aisle while waiting their turn to go up to the altar rails for communion. We soon noticed that most of those near the front were only making the outward signs of being at prayer. Their eyes were wide awake waiting to jump up and move to the rails at the first sign of a gap. What interested us was what we felt to be a noble sense of sportsmanship shown by anyone who failed to get the place and at once dropped devoutly to his knees again with a look that denied that any movement had ever been intended. But the competitive spirit was always rampant.

We were quite a team when the whole family was there together, Lewis singing a strong bass, and usually the bass part, Sybil going great guns in her neo-contralto and the four of us making up in volume what we lacked in skill. After the service was over (even now I find myself wanting to say 'after the show was over') all six of us walked home along the King's Road in that peculiar still mistiness that in those days always seemed to epitomise London on a Sunday.

For lunch we always had one of those enormous sirloins with a great wodge of undercut underneath. Lewis didn't seem to carve it so much, as attack it as a personal enemy. And then there was an equally huge apple pie to follow served by Sybil with the same gusto as she serves everything. In fact when I saw her play Mrs Squeers in the film of *Nicholas Nickleby* in 1947, and she was ladling out the gruel to the young pupils at Dotheboy's Hall, I couldn't help thinking of our Sunday lunches at Carlyle Square.

In the late spring of 1921, the four of us were at home recuperating from chickenpox. We were upstairs in the nursery on a fine sunny morning when we heard the ear-splitting noise of a klaxon horn. We rushed to the window and saw, drawn up at the pavement, what could only be described now as a gigantic bath on wheels, though at that moment it looked like a splendid motor-car with Lewis sitting in the driving seat. It was a 1916 Maxwell, which Lewis had that day bought from an army disposal dump for a little over a hundred pounds. You never saw such a car! The hood was folded up in a flapping heap, the only protection from the wind was a solid straight sheet of heavy, very breakable glass, the upholstery had been cruelly treated for years and the whole outfit was painted a bright yellowy-brown, which was whimsically described on the licence as 'buff'. But she was lovely.

We all rushed to the front door and, chickenpox quarantine notwithstanding, piled into the car and demanded to be given a spin round London. Lewis had stopped the engine by now but he wasn't going to miss the chance of showing off his purchase. Out he climbed and began to turn the starting-handle in the front. Ten minutes later, with a noise like a most irregular machine gun and a cloud of thick black smoke out of the back, the engine started. Lewis ran round, jumped quickly into his seat lest the engine were to stop again, engaged a grinding gear and we were off in 'our car', for a tour round Battersea Park with the wind blowing in our hair. South of the park Lewis coaxed the machine up to the wildly exciting speed of 35 miles per hour, but I fear it was more than this automotive elderly lady could stand and she spluttered back along the Embankment with two cylinders out of action and Lewis getting 'Lookish'!

In the next couple of weeks at a little garage off the Fulham Road, Lewis stripped the engine down to the last nut, cleaned out the carbon, hand-ground the valves, poked about in the magneto, fiddled and tickled the carburettor and then put the whole lot together again. As I was still in quarantine I was with him all the time holding spanners, reaching with my much smaller hand into inaccessible places and getting gloriously covered in oil, which I never washed off until Sybil had seen it and had said: 'I think it's wonderful what you two are doing. It's all such a mystery to me. You must be a great help to Daddy.' Then I went off nonchalantly to the bathroom feeling pleasantly masculine and mechanical.

Some weeks later Bruce Winston came to tea after we'd all been for a drive round Richmond Park. The car had only spluttered twice and Bruce was jovially impressed. Waving a large piece of chocolate cake in the direction of the window he said, in his high-pitched voice: 'Lewis! You must call her "Anxious Annie" because she's so anxious to do her best.' And so Anxious Annie she became, the first of a long line of Lewis's cars. We never went farther in her than the seventy-five-mile run to Dymchurch, and we nearly always had to stop for running repairs or a puncture or both. But, as Bruce had observed, she was always anxious to please and she always got us there. I think we had her for about two years before Lewis traded her in for a dark blue Cubit, and then an Armstrong-Siddeley. All of them were second-hand, of course, not only I suspect because they were cheaper that way, but because he loved to tinker with their engines. A legend has since grown up that Lewis never bought a new car in his life, but there was a period when new cars were bought to celebrate successful productions. He bought his second, but not second-hand, Armstrong-Siddeley with some of the profits from *Saint Joan*. He bought a splendid Austin convertible when they got home from South Africa in 1929, a Wolseley after their Australian tour in 1933 and another one a few years later after he and Sybil had been in a series of highly profitable individual engagements.

Just before the last war he went second-hand again after a local garage manager had talked him into it. This was another Austin which in 1939 he handed over patriotically to the Chelsea A.R.P. The astonishing thing is that it survived the war to be driven by Patricia and me till it fell apart in 1948. Its number was FMT – something or other, and it was always known affectionately as 'Foomt'. After that Lewis only owned one more car, an old and battered Rover, which he ran till he had to stop driving at the age of about 85.

When Anxious Annie arrived we were absolutely convinced that Lewis was the only person in the world who really knew how to handle a car. 'After all,' we thought, 'look at the narrow escapes he has got us out of.' Coming home one summer evening we were bowling along Piccadilly at a daring thirty-five, when a huge limousine swung out from the kerb. Lewis made no attempt to brake – Annie's brakes were on the back wheels only so she wouldn't have stopped anyway – and swung the car out in a great sweeping curve to the right-hand side of the road. Sybil, Kiff and the girls in the back all fell over in a heap. Lewis, having decided not to drive into the gates of a Piccadilly club, swung the car in an equally huge curve back over to the left under the wheels of a bus coming the other way, and then just managed to straighten up again on our own side in the nick of time to prevent our going through the railings of Green Park. By this time Sybil and the rest had been thrown about in a heap of arms and legs from this side to that, and were by now settling down again. Lewis's panama hat was sitting pertly on the gear lever and I was thoroughly enjoying it all. How Anxious Annie stood up to this fierce treatment was one of the inexplicable mysteries. But it was Lewis in 'decisive action' and the crisis was dealt with. 'What a wonderful driver you are, Lewis,' was the only comment Sybil made, and of course we all agreed with her.

Anxious Annie, however, holds a place of honour in the family because, thanks to her, we were all able to go off on Sunday jaunts together as a family. For some reason, I always seemed to sit in the front and Lewis saw that the time was well spent by educating me in the arts of driving. He had a phrase that has always stuck in my mind and that may well be the reason that I am still alive. As we approached a blind corner or the brow of a hill he would say: 'Don't forget that car coming the other way at ninety miles an hour.' It puts a picture in one's mind of a terrifying juggernaut leaping to attack the careless or unwary.

At this time Russell and Rosemary were living in a house called The Old Palace at Wrotham in Kent. It was only twenty-five miles from London and Annie could get us there for lunch provided we started early enough to allow for punctures, overheatings and bits falling off. There was always work to be done on her after lunch, and Lewis, with me as a not very qualified assistant, would spend the afternoon tinkering while the others walked or talked.

'You're so like your father,' Sybil used to say. 'So good at mending things. I'm sure you'll be an engineer one day. Oh, but I forgot you're going to be a sailor.' She had no idea of my engineering skills of course, as she has never known a pair of pliers from a pneumatic drill, but this is one of the secrets of her enveloping warmth of heart. She made us, and everyone, feel we possessed incredible skills that to her were for ever closed books.

Lewis's encouragement to learn was of a different kind. I remember one day he was trying to replace some nut in a very inaccessible part of the magneto. With a screwdriver I was bidden to hold in place a nasty little gadget pressing home on a spring. It could have been a rather primitive distributor. It was certainly a vital part of the machinery and, of course, the inevitable happened. As Lewis gently eased the nut in, my finger slipped and the tiny sprung gadget leapt into the long grass beside the car. I've never seen anyone exercise so much emotional control as Lewis at that moment. He drew a long, shuddering, agonised breath through his teeth, paused long and ominously, and then said: 'Oh my dear John!' It took us half an hour's grovelling in the under-growth to find the gadget, but when he started again he didn't say, 'I'll do it this time.' He gave me the screwdriver, showed me again how to hold it against the spring and then, with infinite caution, gently put the nut on. 'Got it!' he cried, and then to me, 'Well done! That was very tricky, wasn't it?'

It gave me the feeling that we had by sheer skill just managed to save the world from destruction!

It was in that summer of 1922 that the Grand Guignol came to an end. The season had run for nearly two years and the names of Lewis, Sybil and Russell had become known throughout London as dispensers of horror. There were even jokes about it in the music halls. A splendid cartoon drawing was made of Sybil looking like a cross between a latter day Lady Macbeth and the Bride of Frankenstein, and which gave me quite a reputation in the Lower Remove at King's College School.

They were not, however, thoroughly known. One matinée in the last season of Grand Guignol I was in the stalls at one of the milder plays in the bill. As the curtain fell, I heard the voice of a very forth-right lady explaining to a friend the relationships of the Casson-Thorndike trio.

'Russell and Sybil Thorndike are husband and wife and they have three or four children. Lewis Casson, the producer, is her brother.'

'I didn't know that you knew them so well,' ventured her com-panion.

'Oh, my dear,' said the forthright lady, as though to a rather stupid child, 'I've known them intimately for years.'

I must have turned round in some surprise, for a moment or two later I heard the lady say in a stage whisper:

'There! Did you see the boy who turned round? He must be one of theirs and he's the image of Russell. So you see!'

This astonishing triangle was, however, only in the minds of the two ladies and the relationships at No. 6 were entirely normal.

Rather to their relief and to José Levy's sorrow, the Grand Guignol did not become a permanent part of the London theatrical scene and Lewis and Sybil were able to move on to newer and greener pastures. The closing, however, meant something much more exciting for us. They had a few days with nothing to do and so came with us to Dymchurch for a short family holiday. It was the first time that Anxious Annie had ventured beyond Wrotham. All six of us set off down the Folkestone Road and the engine boiled her water away two miles outside the village of Dymchurch. But thanks to Lewis's quick action – by pouring cold paraffin into the cylinders of all things! – the engine was saved.

Tom Kealy came down by train with a photographer and we were all photographed skylarking about on the sands. 'Miss Sybil Thorndike and her husband, Lewis Casson, relaxing on the South Coast with their children.' They even worked Anxious Annie into a picture and, to our shame, there appeared a picture of Sybil holding a cricket bat the wrong way, bowled by Kiff while I kept wicket. It took a long time for us to get over our mistrust of the Press after that. After all she *never* played cricket! They also took pictures of us lying in the sea and trying to appear as if we were enjoying the icy cold breakers that were bursting over us. 'Lewis and I are great swimmers,' Sybil told the photographer, 'so you must have a picture of us in the sea.'

In fact I don't think they ever were 'great swimmers'. Like most people they always enjoyed bathing, but that's not quite the same thing. But that wouldn't have done for Sybil. Her bathing had always to be seen in terms of swimming the Hellespont or battling with gigantic and dangerous seas. She and Lewis swam a good solid breaststroke, occasionally varying it by going into the rather dashing 'side-stroke', as it was called. But I fear I never saw either of them go in for any form of powerful or strong propulsion in the water. They loved to frolic in the water and we loved to frolic with them.

On the first evening after supper the twilight was thickening over Romney Marsh and Lewis said, 'I'm going for a walk. Anybody else coming?'

'You go with your father, John,' said Sybil, 'the rest of us are rather worn out. You two look as though you could go on for hours.'

And so began a custom that lasted all through the time when we had holidays as a family. 'Daddy and John's Walk' it was always called and somehow nobody else ever thought of joining us.

We always went up on to the sea-wall and always walked off eastwards towards Hythe. It was nearly dark when we set out but the deep blue light over the sea was enough for us to keep on the path. Usually nothing was said for a few minutes until we got into a comfortable stride and then off we'd go, talking our heads off. But for some reason we never argued on these occasions. It was much more a sharing of experiences and a mutual delight in the wonders of the world. On clear nights we would talk about the stars. Years before he had explained how if one went to the farthest away star one would be able to see another star the same distance farther on, and from that star another and on and on. 'Well where is Heaven, then?' I had asked.

'I'm not sure that it's a real place at all,' he had replied. 'It's much more like a nice cosy feeling. It's in another world altogether like a kind of dream that's very real.'

Gradually there grew in my mind, during these walks and others, an awareness of his quiet, eye-twinkling wisdom. It wasn't so much the information he gave me as the feeling of his ability to cope with whatever problems might arise. He didn't have slick answers to my endless stream of questions. Rather, he made me feel that we were discovering the answers together. We built up a kind of secret companionship on these walks that somehow not even Sybil was able to enter. We were two men who enjoyed each other's company and the thirty-four years difference in our ages became almost irrelevant.

And yet this very close, almost adult, relationship prevented my being able to talk to him or ask for his help and advice about any childish or adolescent difficulties. It was always to Sybil I went if I felt I was in any sort of trouble, as though any admission to Lewis on my part that I even had such problems would make me feel infantile and incompetent. With Lewis I felt I had to maintain a front of being grown-up, which in some odd way he seemed to expect. I know he got very impatient with me if I behaved in his presence in any way that could be seen as childish. As the eldest I was at all ages grown-up while the others could be tolerated as children. This is both an advantage and a disadvantage to any eldest child, I suppose. He or she is always treated as the adult one of the family from the moment of arrival of the younger brothers and sisters. It helps one to learn more about adult ways but sometimes demands a sense of responsibility for which one's years have not adequately equipped one.

At all events it was from these walks that Lewis became my guide, philosopher and friend as well as my father, and it built up a close relationship between us which lasted all his life.

This holiday was the first of only four or five completely family holidays that we managed to spend all together, and they were tremendous fun, even if, on looking back, I see them as fairly high-pressure affairs. As a family we never considered lying about in deck chairs and taking life easily. Holidays were times of furious and exciting activity. But what was astonishing was that Lewis and Sybil were always as active as we. A deck chair was an article of furniture that was never on our list of holiday equipment. They would sit on the shingle under the sea-wall at Dymchurch and read a lot, but it was part of a programme for the day rather than an orderless 'do-nothing'. That summer we made castles, towns and roadworks in the sand, we bathed, we ate buns, we explored the marsh in Anxious Annie and had picnics in the fields. We joined forces with Athene Seyler and her family, who had a cottage farther along the sea-wall, and all of them talked acting and plays on the beach while we wondered at their inability to see that flying kites and playing bicycle-hockey on the sands were so much more important.

We used to call a lot on that marvellous writer of children's books, E. Nesbitt, or Mrs Bland to give her her proper name. She was a great friend of Grannie and she was wonderfully entertaining with us children. She had married her second husband about this time. He was a tiny stocky man with a beard and his name was Captain Tucker. He had been captain of a Thames barge, we were told, and he was certainly almost a caricature of an old sailor.

'Avast there, me hearties!' he would shout as Anxious Annie drove up to their bungalow. 'Come aboard. Tea's ready in the Long Boat, but Madam's still titivating herself in the Jolly Boat.' Their bungalow was really two weatherboard huts which he called respectively the Long Boat and the Jolly Boat. The corridor joining them was the Quarter-deck Gangway. Nobody ever really knew why or how Mrs Bland came to marry 'The Skipper'. Sybil said it was because he never ran out of incredible stories and because he made her laugh, which are as good reasons as any for marrying someone. She always called him 'Skipper' and he called her 'Madam'. They both adored Lewis and Sybil and we all adored them.

I remember, too, one afternoon having our usual tea round the table at the cottage when in came a vigorous and gloriously entertaining young man who talked theatre, music, songs and plays with Lewis and Sybil without so much as pausing when his mouth was full of cake. We four thought he was marvellous because he talked to us as well as to Lewis and Sybil and made us feel part of it. After he left Sybil said: 'Isn't he a darling? He's a young actor and he's brilliant. He writes music and writes songs and he'll be a terrific success one day. He's called Noel Coward.'

We crammed a lifetime into that short week and then they were off back to London again to begin rehearsals for *Jane Clegg*, which opened at the end of July, and which was to be followed by a new play called *Scandal*, both at the New Theatre. Lady Wyndham had been very impressed by Sybil's performance of Katherine's death scene in a charity performance of *Henry VIII* that June, and had offered to back them if a good play could be found.

They were now in West End management and thrilled to think that they could do some of the things they wanted to do with a bit of money behind them. *Scandal* opened in September and I was taken to see it. But as it was a play about marital relationships it was way above my head. Russell's mother-in-law, Rosina Philippi, played Sybil's mother-in-law, and his wife Rosemary was in the cast, which was headed by that wonderful actor, Leslie Faber. Lewis directed it and it ran till December. All I remember is that it had a happy ending and that the setting was in France. There was a scene at the time of a rose harvest and Lewis arranged for the whole stage to be sprayed with Attar of Roses so that the audience could really smell the atmosphere as well as feel it. And the settee, on which Leslie Faber and Sybil had their reconciliation scene, went all the way to Australia with us and is now in our London home.

What a superb actor Leslie Faber was! He had played the sad shiftless Clegg to Sybil's Jane Clegg, and then her husband in *Scandal*. Even when I was only 12 and often didn't know what the play was about, I found myself completely absorbed by him the moment he came on the stage.

Incidentally it was Leslie Faber in Edgar Wallace's *The Ringer* a few years later that showed us how Lewis always seemed to spot the villain right from the first act. In *The Ringer* there was a jovial Scottish police doctor, played by Faber, and in the first interval Lewis said: 'It's the old doctor.' We didn't agree at all, and when he was proved right we asked him how he'd known. 'Easy,' said Lewis. 'No management would pay Leslie Faber's salary just to play a small comedy relief character. He was bound to have something very important to do in the last act. So he had to be the Ringer! It's just a matter of looking down the cast list and assessing the salaries.'

He did the same when Dennis Neilson-Terry and his wife Mary Glynne were playing in another Edgar Wallace called *The Terror*. Lewis knew at once that only Felix Aylmer could be the villain. It was all very unromantic and not at all in keeping with the proper behaviour of a good audience.

During the run of *Scandal* at the New Theatre it wasn't enough for Sybil, nor indeed for Lewis, merely to go off to the theatre at night and kick their heels during the day. They simply had to be doing something more. And so they asked Lady Wyndham's permission to put on matinée performances of *Medea* at the same theatre. The scenery was simple to the point of starkness and could easily be set in front of the contemporary drawing-room setting of *Scandal*. Leslie Faber played Jason, with Lewis still giving his awe-inspiring performance of the Messenger and Sybil, of course, as Medea. These matinées were packed out to such an extent that they felt justified in taking a chance on a play they had both always wanted to put on, Shelley's *Cenci*. It had originally been banned by the censor as too horrifying for the tender minds of the London audiences, but as a hundred years had passed since Shelley's death, Lewis correctly judged that the ban could be overruled.

Count Cenci was played by that superb actor of strange sinister parts, Robert Farquharson, or Robin as he was always called. Horror or no horror, Kiff and I were allowed to see the production and didn't think it nearly so horrifying as some of the Grand Guignol. We did find Robin the very personification of evil and adored it when he died, falling backwards over a high-backed chair. Sybil was superb as Beatrice Cenci, or so I am told. To us Sybil's performance in anything was the one and only possible performance. She was the actress who knew how to act, and when we heard or read that the 'critics' (whoever they were) found anything to dislike, then they became the real villains of the piece.

'Dreadful men,' we thought. 'How dare they, in their ignorance, say such things about the greatest of all actresses, who was the envy and admiration of the rest of the profession.' We didn't put it quite like that, but that was the gist of it. The 'dreadful men', however, agreed with us about her Beatrice. I still have a cutting from the *New Statesman* of 18th November, 1922, in which Maurice Baring wrote:

. . . from the moment Beatrice sees her course clear, Miss Thorndike's interpretation became clear also, and not only clear but inexpressibly dignified, grave and moving, and at the end magnificent. . . . When (she) spoke the final lines it was clear that not only was Shelley a great poet and that we had lost in him a great dramatist, but that we had found in Miss Thorndike a tragic actress.

There were, however, quite a few theatre-goers who agreed with the original ban on the play. One Saturday morning at breakfast she opened a letter from someone whose lack of stomach for the horrors was only matched by his indignation that they should be allowed on the London stage.

'Oh, those people make me so mad, Lewis,' she cried. 'They will take plays *literally*. Can't they understand that they're symbolic. They can't see beyond their silly noses. There's more to horror than just horrors. If it's poetically done it purges you. That's why tragedy is such *fun*.'

Funnily enough I can still remember her saying it even though at the time I hadn't the faintest idea what she meant. And she sailed on waving the letter in hand and getting it covered in marmalade, while Lewis went on quietly munching toast and bringing her back on to the rails with a gentle word or two every now and again.

This in fact was the fun of Carlyle Square. We were growing up a bit by now and could take some interest in grown-up conversation. There were lots of words that we didn't understand, and which we would giggle about whenever they cropped up, but somehow the enthusiasm, the feeling of pioneering, the drive towards theatrical mountain tops, got through to us. Words like 'personality', 'symbolism, 'dramatic significance', 'emotional tension', 'imagination', 'discipline' were hurled across the table like bombs, conveying no intellectual meaning to us at the time but nevertheless sinking emotionally into our unconscious to emerge years later, certainly in my own case, as we shall see, as theatrical knowledge.

It was not only at breakfast that these conversations went on, and not only to the family. Relations, friends and acquaintances would be invited in to the evening meal, and better still, because there was no pressure of time, to Sunday lunch or Sunday supper.

It is now much clearer to me that there was a new theatrical Jerusalem being planned in those days and at those meals, and I wish I had been more aware of what was being said. Now it is only some of the people that I remember and the atmosphere of excitement that surrounded them. Edith Evans was a frequent visitor and it was best when she was the only guest. Lewis's thrusting logic and disciplined thought underpinned by immense artistic sensitivity and insight, Sybil riding her bounding imagination like a battle-charger galloping over everybody, but making them get up and gallop too, and Edith's gorgeously orchestral voice commanding attention by its more smoothly flowing magic, was all like watching and hearing not a play but a kind of Olympian circus.

Sometimes the talk gave way to music and Sybil would go to the piano and bring another sort of magic to life. Her face becomes quite different when she plays the piano and takes on an entirely ageless look. When I first read Bernard Shaw's *Back to Methuselah* I pictured the Ancients not as withered old ascetics who knew all the answers but as something like Sybil when she is playing the piano. It is the sort of look which makes one believe a person has grown physically bigger as well as spiritually wiser. And it is that part of the character of Sybil that Epstein captured in his magnificently powerful bronze of her. The bronze was made some years after this time, but when it came to Carlyle Square it had to stand on a plinth high enough to make the head appear to belong to a person eight feet high. In the house at the time there was another head of Sybil beautifully moulded in a perfect geographical likeness. And it never came alive at all. If you had actually met the Epstein head on a dark night you would have run screaming for help, but it is alive with the inner fire of Sybil. It fills anyone who looks at it with a feeling of tremendous controlled violence.

Lewis once said to me, 'Russell is the theatrical genius of the Thorndikes, Sybil is a musician first and last. It is her imagination and immense powers of application that have made her an actress. It's hard work rather than flair. Her flair is for music.' No one who has both heard and watched her playing the piano would doubt it for a moment.

Bruce Winston came so often that he was almost part of the family, and when he came the discussion was nearly always about the visual part of the theatre. To Lewis, nothing really mattered at all, except the musically produced sound of the spoken word, and so it was Bruce who saw to it that their work concerned itself also with sight as well as sound. He had a wonderful instinct for colour, scenery and costume and was entirely uninhibited by Lewis's total concentration on words, and by the 'Look' that answered any suggestion of attending to anything else, or by Sybil's perennial belief, which is true for her, that unending practice and unrestrained enthusiasm can overcome any problem. Bruce brought them both back to earth, and then took off again with them on a new and different flight. He was also a superb cook, and when Old Cook had her Sunday night off he would go down into the culinary holy of holies to concoct astonishing dishes for the family supper out of a few scraps in the larder.

But it wasn't all theatrical talk. There were fine old high jinks on Sunday evenings with everyone joining in family charades or some other sort of skylark. During these early years in Chelsea the four of us used to work up short plays together which were played on Sunday evening to an audience consisting of Lewis, Sybil and Vi. Lewis and Sybil never took part in these performances or had any say in how they were produced. They were just told to be ready to see them at a specified time. Only when any of us burst into song did we call for help and then Sybil at the piano would become our orchestra.

Our 'stage' was always the dining-room at the back of the house, the drawing-room at the front the auditorium, and the folding doors between them the 'curtain'. We operated this 'curtain' by an elaborate arrangement of strings and pulleys, which invariably jammed at the critical moment and one of us had to break off the action to free them. We must already have instinctively absorbed some of the professional actors' outlook because we all felt acutely embarrassed whenever anything went wrong with the show, and there was many a court of inquiry in the nursery afterwards if there had been any sort of a hitch in our show. Not that our parents minded in the least. They were the most superb audience I have ever played for, both of them always sitting there with rapt attention on their faces – or at least giving a superb performance themselves of rapt attention. Sybil usually maintained her audience rôle rather better than Lewis. I shall never forget Lewis's attempts to conceal his mounting merriment as an unexpected snag upset the smooth running of the production. The worse the situation became on stage, the more did his sides ache as his laughter built up inside him. Much to our chagrin it did actually explode once when Kiff, wearing a dog's head made of brown paper completely lost his bearings and wandered round the room bumping into everything while the rest of us hissed directions at him in very loud stage whispers.

During the run of *Cenci*, Robin Farquharson had told Lewis and Sybil of the wonders and beauties of Italy in general and of his own beloved Rapallo in particular. So persuasive and enthusiastic was he that when their season at the New Theatre ended the two of them took their first real holiday they had had alone together since they had been married and went off to Rapallo for a couple of weeks. The one extant postcard written at the time in Sybil's ebullient cursive handwriting reads:

My Darlings,
    We do miss you all so. Italy is simply gorgeous and we must all come together next time. We went to a funny little church yesterday and the priest was killing. The Italians are darlings. We'll bring back presents for you all.
                              Tons of love.
                                        Your loving,
                                             Mummy and Daddy

And there were lots of presents when they reached home in time for a splendid family Christmas. Grannie was there too, and Eileen and Maurice came with their newly arrived firstborn, Stephen. We had festooned the entire house with decorations not only for Christmas but also to make an occasion for our parents' return. Anyone would have thought that they had been away for ten years, and indeed there had been a dread that they might be still away for Christmas. That's why they returned home as the Prodigal Parents, who had to produce fatted calves for us all as a compensation for their brief absence.

After Christmas there was much talk of their doing a production of *Macbeth*. While in Rapallo they had run into Gordon Craig and they had obviously all fired each other. But they couldn't get hold of a theatre and had to drop the project, at least for the time being. This didn't stop Gordon Craig, however, who turned up a month later with complete and elaborate designs for the production saying, 'Here I am. When do we start rehearsals?' He was firmly convinced that he had been engaged by Lewis for the production and had a large bill in his pocket for fees and expenses! Such are the fruits of histrionic enthusiasm without a good lawyer's guiding hand! Poor Lewis had to cough up, if not all, at least a good part of Gordon Craig's bill. It was a pity because it rather soured not only their relationship but also Lewis's by no means substantial bank balance.

Lewis and Sybil were not to be daunted by so sordid a problem, however, and after some discussion went into partnership with Bronson Albery to take the Criterion Theatre. This time it was to be neither the drama of *Scandal* nor the high horrific tragedy of *Cenci*. It was an absurd but delightful farce called *Advertising April*. Sybil played a caricature of a glamorous film star called April Mawne, and it was tremendous fun. The critics (those 'dreadful men' again) were rather shocked. They had by now put Sybil neatly into the pigeon-hole marked 'High Tragedy' and here she was, if you please, skylarking around in an idiotic farce. It was too much, too violent a change – and the public loved it. I know I went to see it again and again and revelled in watching Sybil dressed in bright silk pyjamas, with Frank Cellier as her husband, giving a superb, not to say ham, burlesque of an Anglo-Hollywood star. Looking back on it I now believe they enjoyed it mostly for giving her a chance to mock the tinsel world of slick film, which both she and Lewis have always despised.

What was much more important, however, than April and her trapesings was that it marked the beginning of their partnership with Bronson Albery, which was to last until the end of the twenties.

Bronson Albery was about half-way between them in age and he shared many of their enthusiasms for the theatre. But his sensitive imagination didn't prevent his having a very shrewd business brain, which is just what Lewis and Sybil needed as a harness for their ebullient energies. They made a splendid trio as a theatrical partnership which was to reach its highest point of success when Shaw wrote *Saint Joan* with Sybil in his mind for the part. I think they all three regretted that the partnership was allowed to fade away because each of them admired the qualities in the others and they enjoyed each others' company. They certainly did much fine work together and might have done much more if only Lewis and Sybil, and probably especially Lewis, had allowed themselves to temper their theatrical evangelism with some of Bronnie's practicality in winning audiences into his theatres. But in the spring of 1923 *Saint Joan* was a year away and there were plays to produce that would build all their reputations.

Advertising April ran till May and then they went off on the first of their many provincial tours which were to make Sybil known up and down the United Kingdom, as well as in the more sophisticated West End. They took a repertoire of four plays which in its variety provided a theatrical bill of fare to satisfy a whole gamut of tastes. The plays were *Advertising April*, *Scandal*, *Jane Clegg* and *Medea*, and they were away until the end of August.

In the meantime, however, a great change came over my life. Encouraged by Sybil, neither Kiff nor I had ever faltered in our determination to become sailors. On her part, it was probably the spreading of her histrionic talents into realms that, as a woman, she could never enter. With us as sailors she could vicariously experience the joys of a life on the ocean wave without having to turn out for the middle watch. Furthermore her mother's relations were sailors, Eileen had married Uncle Maurice, a naval officer, and there was the example of Captain Holland-Thomas on Lewis's side. Unfortunately for our plans the headmaster at King's flatly refused to let me sit for the examination for the Royal Naval College, Dartmouth. 'English and Latin are your strong subjects, Casson. Your mathematics are deplorable. You'd never pass the exam.'

That should have been that, but he didn't know Sybil as well as he thought.

At a party early in 1923, Sybil met someone whose son was a cadet on board a training ship for budding officers of the Merchant Service. This school for sailors was an old wooden-wall vessel moored off Greenhithe. It was, in the words of the prospectus, 'The Thames Nautical Training College, H.M.S. *Worcester*, for imparting to youths destined for a sea career a sound nautical and mathematical tuition.' Sybil met the young man and came home to No. 6 bursting with enthusiasm and wasted not a second in telling me the news.

'Darling, how would you like to leave school at the end of this term and go and be a sailor on a real ship. It's a training ship on the river not far from Tilbury and I've met such a nice boy who's there and says it's marvellous. You live on board and do all your lessons there, and when you leave you become a Merchant Service Officer. I think the Merchant Service must be much more exciting than the Navy. You meet all sorts of passengers and carry wonderful cargoes all over the world. The Bowers could get you into the Union Castle Line, couldn't they Lewis, and then there are the Seligmans who practically own the Glen Line, or is it the Clan Line, and of course George Booth would be thrilled to have you as one of his officers. And we'd be able to come on voyages with you and it will all be splendid. Oh, I wish I were a man. I'd rather be a sailor than anything.'

It all sounded pretty splendid to me, too. After all what boy of 13 would not want to leave school and go and live in a ship, and with Sybil bubbling over with it into the bargain there was no question ever of my not agreeing with her. A week later she and Lewis took time off to visit the ship themselves, after which there was never a question but that this was the answer.

'The Captain is an absolute darling,' she reported to me, 'and you'll love him. He's got a sweet wife who looks after all the boys and they all have a gorgeous time climbing up the rigging.' This, as it transpired was the wildest hyperbole. The Captain was a highly competent but very tough sailor and his wife never took the slightest notice of any of us. But what did that matter? There was a smell of salt in the air, the wind was whistling in the rigging and Sybil was already seeing me as another Conrad-Masefield-Melville with perhaps St Paul casting four anchors out of the stern.

Lewis and I did have a bit of talk about it on the quiet. 'I think you'll enjoy it,' he said, 'if you really want to be a sailor. The boys seem to be a nice lot and it's a fine ship. But have a good think about it and tell us if you'd like to go there.' And of course I did want it despite my head-master who continued to demur to the last.

At the end of March, I said good-bye to my prep. school and spent the holidays going round with Sybil buying uniform and a complete outfit of accoutrements and, joy of joys, a huge sea-chest to put it all in. Sybil was in a seventh heaven of delight and I was thrilled to bits, while Lewis did his best not to be too depressed at the size of the bills. By the end of April I was fully equipped. Lewis and Sybil were about to start their tour and I was preparing to leave home for the first time and become, as I thought, a man of the world.

In the event their tour began the day before I went off and they very thoughtfully persuaded Uncle Maurice to take a day's leave and come up to London all the way from Weymouth to escort me to Greenhithe. It was the last time, in fact, that I was ever escorted anywhere as a child unable to escort himself. Uncle Maurice took me aboard, had a few highly nautical words with Captain Sayer, R.N.R. and then, after wishing me luck (how much I needed it he would never have known!), left me in the strange, esoteric world of seafaring and seamanship. It turned out to be a pretty rough world for the next three years, but a world I have never regretted because it led me into twenty very happy years with the Royal Navy.

At this time, however, I had reached a milestone which was significant on two counts. First, I had now left home and would in the future look on the family, and indeed the theatre, from the outside, and therefore see it with a rather more detached vision, and secondly, I began to receive letters from Sybil. She has always been the most prodigious letter writer in her large cursive hand which graphologically so mirrors her character. Lewis wrote too sometimes, but not very often. When he did it was very difficult to read, because his writing showed his impatience with the slow pace that a pen demands. Neither of their hands are easy to read for the beginner, as I then was, but I soon discovered that the effort of deciphering was usually very rewarding.

Sybil wrote to me at least two or three times a week and usually more often. Two days after I had joined the *Worcester* she wrote from somewhere in the South of England to say:

Darling John,
Daddy and I are wondering so much how you're getting on in your ship. It must be very exciting but I expect it's a bit strange to begin with. But you're

so good at getting on with people and will soon make a lot of friends. Our tour is going very well and we had a packed house last night. We'll be staying in Streatham in two weeks time and we're coming down to see you on the Sunday after that.

Will the Captain let you off in time for lunch?

Oh, how I envy you doing such exciting things!

Daddy sends his love. Lots of hugs.

Your loving Mummy

All this was very cheering to a rather homesick little boy pretending to be a sailor, and wishing he was. Sybil always made me believe I was, and when she and Lewis came down in whatever was the latest jalopy, it was good to drive off with them, Kiff and the girls, feeling very important in my uniform and enjoying the vast lunch at 'Ye Olde Leather Bottell' at Meopham or going over to Wrotham to have an even bigger one with Russell and Rosemary. In the whole of my three years on the *Worcester*, I don't think they ever missed coming to see me at least every three weeks.

At the end of that first summer term they were still on tour and so couldn't join most of the parents on board the Thames paddle-steamer *Golden Eagle* that always ran on the *Worcester*'s Prize Day from London Bridge to Greenhithe. It was the thrill of the year to sight the steamer coming into Dartford Reach while the cadets manned yards. We came down from aloft when the *Golden Eagle* was safely berthed alongside. As a first-termer I wasn't allowed to be on the yards on this Prize Day, which didn't matter much as Lewis and Sybil weren't there. Nor were they at home that day when I got back to Carlyle Square feeling as though I had just returned from a voyage round the world and finding that Kiff and Vi and the girls weren't at all the sort of appreciative audience that I felt I not only needed but deserved. Somehow they didn't 'love me for the dangers I had passed' and I knew that Lewis and Sybil would.

We all went off to Dymchurch, however, under the watchful eyes of Grannie and Vi, neither of whom had the least idea of the fact that having lived three months aboard a ship I was now old enough to deal with any problem that arose or could arise.

At the end of August Kiff and I joined Lewis and Sybil at Cardiff. They were staying at a splendid hotel at Penarth along the coast, and it was the first time in our lives that we had experienced such self-indulgent luxury. We hardly saw Lewis and Sybil for, as always, they were working like mad on the next, or possibly next to next, production. They certainly had no time whatever to laze around at a seaside resort.

But they had come to know a very charming and well-off family called Mathwin. Mrs Mathwin for some blissful, but incomprehensible, reason thought it fun to look after two boys and stuff them to their eyebrows with delectable foods, and buy them an unending stream of mechanical gadgets, toys and practical jokes like dummy ink-blots.

I'm not sure that Lewis approved of all this prodigality. I do know that Mrs Mathwin's hospitality was too much for me when I woke up one night and was very sick from sheer over-eating. Lewis's lecture to me next morning was short and to the point. 'I don't think it's very admirable to go on eating till you're sick. It's just disgusting.' And that was that.

They were still not very well known in those days – certainly not what are loosely called stars. But Sybil took us to say 'How d'ye do' to a real star, who was also staying in the hotel. It was Marie Lohr and she seemed to us then, what she still seems to me now – a very gracious charming lady and a perfect darling. Sybil took us in rather in the manner of one of the villagers introducing her children to the gentry, and Marie Lohr seemed almost like royalty to us.

At the end of a week the four of us climbed into our Cubit ('Anthony Cubit' we called it), which had replaced our beloved Annie, and set off for Birmingham on a real English summer Sunday. We drove through the Malvern Hills, and they were looking their beautiful best so that when twenty-five years later I heard Lewis say as Professor Linden: 'Long summer days on the Malvern Hills,' I at once saw the four of us bowling along that day in our battleship of a car with our hair blown out by the wind and our faces roasted by the sun. We had lunch at a pub, two or three punctures and a choked carburettor, which we fixed by the roadside, and arrived at The Bull in Solihull with its Tudor bowling-green, in time for a late supper.

'This is one of the really old hotels, darlings,' said Sybil. 'And you can imagine the ghosts of all the Elizabethan people playing bowls in the garden and wandering in and out of the rooms. Look at those gorgeous panels. I expect there are secret passages behind all of them. Wouldn't it be fun if we saw some ghosts.'

She must have said it with enormous effectiveness because I lay awake for hours that night listening to the chiming of the church clock in the village and quite convinced that when midnight struck every grave in the churchyard would open to release its spectral inhabitant. Actually it was Lewis who struck when finally in an absurd blind panic, I woke them both up to say I couldn't sleep. But we had a wonderful week at Solihull, the highlight of which was being taken to Stratford to see where Shakespeare was born.

In September, soon after we got back to London, they opened at the New Theatre in *Cymbeline* with Sybil as Imogen, which unfortunately London didn't awfully like. J. C. Trewin called this play the 'odd and lovely collision of the Renaissance with Snow White and Lear's Britain', and Bernard Shaw made a comment to the effect that 'the English are strange people who return to London in the autumn after killing chickens on the moors of Scotland, to enjoy themselves at the theatre watching a young woman waking up beside the headless body of her fiancé.' But apparently not enough of them were prepared to enjoy this spectacle and the production was taken off in favour of a play by Henry Arthur Jones called *The Lie*.

This was a tremendous success with Sybil at last being able to use her dramatic powers to the full in a play that couldn't be dubbed by people as 'classical' and therefore high-brow. It was a grand play with straightforward human emotions of two sisters in love with the same man and the elder, Sybil, being betrayed by the younger. Sybil's cry of 'Judas sister' at the end of the second act can still ring in the ears of anyone who heard her say it. She was nevertheless a little taken aback after I saw her in it and asked afterwards, 'What on earth's a jute assister?' What's more she did space her sibilants a little more carefully from then on.

All this time Lewis was gradually assembling round him a team of actors who, if they were not all star material, were people who could work with him and liked working with him. In *The Lie* there were O. B. Clarence, Bob Horton and Jack Anderson among others, with Bruce Winston, not in the show but hovering always in the background like a captive balloon, and a stage manager who was to be with them for years, Tommy Hudson.

Tommy had first met Lewis when they were both driving lorries together in the old A.S.C. He had been brought up in a circus and was, in fact, a born clown. He and Lewis had organised a troupe of military pierrots in France and after the war, Lewis took him on to play a small part in *Jane Clegg* and to help with the stage management. He had a cheerful rather impudent face and a quick-witted skylarking sort of humour. The girls of all ranks and classes adored him and he made good use of their adoration. He had been in the second-hand car trade and the techniques of salesmanship, which this profession took over from the much older one of horse-trading, combined with much that he had picked up in the circus, gave him a set of moral values which only he ever understood. The law at times certainly did not. Earning money in wages was apparently only one of many ways by which the stuff could be obtained and this view did from time to time get him into hot water. Lewis was always called on to give him a character and he used to say quite truthfully that Tommy had never let him down in any way whatever. The point was, of course, that Tommy had a dog-like devotion and loyalty to Lewis. When Lewis needed something Tommy believed he had to have it at once. Tommy had learnt the well-known art of stores-scrounging in the army and by only the slightest stretching of this sort of morality he managed to 'win' what he wanted.

With the production of *The Lie* Lewis promoted him to stage manager, at which job he was masterly. And as soon as I appeared backstage in cadet's uniform he won my undying gratitude by assuming that any sailor enjoys climbing up whatever is vertical and in reach. It meant that in every spare moment of holidays he would let me climb the wooden ladder on the wall of the stage up into the 'flies' where the scenery was 'flown' on ropes. Most of what I remember of *The Lie* is the shortened figures of Sybil and the rest of the cast as seen from this platform fifty feet above the stage, and on one blissful day when the curtain fell I slid the whole fifty feet down a rope to arrive, like a pantomime demon, at the feet of Sybil and Robert Horton. This was Tommy's idea and was a pale imitation of his own astonishing feat some years earlier, of going across hand-over-hand on a rope flung across Piccadilly.

The great thing was that Lewis now had a devoted and capable slave who would do anything for him, and who ran his shows for him with a discipline that a sergeant-major would have envied – except of course where the girls were concerned – and who could be called upon for almost any conceivable act of service. When, a few years later,

Lewis and Sybil went to their first garden party at Buckingham Palace, Tommy tore the badge off one of my uniform caps and with this and a smart blue suit became the chauffeur of the plebeian Armstrong-Siddeley for the afternoon.

The Lie ran for six months to capacity business and we had quite an affluent Christmas that year. Not that they had ever seemed poverty-stricken to us, but this one excelled them all. As well as the usual, exciting festivities and with Lewis and Sybil at home a good deal because they were in a successful run, there was something else in the air. Bernard Shaw had written a play about Joan of Arc and there had been much talk and speculation over the supper table. I knew very little about Joan of Arc except that she was French and against us, and less about Bernard Shaw. But their two names kept popping up in conversations and it was clear that plans were being made. We were, in fact, about to enter the 'Era of Saint Joan' and life would never be quite the same again.

Chapter 7

SAINT JOAN BECOMES SYBIL

In the middle of every morning in the *Worcester* we had our 'stand-easy'. The tuck-shop opened on the main deck and then, when the weather was fine, we all trooped up on the upper deck and skylarked around for the best part of half an hour. At some point during this time the head boy, or Chief Cadet-Captain to give him his official title, would climb up on top of a broom-locker with a pile of letters in his hand and call out the names of the lucky addressees. When anyone's name was called, someone answered 'here' and the letter was flicked through the air vaguely in the direction of the caller.

One morning in the late autumn of 1923, a letter sailed through the air in my direction and landed at my feet. To me it was just another, but always welcome, letter from Sybil, and even when I read it there didn't seem to be anything particularly unusual in it.

Darling John,
We had the most wonderful day yesterday. We went to lunch with Mr and Mrs Bernard Shaw at their house in Ayot St Lawrence just north of London. He wanted to read us the play that he has just finished about Joan of Arc. And so Daddy and I drove down in the morning and got there about half past twelve. We had a lovely lunch – chicken for us and all sorts of funny-looking things for him because he's a vegetarian – and then he took us into a nice comfy sitting-room and we all sat down in armchairs. Then he began to read us the play. He read it beautifully – he ought to have been an actor really and from the moment he started we couldn't move! You know how I've always longed to play Joan of Arc and I'd been having the most awful quirks that I wouldn't like the Joan he'd written. But we needn't have worried. It's the most marvellous play and we're so excited we don't know what to do. He says that he wants us to do it as soon as possible and we're going to as soon as the silly old *Lie* is finished. No time for more, Darling. I must fly! Your tin of petit-beurre biscuits is in the post.

Tons of love,
Mummy.

The 'silly old *Lie*' had only just begun so was playing to capacity business, which should have pleased them as much as it did Bronson Albery, and it probably did. But both Lewis and Sybil have always been rather suspicious of a commercial success as it probably means that the audiences aren't learning anything. Nearly twenty years later, when they were touring the Welsh coalfields with *Macbeth*, the noise from the audience before the curtain went up sounded rather curious. Sybil saw Lewis standing on the stage gradually working himself up into his 'I'll show 'em' mood. Sybil went up to him and said, 'Lewis, don't let's try to teach them anything to-night. Let's just do the play.'

And so the highly successful *The Lie* now apparently became almost a tiresome chore – like having to eat bread and butter before getting down to the strawberries and cream. But there was much to do and much to arrange, and it was very good that the money was rolling in while they did it.

I'm ashamed to say that after I'd read her letter I asked a cadet-captain who Bernard Shaw might be. 'Oh, he's that funny looking old codger with a beard. He's always making speeches and talking bosh,' I was told with an air of authority.

'He's just written a play for the theatre,' I ventured.

'Well it'll be no bloody good then,' said my erudite adviser, 'my Dad says he's just an old fool who talks too much.'

And that was that, for after all who was I to dispute the words of a cadet-captain. But I was quite disturbed to think that my parents had apparently been taken in by this mountebank.

When I came home for the Christmas holidays, however, the air was buzzing with plans. *Saint Joan* was about to be produced for the first time by the Theatre Guild of America because Shaw had promised them some time earlier that they could do the world première of his 'next play'. He felt in honour bound to keep his promise and it opened in New York on 28th December without making much of a splash. Not that this made the slightest difference to Sybil and Lewis. Cadet-captains' fathers notwithstanding, the name of Shaw was rarely off their lips. Then there was a comic little man, as we thought, with a pointed beard and a rather high-pitched voice who came to the house one day and we learned that he was a 'wonderful painter' called Charles Ricketts, who was going to design the scenery. He certainly got very excited in the middle of a discussion, as we gathered from our eaves-dropping behind the folding doors of our ground-floor drawing-room.

Mr and Mrs John Foulds came several times. He had been engaged to compose the 'Saint Joan Suite', the beautiful music that was to haunt the whole family for the rest of our lives and send tingles of excitement down our spines whenever we were to hear it.

When I went back to my training ship for the spring term, however, *The Lie* was still going great guns and before long Shaw, Lewis and Sybil began to get restive. It must have been galling for Bronson Albery to have to take off such a money-spinning production when there was no sign of any fall-off in the bookings. It says much for his judgement and for his artistic integrity that he set a limit on this most successful run, and a date for the opening of *Saint Joan*.

Despite all the talk and the comings and goings, the period of rehearsals and the opening itself has left almost no mark in my memory. I don't even remember getting any letters about it, though I cannot believe that Sybil could have avoided keeping me up-to-date about what I know was a most thrilling time. Russell, however, has described it all in his usual racy way in his earlier biography of Sybil:

'Sybil walked on air during the month's rehearsal. The only thing that depressed her was that none of them could act the play as well as Shaw could. He knew every intonation he wanted, and it was always the true, common-sense thing that he did want.

'As a producer he is the most courteous and kindly gentleman imaginable. He never says a word that could possibly hurt anybody's feelings, and as one small-part actor said to me one day, after leaving rehearsal, "Mr Shaw always makes me feel a little better actor than I am, and I think I get better because I feel he believes in me." Sybil has said the same sort of thing.'

In fact Shaw was usually only there with Lewis in the mornings and left Lewis on his own as the producer in the afternoons. 'I shall tell you how I want you to do it,' he said to the actors one morning. 'I expect Lewis will change it all this afternoon.' In an interview for one of the newspapers at this time Sybil said:

'I don't know whether I ought to give the secret away, but Mr Bernard Shaw is a remarkably good actor.

'He plays the part of Saint Joan better than I could ever hope to do. When he first read the play to us I said to him: "It would be wonderful if you played every part." His reply was characteristic, "Oh, dear no. People have quite enough of me as it is. They say I speak in every character, but if I acted every one as well I don't know what would happen."

'At rehearsals, however, he can, and does, if necessary. He knows exactly what he wants. That is why I think he is easy to work for in the theatre. He has such beautiful manners that he never hurts.

'It seems as though he feels it would be an offence against himself to say anything harsh or hard. If he has to, then the criticism is cloaked in such a way that nobody could be offended. He can lay you flat and knock all the conceit out of you without making you feel humiliated.

'That in a man with such a tongue, who can flay institutions and people alive, as he does, is, I think, very remarkable. It is part of his charm.

'At rehearsals he is always quiet, always courtly, but there is about him the suggestion of a volcano. If anyone set himself against him it would be to discover the force in him, but nobody ever does.'

But Lewis confided in me some years afterwards that although Shaw was a very good actor when reading his plays, and superb in showing actors what he wanted done, he didn't know nearly as much as he thought he did about directing actors to project the thought on a scale commensurate with a large auditorium. He was a great help to actors in getting them inside their rôles, but not so good in achieving the large-scale overall effectiveness. This is where Lewis came in. He could and did hurt people's feelings, which no producer can avoid, but he usually knew just how far he could go before he began restoring the temporarily shattered confidence. His directing of actors was always a fight between the fiery evangelist, impatient with anyone making mistakes after they had been told once, and his own inherent kindliness and courtesy.

The play opened on 26th March, 1924 at the New Theatre, and despite some of the critics it seemed to have a feeling of success in it from the start. By the time I came home for the Easter holidays three or four weeks later they knew they had a real smash-hit on their hands. Christopher, Mary and Ann had all seen it two or three times even though Ann was only eight years old. No one, in fact, talked of anything else and even Granny was in it, playing a Casson-built Positive Organ off stage at the beginning of the scene in Rheims Cathedral after King Charles's coronation.

Sybil had arranged for me to see it on the first night I was home and

I sat with some other people in a box rather aggrieved that my brother and sisters had already become, as it were, members of the 'Saint Joan Club'. I had no idea what I was in for except that everyone said it was marvellous. Somehow, though, the feeling of excitement began when I read on the programme, 'Scene I. A fine spring morning on the river Meuse, between Lorraine and Champagne, in the year 1429, in the castle of Vaucouleurs.' Then came the notes of that magical Foulds overture, conducted by John Foulds himself, and suddenly the curtain was up to the sound of Robert de Baudricourt's shouting: 'No eggs! No eggs! Thousand thunders man, what do you mean by no eggs.' The sunlight streamed into the room and, in memory anyway, you could smell the French countryside coming in through the open window of the castle. As a young man of fourteen I had been quite prepared to have to sit through a 'classic' and to wonder what it was all about for three and a half hours. But in the event it was one of the most thrilling evenings of my life. To this day I could tell you the exact layout of the courtyard of that castle, the courtyard that the audience could never see, and from which soon after the beginning, Joan's voice would call up, 'Is it me, Sir?' to be followed seconds later by her entrance up the spiral staircase and her lovely forthright greeting of, 'Good morning, captain squire. Captain, you are to give me a horse and armour and some soldiers, and send me to the Dauphin. Those are your orders from my Lord.' Then on to Chinon with its colour and pageantry and the thrill of seeing Joan's sword flashing out of its scabbard and the whole court crying out, 'To Orleans!' I was crying with excitement by the end of the scene on the banks of the Loire when the pennant blowing in the wind miraculously changed direction as Joan and Dunois go off to pray for a west wind. The hush as they went off leaving only the page on the stage and all the audience watching that pennant change direction, and the whisper that could always be heard rippling through the house. 'Look at the flag,' 'the wind's changed,' made up for me one of those theatrical moments of sheer magic that stay with one for ever.

When Shaw reached this point in his first reading, according to Russell's account, he looked up with a twinkle in his eye and said, 'Well that's the jam. Now the real play begins.' And begin it did, to rise up to those heights that made it the pinnacle of Shaw's multitudinous achievements. Who would have believed that an audience could be held spellbound for forty minutes of politico-theological discussion between the Earl of Warwick, the Bishop of Beauvais and the English Chaplain, John de Stogumber. In later productions I have observed this scene ruined by a lot of fussy and unnecessary movement around the stage because the producer hadn't the nerve to trust Shaw's almost infallible sense of the dramatic in his writing. The lines have only to be spoken with a kind of orchestrated significance and none of the three characters needs to move. And was there ever such a scene of such fascinating talk? Then into the pathos of Joan's rejection by the Court in the Cathedral scene and at last the long high tragedy of the trial at Rouen. Of all the countless times when Sybil has moved me to the core by her acting, I don't think she has ever surpassed the moment when she tore up the recantation and spoke the beautiful words that Shaw had put into Joan's mouth. It was at once her farewell and her condemnation of the world that had rejected her. It was at the same time the beginning of her revolution towards protestantism and nationalism. And it was at the same time Shaw the revolutionary speaking as Shaw the poet. Somehow Sybil managed to say all this and to imbue it with her own special and private magic. For that is what her Saint Joan was – pure, untarnished, theatrical magic. Of those who saw her play Joan none will ever forget the final moment when Shaw's poetry and her acting became fused together in, 'O God that madest this beautiful earth, when will it be ready to receive thy saints? How long, O Lord, how long.' Somehow her Saint Joan has to be seen essentially as she sees herself, or rather as she would like to be able to see herself. It was Lewis who once said, and claimed it to be his only epigram, 'We go through life wishing we were what we hope other people think we are.' An actor, however, doesn't always have to wish and hope. He can find a part that does it for him. When the part is exactly right for him as he sees it, and when he has the technical skill to perform it, then he gives a great performance and attains a supreme sense of fulfilment. This is exactly what happened to Sybil as Saint Joan. Everything was exactly right for her in wish, hope, and belief and she had the skill and drive to express it. It is as sensible to say Saint Joan became Sybil Thorndike as it is to say Sybil Thorndike played Saint Joan. The two people became one and Joan became not only part of the family, but the leading part.

The play itself had a mixed reception by the critics. Most of them agreed that it was Shaw's greatest play, but most of them seemed to be a little aggrieved that Shaw had not made Joan more of a saint and less of a revolutionary. And the Epilogue seemed to infuriate them all. There oughtn't to be any jokes or humour about saints for one thing, and for another it wasn't right for Shaw to point out to them with his own special brand of biting irony just what his point was in writing the play.

But there was no dissenting view about Sybil's performance as these two extracts from newspapers of 27th March, 1924, show:

There may be two opinions about Mr Bernard Shaw's treatment of the story in *Saint Joan*, his new play produced at the New Theatre last night. There are always at least two opinions about everything he does, but there can only be one opinion about Miss Sybil Thorndike's acting as Joan of Arc.

It is superlative. When in the second scene in the Dauphin's throneroom at Chinon, she has induced the Dauphin to allow her to lead his army to the relief of Orleans, and at the close kneels to Heaven and draws her mystic sword, calling to those around her to fight for God and France, she is a figure of the most intense romantic beauty.

She is ablaze with vitality. Her eyes shine with faith. Her courage is as clear as the sun. She is at once the perfect soldier, the impassioned saint, the lovely maid.

And G. H. Mair wrote in the *Evening Standard*:

A great occasion. Sir Johnston Forbes-Robertson, in a box, bringing with him the memories of *Caesar and Cleopatra* and *The Devil's Disciple*; the whole audience expectant and curious; and when the play ended, all of us quite oblivious that we had sat watching and listening, with only a few minutes to rest our minds and hearts, for four hours at the New Theatre.

Miss Thorndike is to be congratulated on the privilege of playing on this great occasion. In all the qualities of memory and diction (and in Mr Shaw's plays these are matters of vital importance) she seemed to me faultless. Moreover she showed an emotional exaltation very beautiful when she was permitted to do so. If sometimes the gaucherie of the peasant was a little overstrained, we must be content to know that this is the way in which Mr Shaw wished the part to be played by her.

The rest of the acting is on a remarkably high level, and in a cast containing so many men and giving so many opportunities for excellence it is hard to single out any name specially.

Mr Lewis Casson, who this time took a part and played it admirably, must be congratulated on a very beautiful production which is distinguished by the collaboration in scenery of Mr Charles Ricketts.

The part which Lewis took and played so 'admirably' was, of course, de Stogumber, Chaplain to the Cardinal of Winchester and private secretary to the Earl of Warwick. Not only did he play it admirably, but he played it with a realism, a humour and a passion that I had never seen in his acting before. Shaw had used de Stogumber's 'invincible ignorance' not only to bring the relief of laughter to his long theological discussions, not only to make his English audiences see themselves as others see them, but to make them feel the stark horror of being presented with the results of their ignorance. Shaw makes the Bishop of Beauvais say in the Epilogue: 'Must then a Christ perish in torment in every age to save those who have no imagination?' and Shaw's answer is clearly 'yes'. When Lewis's de Stogumber returned from watching the burning of Joan his agony was so shatteringly real as to be almost unbearable. I have seen no other de Stogumber who could hold the audience so completely during this scene. Hardly any of them have got through it without getting a nervous giggle from somewhere in the house. When an audience is in a state of high nervous tension there is only a hair's-breadth between their being held spellbound and having all the tension disappear in a laugh. The actor must know exactly how far he can take them without breaking the spell. The timid don't risk it and so make little use of their dramatic chances. The unskilled may risk it but all too often go too far and then complain about the audience when they giggle. Lewis always took his audience closer to their breaking point than anyone else. As he once said to me, 'It's the actor's job to move an audience emotionally to the limit of their endurance without losing his control of them.' As de Stogumber he went way beyond even his own tight limits and the result was a *tour de force* which was devastating. And it made even more poignant his heartbreaking lovely portrait in the Epilogue of the very old and almost witless de Stogumber who had become 'only a poor old harmless English rector'.

What a wonderful cast Lewis had assembled to play with Sybil's Joan, all drilled to the last tiny inflection of voice by Shaw and Lewis. No one who ever saw that first production can ever think of these characters as anyone else. When I read the play to-day the Dauphin is still the impudent and petulant creature of Ernest Thesiger. The Earl of Warwick must have that epitome of aristocratic political power given him by Lyall Swete. Peter Cauchon, the Bishop of Beauvais, could never be anyone else but Eugene Leahy, nor could the deceptively mild Inquisitor with the frightening power of the Church behind him be anyone but O. B. Clarence. They are still all there in my mind, Bruce Winston's La Tremouille, Milton Rosmer's Bluebeard, the then unknown Raymond Massey's La Hire, the beautiful voice of dear Jack Anderson's Brother Martin and even Jack Hawkins's pageboy. From that time on they all somehow became 'our actors'.

The four of us could not only recite the whole play after a few months but we could do it in the accents of the respective actors. We were all imbued with *Saint Joan*, and we were drunk with *Saint Joan*, we quoted *Saint Joan*, we lived, breathed and slept *Saint Joan* and we all learnt a lot of our early political and social philosophy from *Saint Joan* and the preface which appeared with the first edition of the play on 25th June, 1924.

Sybil sent me a copy in the middle of the summer term. It is here beside me on the desk now while I am writing. On the fly leaf she wrote –

> To John
> with love from Mother
> March 1924
> 'I shall put courage into thee.' St Joan

She put the date of the opening rather than the date she gave it to me. Even then I think she knew that something historic had happened in the theatre and that this first edition would be specially memorable with this inscription written by her. It is certainly one of my most prized possessions as is her copy given her by Shaw, in which he wrote, 'Saint Sybil Thorndike from Saint Bernard Shaw.'

Something happened to Sybil and Lewis with the production of *Saint Joan*. It wouldn't be entirely right to say that it represented their theatrical coming of age (Sybil had been twenty-two years an actress by this time) but it was something uncommonly like it. They had risked all their resources to put it on. Just when they were beginning to put a little money into their bank, they took it all out again and added it to Bronson Albery's backing. And despite the name of Bernard Shaw, they never really thought that the play would be a box office success. They just had to do it even if it had meant pawning everything they owned, and they thought they probably would have to pawn everything they owned.

But although the Greek tragedies, the Grand Guignol and one or two commercial successes had made Sybil known as an actress of great power, it was only from *Joan* onwards that she became a household word. It was, for example, great fun for me to hear a musical-hall comedian make a rather ribald joke about her, which the audience thoroughly enjoyed. Lewis, being mostly a producer, was less well-known and more often than not was spoken of as 'Sybil Thorndike's husband'.

Sybil did achieve one signal honour as early as 1923 when an honorary LL.D was conferred on her by Manchester University. I remember this because Sybil sent me a picture of her and John Masefield getting their degrees together. As a budding sailor, I was an ardent fan of Masefield and hoped that Sybil realised how honoured she had been to be in his company. Sybil, who tells everybody she meets about every member of her family, had told Masefield all about my being in the *Worcester*. I knew he was one of the famous old boys of our rival and sister ship the *Conway* on the Mersey, and I was thrilled a week or so after she got her degree to receive a parcel containing a beautiful illustrated edition of his Salt-Water Ballads especially sent to me by the great man himself.

She was 'Dr Thorndike' now, as one of the newspapers had it, and by the time *Joan* had got well under way she was in great demand as a public figure to speak in aid of causes from charitable to political. To-day she must be a member of more institutions than any one alive. She has never stopped joining things and speaks on their behalf even now with the fervour of Joan storming the walls of Orleans. In fact, it has always seemed to me that her passionate evangelical zeal in religion, politics, art and even gastronomy really got under way when every night she could become one of the great rebels of history. As she said of Joan to an interviewer after the opening night, 'To me, she has always been a flaming spirit with the military genius of Napoleon, but with a spirituality that he lacked. Joan was another Abraham Lincoln.'

The play ran all through that summer and in the autumn it was still playing to packed houses. But not in their wildest dreams had they or Bronson Albery thought that it would last as long as this. It might have run for years, but from October the theatre had been let to Matheson Lang and there was not another one in the West End for *Joan* to go to. It had to come off, and they went off on a tour that had been booked for the 'silly old *Lie*.'

The Lie was a smash hit for the whole three months' tour and then

122

they came back to London, or rather the outer fringe of London, to play *Joan* again at that once great barn of a theatre, the Regent, in Euston Road. But even there *Joan* packed them in until May when once again they had to stop because the Regent in its turn was wanted for something else.

They put on Lennox Robinson's *The Round Table* at Wyndham's in May and it flopped. It was one of those plays, and there have been many through the years, that Sybil believes people ought to see and which nobody but herself understands. Her own enthusiasm wasn't enough for London after her Joan and according to Russell, one critic said of it, 'If Sybil Thorndike wants a holiday, why doesn't she take one instead of playing this sort of part.' In any case the two years of 1924 and 1925 and on into 1926 are the first part of the *Joan* years. It was never really out of any of our minds and at the drop of a hat they would put it on again. When *The Round Table* folded up after a week or two, on went the indefatigable *Lie* again to hold the breech until near Christmas when to everyone's astonishment they put on Shakespeare's *Henry VIII* at the old Empire in Leicester Square. They really went to town on this one, and it was a gorgeously splendid production. As a play it is, of course, a pageant, and Lewis saw to it that pageantry had its head. He had wanted to play Buckingham as well, but as in *Saint Joan*, when he had wanted to play the Bishop of Beauvais, Bronson Albery wouldn't have it. He believed, with many others, that one cannot both direct and play a leading part without one of them suffering. And so, thank Heaven, he played de Stogumber in *Saint Joan* and a deeply moving Griffith in *Henry*. Katherine's death scene between him and Sybil is still one of the most exquisitely moving scenes that they have ever played together and they have played it all over the world ever since in their recital programmes. But Sybil was terrific in her earlier scenes when she pulled all her stops out to defy the shrewd, wicked and dignified Henry of Norman V. Norman. Her two pages were Laurence Olivier and Carol Reed.

Despite the forebodings of the theatrical Jeremiahs, London took this Henry to their hearts, not the least reason for which being a bewitching and heart-breaking Anne Boleyn by Angela Baddeley. I was now sixteen and was myself much more than bewitched by Angela. I fell flat for her and used to stand in the wings as often as I could get there during those Christmas holidays and sigh my heart out with

hopeless and frustrated love! And I don't think I was by any means the
only one in the family and out of it. She was really absolutely lovely
and her Anne has stayed as a much treasured picture in my mind ever
since. In fact Patricia and I saw her in *Night Must Fall* on the last night
of our honeymoon and I remember feeling quite guilty taking my
bride of three weeks to meet her after the play.

Henry filled the Empire until March when they were able to return
again to the much more important business of *Saint Joan*, this time in
another huge theatre, the Lyceum. Once again Londoners flocked to
see it, but once again the anti-*Joan* gremlin, which seemed determined
not to let *Joan* have a nice long uninterrupted run, stepped forward in
the form of the General Strike. To us two boys this national disaster
was regrettably a source of unexpected excitement. We were at the
theatre every night to see if there were odd jobs to be done when
members of the cast were prevented from getting to the theatre. It was
during this time we began the practice of getting into ecclesiastical habit
and going on as monks in the trial scene. The monks were usually
played by the girls who were also the ladies of the court at Chinon. If
we put on the habits we allowed the girls to go home early and it was
great fun for us. It became a *Joan* tradition and we even used to invite
the occasional friend to join us. 'Come and be a monk,' we'd say, and
monks they became. It was a beautiful summer and between matinée
and evening shows we would take sandwiches up on to the vast roof of
the theatre and enjoy watching the goings on in the street far below.
Jack Hawkins was usually there and several others from the cast and
stage staff. One evening we heard a terrific shouting from Drury Lane
and all of us rushed to the parapet. On the other side of the street
were the offices of the old *Morning Post*. A huge lorry load of paper was
being unloaded by men, who from their clothes one would have
expected to find in Whites or Boodles. They were the volunteer
workers and some of them had just been attacked by half a dozen
pickets. A fine old bout of uninhibited fisticuffs ensued, which was just
working up to becoming a nice little riot when the police arrived.

A little later we were all bubbling over telling Lewis how the
'Splendid Volunteers' had been beating the 'Silly Strikers' and Lewis
asked, 'What was silly about them?'

'Well, they're striking,' we replied, feeling that this was so obvious
an answer as to be almost elementary.

'What's so silly about striking?' said Lewis quietly. 'They don't think they've got enough money to live on. Nobody would listen to them when they wanted to tell people how poor they are. They and their families just haven't got enough to eat. So they *had* to go on strike. I expect we all would if we were as hard-up as them.'

'Poor dears,' put in Sybil. 'Daddy and I are on their side, you know. We think they're right to strike. It's the only thing they can do. Perhaps we ought to be striking too instead of playing *Joan*.'

When shortly after this the sheer economics, or lack of them, in a General Strike caused *Joan* to fold up, Lewis went off to the north of England with his Armstrong Siddeley, and a huge label T.U.C. on the windscreen, to be a courier-cum-carrier-cum-taxi for any strike officials who wanted themselves or their messages carried from place to place. Before he left he drove me back to the *Worcester*, a week late for the summer term, because there were no trains, and we drove down through the Elephant and Castle and New Cross and Dartford to Greenhithe. This was a 'poor quarter' all the way. Angry looking groups of men stood at street corners and people well-off enough to drive around in motor cars got booed and shouted at. But our T.U.C. label did the trick and we made the journey without getting into trouble.

During the hour's run Lewis tried to explain to me what it was all about and why he was behaving quite differently from all our friends.

'You see John, these people who are on strike don't want a rebellion or even a riot. They just want a fairer share of the things they are making with their own hands in the factories.'

'But the factories don't belong to them. They belong to the owners,' I said with sixteen-year-old certainty.

'Maybe,' answered Lewis quietly, 'but only because our law says so. And anyway they only own a part of what is made in the factory. When you do work on something you give it value. And if you do the work you ought to have a big share of the value. Nothing has value till work is done on it, and we own what all of us agree as a country that we are allowed to own. These strikers don't want to take things away from others. They feel they might own a slightly fairer share, that's all. They're not bad or vicious. They're frightened and hungry people, and their wives and children are frightened and hungry. Just look at their faces as we go by and you'll see what I mean.' And I did look at their faces through his clearer eyes and I did see what he meant.

That was why he volunteered to drive the strike leaders around and why when *Joan* finished he went up north and was thrilled by what he saw. When he went to Carlisle he found people living in a kind of communal society and he wrote to Sybil: 'This strike will go on and on until the government comes to its senses. The spirit of the people is marvellous.' He was right about the spirit but wrong about the strike. When he got back to London he found that, in his own words, 'the pass had been sold by J. H. Thomas' and Labour had capitulated.

Some of this Sybil told me about in her letters during the early part of that summer term when she and Lewis went off to Devonshire to stay with the author of their next play. It was the beginning of their close and deep friendship, and indeed the close and deep friendship of all of us, with Clemence Dane. In another of her letters to me Sybil had said, 'We've just read a thrilling play, one of the great plays. It's called *Granite* and we're going to do it as soon as we can. We met the author the other day and she's a darling. Winifred Ashton's her name but she calls herself Clemence Dane for writing – after the church in The Strand called St Clement's Dane. You know – oranges and lemons said the bells of St Clement's. The play is about Lundy Island and an awful man who comes out of the sea who is really the Devil. Lewis will play the Devil man and I'll be the wife of the man he pushes over the cliff.'

They opened in June and the production was one of Lewis's best. The cast was small – Sybil, Lewis, Nicholas Hannen, Edmund Willard and an enchantress called Florence McHugh. The play gave Sybil and Lewis all the room they wanted for their own special brand of big-scale acting, and they used every inch of it. The setting was a cottage right on the edge of a high cliff on Lundy Island. You walked out of the door, and if you walked three more paces you dropped hundreds of feet into eternity. With a single cyclorama, good lighting and constant reference in word and action Lewis contrived to make his audience really feel the height almost to the point of vertigo. It suited them both because not only was it a play with a good exciting plot but it also carried a tremendous symbolic message. Sybil was the passionate and self-willed wife of a farmer. Staying with them was the farmer's brother, an officer lately resigned from Nelson's navy. At the height of a tremendous storm a nearly drowned man is washed ashore and the housewife makes him her slave. Lewis played this part and the play told the story of the slave's rise to absolute power and the enslavement of the wife. The drowned stranger was the power of evil. From the moment he arrived all the wife's most sinister wishes were fulfilled. The brutal, foul-tempered husband 'fell' from the cliff, helped by a nudge from her slave, and she married the handsome, gentler brother. But he wasn't strong enough for her. She became jealous of the innocent little servant girl and ever more dissatisfied with her life on the island. At the height of a tremendous quarrel, she cursed her second husband and he rushed out of the house along the cliff. And with horror the audience watched the sinister stranger rise up slowly from where he had been sitting unseen by the fire and go slowly out after the husband. Lewis seemed to grow to a height of at least ten feet at this moment and as he left the stage one could see in imagination his awful relentless walk along the cliff towards his victim, which ended with the scream of the husband as he was thrown from the cliff.

The curtain of the first act was a tableau of Sybil with her 'dog' at her feet. At the end of the play it was Lewis towering above Sybil, crumpled in terror at his feet. Each time she had exercised her power to gratify herself and herself alone the terrifying stranger had grown in strength and power. The contrast between his growing influence and the gradual breaking away from her gentleness to the innocent servant girl drew a superb Miltonic picture of Evil overcoming Good. I can still in nightmares hear Lewis's sinister and demoniacal chuckling from his seat by the hearth as he gradually grew in strength. It was this chuckle grown into a horrible and satanic laugh that brought down the final curtain and went on echoing in the minds of the audience.

And incidentally for sheer ingenuity of sound and lighting effects the storm scene would have put Cecil B. de Mille to shame. It was absolutely terrifying and superb.

But *Granite* didn't go. I suppose it was just too much for London audiences to take. It ran for only a few weeks and the Albery/Casson management had to lose some of their hard-earned reserve funds that had been built up by *Saint Joan*. It was, however, a useful sublimation for the non-*Saint Joan* side of Sybil in the middle of the *Saint Joan* period. She has always had her own very clear idea of what real saintliness ought to be. It is a mixture of most of her heroes leaving out that part of each of them which exemplifies what she fears. Granpapa Thorndike, her father, is very nearly The Father. But you can't live in a family with someone and idealise them completely. Her father must have got cross sometimes. I expect he looked like anyone else when he had holes in his socks. Sybil can't bear unhappy endings and so she can't have Father as The Father all along the line because The Father can't be in a bad temper at breakfast or sometimes preach a pompous sermon. If, however, one adds in a spoonful or two of Dean Hole from the Rochester days, whom one never could have seen except 'on show', with one or two other minor prophets thrown in, then there would be Saintliness personified without tying it down to a person. This is the essence of acting. You leave out the bits that you don't want to think about in order to emphasise the bits that you do. Lewis was not really a part of this image. He was rather the exemplification of the image, the image made manifest, if not the image made flesh, and as such his everyday human tiresomeness could be justified, forgiven and indeed loved. She herself could be this image of saintliness in the person of Joan. Judith Morris in *Granite*, I believe, was her vigorous work-out of the violent passions of the flesh that kept on interfering with the most celestial saintly rebelliousness, saintly violence, saintly bossiness and saintly saintliness of Joan.

We four, however, didn't mind very much about the failure of *Granite* because it meant we could all six of us go off together on holiday. That summer term was my last in the *Worcester* and after a terrifying series of interviews and exams, I and three other *Worcester* boys had managed to qualify for naval cadetships. We were to join the R.N. training ship H.M.S. *Erebus* at Plymouth towards the end of September. It had meant quite a few journeys up to London during that term, which is why I had been able to see the ill-fated *Granite* several times and had been able to take my colleagues back stage to show them how a storm was made. To celebrate our passing, however, we didn't feel that 'good theatre' was quite what we wanted and we all trooped off to see Fred and Adele Astaire in *Lady be Good* after a gargantuan blow-out at Frascati's.

And so at the end of July the six Cassons piled into the five-seater Armstrong with all our luggage in a huge cabin trunk strapped on the grid at the back and set off for Newhaven and over to France with the car for five weeks in Brittany. But before we got there we had to

Lewis as President Wilson in
In Time to Come

ybil as Saint Joan with Jack
Hawkins making his stage debut
s the Page

Saint Joan

'do' the 'Joan country', and we had nearly a week on the road doing it.

Lewis was in his element with maps to read, a car to drive and a journey to organise. Sybil had done all the packing and all the letters in French to the various hotels booking our rooms. Having now reached the age of sixteen, I felt myself a cut above the others, who, poor dears, were still 'only kids'. At all events Lewis seemed to assume this because he made me his assistant motor-mechanic-cum-porter-cum-navigator – and what fun that was!

We got aboard the packet at Newhaven late one evening and after supper went to bed in the two reserved double-berth cabins. They had only booked two cabins for the six of us for the perfectly good reason that we only needed two if the sexes were segregated. After all *Granite* had flopped even if *Joan* had succeeded and there was no point in being over-prodigal with cabins in cross-channel packets. Sybil and Lewis had the respective bottom bunks and the top bunks were doubled up with the girls on one and we boys on the other.

Just before we sailed, Sybil came in ostensibly to bid the male contingent good night but actually to ensure that we had been able to get ourselves bedded down in comfort. She has always been convinced, like many another housewife, that no man knows how to make a room or a cabin comfortable for himself.

'Will you be all right there, Lewis?' she said, literally tucking him up as she would a four-year-old. 'You boys look nice and comfy up there. Mind you don't fall out when the ship rolls. Isn't it all exciting! And to-morrow we'll land at Dieppe and be in Rouen in time for tea. Try not to be seasick up there, John dear. Don't forget your father's underneath and he's got all that driving to do to-morrow.' The result of this was that I lay awake for an hour wondering if I'd be seasick. A year or two earlier when we'd been at Dymchurch they had taken Kiff and me on a one-day excursion to Boulogne from Folkestone and I had been as sick as a cat both ways. It was very infra-dig to be reminded of it now just as I had become a proper naval officer. This time, however, the sea was flat calm and we got to Dieppe in good order and good time.

At Dieppe Lewis found the AA man and they superintended the unloading of the car. There were none of your drive-on-drive-offs in those days and it took about thirty minutes to get the car hoisted out of the hold and examined for narcotics by what seemed to be highly suspicious French Customs officials. We all had coffee and croissants in a scruffy little dockside café and then were off on our voyage of discovery, all five of us talking our heads off with excitement, and Lewis weaving his way through the streets of Dieppe, an old Panama hat on his head and the 'Look' on his face as he tried, not always successfully, to remember to keep to the right.

That afternoon we came to Rouen. It was the place where Joan had ended her life and where we began our journey to look for her. All four of us had by now lost count of the times we had seen *Saint Joan* and as near as dammit all knew it by heart. When we all trooped into the circular room in the tower where Joan had been tried we couldn't believe that it was so small. But it wasn't long before we got the feel of it and before you knew it we were practically playing the trial scene all over again. Shaw always said that he had hardly had to write a word of Joan's part because he had been able to get most of her own actual words from contemporary manuscripts. And so when Sybil spoke some of his lines in that room, we almost felt as if we had been in Wells's 'Time Machine' and had gone back five hundred years. It was most eerie. Then we left the room and followed the same route she must have taken straight to the stake set up for her burning in the same market place and where now stands her memorial.

Thanks to *Joan*'s remarkable drawing power at the box office, we were able to spend that night in a very plushy hotel only a few hundred yards from where Joan herself had been chained to a log to 'breathe foul damp darkness, watched day and night by the soldiers of the Earl of Warwick.'

The next day we saw Chartres for the first time and although at our ages I fear we became terribly tired of cathedrals by the end of the holiday, we were completely spellbound by the magic of those windows and the symphonic beauty of the cathedral itself. It has become now for us not only a place to visit but a kind of secret sanctuary inside ourselves which I am sure began on that day when we parked the Armstrong right outside the great west door.

We first saw the Loire at Blois where we lunched one day. But our delight this time was short-lived. For some reason Sybil had been carrying our family binoculars and, of all things, had carried them with her when after lunch she had visited the 'Ladies' with Mary and Anne. When they got to the car Lewis said, 'You've got the glasses, haven't you Sybil?' Sybil suddenly realised she hadn't got them and that she'd left them beside the bidet! Lewis 'Looked' and then swung round and strode back to the restaurant at his express train walk that he always used when he was angry. 'You can't go into the Ladies, Lewis!' shouted Sybil to the astonishment of the Bloisians. 'They'll arrest him you know,' she said to us as though she'd seen it all before. But they didn't, although we never knew whether he had dared the wrath of the lady attendant as well as his own embarrassment. Whatever he did, however, the glasses had gone and to this day Blois has been the 'place where we lost the glasses.' It took Lewis all the afternoon to come out of his frozen calm. If it had been anything else but the binoculars, or perhaps a camera or a telescope, he could have borne it. But he always had a thing about optical instruments of any sort and binoculars were a kind of holy relic to him. Sybil sat in the back seat pouring verbal ashes over sackcloth while the rest of us kept very quiet indeed.

Then towards the end of the day when the light was just beginning to falter, we came to a stretch of the Loire where it was wild enough for us to see a vision of the young Jack Hawkins in his page's uniform watching the kingfishers and suddenly seeing the wind change. We spent that night not on the Loire but at Chinon. To those who know their English history, it may be thought of as the place where Henry II died alone in his castle above the town. To us it is the place where Joan came to meet the Dauphin after her incredible journey across France from Lorraine. Next morning we saw the little inn beneath the castle walls where she had stayed and the church where she had prayed for the success of her meeting with Charles. Then we climbed the hill to the castle and stood on the grass surrounded by the walls that had once been the great reception hall and we saw in our minds Ernest Thesiger, Raymond Massey, Milton Rosmer, Bruce Winston and all the others watching with amazement as the Duke of Vendôme ushered Sybil into the midst of them. The roof and the floors had long since rotted away, but we could see the great stone fireplace half-way up the wall where once the floor had been, and so our imaginations had to have all the members of the court floating ten feet above our heads. We saw the little room in a tower where they had kept her waiting for many days, and we looked down from the battlements to watch the same river flowing past the little houses, which must have looked almost the same to Joan. And before we left we metaphorically drew our swords and shouted, 'To Orleans!' It was a nice statement of intention but the exigencies of our itinerary prevented our carrying it out. We never went to Orleans and had to make do with the various bits of the Loire that we crossed and re-crossed.

We went to Rheims Cathedral where Joan had crowned the Dauphin as the King of France thereby infuriating Bob Cunningham – I mean the Archbishop. It was all so vivid to us that we were surprised not to find Grannie playing the organ in the background. And we went on to see Chateaudun, the castle where Robert Horton's body had been 'comfortably asleep' when all the ghosts had visited Charles in the Epilogue. In fact all that remained for us to do was to call in at Winchester Cathedral on our way home from the holiday, to see that building 'temporarily in the hands of the Anglican heresy' and to gaze at the 'fair statue of the Maid' which had so delighted poor old de Stogumber and which enabled us to quote 'the multiplication of statues to the Maid threatens to become an obstruction to traffic' in loud voices, to the amazement of a Hampshire policeman.

The six of us had a gorgeous time in Brittany, but none of it stands out for me like the scenes from *Saint Joan* that we played in our hearts and minds up and down the French countryside. Even though the noise and dust of cars were already making it difficult to imagine Joan's countryside, most of the roads were still made of white dusty flint with slow-moving farm carts ambling along. The country people were in clogs, and the clogs were hob-nailed. The hob-nails were not hammered in too well, it appeared, because at least once a day we'd pick up one in a tyre and had to stop and change the wheel, or indeed actually mend the puncture. As the car would start to sway ominously on the flat tyre, Lewis would say, 'Blast!' (his favourite expletive, which was hissed rather than shouted). Sybil would take Kiff and the girls off to look at the view, while Lewis and I got down to work. One day the car fell off the jack and Lewis said, 'Damnation' instead of 'Blast' and it took a lot of ingenuity with stones and levers and an hour's hard labour to get the hub up off the ground and the wheel on again. It was at these times that I learnt that although Lewis enjoyed working with his hands on mechanical things, he regarded them all as personal enemies when they didn't perform as he desired. I soon learnt to keep quiet when the job had been trying, and when perhaps blood could be seen mixing with the grease on his kuckles, showing the effect of a slipped spanner.

Sybil, oddly enough, never seemed to realise the need for silence on these occasions. One day, when Lewis and I had had a particularly tiresome job with the third puncture, Sybil said sweetly as she came back to the car, 'Well you two have got yourselves into a nice pickle, I must say.' And Lewis answered with the mild words, 'So would you if you'd had to mend that damned puncture,' but with an acidity in his tone that would have taken the enamel off a cup! From the wisdom of my sixteen years I remember wondering why Sybil, and indeed women in general, should find it so hard to understand the problems that men face in the world of mechanics.

After that holiday it was back to *Joan* again in an autumn tour of the provinces. They took *Saint Joan* and *Henry VIII* and had a fair success with both of them. Sybil had not been seen as Joan out of London before and the big towns of the north lapped it up.

During this tour they rehearsed *Macbeth*, which was to be one of the most thrilling productions that they ever did. It opened at the Prince's Theatre just before Christmas that year, with Henry Ainley as Macbeth, Sybil as Lady Macbeth, Lewis as Banquo and Basil Gill as Macduff. The stage at the Prince's was large and so was the scale of the production. Lewis had persuaded Granville Bantock to compose music specially for this production and it was magnificent. It had the weirdness of the bagpipes in it and passages of ominous and heavy brass that would have scared the daylights out of Genghis Khan.

When I came home on Christmas leave after my first traumatic three months in the navy, they were in the throes of the final rehearsals. Henry Ainley came to lots of meals at Carlyle Square. That glorious 'golden voice' would thunder through the house when, after supper, he, Sybil and Lewis would run through their 'bits' together. And what a dear man he was. Lewis once said to me, 'Harry is one of those actors who cannot work out the intellectual side of a part at all. He just hasn't the brains. But if somebody else does the thinking for him, as I did for him as Macbeth, and can get him to see it, then he adds to it a mysterious magic of his own and can act anybody else off the stage.' I still have the little pocket edition of *Macbeth* which he used in this production, with all Lewis's annotations for the way the lines had to be spoken. Harry gave it to Lewis some years afterwards and Lewis gave it to me when I directed the play at Glasgow.

I went with Kiff to the last few rehearsals and watched Lewis behaving like an avenging fury. He shouted, he snapped, he cajoled, he praised, he applauded (a little). But even though he wasn't still for a second, he played his own Banquo as though he had nothing else in the world to worry about.

'Lewis,' cried Sybil at one moment, 'will you listen to me for a moment.'

'We haven't time for talk now,' he bit back. 'Just get on with it.'

'Oh, he's impossible!' she said in a whispered aside to Harry that boomed through the theatre. 'I can't think why I married him.'

All four of us went to the dress rehearsal which began at 7.30 p.m. and went on till 2 the next morning. It was a night as wild and as horrifying as the play itself. Nothing went right. Scenery got stuck in the changes, backdrops came down in the wrong places and at the wrong time, people put the wrong clothes on and everyone got fratchier and fratchier. At one point, Lewis, only half-dressed in Banquo's battle dress and a Nordic helmet all awry on his head, leaned through the house curtain and had a furious and technical musical discussion with the conductor. As he dodged back with a biting last word, his helmet fell off and rolled into the footlights from where he had ignominiously to retrieve it. The silence in the taxi going home afterwards was like the last act of a Russian tragedy. It went on through the perennial cocoa and bread and marmalade and then Lewis and I sat up till four going through notes that I had made during the evening. At that time I was too young to be flattered when Lewis had asked me to take a notebook and jot down anything I thought should be altered during the rehearsal, and I had filled half a dozen pages. Even to this day I can't quite understand why he appeared to take so much notice of the criticism, and fairly fierce criticism, of a seventeen year old. But he did and even put some of it into effect in the play. I suppose he wanted someone outside the show who wasn't entirely unintelligent, even though young, to give him an absolutely unbiased opinion about it.

Oh dear, they were depressed next day. They had sunk a lot of their own as well as Bronson Albery's money in it and there seemed to be a very good chance that they would lose the lot. But they didn't. 'It'll be all right on the night' is not a very popular motto among professionals, as it can so easily become an excuse for not doing that extra bit of work. This time, however, it happened that way. It was all right, and very all right, on the night.

There weren't going to be very many more times when Christopher, Mary, and Ann and I went together to a Lewis and Sybil opening. We were coming to the end of the years of childhood in the family and we were soon to be moving off on our peculiar (and oh how peculiar sometimes) and individual ways. But we were all at this one and it was thrilling. By some odd chance I had never seen or even read *Macbeth* before and so I was able to see it as though it had only just been written as a new play. It has been far and away my favourite play ever since. I saw it five times from the front during my leave and lots more from back stage. By the end I knew every word of it. It is the only play I have ever seen where the production made me visualise not what was on the stage, but the real events a thousand years ago in the wild vastness of Scotland.

It had tremendous notices and it looked as though they were all set for a success like that of *Joan* when, to everyone's dismay, Harry Ainley was taken ill and had to leave the cast. This was a mortal blow for the production. The understudy was an astonishing character, and character-actor, called Hubert Carter. He was a big, strong man with a huge jaw as massive as the cliffs of Dover. We were told that he literally drank raw bull's blood to keep him strong, and I can well believe it. Whatever it was, he certainly roared like a bull, and when he took over the part of Macbeth he became completely uncontrollable.

One night after the show Sybil, who has almost never been known to complain about another actor, said to Lewis, 'You must speak to Hubert, Lewis. He nearly killed me in the Throne Scene and he wouldn't let go when I had my exit. I'm black and blue all over.' In the fight with Macduff on another night he broke Basil Gill's thumb with a mighty blow from his broadsword. In fact he abandoned all the carefully rehearsed fight routine and went flat-out to slaughter Macduff. And it says much for Basil Gill's extempore skill as a swords-man that he lived through the run. Lewis had to plant an assistant stage manager behind each piece of scenery so that when Hubert came near they could whisper, 'Macbeth has to *lose* the fight Hubert! You've got to *lose*!' But he only roared the louder and plunged into the attack. He even got so carried away at one matinée that he got his cloak all over his head and had to go into the wings to be unravelled by an exasperated stage manager. On one occasion after seeing this outsize performance, or performing lion-tamer, I did say to Lewis, 'That really is pretty awful isn't it?' To which he replied, 'Ye-es. But I'd much rather have it than a lot of this namby-pamby acting that we see so much of. It has got guts and power, if nothing else. He's too big for his acting ability, that's all. It's better than being too small for it.'

But regrettably it wasn't good enough for London and once the holidays were over, the business fell away. The loss of Henry Ainley's splendid performance wasn't sufficiently compensated by Sybil's strong and terrifying Lady Macbeth and they had to take it off.

The success of *Saint Joan*, however, had added enormously to their by no means inconsiderable store of energy and no sooner did the business fall off than they were into rehearsals of a play by J. B. Fagan, *The Greater Love*, a story of intrigue and 'love will conquer all' set in pre-revolutionary Russia. It had a marvellous cast and a marvellous production and I for one adored it. It was chiefly remarkable, however, for the appearance of a young and unknown man who played a comic and very old general. The young man was Charles Laughton in his first job as an actor. During rehearsals he was awful. Dressed in revolting, untidy clothes, forestalling 'hippies' by some thirty years, he was, Lewis said, impossibly difficult to produce. He wouldn't take direction, hardly knew his lines and even when he did he mumbled them. Fagan, the author, and also himself a distinguished producer, was in despair.

'He'll have to go, Lewis. He's hopeless,' he said.

'I know,' Lewis answered gently, 'but wait. I think he's got something important. He'll be all right.'

'I only hope so,' said the unhappy author.

At the dress rehearsal it seemed as if all hope could be abandoned. It was not only insignificant, which wouldn't have mattered; he was glaringly bad, which did. 'Well that's it,' groaned Fagan. 'He'll spoil the show.' And, in the event he stole it. Sybil was noticed by the critics and so was Basil Gill. They raved about the unknown young man, Charles Laughton. How right they were and how right was Lewis to be so patient. Lewis never judged people by normal standards. He could be devastating to people who thought they were good and weren't. But he could wait and wait and wait with astonishing tolerance and gentleness when he believed that an actor had something original in him that was trying to get out.

I've often wondered why they decided to play *The Greater Love*. It was certainly a jolly good play as a straightforward chunk of non-educative romance. It was certainly well cast, beautifully acted and excellently produced. But it wasn't really them, somehow. And it wasn't in keeping with the *Joan* era. As a low-brow, and a seventeen-year-old low-brow at that, I adored it. But then I've always enjoyed theatrical theatre and show business more than the drama. When Lewis and Sybil have gone in for the low-brow, as in *Advertising April*, for example, they have always done it very well. The difficulty is that on the whole, low-brow theatre lends itself to expert techniques rather than to large-scale emotional extravaganza. If the producer can keep Sybil's personality and acting under control, she can then use her very highly skilled technique to captivate those audiences who feel they don't always want to make a journey to the top of Mount Olympus. In the same way that Sybil had said to Lewis, 'Don't let's try to teach them anything to-night, Lewis. Let's just do the play,' he might equally have said to her, though I don't think he did, 'Don't let's exhaust them to-night, Sybil. Let's just entertain them.'

Well, perhaps after all that's why they did *The Greater Love*. They very enjoyably entertained some audiences. But it was to be a long time before the public would again think of Sybil just as Sybil. Certainly in this era every one of her parts was compared with her Joan. The public consciously or unconsciously thought of her as Joan, like Maigret and Alf Garnet to-day. And so her specially ardent fans thought that Nadejda Ivanovna Pestoff was beneath the dignity of Joan, and too many of the others didn't like to risk what they thought might be a play about 'Joan of Russia' urging the Czar to drive the Tartars off the Steppes. This most excellent, thoughtful and charming production certainly didn't bring in the business that it deserved. There couldn't possibly be a *Saint Joan* for Sybil three times a year, and I have a notion that the public's refusal to think of her as anything else at this time caused them both to search in every other direction to find something that the public would accept as well as *Joan*. The public, however, with great obstinacy refused to do anything of the sort. But its refusal did give the perspicacious and her faithful followers, the opportunity of seeing her perform a repertoire of rôles during this decade that could only be described as a gamut, and all of which were in some extraordinary way opportunities for Joan of Arc, not Sybil, to appear on the London stage.

Chapter 8

VIEW FROM THE NAVY

In the spring of 1927 Lewis and Sybil were invited to present *Joan* at the International Festival in Paris and to throw in some matinées of *Medea* for good measure. They managed to get together nearly the whole of the original *Joan* cast, which was lucky because they had very little time to rehearse. Greatly daring for the year 1927, the whole company was flown from London to Paris in one of the old Imperial Airways' Handley-Page airliners. I think this was the first time either of them had flown, and Sybil, never a good sailor, felt a good deal more than squeamish, especially during the descent when the engines were shut off and the aeroplane glided down to Le Bourget.

When she had recovered, and after facing a huge crowd of French actors who had come to welcome her and after making an excellent speech in French, she wrote to me from her hotel in Paris. I got the letter a week later on board H.M.S. *Erebus* in Plymouth Harbour from where I was about to be sent forth as a midshipman after a year's training in the ways of the Royal Navy. Kiff and I had already been flying by this time and both felt rather smug about it. One afternoon the year before, Lewis had taken the whole family out to Croydon to watch the flying and we had quickly spotted that there was a pilot who was offering '10-shilling Joyrides' to the intrepid.

'Can we go, Daddy?' we cried at once.

'Lewis, I don't think they should. It's much too dangerous. You don't know who the pilot is or anything,' warned Sybil. But to our delight Lewis answered, 'Oh they'll be all right. I think they should go. They'll be the first of the family to fly.' And so we had flown in a rattle-trap of an Avro biplane tied up with wire and driven by a rotary engine that shattered us with its noise but made us feel like emperors. Thus Sybil wrote to me as one who had followed the trail of an earlier adventurous pioneer.

Darling John,
    Well!! We've *done* it! We've *flown*! All the way from Croydon to Paris in a *huge* aeroplane, and the whole company came with us – except Lyall Swete

who has to have a cigarette every five minutes and so couldn't bear to go $2\frac{1}{2}$ hours without one – so silly. Think what he missed! When the engines started and we raced across the field I thought I'd die with excitement and quirks. Did *you* feel like that when you flew? Oh, but you're so much braver than me. I was terrified, and thrilled, too, of course. Doesn't the earth look gorgeous from up there. All those lovely fields and the comic little houses. I'd taken lots of seasick pills in case, but they didn't work and I was absolutely pea-green. Half-way over, when I was thinking, 'I can't bear this another second,' Tom Kealy passed me a message which said, 'Note the cultivation of the land.' I could have killed him! I didn't care about the cultivation of anything! But I wasn't actually sick till we went down. Oh, John that awful 'swing' feeling as you glide down. I don't know how you stood it. As we got out we saw a huge crowd of French people waving flowers and hats at us. All those nice actors and actresses. I just had time to dash into the Ladies and be very sick – all my breakfast – put on some make-up and then come back and make a speech to them all – in French! But they were all sweet, and then Captain Boris and his wife came up and we all hugged each other. You remember his coming to Wood Street in the war with all those gorgeous French chocolates. Well let's hope they all like the play. We open the day after to-morrow. How's your ship? Give my love to your nice Captain that we met.

Love and hugs,
Mummy

P.S. Oh, isn't flying gorgeous! Wouldn't you love to be a pilot? Do they have aeroplanes in the navy?

P.P.S. The French are all darlings.

How I wish I could have heard that speech! It would take more than a little *mal d'air* to put Sybil down, but she must have had to give quite a performance to cover up the qualms and quirks of her 'aero-ated' stomach!

The short Paris season was a great *succès d'estime* but I fear they lost money again even though all the company came on shoe-string salaries for the fun and the prestige. The overheads were too high and the great French public in Paris, like their London opposite numbers, didn't turn out to enjoy good drama in a foreign language. So that summer they were once again free for us all to have a holiday together, this time in Wales.

We all knew Aunt Lucy and we knew that Sybil and Lewis had spent part of their honeymoon as the guests of her and Uncle Randal at Bron y Garth, their large house on the hill above Portmadoc in North Wales. Sybil had told us stories of the Welsh mountains and how she and Lewis had walked and climbed all over them, but up till now, none of us had been to Wales or seen Bron y Garth. Aunt Lucy herself made periodic visits to London and always came to tea at Carlyle Square. We remembered her as a tall very gracious lady in front of whom we had to be on our best behaviour. 'Aunt Lucy's coming to tea to-morrow,' Sybil would say, 'so see that you've got clean collars on, you boys, and Vi will help the girls to look nice.'

Now, however, all six of us were going to stay for a month, and we were all a little disturbed by the prospect, despite Sybil's enthusiasm for the mountains. I had been told to bring my newly-acquired dinner-jacket because it was *de rigeur* to dress for dinner at Bron y Garth, something that had been absolutely unheard of in our family. 'It's rather a bore to have to dress up when you're on holiday, darling, but Aunt Lucy likes it and it's sort of right when you're at Bron y Garth,' Sybil explained to me in a letter, thinking that I would be indignant. But the navy had already begun its work on me for a year, and I was able to write back that I was used to dressing for dinner and felt that it was quite suitable to do so when staying with Aunt Lucy.

I didn't get home on leave in time to travel with the family in Armstrong-Siddeley 2, and so went by train, after a prolonged correspondence with Lewis about the train being more suitable than my very small two-stroke motor-bicycle, of which I was inordinately proud but not always in perfect control. So I was met one evening at the Portmadoc Station by the entire family all bubbling over with the wonders of Bron y Garth.

At the front door we were greeted by the legendary Sarah, Aunt Lucy's maid, housekeeper and even, as we believed, 'familiar'. She ushered me into the West Room, where Aunt Lucy held court and controlled her world, and where she greeted me with her favourite term of affection, 'Dear Thing, I hope you had a nice journey.' I never have really been able to separate Aunt Lucy from the West Room. It was her and she was it, this large drawing-room looking out over the terrace and the Traeth to the mountains of Cnicht and the Arennigs.

This is where Lewis was always happy, looking at the ever-changing patterns of light over beyond Penrhyndeudraeth. And it was he who took me out on the terrace to show me his beloved Wales before we all went upstairs to put on our best bibs and tuckers for dinner.

We had a marvellous month and Aunt Lucy did us proud. We climbed

Snowdon by the Pig Track up past the two lakes, and duly sneered at the pathetic philistinism of those who made the journey to the top by the little mountain railway. We went to Caernarvon Castle and on to Denbigh to Lewis's boyhood home, and he showed us the two great trees by the gate that he remembered his father planting. We spent hours on the long flat sands of Black Rock, in the sea and out of it, and Aunt Lucy made us all go to the Conservative Party Fête in the grounds of another great house in the neighbourhood. Lewis and Sybil took this latter in very good part as a necessary duty, but their political views had to be kept firmly in check during the speeches. I have often wondered whether Aunt Lucy had hopes that she would bring them to the pure light of the Right by subjecting them to Suitable Influences. If so she had a tough job on her hands.

But the holiday was not without its influence on us all. We had never lived 'stylishly' as Sybil called it. In fact, the world of upper-class society had always been regarded as a bit of a joke. In this holiday Lewis and Sybil showed us that they could be as entirely at home in this atmosphere of gracious, gentle living, as a performance, as they were in the dynamic hurly-burly of a theatrical household. But there was no doubt about which they preferred. We came back to London knowing something of Lewis's home country, how to behave better as ladies and gentlemen and the joys of a large and adequately staffed country house. We were also all enamoured of Aunt Lucy and not quite so much in awe of her.

Lewis and Sybil came back to London to play for the Old Vic, in temporary quarters at the Lyric, Hammersmith, lent by their old friend Nigel Playfair, while the Old Vic's home in Waterloo Road was being renovated.

Here was a chance for them both to act their heads off and to do it superbly. Lewis for once was engaged only as an actor and so the two of them could thoroughly enjoy themselves, while feeling that they were 'Doing the Right Thing.' They were to play together in four Shakespearian comedies, the *Shrew*, the *Merchant*, *Much Ado* and *Henry V* on cut salaries for popular prices. Sybil, of course, was Katherine, Portia, Beatrice and not only Princess Katherine in *Henry V* but Chorus as well. Lewis had a ball as Petruchio, Shylock, Benedick and Henry V. Maddeningly I was only on leave when they played the *Shrew* and *Much Ado* and of these *Much Ado* was the one I remember most. They somehow played right through it like a beautifully matched pair of dancers, who danced so well that you couldn't believe that it was anything but spontaneous. Sybil's 'Kill Claudio!' nearly killed everyone in the house. And yet even then one got the feeling it was part of the enchanting dance. They didn't really reach me in the *Shrew* and I'm sure it's because as a young man of eighteen one is somehow shocked to see one's revered parents indulging in bawdy horseplay! Or maybe they weren't quite at home with the horseplay themselves and so turned it just too much into a Christmas charade. It was, as they say, 'bravely done', but naughtily done, and a bit too much – at least that's what I thought.

But I wish I had seen Lewis's Shylock which Mary and Ann told me was marvellous and about which the *Evening News* critic under a headline of 'Best Shylock Since Irving' had this to say:

A new Shylock won an exceptional success when *The Merchant of Venice* was revived at the Lyric, Hammersmith, last night.

This was Mr Lewis Casson, the husband of Miss Sybil Thorndike, who played 'the Jew that Shakespeare drew' for the first time in his life.

'The best Shylock since Irving,' people were heard saying as they left the theatre.

Mr Casson has long established himself as one of our most versatile actors, and his Shylock was played upon unusual lines. To begin with, he spoke in the accent of the Jews of the modern East London ghetto. He pronounced 'well' as 'vell' and 'was' as 'vas' – a thing that Irving and Tree, among so many fine actors who have made a success of the part, did not do. But in spite of this he at times made the man dignified, pathetic, fine – the one gentleman, really, of the play, as the character must always be when properly acted.

And his outbursts of rage, hate, and irony were alike finely portrayed.

Miss Thorndike's Portia was well known before last night – she has more than once been seen in the part at the Old Vic. It is sufficient to say that she was again joyous in her lighter moods filled with a spirit of mischief, always delightful.

And I never saw them play the Hal-Katherine wooing scene till they made it part of one of their Australian recital programmes, when they were both well on into their seventies. It was enchanting then as a piece of articulated oral music, enchanting as well-played chamber music. It must have been exquisite in 1927.

They were both in their element in this season as they always have been in Shakespeare or Shaw and they really revelled in it right up to and over the Christmas holiday.

This prodigal self-indulgence in the enjoyment of comedy, however, even Shakespearian comedy, couldn't be allowed to continue indefinitely. I can think of no other reason whatever, that would have made them put on *Judith of Israel*, Baruch's play based on the Apocryphal Book of Judith. Lewis was Holofernes and the production by him helped by Lyall Swete, was on the grandest scale. It was also tragedy on the grandest scale and not a wildly good play at that. I was away on the Spring Cruise to the Mediterranean myself and all I knew of it was a picture Sybil sent me of her making an entrance clutching her husband's severed head by its hair. I do remember, however, standing in the dark on the bridge of a battleship as midshipman of the middle watch and thinking, 'Oh my God, they're at it again. It's bound to flop and they'll lose more money.' And, despite what I heard was superb acting, it did flop and they did lose more money – thousands this time.

By this time as the centuries-old traditions of the Royal Navy began to work on me, I was becoming more and more of a theatrical and artistic Philistine. It seemed to me the sheerest lunacy when you've made a few bob not to put some of it into something safe and not risk it all on 'good drama', that was, I fear, at this time as heavy-going to me as *Tannhauser*. After all even Shakespeare, every time he made a profit, shot off to Stratford and bought some more acres. And so it was with enormous relief that at Gibraltar at the end of February I received a letter from Sybil which began:

Darling,
We're going to Africa! I've always wanted to go there and we shall be off at the end of April. When do you get back from your cruise? They want us to take *Joan* of course and at least four others, so we'll take *The Lie*, *Jane Clegg* and the *Silver Cord*, which you saw Lilian Braithwaite in when we went together, didn't you. The woman in the play's awful isn't she? I get depressed sometimes that I'm like that, bossing everyone about. But still it's a jolly good play. Mary and Ann will come too and they can be pages and things. Fancy our seeing the jungle and the veldt and all those lovely natives. Well, I expect you and Kiff will see it one day with the navy. No more for now. Must fly! Oh Lord, the rehearsals.

Love, Mummy

When I got home on leave early in April, the house in Carlyle Square was like a madhouse. Goings and comings and packings, people rushing about saying parts to themselves even in the bath. The redoubtable Vi, who, bereft of her charge of Mary and Ann for the next eight or nine months, was to be the housekeeper at No. 6, was revelling in the task of getting her girls ready for the great adventure. There had never been the slightest question that it might be better for them to stay at their Frances Holland school. 'They can do lessons on the boat with me,' Sybil had said, 'and anyway seeing all those marvellous places will be much better for them, won't it Lewis? Of course it will.' And that was that! They were 12 and 11 respectively when they went off, and they never went back to school again.

They sailed on 20th April from Southampton in the *Windsor Castle.* Russell, Eileen, Kiff and I all went down in the boat-train and Sybil gave a spectacular lunch party in the ship's saloon. All sorts of people, credible and incredible, were there. Lewis's brother's family, the Randal Cassons, strange unheard of Thorndike-Bowers relations, pressmen from London, Lilian Braithwaite, the Bishop of Somewhere and two members of the Gallery First-Nighters. And sitting beside Sybil was a sweet and rather dumpy old lady whom Sybil had enveloped in a hug and with, 'It's Old Mary. John, you remember Old Mary.' I didn't, but then found it was Sybil's old nurse, who had been induced to come out from behind an aspidistra in the fastness of a Southampton suburb just to say 'Hallo' to Sybil. She must have been a very surprised old lady by the end of the day. I shall never forget Lilian Braithwaite's face when Sybil shouted through the throng, 'Lilian! This is Old Mary. You know, *Old Mary.*' The noise was deafening and how we all got fed God, and a very expert staff of ship's stewards, alone knew. But at last the 'All visitors ashore' cry went round the ship and the move to the gangway began. When an hour later the ship sailed to shouts and cheers from the dockside we were laughing, weeping, bubbling over and completely exhausted. This had been 'Joan' in real life crying, 'Up the ladder and over the wall' with 'Joan' playing Sybil for all she was worth. She is rarely not on top form but this time it was not just over the wall, it was over the clouds and away. I can still feel my blood racing as I think of that farewell party and we all felt very flat on our way back to London. But a midshipman's life was not conducive to brooding and with everyone away I began rather to enjoy a life of an independent man.

The letters from Africa seem to have got lost over the years and al

Lewis and Sybil with Mary and Ann leaving for South Africa, 1928

Three aspects of Lewis

left: The Look
below left: The Producer cogitating
below right: The man himself
leaving the theatre

I can remember clearly is that nearly every letter from Sybil contained the cry of 'I love the veldt.' It appeared like a note from the triangle in an orchestra and occasionally like the tympani. It was clear that the party on the *Windsor Castle* had been continued throughout the southern part of the continent of Africa.

The Lie, Jane Clegg and *The Silver Cord* were, of course, thought of as commercial make-weights for what they regarded as the main point of the tour — *Saint Joan*. In Johannesburg alone the play ran a four-weeks' season to capacity houses. But although they had been told there would be no demand for Shakespeare they had so many requests for it that eventually Lewis cabled London for the clothes of the *Macbeth* production and they built the sets in Johannesburg. Lewis fulfilled one of his dearest wishes to play Macbeth himself, which I wish I had been able to see because his voice is exactly right for this organ-music part. They went everywhere in South Africa — Cape Town, Johannesburg, East London, Pretoria, Port Elizabeth, Durban and then on up into Rhodesia to Bulawayo, Victoria Falls, Livingstone and finally back to Cape Town for Christmas.

They lived at tremendous 'Joan-like' pressure, met everybody from the Smuts downwards, had quite a few rows over not being allowed to play to mixed audiences (and so, of course, insisted on playing some shows to Africans only), got accused by a retired general of being 'clearly in the pay of the Russian Government' and altogether had themselves a kind of permanent drama festival. One of Sybil's favourite boasts is that during this tour she had a letter from England delivered to her addressed —

Miss Sybil Thorndike, Africa.

Some farmers also managed to get her on to the back of a horse. In fact she, Lewis, Mary and Ann all got on to horses and galloped across the 'I-love-the-veldt.' I remember Ann writing to me that they roared with laughter when they heard that the Boer or Dutch for 'mount a horse' is something like 'klomber op de beeste!' She said that this is exactly what Sybil looked like while doing it.

Somewhere they went to a circus where there was a highly philosophical lion-tamer who used yoga and other allied techniques to hypnotise his lions into submission. He was also a 'student' of Shakespeare and gave Lewis the idea that when Macbeth says, 'vaulting ambition which o'er leaps itself' the word should not be 'self' but 'sell' which the lion-man had found to be an old English word for 'saddle'. 'Vaulting ambition which o'erleaps its saddle' makes much more sense of the line, which is otherwise one of those mysterious Shakespearian statements that defy analysis and can't be altered because it is Holy Writ! From then on Lewis always used this idea.

His Shakespearian-cum-Yoga technique did not prevent a lion lifting its leg, or whatever mechanical equivalent a lion uses, near the side of its cage and spraying Sybil from head to foot, to the gleeful astonishment of the rest of the audience. Sybil was apparently undismayed and roared with laughter herself, to the even greater general amazement. Her letter to me about it read:

My dear, a killing thing happened during the lion act. One of the lions came right over near us and did its business all over me! The audience roared with laughter and so did I. Was there ever such a scream? And do you know when it dried off there wasn't a mark on my clothes or even a smell. Such lovely clean beasts they are.

In November, Mary had returned to London to play Wendy to Jean Forbes-Robertson's *Peter Pan* for the second year. She had played it first the year before when she had been only 13 and had been enchanting, so much so that she played it for five years both in London and on tour until not only she but all the rest of us could recite the whole play from beginning to end and were sick to death of it – including Mary.

The rest of them got back to London in the early spring of 1929. I know it was before April because Lewis was so depressed at having to pay double income tax. Carlyle Square had been their official residence all this time and they had been away for less than a year. But tax or no tax they plunged into work at once. Not only was *Joan* still with us but she was by now a British Empire builder as well. She had carried her sword and banner across the veldt and had championed the repressed natives in place of the repressed French. But the spirit was the same. I was on the high seas somewhere or other when I was told that their next production was to be *Major Barbara* with, of course, Sybil as Barbara, who as everyone knows is really only a latter day Joan playing the part of a rebel society girl in the Salvation Army. It opened in April in Wyndhams and got some marvellous notices. Somehow though it didn't ring a bell with me. It may be that I was at the age when it didn't seem right for my parents to be playing young people, and when Baliol Holloway as Undershaft at the end of the play said to Lewis, as 'Dolly', 'six o'clock to-morrow morning my young man' it always seemed to me to be outrageously impertinent. It was all played with what we used to describe as 'The Old Vic heartiness', that is actors and actresses going through their parts with a kind of self-consciously self-confident relish, a kind of arrogance, like the members of a rather exclusive club having fun at a country fête. But when you add to this confidence the blazing enthusiasm for a 'Cause' that Lewis and Sybil have always had in abundance, then you get a kind of acting that exactly suits the plays of Shaw. They all seem to need a bounciness of manner and speed to bring out the ideas that were regrettably not wildly important to a young midshipman of 19. And it didn't appeal very much to the public for it only lasted just over a month during which time they were rehearsing for another play by Clemence Dane.

Where *Granite* had been grimly dramatic to the point of melodrama, *Mariners*, the new play, was grimly tragic to the point of unrelieved gloom and misery. I was always told it was a fine play but I loathed it. It gave Lewis a wonderful chance to play his best sort of part, that of a kindly gentle and patient man, but there seemed to my youthful eyes not one redeeming feature. It's true there was a moral, that the young couple in the play could learn from the tragedy of their elders how not to run their marriage, but they were such a dreary pair that I never felt the lesson mattered.

As the years went by Clemence Dane became a closer and closer friend of the family. She was a huge woman not only of stature but of ideas. Everything about her was on the most gigantic scale. We used to have fascinating supper parties in her flat above a greengrocer's shop in Covent Garden, and instead of boiled hen's eggs she used to give us boiled goose's eggs, only because, I'm sure, she couldn't get ostrich eggs. Her salad bowl was as big as a small bath and the sofa in the sitting-room could have provided accommodation for a regiment. She was also quite uncanny in her ability to know what other people were thinking and feeling, and to sense an atmosphere, sometimes when the people concerned were even unconscious of it themselves.

This is why I have always had a strange notion that the two plays she wrote ostensibly *for* Lewis and Sybil were in a certain way written *about* them. She adored them both but she had particular adoration for

Lewis. In *Granite* she showed how Lewis dominated Sybil and in *Mariners* how perhaps *she* thought Sybil might have dominated Lewis. I'm probably entirely up the pole about this but they were all three so close to each other that I can't help feeling that at least her subconscious was at work when she wrote the plays.

The heavy air of doom about *Mariners* was again too much for London and they replaced it with a quick emergency revival of two plays in one evening, *Jane Clegg* and *Medea*, both tragedies again! They were beautifully directed and played, of course, but one simply can't avoid the thought that there was an element of histrionic masochism about it.

The notices were mixed. For example, under a headline of 'Double-Barrelled Gloom', A. E. Wilson wrote in *The Star* –

Clemence Dane's *Mariners* failed to attract the public because it was considered to be too gloomy. I wish Sybil Thorndike better luck with her new bill, but what is to be said of a programme that embraces St John Irvine's study in drabness and the austere tragedy of Euripides? If it is to capture the public it will not do so by reason of its gaiety and lightness. But it is a generous entertainment for those who take their theatregoing seriously, and though it is rather heavy going, it is one excellently composed to show Sybil Thorndike in the moods that suit her best.

It takes something like the *Medea* to show the real scope of her tragic powers, the true grandeur of her style, the full magnificence with which she can take command of the stage and stir the deepest feelings.

Lewis became very depressed about it all and even wrote me a long letter about the dangers of extravagance when I bought a battered, but fast and roadworthy, secondhand motor-bicycle for the huge sum of thirty-five pounds. He had every reason to be concerned and even more to tell me off because he had opened my first bank account for me with twenty-five pounds when I joined the navy and had given me this amount as a quarterly allowance thereafter. He felt, and I thought rightly of course, that a midshipman's pay of five shillings a day wouldn't allow one to have an awful lot of fun. And, thanks to this allowance, I had a lot of fun as a midshipman. I fear, however, that my only reaction to his remonstrances was astonishment at their apparent inability to be careful of all that beautiful money that *Joan* had made for them.

At all events we all went to Dymchurch together that August and Lewis's disapproval of the extravagant motor-bike turned to joy in the feeling of mechanical power when he rode pillion behind me at breakneck speeds across Romney Marsh. Our family cars had never been anything approaching 'sporty' and this was the first time he had really felt the kick of explosive acceleration. Greatly daring I even allowed him to ride it by himself, which nearly caused a major disaster. In explaining the controls I had completely forgotten to warn him that on such a bike it is necessary, when accelerating, for the rider to press his knees hard into the rubber pads on the side of the petrol tank. And so he didn't think of it, and when he opened the throttle rather quickly the bike leapt forward like a rocket, and he ended up right on the back of the back mudguard! Fortunately his first solo was on the wide hard sand of the beach and he managed to struggle back into the saddle while the bike performed a most spectacular *pas seul* over the sand. It was the first time that I had ever found something mechanical that I could do better than Lewis and I was thrilled.

Towards the end of the holiday there was one more occasion when I moved a step nearer to treating Lewis as my father who was a fellow human being rather than as my father who was only one step removed from the Almighty. We had gone out after supper for one of the last of our sea-wall walks. Somehow we got talking about my job as a sailor and I was telling him about some night manœuvres in the Bay of Biscay during which I'd been on the bridge of a destroyer. 'The whole fleet was darkened and you couldn't see a thing except the next ahead in the line. We were carrying out a dummy torpedo attack on the battleships and were racing along at about twenty-five knots. Then we got the signal to go into quarterline to starboard, and –'

'How do you mean quarterline to starboard,' interrupted Lewis.

'You know,' I answered, 'each ship being on the starboard quarter of the next ahead. Ordinary quarterline. You know.'

'But I don't know,' said Lewis with a laugh. 'I've never been at sea in a destroyer.'

I stopped dead in my track and said, 'Good lord! Nor you have. I never thought of that.'

I had never realised until this moment that I, too, had been becoming a professional in my own right in a world that neither Lewis nor Sybil knew anything about, a world of private jargon, of men and ships and high seas and harbours and routines and navigation and seamanship. 'This is my world,' I thought, 'and they will never know anything about it. Poor dears.'

We walked much further that night and for the first time we talked as men who are equal to each other and not as father and son. It was pitch dark when at last we got back to the cottage.

'Where have you been, you two?' said Sybil. 'I was getting quite worried.'

'Oh, we've been talking a lot, haven't we John?' answered Lewis and caught my eye.

'Yes, a lot,' said I and we smiled at each other, as friends who suddenly know they are friends.

'Well you are a pair,' said Sybil. 'Let's all get off to bed or we'll never get up in the morning.'

That autumn was my last three months as a midshipman. When I came home from Portsmouth just before Christmas, I was able to tell them all I had become a sub-lieutenant and was joining the Royal Naval College, Greenwich, in January. I was also just in time for their opening night of an entirely different kind of play. Probably as a sop to the theatre-going public, or to try to make some money, or both, they went completely to the other end of the scale and put on an absurd and very amusing play about Napoleon called *Madame Plays Nap*. The plot was about social intrigue just after the Revolution. It was romantic to the point of sentimentality, rattling good entertainment and, of course, the critics hated it. This was *Joan* in reverse, a kind of clownish hair-shirt, I believe, to demonstrate an ironical snook-cocking repentance for their theatrical evangelism of the past few years. We four and all our friends loved it, and when I took some of my brother officers to see it, one of them exclaimed: 'I didn't know your people did this sort of stuff, John. Bloody good! It's what I call a real play. Plenty of laughs.'

But Ivor Brown, who was ever their friend, felt that he couldn't let them get away with it. *Joan* was still with us and should not be frivolous. In the best of his inimitable style he had this to say in *The Saturday Review*:

The new play at the New Theatre is sub-titled 'romantic comedy'. But is it anything of the sort? Romance has many definitions, of which I take to be the best Meredith's 'fiddling harmonics on the strings of sensuality', a phrase which prophetically drives at the very heart of half the films that were ever made. Nothing sensual, surely, about this astringent piece brought to us by Miss Thorndike and showing Purity Triumphant. But romance is a hard word. In its time it has been, like Caesar's wife in the discourteous adage, all things to all men. Let us, therefore, leave romance out of it. Comedy then? But Miss Thorndike has decided that the pawnbroker's wife who made rings round Napoleon is a figure of farce. At any rate, she plays it as such, for her performance is a demonstration of energy, of antics, of skippings, of hoppings, of furious frivolity – in short, of what the vulgar would call 'getting away with it'. A critic should always salute efficiency, and on the first night Miss Thorndike did get away with it. Accordingly I tender my salute. But my obeisance is made with reservation. I am perfectly prepared to admit that at Christmas much must be forgiven and that play-goers are then jolly simpletons whose only purpose at the box-office may be summed up in the billboard phrase 'a continuous scream'. Even so, I must temper my seasonal salute with some form of critical remonstrance. Miss Thorndike should not be so seized with the spirit of the festive season as to confuse Madame Bertrand of Paris, 1793, with that group of noble dames whose home is in pantomime. The part, to put it with a more seasonable politeness, is over-played.

On the other hand an unknown critic writing for *The Sackbut* took a view which more nearly corresponded with my own.

We went to see *Madame Plays Nap* at the New Theatre, because the title intrigued me partly, and also because I never can resist seeing anything that Sybil Thorndike does.

The play itself is nothing much without fine costumes and good acting, which is like saying, a piece of music sounds bad unless it is well sung. But for me it was an evening of pure enjoyment. I adore Sybil in comedy, and there was a little girl of about fourteen sitting next to me (American I should think because she said 'Saint' instead of 'Snt') who could not believe that the Sybil of *Saint Joan* was the gay, laughing bunch of fascinating humanity in *Madame Plays Nap*. How wise Miss Thorndike is to vary her parts! I know there are people who say that she should never play anything but great dramatic roles; but such people are mostly writers, not doers. We should not have had so many of our great comedians go mad through the ages if they had been allowed to play other parts; and I am firmly convinced that when we see Miss Thorndike in a drama again she will have regained a lightness of touch which she is a little apt to mislay.

. . . this I do know, I shall take all my family, or as many as I can collect, and sit in the front row.

(The writer continued *after* he had taken his family):

My family became so large that we not only filled the front row but spilled over into a bit of the second. It was a curious experience. I have rarely been to a play twice, though one goes to an opera a number of times in the course of one's study. And I was at once more critical and more appreciative. For one thing, Miss Thorndike was even more fascinating, and a distinguished foreigner who had but recently come here said: 'But what an adorable young woman. So rarely can young people portray the joy of youth and its bouncing, bubbling qualities.' And I said, 'She is considered our greatest tragic actress. Indeed, the big critics, who are very powerful here and can shut up our theatres with the stroke of a pen, will not allow her to play *comedy*. They *say* she is no good at it.'

'But they cannot have seen her in this play! I personally find it impossible to imagine her in tragedy. She has nothing of the heavy manner,' said he.

'Have you seen *Saint Joan* in Germany?' I asked.

'But of course,' he replied.

'Well Shaw wrote it for her.'

His air of shocked surprise was one of the loveliest tributes to a body's art I have ever known.

I suppose it was a pity that when they temporarily abandoned the classical for the commercial they didn't find a work of literature in which to have their fun. Did audiences and critics complain bitterly about the play when Irving did *The Bells*? It's a frightful play but a marvellous vehicle for a good actor to show his skill and to tax his audiences' emotional, but not their intellectual, powers. Surely the question to be asked is, 'Does the play entertain?' because that's what actors try to do. If it also has a high intellectual content then so much the better, but I wouldn't have thought that this was a pre-requisite. Anyway it only ran till the end of January and then did a short tour of the suburbs. And when they played at Lewisham they did excellent business with all the sub-lieutenants who came to it from Greenwich.

But now I was almost living at home again because Greenwich is only eight miles from London and I was the proud possessor of an Austin Seven. Classes for the young officers finished at 4.30 in the afternoon and I could be at Carlyle Square in half-an-hour at the most. By now the evening meal at six o'clock had become quite a function and Lewis and Sybil were wonderfully hospitable. I had but to telephone to say there would be two or three more for supper (it was never called dinner) and the extra places would be laid and the red carpet, as it were, rolled out. As cocktails were in fashion at this time I was able to persuade Sybil that it would really be quite a good social investment to have a cupboard stocked with the necessary ingredients. Naturally I was only too delighted to take on the onerous task of being the store-keeper and, with the aid of the Savoy Cocktail Book, do such mixing and concocting as might be desired.

One night I persuaded Lewis to come with me on one of those splendid, though I believe illegal, motor car treasure hunts. It was really very brave of him. We assembled at Greenwich about 8 p.m. and on receiving the first clue about twenty cars set off for London via New Cross and the Elephant and Castle. I drove and Lewis sat beside me in this minute but lively Baby Austin. Whether I was a good driver or not, I fear I was certainly a fast driver and I did know my little car to the inch. We plunged into the traffic, dodged round trams, squeezed through between lorries, indeed almost under them at times. While I drove Lewis exercised his encyclopaedic knowledge of the highways and byways of London. We were jolly nearly the first car home, but the last clue defeated us. It was something to do with an exclamation and fire and I know we had assumed it was Holborn. Lewis led me a fascinating route through little-known backstreets of the City. But, alas, it was not Holborn but Woburn we should have been making for and we were pipped at the post. But we had a most exciting evening together, two and a half hours of high-speed thinking and trafficating and only twice did Lewis suck in his breath very loudly and mutter something about 'a bit too close for me' or 'that was a near one'. On another night I invited him down to a full Officers' Mess Guest Night. He had to put on tails for this as our monthly guest nights were very spectacular ceremonial affairs even though it was before the days when the Painted Hall became the Officers' Mess. The order was 'Miniatures will be worn' and Lewis of course, being Lewis, had never even thought of having a set of miniature war medals. It gave me a great thrill when at his request I went to Gieves and got him a set, the Military Cross and the three war medals, 'Pip, Squeak and Wilfred.' I called for him in the Baby Austin and before we left Sybil looked at us standing together in the drawing-room and said, 'Well you do look a fine couple of boys, the pair of you. Don't drink too much port,' and off we went.

Lewis absolutely adored this occasion. We sat together in the middle of one of the long polished mahogany tables, glittering with one of the finest collections of silver in the country, glowingly lit by shaded candles. There must have been at least a couple of hundred diners, most of us in uniform, waited on by a magnificent body of Royal Marines.

At the end the Commander of the College as President of the Wardroom Mess, rose to his feet, raised his glass and boomed out,

'Mr Vice, the King.' The Vice-President at the other side of the room got to his feet with glass raised and answered, 'Gentlemen, the King.' Then everyone in the room rose up, the Royal Marine Band played the National Anthem, and as it died away there came the concerted call of 'The King' from every one of us. I stole a glance at Lewis and saw him standing very still with his chin thrust forward, his lips pressed so firmly together that they almost ballooned out of his face, his eyes smiling and blazing with pride and tears pouring down his cheeks.

It was a wonderful time. Lewis and Sybil were on the top of their form and leaping out of one play into another. Sybil played her very best and most moving performance in any play other than *Joan*, when she played Mrs Alving in Ibsen's *Ghosts* at the Everyman up at Hampstead. It's very difficult to watch members of the family on the stage and be able entirely to dissociate oneself from the person one knows. I think only as Joan and Mrs Alving have I been able to do it with Sybil – except perhaps when she played with Edith Evans in *Waters of the Moon* in 1951. But as Mrs Alving she held me rigid in my seat. For sheer controlled power I had never seen anything like it. I came out into the street afterwards quite unable to speak and feeling as though I had just survived a psychological blitz.

But a month earlier she had done *Phèdre* in French at the Arts, which I went to see because all the family went and I didn't understand a word of it, and a play called *Fire in the Opera House* at the Embassy at Swiss Cottage, which was in English and so subtle in innuendo and symbolism that again I didn't understand a word of it, and nor did Sybil.

At the same time on a Sunday night Lewis played Socrates in Clifford Bax's play of that name. His performance had a beauty in it that was almost beatific and I have rarely if ever been so moved by a single performance. Even after all these years I can still hear his, or rather Socrates', gentle and moving voice speaking those last lovely words after he has drunk the hemlock.

Then in April, Sybil gave another tremendous performance, this time as Emilia in the famous Paul Robeson-Peggy Ashcroft production of *Othello* at the Savoy. She wasn't offered the part, she offered herself for it as soon as it was announced that Paul Robeson was to play the Moor. In fact, she took off like a rocket. With a Negro in the lead and a Negro who was a fine artist and a great man, the production was for her a cause and a crusade. This was a breakthrough in race relations and she had to be in it and with it. Maurice Brown was the *entrepreneur* who some years before had been the only manager who would look at the famous war play *Journey's End* and so had made his fortune, and was now, like many others before and after him, prepared to squander some of it on a lavish production. The fact that he cast himself as Iago no doubt helped his decision, but thanks to him we did get a chance to see Paul Robeson, even though Iago did not appear to be any more villainous than the Rector of Stiffkey. It was directed by Ellen von Volkenberg, an American lady, who later became Sybil's very good friend, and so perhaps I can be allowed to tell the story of their first meeting. Sybil denies that it's true but I'm sure she has just conveniently forgotten what might now make Miss von Volkenberg blush for shame. When Sybil offered to play Emilia the producer summoned her for an interview. When Sybil sailed into the room she was asked:

'Name?'

'Sybil Thorndike.'

'Would you spell that please?'

'S-Y-B-I-L T-H-O-R-N-D-I-K-E.'

'Have you had much experience?'

If Sybil now refuses to remember it then she has also forgotten the glee with which she told us about it that evening at family supper! In any event, once Sybil gets to know and like someone, which given time is nearly every one, then she sponges her mind entirely clean of any blemishes that might spoil the pictures. That is why, of course, every relation of either the Casson or Thorndike family, and even to some extent their respective distaffs and sad, forgotten, eccentric and distant cousins in a remote quarter of Latin America or the Balkans, are each and everyone a peculiar genius in some fascinating skill or profession. 'Yes I know he's rather a bore, darling,' she will say, 'but he's got a marvellous way of cooking rhubarb. He's brilliant at it.' It's one of the most endearing things about her, but if you live close to it, very difficult to live up to.

The great thing about this *Othello* was that it introduced us to Paul Robeson. His huge figure and even more huge voice completely filled our house at Carlyle Square and he had the most heart-warming uninhibited laugh. And who knows that Sybil may not have been right in her ideas about race relations. The following year, I was the sub-lieutenant in a destroyer which put into Bridlington for the weekend, and among the summer attractions was a recital by Paul on the Sunday night. Unfortunately I happened to be the Duty Officer and so couldn't go to it, so I asked our skipper, a lieutenant-commander, if he would like to invite Paul back on board for supper after the show. The skipper was a man who on the whole referred to Negroes as 'black fellahs' and felt that they should know their place. But his feelings about it took second place when it came to having such a famous man aboard his ship. And so at eleven o'clock that evening when our boat came alongside from shore, out of it stepped Paul grinning like a schoolboy and obviously delighted to be our guest. The last thing I remember of that evening is the picture of Paul and my revered captain playing American football together on the deck of our very small wardroom mess at three o'clock in the morning.

During the summer I had my first and only experience of a London Season and all the routs, balls and assemblies that it involved. There was at this time a very charming family called Foster, who lived near Weymouth where the Atlantic Fleet went regularly. They were very hospitable to young midshipmen, and there were three enchanting daughters, one of whom I found very specially enchanting. Thanks to them I was lucky enough to be swept into the London social round. The fact that we were in the midst of the Great Depression seemed to have little or no effect on the gaiety in all those stately homes. Despite Lewis's and Sybil's socialistic views, which as an ardent young naval officer I could not possibly have espoused at that time, they were both of them enthusiastically charming to all the young things that used to assemble at cocktail time at Carlyle Square before we went off to the dances, and Lewis and Sybil to work. They had never, and have never, been part of 'Society' society and only got into the *Tatler* when their plays were reviewed in it. But that didn't stop them being a most jovial host and hostess to all of us, and Sybil always gave a superb performance of a society hostess as if she had been that and nothing else all her life.

One of the highlights of the Season in those days was the Greenwich Ball, when the navy opened up the whole of that beautiful college for the sort of ball that the navy always does so well. Mary was just 16 that summer and so Sybil allowed me to take her in our party, 'as long as you keep an eye on her, darling,' which of course I didn't. A party of eight of us assembled at Carlyle Square at six o'clock and I mixed a daring Sidecar Cocktail. The four girls were a *patine* of bright stars (Mary had a huge pink ribbon bow on the back of her hair) and we four young men were all over-nonchalantly blasé, wearing our sub-lieutenants' mess dress for the first time in public and, in fact, thinking that we looked terrific. We were taking the party out to dinner first and had wanted to do them impressively proud. On a sub's pay of 8s. 6d. a day this wasn't too easy. Rather rashly as it turned out, I had asked Lewis to recommend us a suitable restaurant in Soho. After all we could then do it cheaply and tell ourselves and the girls that we were really 'seeing life'. Even more rashly, none of us checked the place over after I had telephoned to reserve a table. When we arrived in all our splendid finery, we discovered that the place was little more than a cheap joint. I was covered with confusion and my three brother officers were furious. It wasn't until years afterwards that Joan Foster told me that they had all been thrilled to dine in a 'dive'. Lewis, I fear, lost a lot of face as a result. He had known the place when he had first come to London with hardly a bean in his pocket and I suppose he had remembered it as a place of relative glamour. But I never told either of them and when Mary and I got home at five in the morning, after we'd all had bacon and eggs at Lyons Corner House in the Strand, we woke them both up and regaled them with every detail of our 'absolutely marvellous party'. That, incidentally, was rather a nice thing about them. I never remember their waiting up for any of us after parties. Somehow it was always assumed that we would come home in good order and wake them up if we thought the party was worth telling them about. And when we did they never seemed to mind being woken up.

At the end of the summer they set out on a provincial tour again, this time with *Ghosts*, Ashley Dukes' *The Matchmaker*, *Granite* and a fine old piece of dramatic romantic soap-opera-sobbery called *The Squall*, set in Spain. I had gone off on my own in my Baby Austin to have part of my leave at Bron y Garth with Aunt Lucy. In the first week of September I drove down from North Wales through the Wye Valley and joined the family at Southampton. Mary and Ann as usual were part of the tour, and Kiff was there too. He and I slept on the floor in one of the rooms of the Randal Cassons' house at Upper Bassett and we all went to see *The Squall* together at the Empire Theatre. The manager of this theatre, Ernie Lepard, was a great character. One morning he was to drive Sybil to some civic function at the Town Hall. As she got into the front seat of the car beside him she heard a loud and unfriendly voice, as she thought behind her, saying, 'Miss Thorndike, what are you doing?' She turned round and saw a sad little man with rimless spectacles gazing at her. Smiling her best leading lady smile she said to him, 'What can I do for you?' The little man gave one look of stark terror, muttered, 'Nothing. Nothing at all,' and ran for his life. Somewhat astonished Sybil turned to get into the car to find Ernie Lepard doubled up with laughter. Unbeknown to any of us he was an accomplished ventriloquist!

Later in the tour on a week-end from the naval gunnery school at Portsmouth, I joined them at their hotel in Cambridge and saw *The Squall* a couple more times. Kiff was away at sea somewhere but Hugh Casson was there doing architecture at Jesus and we were still a large family party.

Sybil looked magnificent in this play in a huge jet-black wig topped by an enormous Spanish comb and mantilla. Lewis somehow wasn't quite so happy as her Spanish bewhiskered husband, bewitched by a bewitching little gipsy girl – which of course provided the conflict for the play, especially as their son in the play was also bewitched by the gipsy. It was all very well done and the provincial audiences lapped it up. But I'm afraid none of us took it really seriously. It was full of rather hammy dramatic clichés, which we all burlesqued outrageously. Ann used to give a wicked performance of Sybil's dramatic statement, which always brought the house down – 'Pedro, God sends us storms that we may the better love the sunny days' or something as deeply profound as this.

'You little beasts!' Sybil would say. 'Tell them how horrid they are, Lewis. It's a beautiful play.'

To Sybil's delight one of the girls in the company was a Quaker and therefore a pacifist. 'They are absolutely against war,' she had written to me, 'and they're such wonderful people. You'll adore her, but what she'll say about your being at the Gunnery School I don't know. Still you're all very nice *people* in the navy. You must talk to her about it.' When I arrived for the week-end I'm afraid I gave her a present of a toy howitzer with a card on which I had written the motto of the Gunnery School '*Si vis pacem para bellum.*' The next day she handed me a parcel. In it was a gorilla carved in wood and a card saying, '*Si vis bellum para bellum* – Beware lest ye revert to type.'

'Well that's one in the eye for you,' said Sybil, delighted that the pacifist had beaten the warmonger!

In November, Christopher resigned from the navy, or rather Lewis, after some haggling which would have delighted a Persian carpet-seller, bought him out for several hundred pounds. Up till this time he and I had always seemed to agree about most things and we had rather taken each other for granted. Kiff was just there as Kiff and I never gave a thought to whether he was much different from me. He had been very homesick at Dartmouth to begin with, but by the time he went to sea at 16, and afterwards, he had, I gather, all the makings of a very good naval officer. We were both in the Atlantic Fleet together as midshipmen for a time, he in *Tiger* and I in *Emperor of India*. But sometime during this year Lewis and Sybil had a letter from his captain which said:

I don't think your son is cut out for the navy. I feel you should take him out of it or you may do him real harm.

Somehow Kiff had not really thought of the navy as an institution which would require its members, among other things, if necessary to kill people. When he did realise it he knew with absolute certainty that he couldn't go on with it. It was a great blow to me because it had been fun having a brother in this very esoteric profession that had nothing to do with the rest of the family. I still sometimes wonder what would have been the answer if Sybil had not been such a staunch and convinced pacifist herself. It seemed so right to her that one of her sons should take a stand on this issue, especially as it meant that without question he would become an actor. I don't think there ever was a question about it, but I've often felt that there should have been at least one or two very pointed questions asked.

To ask the question now is in any event entirely pointless, but when I came up to London one week-end in November, there was Kiff in plain clothes and standing by to start work at the Central School then located at the Albert Hall under the strict and watchful, but delighted, eye of Elsie Fogerty. And oddly enough it gave me a chance to meet some young actors, and even better, young actresses as my own contemporaries rather than as people connected with the older generation of Lewis and Sybil. And so for a few more months Kiff and I went about together to concerts, plays and parties as brothers. But now he was in the family profession and I alone was, as it were, the outsider who was doing something quite different. I never really knew what Lewis felt about it. Part of him was certainly delighted that one of his sons was doing his job. I suspect, however, that another part wasn't so happy that Christopher's economically assured career had been abandoned, especially as we were in the Depression at the time and there were family financial worries again. He would certainly never have said anything discouraging about it once the decision had been made. He was always one for backing any of our decisions as long as we had thought about them and then taken the plunge ourselves. What I don't think either he or Sybil realised was that Kiff had not been away from home long enough to be independent of their influence, independent enough to learn from and use their experience and their skills without being swamped by the tremendous force of their personalities. The following year Mary was to make a break the other way and give up the theatre as a profession when the question of the Australian Tour was mooted. Years later she said to me, 'I think what suddenly got me down was that Mummy and Daddy took it for granted that Ann and I would go with them. I don't think we were ever consulted. They just assumed we wanted to act, and would want to act with them. In a way it was true, but not to be taken for granted. So I said I wasn't going to Australia and there was quite a dust up.'

No one could have lived in a household with Lewis and Sybil without acquiring the urge to perform in some way or other. We were all taught the piano, of course, but somehow I never took to it. This left Lewis and me as the two non-players of the family. Mary also studied the violin for a time, Ann the cello and later on Kiff the Celtic harp. And naturally we could all, and would all, do 'turns' at the drop of a hat to anyone who would care to listen.

By the time I was 20 I was very much the odd one out as a performer until one evening just before Christmas 1929, a distant uncle by marriage, Eileen's brother-in-law the Rev. Harold Ewbank, taught me a few of the elements of sleight of hand with cards. The very next morning I went down with German measles and had nothing to do for the next two weeks but lie in bed and practise. When I came out of quarantine I was quite an accomplished conjurer and went off and had

half a dozen lessons from a man in the conjuring department at
Gamages. From then on I had my own performing skill, and, like the
navy, it was an esoteric world from which the rest of the family was
barred. Poor dears, they all had to put up with 'taking a card' for weeks
and weeks. To give them their due they stood up to it very well and
even appeared to enjoy it. That's one lovely thing about nearly all
actors – they make the most marvellous audiences. Lewis was particularly delighted by it, because it was a new form of acting and show-
manship combined with the planned ingenuity that has to be used in
the routine of a conjuring trick.

It had even more far-reaching results for me because for the first
time I had a performing skill that the family couldn't challenge. There
must have been in me a very strong desire to better the family in skills
that were demonstrative, not to say 'show off'. The navy itself has
always been a very theatrical profession with its 'props', its 'costumes',
its 'scenery' (a man-of-war is a superb setting for drama) and, above
all, excellent 'plays' or 'ploys' to perform. Now I had a performing act
that was as popular a turn in a wardroom mess as anywhere else and I
made shameless use of it over the next decade. If I had not left the
navy and had been lucky enough to become an admiral I am sure it
would have been the result of my conjuring rather than my seamanship.

The point is, of course, that we couldn't really help working off
the histrionic urge in some way. It became too much of a good thing for
Mary and she gave it up completely. But Kiff and Ann still earn their
living by acting, and I – well I act in the process of earning my living in
ways that lend themselves to acting. But, as they say, all this came later.
At this time I had kept my independence by keeping out of the theatre,
and Kiff had in a sense lost his by getting into the theatre.

But if the tremendous strength of the personalities of Lewis and
Sybil were at times apt to be more than a little overwhelming, they
had the saving grace of being, even more than most actors, the most
endearing people to play to. They were always fascinated by whatever
we did and were never in the least hesitant at showing it. The whole
family set a high standard, but one which was fun to try and beat. Sybil
is always the best audience because she effervesces with enthusiasm for
whatever she sees and hears. She has that heart-warming ability to fill
in inside her own mind the inadequacies of someone else's performance,
and then believes that this is the performance she has seen. And so

unless something is so bad that there is no point of contact at all, she sees, enjoys and applauds in others what is, in effect, partly her own performance. One always feels much more competent during and after performing before Sybil.

With Lewis it wasn't quite the same. He was always encouraging, but never uncritically so. Kiff and I always said that to make Lewis bellow with laughter with a story or a turn was the acme of theatrical success. Where Sybil encouraged us by reacting always in the way we hoped (and her genius is still that of knowing what people hope), Lewis encouraged us by reacting as he felt, and helping us to learn how to get the reaction we wanted. Sybil enjoyed and applauded almost uncritically. Lewis enjoyed and taught very critically indeed.

And so at the beginning of 1931 we were a very close family, all pretty well grown up and all so full of ourselves that no one else ever seemed to get a word in. Ann was 15 at this time and was already showing us that she had a theatrical talent for comedy that was peculiarly her own. Furthermore, she was writing her own scripts and the previous year had written a one-act thriller for the four of us to perform at Christmas. It was called *Louis the Strangler* and was a send-up of all the thrillers that were the rage of London at this time. Later on she wrote a sketch called 'Clichés' which Lewis, Sybil, Kiff and Ann performed somewhere at a greenroom rag. The clichés were theatrical clichés of line and situation such as:

'What do you mean to suggest?'
'I suggest nothing. I'm merely stating a fact.'
'Then she can't quite –'
'No.'
'You mean – .'
'Yes.'
'I understand.'

This sort of dialogue went on for twenty minutes with intense seriousness and a kind of 'hamming' false sincerity. Both Lewis and Sybil were seldom better in any comedy, and any two members of the family could turn on scraps of it at any time, at a party or on top of a bus, to the astonishment of anyone who happened to be listening.

It was great fun, but it tended to make us perhaps rather too close as a family. We didn't really need anybody outside. Other people were lovely, charming, entertaining, boring, sad and all the rest of it, but I think we observed them as though they were doing a play as a command performance for the Casson family, while we got on with performing ours.

Then in April *Joan* was revived at His Majesty's in the Haymarket, with all the splendour of the original production of seven years before. At the first night we four had one of the dress-circle boxes and when the overture began we were inundated by great waves of anticipatory joy. We knew every line of the play like a favourite piece of music and were highly critical of any new member of the cast, who, as it were, played a different tune. One new member, however, we all agreed was better than the original. He played the part of Dunois and had been sent to Lewis from Liverpool by Margaret Yarde as 'a young man who shows some promise'. He was Robert Donat and this was his first part in an important production.

By now I was back at sea again, having joined H.M.S. *Velox*, a destroyer based on Chatham, within a few days of *Joan*'s opening. I used to bring an occasional brother officer up to London and we would go on as monks together in the trial scene. The two of us might be having dinner and I would say, 'Come up to London this evening and be a monk in *Saint Joan* with me.' An hour and a half later the astonished fellow would find himself in a dressing-room at His Majesty's being fitted out with a white robe of the Dominican order and a tonsured wig.

Two very distinguished naval officers, now retired, Admiral Sir Fitzroy Talbot and Rear-Admiral Finch-Noyes have been able to boast that in their youth they appeared on the London stage in *Saint Joan*. When Lewis, as de Stogumber, shouted his line, 'I know there is no faith in a Frenchman!' at us he was facing up stage while we hurled abuse at him. He always tried to make us laugh by shouting utterly incongruous statements back at us. One evening he finished us with 'What have you done with the pork and beans, I should like to know. Why didn't you have them in the bath?' The agony was that the audience could see our faces but not Lewis's, and woe betide us if we even looked like laughing. We just had to hold on for a few minutes till the shouting match ended and we could bury our faces in our hands in seemingly devout prayer!

One Sunday when I was Officer of the Day, and therefore on duty, the entire family drove down to Chatham Dockyard and lunched with me in the Wardroom. I was the only officer on board and we spent the afternoon eating, drinking and seeing over the ship. This was the first time they had ever visited a naval ship in which I was serving and Sybil was bowled over by it all.

'Do you mean you understand all this?' she said, standing on the bridge and embracing the whole ship, and indeed most of the dock-yard, as she swept an arm through the whole thirty-two points of the compass. 'I don't see how you can, can you Lewis? It must be terribly difficult. Is your captain a nice man? He must come and see the play one night.'

Lewis was thrilled with it all and I had to explain all the navigational instruments, the torpedo firing apparatus and the guns to him. Mary and Ann were ogled suitably by the sailors, and Kiff was a bit wistful as it was only just over six months since he'd left the navy.

It was on the bridge of this same destroyer at 9 a.m. on 1st June that I got the news that Sybil had been made a Dame of the British Empire. We were doing manoeuvres and exercises in the middle of the North Sea, racing along at twenty-five knots in a fine formation of nine ships on our way in to make a dummy torpedo attack on four battleships. It came in a news bulletin handed to our captain by a signalman.

'Your mum's been made a dame, Casson,' he called across to me. 'That's great news. We must send her a signal from the ship as soon as we finish this exercise.' Which is why one of the hundreds of telegrams that greeted Sybil on this day read, 'Heartiest congratulations from Captain, Officers and Ship's Company, H.M.S. *Velox*.'

By now the revival of *Joan* had come to an end – it had a run of only seven or eight weeks this time – and Sybil was playing at the Embassy with Donald Wolfit in a not very good play called *Marriage by Purchase*. In fact it was a hell of a play and one of the very few, as far as I know, that Sybil was unable to rationalise into a Symbol of Higher Things. It was a straight-out piece of sexy melodrama with Donald Wolfit playing a kind of gigolo held in thrall by Sybil as a wealthy but unattractive lady of immensely frustrated passion, who bribed the man into marrying her and then by threats of violence from her stalwart henchman, and a bit of blackmail thrown in, forced him into reluctantly performing his marital duties. Lewis had a small part in it too, I think as her father, and Margaret Webster astonished herself and the rest of us by playing a not wildly convincing demi-mondaine. God knows why or how they got themselves into this incredible play, but there was something almost comic in the irony of their both, as it were, being 'caught in the act' of performing this piece of absurdity at the moment of Sybil's entry into damehood. It was like a parson being told of his elevation to the purple while playing a roguish game of hide-and-seek at the village picnic.

In Sybil's case, of course, it didn't matter a button. She was thrilled to bits and all her family was thrilled to bits. And to judge by the telegrams and letters so was the whole of the British public, theatrical and otherwise. Lewis, of course, had been the only person who had known it was coming, although we had been given hints that a secret but exciting something was going to happen on 1st June. But neverthe-less we, and all her friends and relations, were surprised and delighted. I say 'surprised' and don't mean 'astonished'. We were all caught un-prepared for it, because we thought it would take the powers that be much longer to recognise not only her greatness as an actress but, even more important, her genius for inspiring people and for making friends. She herself was particularly delighted to be awarded this honour at a time when Ramsay MacDonald was the Prime Minister of a Labour Government. Both she and Lewis have always been strong socialists, not then so intellectually and socially respectable a thing as it has since become.

At the end of the year Sybil went to the Old Vic again but now they were back in the Waterloo Road. It was *The Knight of the Burning Pestle* and I remember I didn't think much of it. The 'Old Vic heartiness' was in great evidence, for one thing, with people bouncing about the stage as though it were a hockey field, and for another I had proposed marriage to a most charming girl, who had turned me down flat. Lewis and Sybil were very sweet about this latter, and were, I believe, rather worried about me. They needn't have been because, in a way sad to relate, one's heart mends awfully quickly at 22. And in any case it was to be a very eventful Christmas time.

In the middle of the summer I had requested Their Lordships of the Admiralty to allow me to be trained as a pilot in the then very small Fleet Air Arm. In December I was ordered to go to the R.A.F. station at Leuchars near St Andrews with effect from the middle of January, and by Christmas I was very agog indeed. In the autumn Lewis and Sybil had been asked if they would take a company to Australia and New Zealand early in the New Year and they had accepted the invitation. They were to take a repertoire of seven plays – *Saint Joan*, *Macbeth*, *Captain Brassbound*, *Granite*, *Advertising April*, *Milestones* and the plebeian *Madame Plays Nap* to give the whole thing a commercial flavour. In the event, of course, it was the classics that turned out to be the money-spinners. But this wasn't by any means all that was to make this Christmas and New Year so dramatic.

The eleven years lease of Carlyle Square was about to run out and the family had got to move. Some years earlier Granny Donnie had taken on a lease of the nearby 74 Oakley Street. The house was quite large – a basement and four more floors – and so had countless spare rooms for odd relations and friends that needed boards, lodgings, beds and breakfasts. She was watched over by an incredible character called Mrs O'Connor, who was clearly the Third Witch having a working holiday before returning to her native and blasted heath. The two of them used to get together and, as it were, celebrate any event which appeared at the time to be a good excuse for celebration. Granny had always believed that a well-equipped larder should include a bottle of brandy, strictly for medicinal purposes ('The doctor says it's a wise precaution,' she would say), which meant that during their increasingly frequent celebrations they could be confident in the knowledge that their health was being improved. Granny's indefatigable energy had to have an outlet and, until the neighbours complained, she and Mrs O'Connor would sometimes go far into the night singing through Hymns Ancient and Modern until the empty bottle assured them that their health was fully restored.

It was all done with great decorum, but about this time we all began to be alarmed about her safety. One evening just after I came on leave, Lewis and Sybil were working at home on one of the plays for the forthcoming Australian Tour and the telephone rang. I picked up the receiver and heard the voice of Third Witch O'Connor asking:

'Is Missaloowisatome.'

'Well, yes, but he's very busy just now.'

' 'Eortacumround. Mrs Thorndikesaddafall. But she's or-wry. I carn pickerup. She stoo evvy.'

Five minutes later Lewis and I opened the door of 74 with our spare key to find Granny sitting on the tiled hall floor at the foot of the stairs laughing her head off and with one eye rapidly turning into a first-class shiner.

'Lewis,' she called with a yell of delight, 'how nice of you to call. And John too. I can't get up. These stairs are a disgrace and there's something the matter with the carpet at the top. It tripped me up! I've rolled all the way down, my dears, all the whole way down, down, downsie.'

As we each took an arm and lifted her up, she turned to me with a sweet smile and said, 'John dear, tell your father not to be so solemn. It's all such fun having a man on each arm.'

An hour or so later Lewis and I departed. We had summoned the doctor, who was astonished to discover that an old lady of well over seventy had fallen down seventeen stairs and had suffered nothing worse than a few bruises and a huge black eye. When we got back to Carlyle Square and reported to Sybil she said, 'Poor Mother. It's her rheumatism, Lewis. It makes her unsteady on her legs, and Mrs O'Connor isn't much help.'

'It's lucky we're moving from here into Oakley Street. We shall be able to keep an eye on her,' answered Lewis, not too sure whether to twinkle or 'Look'. At any rate, move to 74 Oakley Street we did during the first week of January and had a fine old time with the whole family taking their coats off and joining in with the furniture removal man.

Eileen and her family had spent Christmas Day with us. Uncle Maurice had recently retired from the navy and had taken a job in the personnel department of John Lewis's. Somehow after a lifetime as a sailor he couldn't adjust himself to commercial life and had been worrying a lot about his future. One night, just before we moved to Oakley Street, he was carried off to hospital with a perforated ulcer. Two days later he died with Sybil, Eileen and Lewis at his bedside. He was 42 and as he had commuted most of his pension to buy the lease of a house in Bayswater, he left Eileen and her four children almost penniless. She adored her 'great big Maurice' and she couldn't really believe that he had gone. For a time she just couldn't cope with life at all. But the Thorndikes are a tough lot and cope she did, with everyone in all the families rallying round to help her.

All through these weeks Lewis and Sybil were rehearsing for their Australasian Tour. The heavier burden fell on Lewis of course. He had seven plays to prepare and cast, and all the travelling arrangements to organise. He was not only directing the plays but himself taking a leading part in every one. I had noticed that he had been becoming very morose and grumpy and had been tending to snap at people. One night I came home late from the theatre and went into the drawing-room to find Sybil alone and in tears.

'It's Lewis, John darling,' she sobbed. 'He simply won't rest and he gets more and more fussed and worried. He's not a bit like himself and he gets so cross with everybody. I'm sure he's going to have a breakdown. He won't listen to anyone. Can't you do something? He always listens to you.'

I managed to calm her down and kissed her good night, and then sat up for another hour brooding about it all. I suppose most of us are blissfully insensitive to our elders' worries when we are young. It certainly hadn't occurred to me that Lewis and Sybil had a care in the world. Lewis especially had always appeared to be in complete control of himself and all his doings. It was astonishing to think that I might be the one to help him, and I was frankly rather thrilled by the thought. And so with all the cocky assurance of my 22 years I tackled him after breakfast next morning. Without beating about the bush, and after all who had heard of 'human relations' in those days, I asked bluntly, 'What's going wrong?'

'How do you mean, "What's going wrong"?' said Lewis coldly.

'Well something's not right,' I went on. 'You don't seem to be yourself at all.'

'No I'm not, and I haven't time to do anything about it.'

'You might have to do something about it.'

'What for instance?'

'You could go and see the doctor for a start. And you could take a week or two off.'

'How the devil can I do that?' he shouted, jumping to his feet, and then began pacing up and down making a high kind of humming noise, which sounded like a bottled-up scream. 'I can't go away. I can't. There's too much to do,' he cried again, 'and it's so unfair on Sybil if I stop.'

'It'll be a jolly sight unfairer on her if you crack up,' I put in. 'Look here, I'm going to phone the doctor now and make an appointment for this morning.'

'But there's a —'

'Yes I know there's a rehearsal. But Matthew Forsyth can take it perfectly well. Go and have your bath. I'll fix it all up and take you round in the car.'

To my amazement he went off like a lamb and I began telephoning.

The doctor told him he was right on the edge of a bad breakdown and that he had to go away and forget the theatre for at least a fortnight. And for once he did as he was told. He took Ann with him and the two of them went off to Lyme Regis together, and they spent two weeks striding around Dorset with Ann hearing him his lines – the one bit of theatre he wouldn't drop. When they returned to London full of fresh air and good food, they were both fighting fit. Lewis had the old demoniacal look in his eye and was raring to get to work. He plunged back into rehearsals like one possessed and gave everyone hell for not having done more work while he had been away.

Two days later, my naval friend Roy Talbot arrived for the night and in the morning he and I loaded our belongings into his battered old Alvis. We were off together to Scotland to be taught to fly. Lewis saw us off at the door – I think Sybil had gone off early somewhere – and just before I got into the car he caught my arm.

'Take care of yourself, won't you? Don't do anything silly in that aeroplane of yours. You're rather a precious person you know.' His hand tightened on my arm like a vice and he gave it a little shake, then 'Well this is the end of a chapter, isn't it? We're off to the other side of the world and you're off to start your flying. We'll all be quite a bit different this time next year when we come home again. Good luck.'

As Roy and I drove up the Great North Road I had time to think about this now closing chapter. Our Carlyle Square childhood was over and we were all moving off on our separate ways. Lewis, Sybil, Kiff and Ann were sailing in a few weeks for Egypt where they were to start their tour, and after which Ann was to return home while the other three went on to Australia. There was a feeling of adventure and great beginnings in the air, and the world seemed to me to be a most exciting place on that crisp January morning.

What I couldn't have known then was that 1932 marked the end of another and rather longer chapter for Lewis and Sybil, and perhaps especially for Sybil. It was not just the end of their climbing. They had by now reached a high plateau of theatrical and artistic success. Before them stretched the splendid pastures in which they would wander, explore and indeed rampage for many more years than they had spent in climbing up there. But they had reached that kind of plateau which most of us seem to reach eventually, where we can use and enjoy the results of our climbing but don't do very much more climbing. Their plateau was a good deal higher than most of us can ever hope to reach, but it was a plateau.

It would be absurd to say that either of them had come to the end of their creative life and yet somehow there weren't going to be any more great leaps forward. When they came back to England again, Lewis began to move away from producing towards acting and sometimes I wish he had only been an actor. He never became impatient, he never had the 'Look' when he was acting. And yet if he had never been a producer, who would have brought the 'Greeks' to London, from whom would so many actors and actresses of the present day have learned to speak words with the 'significant music' of William Poel and where would *Saint Joan* have been? He was to go on producing until just after World War II when he produced Ann as Saint Joan. But although there were many beautiful productions from him, they were no more to be part of a Great Theatrical Revolution, which up till now he had rightly believed all his work to be.

Sybil was to go on playing a wonderful variety of parts and would bring to each of them her own special brand of explosive and un-quenchable fire. She would go on growing in the skill and craft of her trade and bringing to it an ever-deepening sensitivity and under-standing. Though she was to continue holding to her own special motto of 'with the help of my God I will leap over the wall', there weren't going to be quite so many walls to leap over and the walls weren't going to be so high.

Like most chapters of our lives it would be difficult to find a moment when this creative period ended. Indeed it hasn't ever come to a standstill. It was more a matter of the roaring rapids becoming a smoothly running river that could be used for navigation. If a suitable 'curtain' for the period is wanted, and all theatre people like to have good 'curtains', it probably came at Invercargill, the southernmost city of New Zealand, when early in 1933 at the age of 50, Sybil played *Saint Joan* for the last time.

Lewis and Sybil had by now become great people of the theatre. They would go on to become great people of the world.

Chapter 9

THEY BECOME PARENTS-IN-LAW

WHATEVER Lewis and Sybil did in Australia, however fascinating it may have been to them and to the rest of the family, to me 1932 was the year when I was learning to fly. It was such a supremely exciting and new world of experience that I regret to say I didn't think very much about what the others were doing. Lewis, Sybil, Kiff and Ann had a high old time in Egypt that spring and I had letters telling me about the Pyramids and the Sphinx, with pictures of them all mounted on camels outside the Mena House Hotel. They played their shows at night and in the daytime did everything that good tourists should. King Fouad came to see one of the shows, and they took part in the social rounds of Alexandria and Cairo, which in those days were very social indeed. They frolicked with the British Services, enveloped Egyptian officials with their charm and had tremendous arguments and discussions with the pashas and their wives. They made a great hit it seems from all accounts. I caught the backwash of it myself a year later when, in the aircraft-carrier *Eagle*, I visited Alexandria where their names were still on everyone's lips.

After Egypt they went to Israel and played in Jerusalem. To Sybil, to whom of course the Bible is more familiar than the history of the Kings and Queens of England, this was a real traumatic experience. It began when the train pulled into a station and she looked out of the window to read the name 'JERUSALEM'. She wrote long letters to me describing everything from the Wailing Wall to the Grand Mufti and saying that the Arabs and Jews all seemed equally delightful people.

When they sailed from Port Said for Australia in April, Ann came back to England with Matthew Forsyth as her escort and guardian for the voyage. She was now sixteen and was to play in *The Way to the Stars* that autumn. We were sent a picture of the company rehearsing *Saint Joan* on the forward cargo hatch of the ship in the middle of the Indian Ocean. After all a month's sea passage was not just a holiday for actors, not in Lewis's book anyway. They had to be ready with a repertory of eight plays a few days after their arrival in Australia, and that meant there was work to be done. Deck tennis and other such frivolities had to wait.

The awful thing is that I can hardly remember anything they said to me about Australia, and later on New Zealand, except that they used to walk round and round Albert Park Lake in Melbourne learning their lines and that they were wildly enthusiastic about the country, and life and the people they met. But as they have always felt this at all times, wherever they have happened to be, this occasion was thereby not made specially remarkable. My head was quite literally in the clouds, several thousand feet above Scotland. I sent them a cable on the 17th August saying, 'Got my wings. Love John' and received an explosively congratulatory telegram from Sydney, as though I had been working with the Wright brothers and had been the first human being to get his feet off the earth. And as if flying wasn't enough, I alarmed Sybil even more, by spending the first two weeks of my summer leave in Cumberland learning about rock-climbing, and the last two weeks with Aunt Lucy in Wales climbing some more, but without Aunt Lucy. With great generosity and not inconsiderable courage, Lewis had handed his car over to me 'to look after while we're away' as he euphemistically put it. I am fairly sure he bitterly regretted having been so large-hearted. It was a large Austin family saloon with a most ingenious roof that folded up when you wound a handle at the back, and was his joy. I flogged that car at maximum speed up and down the length and breadth of Great Britain. When Lewis eventually got back, and got it back, it wasn't at all the car that it used to be. I learnt ages later from Sybil, that Lewis had been very cross about it, but he never said a word to me. He sold it in part-exchange for a brand new Wolsley Hornet, which he drove with great dash and fury to the alarm, but not to the actual physical detriment, of other road-users.

In the autumn I went back for a final term at the R.A.F. flying school to learn about deck-landing, dive-bombing, formation flying and generally to acquire the final polish that would be needed for a Fleet Air Arm pilot. I suppose we all exchanged letters regularly, because we Cassons are prodigal correspondents within the family, but not one jot or tittle of the letters have survived the years. I did get one telegram from Sybil asking, 'Are you all right, Darling?' and was unable to decide whether she was anxious about my finances or my safety. So I sent a reply, 'See John, chapter 3, verse 24. Love John.' The passage reads: 'For John was not yet cast into prison.'

I went home to Oakley Street two days before Christmas bursting with a swaggering pride and bored Mary, Ann and Grannie to death with aeronautical fables in between writing them in letters to Australia. By now Grannie was spending most of her time in bed and she didn't join us for the fine Christmas dinner prepared and served by Vi and one of her innumerable relations. At noon of that day, just before we sat down to the feast, the telephone bell rang and Lewis came on the line from Wellington, New Zealand. In 1932 this was something of an event and we were all flabbergasted at the wonder of it. Lewis, Sybil and Kiff were in their hotel at midnight and at the end of their Christmas Day. Mary, Ann and I were in London and so we had to get in nine conversations in the three minutes, twenty seconds for each one of us to speak to each of the others. We just made it with Ann only managing, 'Hello Daddy', before the line went dead. We were all much too excited about hearing each other from 12,000 miles away to say anything coherently. But I did have time to tell them that I had just been ordered to join a 'fleet-fighter' squadron being formed at Netheravon on Salisbury Plain, preparatory to its being embarked in H.M. aircraft-carrier *Eagle* and that we would be sailing in April for two years on the China Station. Would they be back in time? That was the question. They hoped so and we'd all keep our thumbs crossed. In the event they were, but before our most joyful family reunion, there were to be two very far from joyful happenings.

One evening Vi telephoned me at Netheravon to say that Grannie was unconscious and sinking fast. I rushed up to London early next day to find Russell and Rosemary already in the house, but Grannie had died that morning. The news reached Sybil when the company was on its way home in the middle of the Pacific. She and her mother had never been intellectually in the same world, but they had the same devastating energy, the same enthusiasm and the same way of cocking a snook at everything and everybody that remotely smacked of the pompous. Almost the last piece of news that Donnie heard was that her beloved Sybil was on the way home again and, bless her, she drank a whacking great glass of port with me on the strength of it. She was buried beside her dear Arthur in the churchyard at Aylesford.

Then, two days before they reached England, Uncle Randal telegraphed me to say that Aunt Lucy had unexpectedly and suddenly died in her sleep, which meant that Lewis was now the owner of Bron y Garth and of all Aunt Lucy's goods and chattels.

I wrote a final letter which got to them while they were in the Panama Canal. I ended by saying, 'By the way if you arrive in daylight and during working hours, I might be able to fly out and meet you over the Channel somewhere. Let me know your time of arrival if you can,' and then never gave it another thought. I knew that they were due in London from Southampton in the evening of a day in April, and I had arranged to have a final week's leave with them before going off to China. On the morning of their arrival, as I ate my breakfast in the mess at Netheravon, an orderly brought me a radio telegram. It was from Lewis and was in professionally nautical style. 'o-three hundred Bishop's Light abeam speed 14 knots. Love Daddy.'

It was pouring with rain and there didn't seem to be much chance of a reconnaissance sortie out over the sea that day, but I went across to the flight office and got out the chart of the Channel. With a pair of dividers I began stepping off fourteen-mile intervals from Bishop's Light and muttering, 'Four o'clock, five, six, seven, eight, etc.' as I did so. When I got to St Alban's Head, just west of Swanage, I was at 16, four o'clock in the afternoon. It was very tempting and so I succumbed to the temptation. My flight-commander was away anyway, so in the middle of the afternoon, with the clouds down to about six hundred feet and still raining, I took off in my two-seater Hawker Osprey and hedge-hopped down to the coast, following the railway. Visibility was very bad and the sea, cloud and rain merged together into grey nothingness. But I found St Alban's Head and circled it a couple of times. There wasn't a sign of a ship and I began to think I should call it a day and head for home. And yet what an 'entrance' for a Casson to throw away! After all when they had left the year before I hadn't even done my first solo. Which was why I suddenly decided, against all commonsense and certainly the regulations, to leave the land and fly out low over the sea. St Alban's Head disappeared into the mist behind me and then there was only greyness. Suddenly I saw a dark splodge which quickly became a Shaw Savill liner, as I rushed towards it scudding along low under the stern to read her name. And miraculously it was their ship! Up into a low climbing turn I went, round and down again past the ship and there they all were on the boat-deck, waving and dancing about. It was one of those things that rarely but really come off. I stunted round that ship for a full ten minutes at a height over the water that was downright stupid. It was only the kindness of Fate to the inexperienced that prevented my grand spectacle from becoming my grand disaster. Finally I roared past low, waved and headed off into the driving rain for Netheravon.

In fact it was the beginning of a family fortnight in which somehow everything 'came off'. It happens that way sometimes, as though the whole thing has been produced by whichever of the gods looks after variety shows. I got back to Netheravon in about half an hour, flung my suitcase into the back of the family car and was at Waterloo in time to meet their train from Southampton with Mary, Ann and all the relations who happened to be in London. None of us stopped talking at the tops of our voices for at least twenty-four hours. We all sat round the large rectangular table in the basement dining-room at 74 Oakley Street, eating, drinking, exchanging news and arguing till three the next morning. We were drunk, not with alcohol but with sheer excitement and high spirits, and none of us broke surface next morning till ten o'clock. But because I was going off to China in a few weeks time and had only this one week's leave, all the jollifications of their return centred round me. The others could take it up after I had gone.

We gave ourselves a day for talking and I don't think any meal took less than a couple of hours. And then the next day I took the whole family to the flying club at Hanworth. It was in the early days of the Royal Naval Flying Club, the members of which were able to hire an aeroplane from almost any flying club in the country. This meant that Hanworth had become a handy place for me and a few pilot companions to give our respective girl-friends a treat or two. Being as impecunious as most young naval lieutenants, I had for this day persuaded Lewis to hire a DH Moth for the whole afternoon, or rather to finance my hiring of it, so that I could take the whole family flying. I'm not sure if Kiff, Mary and Ann were all there that day, but I very well remember taking Lewis and Sybil. A Moth had, of course, only room for two people, each one in a separate cockpit with the pilot in the rear one. The machine we got hold of was, however, fitted with dual control and I was able to give Lewis a flying lesson. Those were the days when we wore flying helmets and communicated through voice pipes connected to each other's earpieces. I took Lewis up first and as an ex-engineer he was enthralled by the sheer mechanics of controlling an aeroplane. Our conversation was soberly unemotional, but we allowed ourselves to unbend before landing and I gave him a stall turn, a spin and a loop. When we got on the ground he jumped out of the cockpit beaming like a schoolboy and, to my amazement, with his flying helmet on back to front! Then it was Sybil's turn. Even as I strapped her into the cockpit and showed her how the voice tubes worked she began to bubble with excitement and her voice took on a sort of breathless awe-filled quality, which is always a sign that she is on the brink of ecstatic excitement. Once we began to taxi out, however, she surprised me by maintaining such a total silence that if she had not been sitting in front of me where I could see her, I would have thought she had fallen out. So I called through and said, 'Are you all right?' She nearly jumped out of her skin when a voice from nowhere came through above the noise of the engine. 'It was like the voice of the Lord,' she said afterwards, which, even for her, was perhaps something of an exaggeration. However, we managed to establish communication and I gathered that her silence was merely her following the age-old injunction of 'Don't talk to the driver.'

When we took off she didn't so much talk as keep up a running exclamation of wonder and delight. I led her into it gently by moving from gentle turns to steep turns and then into a stall turn. Finally, because I didn't want her to feel that Lewis was one up on her, we did another loop. As a final bit of excitement we came in to land with a broad swishing sideslip that always looked more dangerously daring than it was. She had sung, shouted, exclaimed and laughed into the voice-pipe for the whole of the twenty-minute flight, but as we helped her out of the aircraft I had wondered if the prolonged excitement might not have been a bit too much for her. I should have known her better.

'Glory, Alleluja!' she shouted from the step on the wing. 'That was gorgeous! Oh how I wish I could fly myself! How I envy you, John. Fancy earning your living by doing something so glorious. Isn't it wonderful, Lewis? I can't think how a child of ours has learnt how to do it. And now you're going to do it all over China!'

She went on and on at the top of her voice while Mary, I think it was, had her turn, and then Ann and Kiff.

There followed a crowded and happy week for all of us. Nearly every night we went as a gang to a theatre but the only one I can remember was a Gracie Fields revue when we all sat in the dress-circle and had coffee and cakes with Gracie and her then husband, Archie Pitt, in her dressing-room during a long interval. We laughed till we nearly burst at the show and Lewis slid off his seat with tears streaming down his face.

At home at 74 we somehow began a custom which was to last till Lewis and Sybil went to live in a flat five years later – eating, drinking and talking in the basement dining-room. The table could seat eight people comfortably and often sat fifteen uncomfortably. The custom, which now began, was for any of our friends to drop in for some food and an argument, and I believe mainly for the argument, at any time they felt like it. Supper on Sunday evenings was the best time because Lewis and Sybil were always in and there was always a joint of cold roast beef on the sideboard and the table was strewn with bread, butter, cheese, salad and a seemingly unending supply of bottled beer. By the time I came home again, after two years in China, complete with a fiancée, the institution was in such full swing that the high pressure of a 'Casson Sunday evening' nearly lost me the fiancée, who didn't know what had hit her.

At the end of the week I returned to work at Netheravon and the next day the whole family came down to have lunch in the mess and look at our squadron. I was allowed to take off in my Osprey and do a bit of mild stunting for them and they all stayed on to watch night-flying by flare path. Flying in the first part of the thirties still had something of the air of a picnic about it. It certainly hadn't developed into the very earnest and necessary professionalism of to-day. If you lost your way flying over the country you could land in a field to ask a farmer where you were. There was little or no serious air traffic control except at Croydon and all we did was to send a telegram to our destination before taking off on a cross-country flight. And so nobody seemed to mind when Lewis and Sybil stood on the flare path to watch the Hawker bi-planes swooping in out of the dark and picking up the orange glow from the flares as they bounded their way over the grassy aerodrome.

A few days after this our squadron took off and landed on the deck of the *Eagle* as she steamed up Spithead. Of course they all came down to Portsmouth too, and came aboard the *Eagle* for tea and a look round on the day before we sailed. I made sure they all realised what deck-landing involved and it was fun to be the 'leading man' in a bit of show put on for their benefit. For a short time they were in unfamiliar territory and I could be host, guide, expert, actor and showman, while they, bless them, were a wonderfully appreciative audience.

But the final act of this particular play was to be theirs. Just as we were about to weigh anchor a little cabin air-taxi plane came scudding along low from the direction of Southsea. When we had said our family farewells the night before, Lewis had told me that they had made a tentative charter from the Portsmouth flying club and that I should keep a look-out for it next morning. It had to be a beautiful piece of timing, of course! The little machine circled the ship and I stood on the after end of the flight deck and waved my cap in the air. I'm afraid it wasn't very popular with the commander of the *Eagle*, because the sailors were falling in for the ceremony of leaving harbour. But who were we to care about that. Lewis always loved some sort of ceremony or a dramatic gesture to mark an occasion and this was his throwing of an aeronautical bonnet into the air to wish us all 'bon voyage'. And a bonnier voyage of nearly two years we could not have had.

Now I was away and whatever news or knowledge I was to have of the family was to come by letter and mostly from Sybil. A particularly annoying bomb on South London in 1941 destroyed Lewis's scenery store, which contained a box of our letters. That's why we don't have very extensive family archives till after the war, except for an odd letter or two accidentally left at the back of a chest of drawers. Sybil kept me posted, I remember, about all the plays they were doing, but they didn't mean much to me. I was far too busy enjoying myself in Hong Kong, Wei Hai Wei, Japan and all the other fascinating places of the Far East.

For the next three years they didn't play in a show together and for two years Lewis acted rather than produced. Sybil wrote to me about his performance as Sir Jafna Pandranath in Shaw's *On the Rocks* and said something like: 'Sir Jafna is an Indian and it suits Lewis because he has a lovely speech in which he's frightfully rude to all the English high-ups. So like him.' He must have liked it because the next thing I heard was that they'd bought a dog for Bron y Garth from the Battersea Lost

Dogs Home – a black so-called Dutch Barge Dog! – and they had named it 'Jafna'.

He also played the part of Dr Braddock in a moving play about the medical profession called *Men in White*. I remember Ann telling me later what a beautiful performance Lewis gave. Although I never saw it myself, I heard something about it thirty-five years later, when Sybil gave me a letter to read, which she had received from a distinguished Harley Street surgeon a few days after Lewis's death. The writer had been so moved by the performance of Dr Braddock that the morning after seeing it he decided to abandon his career in the Colonial Service and become a doctor. He said he had modelled himself on 'Dr Braddock'.

Despite Lewis's tremendous powers for large-scale classical acting, despite his undoubted violence of personality, albeit a violence held rigidly under the even stronger power of his will, it was in parts where gentleness or quiet pathos were needed that he was, for me, at his most moving. I noticed it first when he played the old and witless de Stogumber in the Epilogue of *Saint Joan*. But through the years there was a long line of performances of this sort which, in Christopher Fry's phrase, caught me 'by the scruff of the heart'. There was his Griffith to Sybil's Katherine in *Henry VIII*, his exquisite Socrates which he played for the Stage Society one Sunday night in 1930, and which was not only one of his finest performances but his own favourite, and a year later in *Late Night Final* the sad little American husband whose wife commits suicide after a tabloid has raked up some past scandal. He got something like it shortly afterwards into his Walter Fane when he played with Gladys Cooper in *The Painted Veil*. She must have felt the same because one of my most prized possessions now is a gold cigarette case which she gave him at this time. It is inscribed quite simply, 'To Lewis Casson, in appreciation, from Gladys Cooper.' He told me that he used to take it out and look at it whenever he felt depressed with himself. I never saw his Mayor Orden in Steinbeck's *The Moon is Down* because that was in 1943 and I was locked up in Germany, but Patricia told me all about it in a letter she wrote to Stalag Luft III. There are others, too, that I missed like his Friar Lawrence, and Telyegin in *Uncle Vanya*, which I'm sure had in them the quintessence not of human tragedy but of human pathos, and a plea for compassion for the little people who cannot aspire to Olympian tragedy. All of his skill, understanding and wisdom which he distilled into these rôles were, I believe, brought into focus, almost summarised, by his performance of the old country peasant when he recited the poem 'Carcassonne'. The sad thing about it is that his success in these parts, especially in 'Carcassonne' rather depressed him. I believe he felt they were too easy, as though people were liking him better in simple charades than in serious drama. He never really accepted that he had so much more human understanding than most people, and so could not see why people were impressed by what he regarded almost as theatrical jobbery.

At all events through most of the thirties, and certainly while I was in China, he and Sybil went their separate theatrical ways. In September of 1933 while Lewis was in, first, *Ballerina* and then *On the Rocks*, Sybil went into *The Distaff Side*, followed in March by a real piece of good old melodrama called *Double Door*, in which she played a blood-proud aristocratic lady who tries to murder her half-sister by locking her in a safe, and who, as the final curtain came down, was left a raving lunatic drooling over the family pearls. It was in this play that there occurred a remarkable example of what some might call E.S.P. and others, more suitably perhaps, artistic insight.

When Sybil was rehearsing the play she did what she has often done before in building up a character. She invented for herself another character, not in the play but who she believed would have influenced the character she herself was playing. In this case she felt very strongly that Victoria Van Brett was as she was because of the influence of her father. So she invented Mr Van Brett. After the play had been running for some weeks, a Harley Street psychiatrist came round to see her after the show.

'Have you had medical advice about your performance in this rôle?' he asked.

'Oh no,' said Sybil. 'I've just played her as I felt the author saw her.'

'That's really very interesting,' said the psychiatrist, 'because you gave all the classic symptoms of a well-known mental disease. I "diagnosed" it in the first half-hour and from then on you gave me all the continuing symptoms as the disease progressed, right up to the entirely predictable collapse at the end.'

'How absolutely fascinating,' said Sybil, naturally thrilled that her performance was so medically correct.

'Yes,' went on the doctor, 'it may be of further interest to you to know that it is a disease almost invariably inherited from the father.'

In June of 1933 my ship arrived in Hong Kong on passage for summer exercises at Wei Hai Wei. It was a Sunday and when, a few hours later, I went on board the home-bound aircraft carrier *Hermes*, that we were relieving, to have lunch with a friend, I saw in his cabin the photograph of a most fascinating girl. As I knew he was to be married when he reached England to a lady who was not this fascinating girl, I asked who she was and was told that her name was Pat Master and that she was living in Hong Kong. And so he gave me a letter of introduction. Six months later, after much gaiety in the Hong Kong social round, we became engaged. On the following morning my ship sailed for three months to Singapore and in something of a whirl I started buying time on the ship's wireless to send radiograms hither and yon.

The one I sent to Oakley Street read 'Engaged Pat Master. Love John' which for economical succinctness would have taken some beating. The reply I received forty-eight hours later did, however, beat it and managed to be not only economical but very encouraging. It said simply, 'Thrilled. Love Family'! I heard later that there had been some confusion at first when the radiogram arrived. Susan Holmes, who was not only secretary to Lewis and Sybil, but, though unrelated, as near a beloved member of the family as made no difference, was the one who opened it. The Post Office, in transcribing the message, had omitted the letter 'd' from the 'engaged'. Susan at once assumed that I had become enamoured of a lady who had aspirations for the theatrical profession, and that I was requiring Lewis and Sybil to 'engage Pat Master'. Fortunately Susan rang the Post Office and received the corrected message.

I must say they all took it very well. It couldn't have been easy for them. I had mentioned her name among, may I say, many others in my letters home, but I don't think I had even hinted that, to coin a phrase, my regard for her was growing into a deeper and more lasting emotion. They had absolutely no idea whether my engagement was suitable or not. But that would have made no difference to them. 'If it's right for John it's right for us' was what their cable told me and I blessed them for it.

In the meanwhile Patricia, her full length name was Patricia Chester Master, had written to me to say that she had cabled the glad news to her parents, who were having a holiday in England. 'Aha!' thought I. 'This is where my parents can oil the wheels for me,' and I sent off another cable with addresses, and asked them to make contact. My mother-in-law-to-be was invited by Sybil to meet her at the theatre in Liverpool where she was playing in the try-out tour of *Double Door*. I wouldn't have thought it the ideal play in which to see your only daughter's future mother-in-law for the first time. But Betty Chester Master did see it and apparently rose nobly above the villainies of 'Victoria Van Brett'. For when the two of them met in Sybil's dressing-room after the show they completely captivated each other. Sybil's letter to me said something like, 'Your future mother-in-law is a darling and we got on like a house on fire. If your Pat is anything like her she must be lovely. We spent an hour together praising our respective offspring to the skies.'

Lewis was in London and Reggie Chester Master was in a hotel at Surbiton. Reggie invited Lewis to dine with him and the two of them dressed for the occasion. But Lewis went even farther. He always hated evening clothes yet to meet and dine with his son's father-in-law-to-be he solemnly put on the full regalia of white tie and tails – to dine, if you please, at Surbiton! Lewis wrote me one of his rare and almost indecipherable letters about his evening and said, 'He's very distinguished looking. He's rather like Bob Horton.' (The actor who played the first Dunois in *Saint Joan* – as I said, everything was at this time related to *Saint Joan*!) 'You know he's a lawyer, but he looks like a diplomat. We had a very nice dinner together and I was slightly one-up on him because I had put on tails and he was only in a dinner jacket. I think I've convinced him that you'll be a suitable son-in-law! Do send us a picture soon.'

In April, when I met the Chester Masters in Hong Kong, I had what must have been one of the pleasantest interviews that any young man could ever have had when asking for a daughter's hand. Neither of them talked about anything except the charm of Lewis and Sybil, and our engagement almost took second place. But they did feel we were both rather on the young side (we were 24 and 19 respectively) and thought that we should plan to get married in London in the summer of 1935. And that is what we did in what might almost have been called a spectacular production. Reggie sent word back to Lewis and Sybil that the whole thing could now be made public, and very public it was indeed made, with Sybil telephoning and writing to everyone who was even remotely a relation or a friend, and a good many more who were neither. And one day, when Lewis went out to get his evening paper, he was astonished to see a placard saying, 'Sybil Thorndike's son engaged', which he promptly bought from the paper-man for the sum of sixpence.

In September Sybil went off to New York in a new production of *The Distaff Side* and Lewis stayed behind playing in *Men in White* and living with Kiff, Mary and Ann at Oakley Street.

I got back to London in the middle of February having travelled from Malta by P & O. Lewis, Kiff and the girls came down to Tilbury to meet me and I can still see Lewis racing down the length of a go-down shouting 'Here he is!' when I appeared through an unexpected door. There were great embracings and jollifications on the wharf and then we all drove back to London in Lewis's Wolseley. Once more the Cassons' insatiable appetite for talking was given full rein and we all talked our way through meals and on far into the night. Two days after I arrived Patricia and her mother set off from Shanghai for Mukden where they boarded the Trans-Siberian Express for the fifteen-day journey to London.

Lewis at this time was about to open at His Majesty's in Robert Atkins's production of *Henry IV* part I, in which he was playing Owen Glendower. It gave him the chance to be gloriously and exaggeratedly Welsh with his voice spanning at least a couple of octaves when he said:

> . . . at my nativity,
> The front of heaven was full of fiery shapes
> Of burning cressets; and at my birth
> The frame and huge foundation of the earth
> Shaked like a coward.'

He played it like an old druid magician, thoroughly enjoying himself in weaving spells and enchantments.

The production was a piece of real extravaganza in the old Shakespearian tradition of Irving and Tree. John Drinkwater was the King with Patrick Waddington as Prince Hal, Edmund Willard as Hotspur, John Laurie as Douglas and, a piece of apparently lunatic casting which came off superbly, George Robey as Falstaff.

One night I was standing in the wings with Lewis, watching an actor thundering his way through a couple of speeches while Lewis snarled, groaned and gnashed his teeth with rage.

'The lines will say themselves if only he'll let 'em,' muttered Lewis. 'He's murdering it.'

At that moment old George Robey came up beside us and, in a heavy stage whisper that nearly knocked over the scenery, said to Lewis, 'God! I wish I could act like that. That's *real* acting that is. All I can do is talk to the audience.' And a couple of minutes later that's exactly what he did. He walked down to the footlights as he had done on the music-hall stage for years and gathered the whole audience in under the comfortable cloak of his charm.

'That's it!' said Lewis. 'That's the real Shakespeare Falstaff. Warm, vulgar, huge and outrageous, talking to the audience as his friends and fellow conspirators. He doesn't have to *try* to be an actor. He *is* an actor. If only some of these others would stop ranting and let Shakespeare do the work for them.' And off he went growling to his dressing-room.

He could hardly wait to take me to see what he'd done with Bron y Garth and so on the first Saturday I was home I collected him at the theatre at 11.30 p.m. and off we went for Bron y Garth. This was the first of the famous night drives that I went on, leaving London after the show and reaching Portmadoc at about six in the morning to be met by Sarah, who always had a fine breakfast waiting for us directly we arrived. Half an hour earlier we always used to stop for a moment at Pen-y-Gwrid, sniff the Welsh air and, if it was a fine morning, refresh our souls with a look at Snowdon.

On this particular morning it was completely clear and we watched the light of the dawn slowly spreading itself down the mountainsides and into the valleys. Lewis stood beside me with a look of breathless, smiling ecstasy on his face. 'What a lovely welcome for you,' he said as we got back into the car for the final fifteen miles to Bron y Garth.

They had done wonders with the house, and Hugh Casson had been their architect. The biggest change had been the knocking down of a wall so that when you came in through the front door from the landward side you were at once in an immense hall that went right across the house, and you could see right over the Traeth where my grandfather had got his feet wet walking across to court my grandmother at

The Thorndike family
Left to right: Russell and Eileen with Sybil and Lewis

CHARACTER MAKE-UP
Left: Sybil in a make-up of her own devising for *Britannia Mews* (see page 298)
Right: Lewis as Dr Gortler in *I Have Been Here Before*

DRAMA AND COMEDY
Above: The author producing his parents in *Douglas* at the Edinburgh Festival
in 1950. *Below:* Sybil (left) as The White Queen and Zena Dare as
The Red Queen in *Alice in Wonderland*

Carfynnen, and to where Harlech Castle stood at the foot of the mountains. Lewis was like a little boy showing off his prized possessions to a parent.

After we'd had breakfast and a snooze for an hour or so, he took me all over the house and the grounds, telling me what his plans were and what fun we were all going to have with it in the future. Alas, we couldn't have known that the war was going to put the kibosh on most of the plans, and we were only going to have about four and a half years of the sort of fun that he was imagining. But we really did enjoy those years and here it was just beginning.

We had brought one extra passenger on this trip in the form of Epstein's bust of Sybil who (or which) had stared disapprovingly at us all the way from London, and at one moment had given Lewis a sharp crack on the back of the neck as a kind of marital remonstrance when he pulled up rather too suddenly in the middle of Llangollen. And she (it) was to stand on a plinth and keep us all in order till the sad day came in 1949 when Patricia would oversee the sale of Bron y Garth.

At this moment, however, Patricia with her mother was lost somewhere in the fastnesses of the Russian steppes, in Irkutsk, or Omsk, or Tomsk. But at the end of the month she sent me a telegram from Warsaw to say that she and her mother would arrive in Harwich in two days' time at six o'clock in the morning. When I told Lewis he immediately offered to drive me down to Harwich. 'We'll leave London at four and take some food and a Thermos. Two hours should give us quite enough time.'

In the event it was only just enough and we drove on to the dock as the packet from the Hook of Holland was coming alongside. We both rushed to the dockside and as we got there Patricia came out on the deck wearing a very long fur coat as befitted a traveller from Russia. I was quite surprised not to see snow on her boots.

Then Lewis did something which was so endearingly like him. He took a look from about thirty yards range at his daughter-in-law-to-be and then said to me, 'It wouldn't be fair to either of us to meet on a cold dock at six in the morning. You come back in the train with them. Pat and I will meet properly at Oakley Street this evening. She looks adorable.' With that he turned on his heel and drove back to London all by himself.

Twelve hours later, Patricia was flung not to the wolves but to what may easily have been just as traumatic – the Casson family. Kiff, Mary and Ann were already there and made her, as they and I thought, welcome. But of course none of us could imagine that there was anything particularly alarming for a girl brought up in Shanghai having to face, for the first time, a completely theatrical family. 'After all,' we felt, 'we're all perfectly normal people!'

At 6.30 Lewis came in, kissed her warmly on both cheeks and said, 'How lovely to meet you at last.' And that evening he cabled Sybil in New York. 'Pat a darling. Just what we expected.'

However, her greatest ordeal was yet to come. In the first week of April she and I, in Lewis's car, were spending the last fortnight of my foreign service leave going around seeing her relations. We were in Warrington when we got another telegram from Lewis: 'Sybil arrives Plymouth to-morrow. Please meet her.'

So we set off for Plymouth and went out in the tender to Cawsand Bay to find Sybil. We saw her on the deck and waved. It was at this moment, Patricia told me later, that she nearly dived overboard and swam for the shore because being about to meet her mother-in-law-nearly in the person of the famous Sybil Thorndike was almost too much for her.

But we got on deck and fell on each other. 'Darlings,' Sybil cried. 'How lovely of you to come. And this is Pat! How nice you look, and oh, isn't it all gorgeous. My dears you must meet Louis Bromfield, you know, the novelist. Marvellous man and an absolute pet. Louis! This is my son John, the sailor, and this is Pat, his fiancée, and they met in Hong Kong, where I've always wanted to go and they're going to be married in June. This is the first time we've met. How's that dear mother of yours, Pat. Isn't she pretty? Louis! Pat and her mother have just come all the way from Shanghai by train across Russia. My dear, I would have been terrified. All that snow. Weren't you frozen? Let's all go and have a drink to celebrate before we go ashore. I'm catching the train to-night from Plymouth so's to be home quickly. Will you come and see me off?' And so she went on enveloping Patricia, me, the Bromfields, half a dozen other passengers and a couple of ship's officers, in what could only be described as a vast mantle of enthusiasm. It knocked Patricia edgeways and hindside before.

At some point Sybil handed me a telegram and said, 'Look at this lovely wire from Lewis.' I took it and read: 'Pat and John meeting you

Plymouth. What know they of harbours.' I was rather astonished at his assumption that the well-travelled Patricia and I could know nothing of seaports until Sybil added, 'Don't you know the poem by Ernest Radford?

> *Oh what know they of harbours*
> *That toss not on the sea!*
> *They tell of fairer havens*
> *But none so fair there be*
> *As Plymouth Town outstretching*
> *Her quiet arms to me;*
> *Her breast's broad welcome spreading*
> *From Mewstone to Penlea*
> *Ah, with these home-thoughts, darling,*
> *Come crowding thoughts of thee.*
> *Oh, what know they of harbours*
> *That toss not on the sea!*

Isn't he a *love*?'

Once again Lewis, as was his wont, had managed to find a quotation which enabled him to say what was in his heart with telegraphic economy.

Then we went ashore, put Sybil on the train and set off for our 250-mile drive to London. We were of course almost at our last gasp from the emotional pressure, so much so that we could only get relief by having a blazing row for the first hour of the journey. We reached Oakley Street at one in the morning, to find the entire family waiting up for us, and once again we all talked and talked until we fell into our respective beds at about three.

And so, a couple of months later, we had our wedding in London. The run-up was the usual whirl of mad pre-nuptial gaiety. Being back at Netheravon again getting ready to go, in August, to the Mediterranean, meant that I could be in London nearly every week-end to help or hinder the arrangements.

My father-in-law had let it be known that as Patricia was his only daughter he would like to have a big stylish wedding, if we were agreeable. We were indeed agreeable and grateful. But I don't think he quite realised what it would mean to give Sybil almost carte blanche for theatrical invitations. She must have asked the entire list of actors in

Who's Who in the Theatre, not to mention all the uncles, aunts, cousins unto the third and fourth generation and all the staffs of any house we had ever lived in. And they brought Sarah down from Bron y Garth to 'dress the bride'.

The very evening before the wedding Sybil opened in a play by Merton Hodge called *Grief Goes Over*. The title doesn't sound very much like the prologue to a wedding and indeed it wasn't. But of course we all went. Patricia and I, Kiff, Mary, Ann, the Chester Masters and my best man sat in the third row of the stalls and sobbed our hearts out at this play. I can't remember anything about it at all, except that it was the first time Owen Nares's son, Geoffrey, appeared in the West End and that in the play his girl-friend died in childbirth. One could hardly imagine a less suitable play for the occasion. There was a tremendous crowd in Sybil's dressing-room afterwards with all the theatrical nobs there besides ourselves. And Sybil gloriously handed over her leading lady's position to Patricia and me.

'Darlings, how sweet of you to come round' she said to everyone. 'This is my John and his fiancée. They're being married to-morrow. It's a naval wedding and everybody will be there. Didn't you get an invitation? Oh but I'm sure you were on the list. But of course you must come. Betty, you don't mind, do you? This is Mr and Mrs Chester Master, Pat's parents. Of *course* it's all right.' And by the time we all went off to a jovial supper, there must have been at least another dozen guests added to an already overflowing list. I must say Reggie Chester Master took it very well, like the gentleman he was, but it all confirmed what he had always suspected, that every actor is as near certifiable as makes no difference.

On the day, Friday 7th June, Sybil gave a kind of picnic buffet lunch in the basement of Oakley Street. My best man, Lieutenant Peter Bramwell, and I dressed in the pre-war and very theatrical naval full-dress, drank beer with the Bishop of Southampton, who told us wicked stories of his life as a Missions to Seamen padre in Buenos Aires. We were all somewhere up in the clouds and the meal had an air of a green-room during a break in the dress-rehearsal. Everyone was dressed up to the nines but the clothes were obviously in the wrong setting!

Eventually my best man drove me to St Paul's, Knightsbridge, where we waited in the wings/vestry while the cast/congregation assembled in the church. Someone said afterwards that it must have been 'one of the most star-studded crowd-scenes ever produced'. But then there was also, as it were, a second part of the crowd scene consisting of all the 'China-siders' who were in London. There was only one civilian usher and that was Kiff. The other five were my friends in the Royal Navy, the Royal Marines and the Royal Air Force, backed up, of course, by a large body of service people all in full dress.

The church was packed to the roof, with Lewis and Sybil, all our relations and the supporting cast of actors sitting on the prompt side, while the Chester Masters and the China-siders were on the O.P. The uniformed service personnel seemed to spread themselves throughout the auditorium.

Then suddenly the 'curtain went up' and the organ began to play 'A Trumpet Voluntary' (no longer, they tell me, by Purcell) with an actual orchestral trumpeter standing in the chancel lifting the roof with those gorgeously joyful trills, as Patricia on her father's arm, made her entrance at the end of the aisle, followed by her six bridesmaids in bright emerald green. It was an entrance that needed Enobarbus to describe it. Godfrey Tearle said to Sybil later, 'There are very few actresses that I know who could have walked down the aisle with such real style and dignity.'

We had picked all the hymns and music ourselves and even had Paul Robeson a few rows from the front joining in the singing. The service had naturally been fully rehearsed some days before with everybody, including Lewis and Sybil, in attendance. As a hostage to superstition, however, the bridegroom was kept out and an up-ended hassock took his place in the aisle.

We both had the usual 'opening nerves' but the 'show' itself left nothing to be desired in splendour, joy and theatricality. The Bishop of Southampton officiated, assisted by our own vicar and the vicar of St Paul's. I must say the Mendelssohn Wedding March was given a tremendous lift when the trumpeter went beyond the terms of his engagement and accompanied the organ. We were almost blown down the aisle to the door.

We came out of the church into the sunshine under a long archway of swords, to find a huge crowd waiting in Wilton Place and a couple of pedlars selling specially printed souvenir napkins. There and then there was a 'photo call' for the whole cast, with much laughter, shouting and gaiety, and the curtain to the first act was our being swept off in a large limousine to the Rembrandt Hotel.

The reception, or second act, went by in such a flash that almost nothing registered with me. I know that it took us an hour-and-a-half to shake hands with almost a thousand guests. I remember that Lewis inadvertently stood on Patricia's veil and nearly had the whole head-piece off. I know that Sybil had a ball and that my in-laws were the most superb hosts. And I remember seeing old Ben Greet sitting in a chair in the vestibule at the end, determined not to miss saying farewell to 'Syb's boy and his wife'. Nearly a year later, and a month before he died, Patricia introduced him to 'Syb's first grandchild', our Anthony.

Then off we went to Great Fosters at Egham for a couple of days, before going on to Bron y Garth for the main part of our honeymoon where Lewis and Sybil had spent part of theirs over twenty-six years before.

The wedding party took themselves off to see a musical that evening and most of them slept through most of it. But they were thus all very lively when they were the guests of Lewis and Sybil at the Savoy for supper. Next morning, in the rather overdone Italian Suite four-poster at Great Fosters, we were given a telegram with our breakfast, 'Champagne in our heads, Egham in our hearts. Love from all at Savoy.'

We spent the last evening of our honeymoon going to see *Night Must Fall* and then went back to the Rubens Hotel, where next morning Lewis, Sybil, Kiff, Mary and Ann joined us at 9.30 a.m. and sat on our bed drinking coffee. 'Here's another chapter beginning,' said Lewis. And then we all went back to Oakley Street for our beef and a raspberry and red-currant pie. As usual there was much argument and discussion at the table until it was time for us all to go for a walk together round Battersea Park.

It was the time when Mussolini was beginning to go much farther than casting an eye on Abyssinia. He was moving his troops over there in order to 'civilise' the Abyssinians, or 'liberate' them, or 'to remove the danger of their arrogance towards Italy' or whatever the phrase was. We hadn't heard much of this sort of talking in 1935, and in England I suppose we still thought that uppity foreigners should be put in their place.

In our family we were at various levels or degrees of pacifism. At the extreme end of 'no killing of anybody ever', a belief, of course, that one would think was almost basic to Christianity, were Sybil, Kiff and Ann, with Kiff perhaps farther over than the other two and entirely unequivocal about it. I tended to be on the other end of the scale most of the time, because after all I was a member of the fighting services, but I combined it with a kind of religio-moral sentimentality which conveniently allowed me to change sides sometimes if the going got rough. Lewis and Mary were in the middle; Mary because she didn't like argument as much as the rest of us and so tended to be the most peaceful one, and Lewis because his honesty compelled him to compromise. His fierce pre-war socialistic pacificism had been considerably tempered by the practicalities of fighting in France. As I have said, he had violent energy and hated violence. He was also a highly sensitive artist with the practical training of the engineer.

Patricia didn't know what to make of it all. She had been brought up in a family, none of whom had ever questioned that, in the words of Ogden Nash, 'what the world needs is what is right for Great Britain.' If foreigners didn't understand this principle, then the ships of the British Navy and garrisons of the army backed up by flying machines, would have to see to it that they learnt it as soon as possible. And as befits a bridegroom of about three weeks seniority, I agreed with her when she put forward this view. But the sight of this closely knit family tearing into each other at every meal and obviously enjoying both the talk and the food, was very different from what she had known in the society of Shanghai. And so I was caught between two fires. 'You all shout at each other all the time,' she said to me one day, 'except Lewis, who sits there listening till you've all tied yourselves in knots and then quietly tells you the answers. You're worse than any of them. Why can't you be more like your father? It's all so exhausting the way you go on.' It was an opinion shared with Vi Ings who used to sum it all up in her favourite phrase when she was exasperated by the family: 'Oh you people!'

There would have been a danger at this time of my remaining a unit of this family, as I had always been, and Patricia's being drawn into it as another daughter. It was very easy to be not so much overwhelmed by the family as to be carried along willy-nilly by its enthusiasm without being aware that there could be other directions to move in.

Mussolini, the British Government and, as far as I was concerned anyway, their Lordships of the Admiralty, were now, however, going to take a hand in it. The whole of the not inconsiderable Mediterranean Fleet, of which my ship the *Glorious* was to become a part, was now ordered to Alexandria to keep watch on those Italians and if possible to prevent their getting up to any sort of Latin nonsense. The fact that British economy measures had seen to it that the ammunition of our guns was only enough for each ship to fight a ten-minute action in no way interfered with our confidence. I have no doubt that it was of some concern to their Lordships, but to Patricia and me it meant that our life together as young naval marrieds was to begin in Alexandria.

But before we left for Egypt we set up our first establishment near Netheravon, two rooms on the ground floor of a semi-detached house in Amesbury. We were there for a month and Patricia joined the Old Sarum Flying Club at High Post. We had decided that as I was a professional flyer she ought to fly too, and that if we got enough money in wedding present cheques we would spend some of it on her lessons, which we did and she did. She still, I believe, holds some sort of record in having gone off solo after only three-and-a-half hours' dual instruction. Lewis and Sybil had visited Netheravon two years earlier to watch their son demonstrating his so-called aeronautical prowess. Now they came again, this time to watch their daughter-in-law put a De Havilland Moth through its paces, which surprisingly, in view of her somewhat limited experience, passed off without any untoward incident.

A few weeks later, in August, my squadron embarked in the carrier *Glorious* and we sailed for Alexandria. Patricia followed on her own and arrived during the first week in October. I had been around with Lewis and Sybil for over twenty-five years and now Patricia and I were starting another family of our own. I had come out from under the very gay, splendid, but nonetheless, protective, family umbrella and it was all very exciting, especially as before either of us left England both our families knew that Lewis and Sybil's first grandchild was on the way.

Chapter 10

THE LAST OF THE OLD DAYS

IN 1935 the Admiralty did not pay marriage allowance to naval officers. Our wives were in fact not recognised until we became admirals. Thus it was that in the Abyssinian war the army and the air force were in a position to forbid officers' wives to go to Alexandria, and forbid them they did. The Admiralty could only advise naval officers' wives not to go, and their advice was not taken. Patricia was one of the first to arrive and before long the navy's social life in Alexandria was almost the same as in Malta. But the navy had an answer to this. There was an 'emergency' on and so no all-night leave was granted either to officers or men. We were, however, not to be daunted. There were six couples at the Pension Astoria and the husbands took it in turns to be 'Duty Boy'. We came ashore at 1600 hours and after a swim or a game of tennis we had our evening meal at 1800 hours, went to bed at 1900 and were all called by the 'Duty Boy' at 2300, which gave us just enough time to get dressed, kiss our wives good night and catch the 23.30 boat back to the ship. We were nothing if not adaptable. We exchanged letters with our families and all told each other what splendid times we were having.

While we were settling down to this rather strange routine, Lewis and Sybil were also off on their travels. In November, Sybil went into a play with Marie Tempest, Robert Morley's *Short Story*. We had been told about it in letters at the time but had not given it much thought. What we had not realised was that it was a meeting of two queens, neither of whom was prepared to be dominated by the other.

Years later, when Sybil was staying with us in Glasgow after the war, she told us a bit about some of the fireworks. 'My dear, *Short Story* was Tony Guthrie's first important West End production,' she told me, 'and Marie Tempest was being very naughty. She was really such a darling but also a bit of a bully. She would try to make you her slave and if you gave way she despised you and treated you like dirt. One day when she'd been awful Tony suddenly snapped his fingers and we all stopped. He came striding down the auditorium (you know how tall he is) while we all waited. Then, in a loud voice, he said, "Miss Tempest! Why are you being such a bitch?" There was an awful silence and we all thought, "Poor young man! Such a promising producer and that's the end of it." They looked at each other for a long time and then suddenly that gorgeous smile of hers spread across her face and she said very sweetly, "Very well Mr Guthrie, shall we go on with the rehearsal?" And after that she never argued with him again. But you know Tony was very clever. Ten minutes later he was trying to get Rex Harrison to do a bit of comedy business on the telephone. Rex was very young and inexperienced at that time and just couldn't get it right. Suddenly Tony said, "Miss Tempest, I wonder if you'd mind showing Rex how to do it." And of course she was gorgeous and had us all in fits. "There you are, Rex," said Tony, "Do it just like that" and Rex said, "Don't be silly, I couldn't do it like that in a hundred years." Wasn't that marvellous of him, knocking her down for being silly and building her up for being a marvellous actress? Then later on she had a go at me. I had some amusing things to do at a writing-desk up stage. It got terrific laughs for the first few nights and then came a night when they weren't laughing in the right places. I looked downstage and there was Marie doing brilliant things with a handkerchief and the audience was lapping it up. So the next night Marie found that she wasn't getting the laughs and when she looked round she saw that I had got out a pack of cards and was playing patience on the floor! As we went off the stage she whispered, "You're a very clever actress, aren't you?" I said, "Not specially, darling, but clever enough to act with you." Do you know, after that we were the greatest friends and I adored her.'

Marie Tempest developed quite a passion for Lewis, too, and her forebodings were reminiscent of Cassandra when she warned Sybil not let him accept an engagement in New York that December. We are often very blind to the potentialities of our parents. Lewis at this time was just 60 and it would certainly never have occurred to me that he could at that age get up to any sort of behaviour that could be described as 'dangerous', though he had always been a very good-looking man and most attractive to women. Now that I am beyond this age myself, I can see what Marie Tempest meant, and indeed I now know that her forebodings were by no means exaggerated. The show in New York was the very controversial *Victoria Regina* by Laurence Housman, in which Lewis was Lord Melbourne to Helen Hayes' Victoria. It had been banned by the Lord Chamberlain in Britain because he thought it went too far for the susceptibilities of the loyal subjects of King George V. And so we never saw Lewis play what was, I believe, one of his best performances. Moreover I would have loved to have seen the female, or should I say feminine, members of the cast so that I could look back now and speculate about which of them could have been the danger that Marie Tempest foresaw. It was in any event all over, as far as I know, by the time he returned to London in the following May. Whatever storms and crises may have occurred in their married life, they always managed to rise above them with the minimum delay, and always most successfully managed to 'keep it from the children'.

In the first week of March, while Lewis was away, Patricia and I somehow got cold feet about the risk of our firstborn's arriving in Alexandria. In the light of some of the present-day passport regulations this is probably just as well. At all events I took her to Port Said and put her aboard the *Esperance Bay*, a not very comfortable and very crowded ship. She reached London a fortnight later with little time to spare for the baby's arrival, but in time to attend Mary's wedding to the actor, William Devlin. Lewis couldn't be there himself and so he telephoned London the night before. On the day, the whole cast of *Victoria Regina* drank champagne toasts to the couple and to Lewis on the stage at the end of the show.

Anthony was born in London on 24th March. Sybil was in Shrewsbury and cabled to me her joy in becoming a grandmother, while Lewis sent his congratulations from New York. They were very thrilled, and very sad that Patricia was determined to return to Alexandria as soon as possible. They were specially concerned that she was going to take the child on a sea voyage before he had been baptised. We, however, were determined that Anthony should be christened on board *Glorious* in the traditional naval manner, with the upturned ship's bell as a font.

Sybil wrote to me, 'Darling, do you think it's all right for Anthony to go all that way on a ship without being baptised? Father Whitby was very upset about it when I saw him yesterday. He said the risk is too great.' I have never really understood this sort of risk nor has Patricia.

Was there some sort of angel, good or bad, watching closely, and ready in the event of shipwreck immediately to claim this child, who had been rash enough to venture on the ocean without having the qualifications for a celestial insurance policy? I can't really believe the Almighty is like that. Nor can Sybil in her heart, but sometimes the more complicated superstitions attached to Christian theology planted in her at Rochester, are too strong to be ignored.

At any rate Patricia was prepared to run the risk, while on a much more practical note, Sybil thought that Ann might accompany her, help with the child, stay for a bit in Alexandria and have fun with the navy. But, as always with Sybil, a big decision like this had to be referred to Lewis. Accordingly she sent a cable to New York, 'May Ann go Alexandria with Patricia and baby?' to which Lewis replied, 'Arise and take the young child and his mother and flee into Egypt.' Which is just what she did. Anthony's name was placed in the ship's log of *Glorious* as having been suitably christened on board. And in the meantime Ann, as far as I know, had a splendid time of it with the navy. She was eventually relieved by Patricia's chief bridesmaid, Pauline de Boinville, who came with us when, thanks mostly to unusually heavy rain rather than British arms, Mussolini's Abyssinian dream faded, and the fleet proceeded to Malta in July.

At about this time, Lewis, Sybil, Kiff and Ann went on a tour with a very odd repertoire of one-act plays, a sort of Grand Guignol programme without the horrors. D. H. Lawrence's *My Son's My Son*, Noel Coward's *Hands Across the Sea* and *Fumed Oak* and Shaw's *Village Wooing*. To make up for the lack of a horror play they did the much stronger meat of *Hippolytus* for matinées, and as usual Sybil wrote us long letters about how good Kiff, Ann and indeed Lewis, were.

Fortunately for us the tour was a short one, so that at the end of December they were able to leave London to come and spend Christmas with us in Malta.

We met them late one night at the wharf in the Grand Harbour just beneath the Castile. I remember calling out, 'Hallo-o,' over the water as the little steam packet from Sicily drew in, and hearing Lewis's voice echo mine. It was a crisp and clear night, and when they got ashore and through the Customs we all piled into our old open two-seater Morris that we had acquired for £11. Lewis and Patricia sat in the dickey holding the luggage and Sybil and I were in front. There was a breathless Christmassy feeling in the air and I can still feel the delight of driving up the steep little streets to Valetta and hearing the noise of our aged engine bouncing off the stone walls of the houses. And then we arrived at our ground floor flat just by the water in Sliema Creek and our holiday had begun.

They joined in everything. On Christmas morning we all went aboard *Glorious* and sang carols at the service in the aircraft hangar. We drank champagne afterwards in the cuddy with Captain Bruce Fraser, later to be Admiral Lord Fraser of North Cape, and went back to Sliema to sleep it off. Patricia had cooked her first Christmas Dinner – the previous year I had been away on a cruise – and our marriage nearly came to an end because Lewis and I argued politics all through the meal and hardly noticed what we were eating.

One afternoon they were to drive out to the aerodrome at Hal Far and have tea at the mess. I was flying a single-seater that afternoon and I flew over the road from Valetta to spot them. But as I couldn't find them I flew over to Sliema and there they were far below me, peering into an open bonnet. And so I called up the aerodrome on my radio and said, 'Would you ring Sliema 024 and tell Mrs Casson she probably needs to pull the wire leading to the choke, and that I am watching from above.' Sure enough, two minutes later I saw Patricia run into the house. When she came out she waved, fiddled with the car, caused a burst of black smoke to come from the back and the car was away, to be met by me at Hal Far half an hour later.

They came to see the Christmas Revue of the Malta Amateur Dramatic Society called *Show Goat 1936* in which both Patricia and I were performing. Their presence caused something of a flutter among the rest of the cast, who could cope with admirals but weren't too sure of stars. But they sat in the front row and laughed in all the right places. We took them to the Sliema Club Ball and they both danced on and on till all hours. At one point one of my colleagues, who was an ardent fan of Lewis, said to me, 'Look at the wise old bugger sitting there smiling. He's got us all absolutely taped, but he's not saying anything – just goes on smiling. He's a great one, your governor.'

They had New Year with us and then went home to begin rehearsals for *The Six Men of Dorset*, which gave them both a chance to do a play with a strong socialistic message. It had been discussed in Malta and I think our Christmas Dinner argument probably arose out of Lewis's socialism and my half-baked socialist-naval-conservative-love-thy-neighbour-but-keep-law-and-order-and-everyone-fed-philosophy. At this time it was taking the form of an almost blind belief in Social Credit. In Malta at the end of 1936 the idea seemed to me to be the gateway to Utopia. Lewis had clearly seen that it wasn't, but looking back on it all, I am convinced he wanted me to get it off my chest and come to a more sensible view on my own.

When we ourselves got back to England in February and went to stay in Oakley Street, because we hadn't got a home of our own, *The Six Men of Dorset*, the story of the Tolpuddle Martyrs and the beginnings of Trades Unions in this country, was filling all our minds. Once more the supper-party arguments bounded off the walls and shook the foundations of No. 74. Lewis continued to sit at the head of the table with a smile on his face, leading us all up the garden path until we had defeated our own arguments without his gainsaying us at any point. Sybil was always infuriated by this habit of his. 'Lewis!' she would shout across the room. 'You don't believe in all the privileges of the rich. So how can you say So-and-So is a good leader. Look at what happened in Glasgow! He's awful! I can't think why I married you when you go on like this.' And then everyone would join in at once and pandemonium reigned supreme.

In the play Lewis was George Loveless, the Dorsetshire farm labourer who dared to challenge the power of the landed gentry in the year 1834, and for his pains was transported to Van Diemen's Land with five of his mates. It was the story of their trial, the tribulations that they suffered down under and their eventual release after explosive agitation in Britain. For almost the first time, Sybil played second fiddle to Lewis in a production. She was George Loveless's wife, while Miles Malleson, the author, and a lifelong friend, directed it. It toured all over the country that spring, thanks to the sponsorship of the T.U.C. and to the good offices of Ernest Bevin and Walter Citrine. I saw it in Portsmouth because by now I was attached to the naval air station at Lee-on-Solent. The play itself I don't think was good enough to make the kind of impact that they had hoped it would. To me it seemed to be a series of very good sketches strung together into a documentary. The sketches moved me individually but the play had little or no dramatic suspense in it. But it did give Lewis the chance once again to create one of those little gems of human character into which all his compassion and understanding for oppressed people was instilled.

At the end of August our Penny was born in London and soon afterwards we took a minute house in Lee-on-Solent to which Lewis and Sybil would come for Sunday lunch whenever they could get away. By now I was in charge of the three aircraft carried in the cruiser *Glasgow*, which was based on Portsmouth. On a Sunday in late September, we had Penny christened on the quarterdeck, once again having the ship's bell as a font. Lewis and Sybil drove down from London and the Captain allowed us to use his cabin for the small celebration afterwards. We had lunch on board and then I took them all round this very new modern ship with its shining aircraft catapult. 'I can't believe that you can understand all this,' said Sybil. 'Why do men always have so much more exciting jobs than women. I'm green with envy at yours. Though I don't think I'd like having to fight battles.' And then we went back to the little house at Lee and they played with Anthony in the garden while Penny gurgled in her cot until it was time for them to go back to London.

That same month Lewis directed one of Priestley's perennially fascinating time plays, *I Have Been Here Before*, and made it one of his best productions. Lewis also played Dr Görtler and that superb actor, Wilfrid Lawson, was in the lead. I think Lewis enjoyed it specially because the theme of the play was taken from the metaphysical theory of 'eternal recurrence' put forward by that strange Russian mathematician and mystic, P. D. Ouspensky. It was also the period of J. W. Dunne's *Experiment with Time*. Time had been a favourite topic for discussion for quite a while at 74 during that year. We had seen *Dangerous Corner* and had been most intrigued by Priestley's ingenuity in making a good play out of this new theory of time.

Looking back now on this period, the end of the thirties, I find the whole thing seems to have been telescoped in an odd sort of way. The months seem to have rushed by without much actually registering on my mind. Patricia and I were very busy with our own affairs, two babies and the pre-war naval life. We had a really very gay time and bumped into Lewis and Sybil from time to time, like touring theatrical companies that pass in the night at Crewe.

In April of '38 Lewis directed *Coriolanus* for the Old Vic with Laurence Olivier and with Sybil as Volumnia. He somehow got the two of them sparking off each other and did it, for once, without getting too impatient with either of them. By now, however, I had become much more nautical and aeronautical than theatrical and our life as part of the Home Fleet was completely absorbing; while in between cruises and exercises I returned to 'Waltonholme', the two by four house at Lee. We went to Bron y Garth for the summer to walk the hills and climb the rocks and Lewis and Sybil appeared for the occasional week-end.

During this year after much pushing from all their offspring, Lewis and Sybil decided to give up the house in Oakley Street and move to a flat in Swan Court at the top of Chelsea Manor Street. From then on 98 Swan Court, or '98' as we have always called it, became the Casson base. The move was far more than a mere change of dwelling. From this time on the 'family' would continue to be united by all the filial ties of affection and mutual admiration, but not by geography. The move also meant that they would no longer require a staff. Sybil would do the breakfast and the late-night cocoa; there was, and still is an admirable restaurant in Swan Court; and a lady could be engaged to clean the place up in the mornings. It has always been a point of honour with Sybil that, wherever she is, she personally makes the bed or beds that she and Lewis have slept in, even in hotels. And it now looks as though this move was to be the last move. 'Ninety-eight' is still a kind of centre as well as being Sybil's home, and apart from a brief period when they were bombed out of it, it has been 'home' to them for over thirty years.

The move didn't seem to be much of an event at the time. We were at Lee-on-Solent very deeply engaged in the task of building and establishing our own family and didn't pay an awful lot of attention to what the others were doing. They were there all right, and we all liked having each other somewhere around, but we were also getting on with our own businesses in our own way. Kiff had gone off to Ireland to play at the Gate Theatre for a season, but he appears to have liked it so much that he has been there ever since. He was received into the Catholic Church and married Kay O'Connell in 1941, and became a full-blown Irishman in 1946. His two daughters, Glynis and Bronwen are therefore Irish, half legally by Kiff and half by birth from Kay and are as Irish as the Blarney Stone in thought and behaviour. Perhaps in generations to come, however, their descendants may show some unexpected Welsh and English traits which cannot be stifled by a legal naturalisation. Not that it matters of course. Ann was beginning to make a name for herself in her own right as an actress and would shortly join the cast of the long-running *George and Margaret*. But she would also have continuously to put up with critics pointing out on almost every occasion they mentioned her, 'How like her mother she is.' As our own daughter, Jane, was to discover twenty years later, it can be very irritating not to be allowed to have an identity of one's own. It tends to make one try just a shade too hard to demonstrate one's own characteristics and this doesn't help one to win friends and influence people. Mary, having married Bill Devlin, gave a sigh of relief and became a housewife who was also an excellent pianist and singer. It did for her what the navy, flying and conjuring did for me. It established an area of living all on her individual own.

I don't think any of us realised at this time that throughout the thirties Lewis and Sybil had begun to establish themselves not merely as theatrically important people, but as nationally important people. They were always political as well as dramatical animals and believed in their duties as citizens as well as actors.

This is not to say that there was anything the matter with their work. It was as vigorous and as imaginative as ever. But they were moving in other directions as well. Way back in 1930, in company with Ben Webster and his wife Dame May Whitty, Godfrey Tearle and others, they had formed the actors' union, British Equity. This was no easy task because not unnaturally the theatre managers were against any move that gave actors more bargaining power. Lewis was very seldom, if ever, discourteous, but he was very often far from tactful. Smooth-tongued diplomacy was not for him when there was a cause to promote. Thus his strong unionism, his socialist beliefs, his passionate evangelical temperament and above all his absolutely terrifying, unequivocal honesty of purpose, did not endear him, or indeed any of them, to the theatrical moguls. He had quite a lot of battles before the union, and a closed shop union, was established in London with Godfrey Tearle as its first president.

Sybil, too, had been discovering that a good actress can also be a good public speaker, and she became much in demand to speak for any sort of cause in which her broad humanity could be used to gain followers. She spoke at settlements in the East End, she spoke to miners' political gatherings in Wales, she sat on platforms with distinguished men and women of India and pleaded for their country's independence, and above all she spoke for the cause of pacifism.

Sybil has always been a great 'joiner'. She is for ever joining clubs, institutions and associations for the promotion of every cause from saving the lives of multi-coloured guinea pigs in Persia to petitioning the Archbishop of Canterbury to lead a delegation to talk to Hitler. Some of her memberships have led her into hot water, but, oddly enough, not many. She is quite superb at explaining how there is no inconsistency between being a subscriber to *The Daily Worker* ('because the editor is such a pet') and being one of the governors of an exceedingly posh girls' boarding school ('after all the headmistress is almost a socialist. She said so herself'). While underneath all these apparent overflowings of energetic eccentricities is the sane, high-minded, intelligent woman, who appears to know by instinct – and I'm sure it is the instinct of the artist – what is the most human and humane way to behave in almost any circumstance. What is fascinating to me is that Lewis's contradictions, of violent impatience and huffinesses with above all things his love of beauty and belief in courtesy, and Sybil's contradictions which are the core of her life, had not in any way prevented the growing awareness and recognition by the public of something much deeper in both of them. This is not a greatness of professional skill, which they both have anyway, but which they share with many others. Rather it is a greatness of heart which compels each of them to put themselves and their comforts at the bottom of the list.

Lewis put the case for being independent of what other people thought of him when he performed the opening ceremony of the Bradford Civic Theatre School. When he had performed whatever symbolic gesture had been arranged, like cutting a tape or cracking a bottle of champagne over some footlights, he addressed the newly assembled pupils:

'I wonder how many of you young people', he began, 'have come to this school because you want to be great actors.' And with a warm twinkle in his eye he beamed on them. They, not unnaturally, beamed back at him and nudged each other. Of course that was the reason for their being there! 'Because if there are any of you with that idea in your heads,' he went on, still smiling, 'I can only say to you that the

sooner you get out of this job of acting the better for everybody concerned.' That rocked them not a little! 'But,' he added, 'if you are
prepared to work hard to develop and train the abilities that you now
have so that you can *do* something worthwhile in return for what your
audiences are going to pay you, then you're going to be so jolly busy
that you won't have time to worry about *being* something. Do you want
to *be* something or to *do* something? Do you want to be admired or to
do good work? Do you want to get or to give?'

I don't think it has ever occurred to either Lewis or Sybil to work
in order to *be* something. They never think of anything except what
they have to *do*. They have never been self-concerned in their work and
have, therefore, never stood on their dignity, never been pompous.
Lewis was for ever driven onward by an inexorable sense of duty,
which allowed him no time for pause, no time for what he called
'slacking'. Even during holidays, time was for using, not for idling
away. His inner drive always made me think of Francis Thompson's
Hound of Heaven. Whatever it was, this fury within him never let him
alone for a second. But it gave him his energy and it gave him his
singleness of mind. His mother's Welsh discipline in his upbringing
held it under control, and his father's artistry helped him to cock an
occasional snook at it all, so that he could laugh at it and laugh at
himself, which he did often.

Sybil's drive comes from something different. I'm sure that her early
success in music combined with a certain stability in vicarage life,
instilled in her an absolute belief that essentially the universe, that is
the whole bag of tricks, is all right. We don't know what it's all about
but at heart it is benevolent and splendid. She believes that for her
things can never go badly wrong and so she can fling herself into
anything and everything with her ravenous hunger of enthusiasm and
with little or no fear of consequences. Her father was there to begin
with, and later on Lewis was there, both of them in their own way and
respectively representing the God the Father of her Church on an
only slightly lower scale. Through her music she learnt the absolute
necessity of discipline in order to do what you want to do. She has a
firm conviction that any problem can be solved by more and more
rehearsal and practice. In her early letters to Russell again and again
appear phrases like, 'I'll practise and practise,' or, 'I mucked it up last
night so I've decided to do two hours extra practice every day this

week.' Once when her dentist told her she must be careful of her teeth she told him, 'I'll scrub them three times as hard and three times as often.' She doesn't believe in evil, only that people and scenes are under-rehearsed and so dramatically bad. Her energy – and what energy that has always been! – comes from her sheer enthusiasm for glory, and her certainty that glory can be found in everything. This driving power also has its snags. When you come within range of it, you suddenly notice that the work you do, the way you use your leisure, your hobbies, your home, your family, the very world itself have all become three times more exciting and invigorating than you thought they were. That's wonderful and you don't want to let go of it. But it's like whisky. The first and the second tot are nectar, so you want to keep going and of course if you do, you eventually pass out. You have a wonderful time while you're with Sybil, but unless you can ration the doses and give yourself some time off, you suddenly wonder why you're so tired.

When our third child, Jane, was born, for example, Patricia had rather a bad time and for a while was very sick indeed. Sybil was most upset when our doctor forbade her to see Patricia for the first week. 'No, my dear,' he said, 'you'll tire her out. You get people to use up all their strength in keeping up with your own ebullient energy.' And a week she had to wait, though she has yet to understand why.

In the autumn of 1938 Sybil found a part for herself, or rather Emlyn Williams wrote it and offered it to her, that was right up her street, Miss Moffat in *The Corn is Green*. The play was based on Emlyn's own early life and Miss Moffat was drawn from his teacher, Miss Cook, whose photo Sybil had on her theatre dressing-table throughout the run.

Apart from *Saint Joan* (and I would think you'd be lucky to get even one part like that in a lifetime) Sybil is always at her best when, instead of exploding violently all over the stage, she uses her skill in controlling the violence within her and makes the character appear to be natural, but at the same time, a much more alive and exciting natural character. So it was with Miss Moffat. She was as multi-dimensionally herself in it as she was in *Saint Joan* and in a way that she never had been since *Saint Joan*. Of course it was an entirely different performance. When Shaw saw the French actress Ludmilla Pitoeff play Joan in

French (an exquisitely beautiful but sad little Joan, I remember), and was asked to compare her with Sybil, he said, 'When Ludmilla played Joan I wanted to give her a double whisky and soda. Sybil needed a soporific.' Whereas her Joan burst out all over the place, and the very immaturity of it made it such a wonderful Joan, her Miss Moffat appeared to be about to burst out, holding one on tenterhooks from beginning to end, and the maturity of it made one awfully glad to have met Miss Moffat. And apparently London thought so too because the Duchess Theatre was packed for a whole year till the theatres closed on the outbreak of war.

Almost at the same time as *The Corn is Green* opened, Lewis did one of his most splendidly spectacular productions. He was asked by Ivor Novello to direct a full-scale *Henry V* at Drury Lane and he went at it with all his heart. To his delight he found Ivor Novello not only willing but eager to learn everything he could from Lewis about how to speak Shakespeare and make it meaningful. As a musician and a fellow Welshman he could understand the subtleties of Lewis's musical inflections and he gave a most thrilling performance of which Shakespeare would have been proud. Dorothy Dickson was the French Princess and so the wooing scene in the hands of two such experienced and admirable comedy artists was sheer delight. But it was in the sweeping continuity, with only one interval, the huge scale bravura with plenty of rip-roaring trumpets in the music, a cast of two hundred and the courage to make a Cecil B. de Mille epic of it that was Lewis's triumph. It didn't open till I had sailed for Scapa Flow in H.M.S. *Glasgow* where we were at the 'Stand-By' for the Munich crisis, but I managed to see half the dress-rehearsal after a dash to London from Portsmouth.

Alas, Ivor's fans refused to see him as anything other than the Ruritanian monarch or aristocrat of his many fairy-tale operettas and the show was a failure. Some people said that it was ill-timed and Lewis felt that the rather hysterical relief after Chamberlain's return from Munich with his sad little scrap of paper made any sort of war-play or sabre-rattling a complete anathema. I don't know, but I feel it to be more likely that the public just could not think of the palely handsome face of their dream prince as the fiery, vigorous, fighting King Harry. This was a great pity, because he was very good, and Lewis had excelled even his own exacting standards.

One Sunday morning I went down the road before breakfast to get the papers and saw the headline 'Sybil Thorndike in emergency operation'. She had been taken ill with a fearful pain during the Saturday matinée and by sheer good fortune Ann went in to see her between the shows and insisted on sending for our doctor. He made his diagnosis with Sybil lying on the dressing-room floor and told her she had very acute appendicitis.

'You must go to hospital now,' he said.

'Rubbish,' retorted Sybil. 'I'll play to-night and go to hospital afterwards.'

'Then you'll die,' said the doctor.

At that Ann very sensibly went to the telephone and called Lewis. The bell rang for a long time and then, to her relief, she heard Lewis's voice. He had actually left the flat and was walking along the corridor to the lift when he heard the bell and he very nearly said to himself, 'Oh let it ring. I've gone.' It was touch and go. Once he got to the theatre there was no more argument and Sybil was whisked away in an ambulance. The appendix actually burst during the operation, and the nurse told us afterwards that when the surgeon saw the situation in the operating theatre, he shook his head and shrugged his shoulders at the apparent hopelessness of his task. Luckily for us all he was a man who didn't believe in hopelessness and she was pulled through by the skin of her teeth.

Lewis went off within a couple of weeks in charge of an Old Vic tour of the Mediterranean. From Rome he wrote to me to say that they had been given a huge formal reception by the Italian Theatre and he had prepared a suitable speech praising the achievements of Italian artists. 'But before I could speak, the senior Italian actor got up and did all the praising of themselves leaving me nothing to do but praise ourselves.'

On this trip he went all by himself on a pilgrimage to Rapallo where he and Sybil had spent that wonderful holiday in 1922. He climbed up on to the cliffs and then suddenly took off his expensive wrist-watch, which Sybil had given him, and flung it into the sea. In his letter to Sybil telling her about it, he simply said, 'I wanted something that belonged to us both to become for ever part of Rapallo.'

In July 1939 Lewis was rehearsing to play Colonel Pickering in support of Basil Sydney and Margaret Rawlings in *Pygmalion* at the Haymarket. I was in my ship, the training cruiser *Vindictive* at Quiberon

Bay in Brittany, when I was called home to Bron y Garth because Patricia was having an emergency operation for the arrival of our youngest, Jane. It was an unpleasantly near thing for her, as it happened, and the Bron y Garth family holiday that we had planned had a certain anxious edge to it.

But at the end of the month all Service leave was cancelled and I was ordered to join the cruiser *Southampton* at Grimsby. On Sunday 3rd September I heard Chamberlain's broadcast from somewhere out in the middle of the North Sea, and next morning I was catapulted off from *Southampton* in my Walrus aircraft for my first war-time reconnaissance.

Lewis, at the age of nearly 64, at once joined the motor transport section of the Chelsea A.R.P. with his Austin saloon 'Foomt'. He wrote me a long letter that week which eventually reached me at Scapa Flow. He was very depressed by what he called 'the failure of my generation' and he seemed to be taking quite a lot of the burden of guilt for the war upon himself. This feeling of guilt for the things that went wrong, not only in the family and the country, but even the world, grew stronger in him as he grew older. Now it was more of a feeling of disappointment that the promises of 1919 had disintegrated into the disaster of 1939.

In a letter to me in October, however, he complained in almost the same terms as he had complained to his Colonel twenty-five years before at St Albans. He couldn't think of enough ways of keeping himself and his staff occupied at the Chelsea A.R.P. Depot. My reply to this letter, which was also to send greetings for 'his sixty-fourth birthday on 26th October, has survived. The move to Swan Court combined with the outbreak of war had apparently persuaded me that they should divest themselves of even more of their property. The week before, my ship had been at anchor just below the Forth Bridge when we had been the target for the first real German bombing raid of the war in an attack by a dozen dive-bombers. A few days later Sybil had come to Edinburgh for some reason, while I was looking after my Walrus aircraft at the naval air station at Donibristle. She had travelled over the Forth Bridge to have lunch with me and we wandered together round Dunfermline discussing the war and ourselves until it was time for her to watch me take off and fly to my ship up at Rosyth. I answered Lewis's letter a few days later as follows:

H.M.S. *Southampton*
23.10.39

Dear Daddy,

A line to wish you very many happy returns. I saw Mummy yesterday and had lunch with her as I expect you've heard by now. She will tell you all about our raid last week. You, of course, know only too well, from the last war, what it all sounds like and how one feels at the time, and so I'll say no more than that I was certainly the same! Most unpleasant I thought it was!

We had a long talk about Bron y Garth. Don't you think you might sell the place? No one loves it more than I do, as you know, but the expense and responsibility is out of all proportion to the amount it can be used. . . .

It must be desperate for you trying to find work for your A.R.P. chaps to do. As you say, though, once there has been a raid things will probably be different. . . .

And how right I was! But by the time the 'phoney war' was over, Lewis was no longer with the A.R.P. Patricia and I saw each other for odd snatched, rather desperate, hours in unexpected parts of the country, and in December she rented a house in Golders Green for herself and the children.

While she was still in Wales, however, and not yet fully recovered, Sybil went down to Rainham in Kent to pack up our things for us and to hand the house we had rented back to our landlord. It was here in the house that she had for a short while, what has been described by a researcher in this field, as a genuine mystical experience. She wrote to this friend of hers some years later:

I was packing up a house for my son – he had gone off to sea, and his wife and family had gone off to our house in Wales. The furniture van had left, the house was empty and I, feeling a little forlorn, was wandering round the garden thinking of the happy jolly times we'd had while they were living there. I caught sight, in a flower-bed, of a bright-coloured ball, which suddenly made me cry, and all at once I seemed to be in a changed atmosphere. It was a little alarming at first. Everything looked the same but seemed charged with something more real – very hard to explain. It was as if suddenly, for a flash, I was seeing the significance of things – material things being just symbols – like seeing familiar things on another plane of existence. This curious feeling lasted about ten minutes, and then I was back to normal – but in those few moments I had sensed great happiness and a sureness of something that I felt was eternal life.

On the day before Christmas Eve I was on watch on the bridge of the *Southampton* shepherding a convoy across the North Sea from Norway. I was thinking what a hell of a Christmas this was going to be, when a signal arrived. 'To *Southampton*, from Admiralty. Proceed Newcastle with all despatch for one month's docking.' We reached Newcastle on Christmas Eve and I caught the night train to London after drinking far too much that evening with the Resident Naval Officer, Newcastle, who turned out to be the actor George Curzon, who had rejoined his original profession.

I had been able to phone Patricia but we decided to spring a surprise on Lewis and Sybil. I got to Golders Green at seven in the morning and at 11.30 Lewis, Sybil, Mary and Ann came walking down the road to join us for the day's celebrations. We weren't going to have a family Christmas like this again until 1945. But we wouldn't know that and so we had a wonderful day, with our children providing the excuse for lots of toys and idiotic presents and games for all.

Six weeks later I was away again for the rather dreary round of eight-day long patrols between Iceland and Greenland. It was followed by a period on shore when I used my Walrus to look for submarines round the north of Scotland. And then, joy of joys, I got a new job training midshipman Fleet Air Arm pilots how to begin their deck landings. For six blissful weeks we all, Patricia and I and the three very small children, lived on a farm near the edge of Worthy Down aerodrome near Winchester. We didn't know then that the real war was about to begin, and so despite the rather primitive facilities of the farm and despite the hard work in looking after the children, we had a kind of holiday before it all hotted up and the world we had known disappeared for ever.

Lewis and Sybil came down by train to see us at week-ends, and the train from London to Winchester ran across the back of the garden. We all used to run out when the train was due, and they had been briefed to look out and wave to us as the train rushed by. Not only was 1940 a golden summer, it was also a warm and lovely spring too. But of course the idyll couldn't last. At the end of April I was appointed to command a fighter-divebomber squadron of twelve aircraft stationed at Donibristle and later to embark in H.M.S. *Ark Royal*.

Patricia found a baby-sitter and came to London with me and Lewis and Sybil met us at Waterloo. I suppose it's easy to see significance in things after they have happened, but when we all went into the station buffet for a valedictory drink together, there was without any doubt an air among us of 'This is it!' Obviously we couldn't have known that this was indeed it, and in any case to go off to sea as a Fleet Air Arm pilot in an aircraft-carrier in 1940 did have an ominous side to it. I was torn between this feeling and a more predominant one of the thrill of having my first command. But it was not a very happy little gathering. The last I was to see of the two of them for five years was when they stood together waving as Patricia and I went off in a taxi to Euston.

Alas, my first command was to be a very short command. I took my squadron on to the deck of the *Ark Royal* ten days later to the west of the Orkneys and we set off for the vicinity of Narvik, where, with *Ark Royal* in 'the long grass' a hundred miles to the north of Norway, we gave some sort of air cover for the evacuation of Narvik over the next few days. Then the whole convoy of six or so merchant ships, containing 24,000 of our soldiers, the *Ark*, the *Glorious*, *Southampton* and three destroyers set off south for Scapa. The *Glorious* had been running short of oil and was finding her own way home when she ran into the battleships *Scharnhorst* and *Gneisenau*, who sank her in five minutes. Three days later nine of my squadron and six of another were sent in to dive-bomb the two German battleships in Trondheim. At 2.15 a.m. in broad midnight-sun daylight on 14th June I led my nine boys down one behind the other in a dive at the *Scharnhorst*. My bomb was a near miss, I fear, and then I started home down the fjord. After clearing the heavy flak I was just beginning to think I'd got away with it, and hoping that the other eight behind me would be as fortunate, when I ran into bad trouble with a Messerschmitt 109. Fifteen minutes later, after a mad running fight low down in and out of the mountains of the fjord, I made a forced landing of my damaged plane at 120 knots on the waters of the fjord.

As the wings touched the water and the aircraft skidded to rest in a flurry of spray, with her tail in the air, the whole of the life of England, my home, Lewis, Sybil, the family, everything, was cut off clean like the severing of the umbilical cord. This was not just the end of a chapter but irrevocably the end of the kind of life that we had always known. It was like being born, suddenly to be taken out of a life of relative comfort and security and to be pitch-forked into a completely new unknown world where few, if any, of the old standards would apply. A completely new life was starting for me, which would change my relationship with my wife and children and with my parents. From now on I would begin to see them all quite differently, and so for me they would become quite different people.

In the meanwhile we all had to try to survive or try to help others to survive, so that eventually we could all come together again and try to discover a new way of doing things. It was going to be very difficult and it was by no means in the bag. In the meantime, however, I myself was going to be very much 'in the bag'.

Chapter 11

IN WARTIME

In a way it might have been better to have ended the last chapter with the Christmas at Golders Green. This, very accurately, was the end of the thirties, the end of our growing-up, the parting of the ways. On the other hand, my being shot down and taken prisoner is much too good a dramatic curtain to throw away. My observer and I were captured after a brief swim, and a few weeks later found ourselves in Dulag Luft, a small camp outside Frankfurt where I was to remain for the next two years.

At the time of my capture in the first part of June, tens of thousands of prisoners were pouring into Germany from Dunkirk, and so any news of me was going to take a long time to reach England. When seven out of our fifteen aircraft had managed to get back to the *Ark Royal*, someone reported seeing me go down in a dive pursued by a Messerschmitt. He was not to know that I had dived down to the level of the fjord in the hope that I could outsmart my opponent in low-level crazy-flying. But that was why my observer and I were reported as 'missing believed killed'.

Even though I had been careful to fill in my 'next-of-kin' form correctly, giving Patricia's address as the farm at Worthy Down, the Admiralty did not give the news of my going missing to her. They telephoned Sybil. This could have caused the most awful mess-up in family relationships had we been a family with a propensity for striking attitudes. Fortunately, however, actors normally only strike attitudes about trivialities and Patricia has never struck one in her life. We were all rather surprised, however, that staid Admiralty officials considered an officer's wife was of secondary importance compared with his mother, when his mother was as well-known as Sybil. We didn't mind. We were just astonished that some of their Lordships' minions appeared to be theatre fans.

I heard all about it months afterwards when I began to receive letters from home. Sybil had been alone at 98 when the Admiralty telephoned the news. She went at once to the Old Vic where Lewis was playing Gonzalo in *The Tempest*, the man who has to comfort Alonso for the supposed drowning of his son. In her letter to me she said, 'Lewis just stood there with tears streaming down over his make-up, but all he said was, "You must go and tell Patricia." ' Lewis played that night, as John Gielgud told us, 'without faltering' and Sybil took the train to Winchester.

Patricia was in hospital having a wisdom tooth removed and when Sybil told her I was missing all she said was 'Damn,' but it didn't sound as trivial as it appears on paper. Lewis and Sybil didn't feel that the 'believed killed' allowed much room for hope, but Patricia always said she would have known if I had been killed and so she never even accepted the possibility.

On 11th July, a parson in a remote part of Wales telephoned Patricia at Bron y Garth, where she had taken the children and herself to live, to say that he had just heard Lord Haw-Haw announce that I was a prisoner. This time Sybil's fame turned out to be a great help to us, because it allowed my name to jump the queue. It made a good news story for the sad and infamous Joyce. A month or two later, we were all once again in rather tenuous contact with each other through the very slow, though not too unreliable prisoners' mail.

The time between my flying off to the *Ark Royal* at the end of May and being introduced by Lord Haw-Haw as a prisoner of war, was one of those mysterious periods of time that somehow doesn't exist because the time itself was out of joint. Any thoughts that any of us tried to communicate to each other by letter were so wildly irrelevant by the time the letters were received that we wondered who had been talking to whom. It doesn't matter so much how long letters take in transit as long as there is some order in the chronology and in these few weeks there was none.

For instance there were letters that had been addressed to me in the *Ark Royal* and had not been delivered before I was shot down. Lewis and Sybil had both written and their letters had been returned with the grim, stark words, 'Addressee missing' stamped on the envelopes. I didn't see them till five years later when the news was a little stale. One of them, however, is particularly interesting because in it Sybil had expressed herself very strongly about the Christian religion. Always inclined towards religious discussion, the whole family had gone to town on it when the war broke out. We had discussed the relation between the Church and war, Christ and pacifism, courage and suffering and how we could try to keep some sort of philosophical sanity while taking part in a war.

I remembered that on my journey north at the end of May, I had found time to have dinner with our dear friends Charlie and Ruby Warr. He was Dean of St Giles Cathedral in Edinburgh and whenever any of us met him we had always plunged into enthusiastic theological discussions in the earthiest and most forthright way. On this particular evening a young and very orthodox army chaplain had been present and I must have written to Lewis and Sybil about the verbal jousting that had taken place. In a letter dated 2nd June 1940, and read by me in June 1945, Sybil wrote:

Darling John,

We were so thrilled to get your letter yesterday morning, and we won't worry. We'll just hold on to the splendid thought of all being well with you. We loved your arguments with Charlie and the army chaplain – your having not a bar of the old theological arguments. I find churchmen's talk quite irritating – except Charlie's. Ann brought me a pamphlet yesterday about fortitude and suffering and death being sacramental, etc. Honestly I think that begs the whole question. If Christianity is this superstitious thing then the sooner it's overboard the better. I find the thing I'm striving towards is at once much simpler and much more profound – and *in* everything, as you say – the god of the 'something – calculus' in mathematics, the utter rightness and beauty of a complicated bit of counterpoint – well – well! I'm very glad 'Good God' exalted you as it did me. I think Charlie should read it, don't you?

Good luck, darling. Father Whitby is writing to you. Poor Father Whitby. They are so muddled, I think, his old-fashioned sort.

Your loving,
Mummy

Wasn't the evacuation of troops from Dunkirk amazing? Eye-witnesses say it was like a sort of regatta. All those tiny boats.

On the back of the last page Lewis had added a short note, which, if I had received it, would have put much heart into me at a time when I badly needed it.

My Dear John,

What a lovely letter! I have no fear of your courage nor your instinctive power to do the right thing whatever the circumstances. God bless you.

Your loving,
Daddy

Well, my 'instinctive power' had now put me in a prison camp, where for the first year I decided to occupy my mind by studying theology and wrote home asking for books.

On the whole we were allowed to have whatever books we wanted, which were sent to us through the Red Cross or Y.M.C.A. They were only withheld by the German censors if the author had ever written anything at any time against Germany. My decision to read theology was, I must admit, triggered off by a vague idea that, after the war, I might become a parson. I wanted to have a look at the whole proposition, brood about it and study the subject. But the moment I hinted at the possibility when I asked for theological books, Sybil took off. Within a week the whole of theatrical London, not to mention our friends and relations, were aware that John was becoming a priest. Sybil could now not only vicariously become a sailor and so fulfil her destiny as a Bowers on her distaff side. She could also, as it were, follow in her father's footsteps by having a son in the Church. I can almost believe that if I were to show a strong interest in the fishing industry Sybil would begin to wish that she had called me Peter. But, bless her, she sent me books by the cartload. Lewis never mentioned it at all. But when a year later I went on to philosophy, semantics and languages, he wrote to say that he had never believed that my way of thinking would have been any good for a parson. He added one of his best epigrams when he said, 'I annoyed one or two people the other day when I said at a meeting that I thought it was impossible to be both the Archbishop of Canterbury and a Christian. Not that I don't think Fisher is a splendid fellow. But I expect he has discovered by now that his job requires more generalship than theology.'

At the end of the year their letters began telling me about their touring the mining villages and towns of Wales, under the auspices of the newly formed Council for the Encouragement of Music and the Arts and the Old Vic. Against the advice of the Old Vic they took *Macbeth* in a simplified form. They didn't have costumes, but what

Sybil described to me as 'clothes for acting in – a sort of battledress for the men and unadorned robes for the women. Then we can add cloaks, hats, gloves, swords and things as we need them. Much easier for us and jolly good too for all of us, including the audience because we have to use our imaginations.'

Lewis got together a small company of enthusiastic, have-a-go-at-anything actors and they must have been a merry band. They had a lorry for the bits of scenery, the props and two hampers for the 'acting clothes'. The company travelled in a small bus. Each afternoon they would arrive at the new place, find their billets with mine managers, foremen and miners and then set up the very simple set and lighting in what was usually the scout or parish hall. I would have loved to have seen this really theatrical production in the convention of strolling players. The scenery consisted of a couple of screens, a bench, two 'throne' chairs and perhaps a drape or two at the side. But what more do you want when you have real actors acting?

Lionel Hale had written an introduction explaining what the play was about for the benefit of some of their audiences who had barely heard of the play. Lewis and Sybil would walk on to the stage in their everyday clothes, followed by two actors carrying a hamper. I have in my possession what is probably the only extant script of this version of *Macbeth*, which Lewis gave me after the war. The 'plain-clothes prologue' was obviously written in conjunction with Lewis and Sybil because it is just the sort of conversation they would have had about a play and what it meant to them. Lewis began the dialogue:

Lewis: Come along – here's the stage. Put the basket down there.

Sybil: Come to think of it, this is the way Shakespeare's actors used to travel about – just carrying their baggage around with them and playing the play wherever they could in palaces and pubs and places like that. We're about three hundred years out of date!

Lewis: Well if it was good enough for them it's good enough for us.

1st Actor: Just a minute.

Lewis: What is it?

1st Actor: We're going to do *Macbeth*, aren't we?

Lewis: Yes, of course.

2nd Actor: Why 'of course'?

Sybil: It's up on the posters. Can't you read?

1st Actor: No, we don't mean that. It's like this. We've come a long way to do a play here. Why *Macbeth*? Why not *Hamlet* or *Othello* or one of the historical plays?

Lewis: Well that's a fair question. Now I'll ask you one. What sort of play do you think we ought to do?

1st Actor: It has got to be Shakespeare.

Lewis: Yes.

2nd Actor: But this particular play?

Sybil: I'll tell you. We want a good play and this *is* a good play. But we want something more than that. Though it was written over three hundred years ago it has got to mean something to-day. It has got to be true for 1940.

1st Actor: Yes. I see.

Sybil: Well when did this Macbeth live?

1st Actor: That's just it. It's about a thousand years ago in Scotland and I still can't see what that's got to do with us in 1940.

Sybil: Just go on a bit. What do we know about him?

1st Actor: Well, it's a legend about a savage time –

2nd Actor: Macbeth was a chieftain. He murdered King Duncan and made himself King.

1st Actor: He had to go on murdering to keep himself in power.

2nd Actor: With a spy in every house in Scotland and so on.

Sybil: And you still don't see what this has got to do with 1940?

1st Actor: No.

Sybil: Don't you? You've just given a perfect picture of a dictator.

1st Actor: Yes, but. . . .

Lewis: You needn't always think of dictators in terms of concentration camps and tanks and aeroplanes. Men don't change in a thousand years. What Macbeth wanted, what all such people want, is power. This is a play about a tyrant, a dictator.

Sybil: Yes, and his wife too. Macbeth isn't the only part in this play remember.

Lewis: Sorry.

Sybil: There's Lady Macbeth – that's me! She's the sort of woman who encourages this sort of man. You can meet her anywhere. The wife who wants her husband to get on in the world, always pushing him along from behind. And then when he *has* got on, he grows beyond her and above her. So that's the woman's side of this power business.

Lewis: Well, let's get on with the play.

1st Actor: By the way, you haven't given *us* any parts in this.

Lewis: Yes I have. You're to be the scene-painters.

1st Actor: Scene-painters?

Sybil: Oh you tell them! I've got to dress. (Exit)

Lewis: I want you to sit there (1st actor to right), and you there (2nd actor to left). This stage has got to be a Scottish moor, a castle, a cavern, a battlefield and out there in front they've got to believe it. You've got to tell them what to see. Can you do it?

1st Actor: Leave it to me. Over there is Macbeth's castle, near Loch Ness, wild hillsides looking down on deep black water. The road runs along here through a mountain pass. Over there is Forres on the north-east coast about three miles from the sea. How's that?

Lewis: Good. Ladies and gentlemen we play for you, or rather we will play *with* you, The Tragedy of *Macbeth*. (Exit)

1st Actor: It is a time lost in legend, a thousand years ago.

2nd Actor: Over the wild land of Scotland battles are being fought.

1st Actor: Three weird sisters, the evil spirits to whom a man may turn for strength, meet on a wild moor.

2nd Actor: The wind over the moor is high. (Curtains open)

1st Actor: The air is cold.

And they went straight into 'When shall we three meet again'. Sybil doubled Lady Macbeth and the First Witch, Lady Macduff was also the Second Witch, and the Gentlewoman was the Third Witch. By making the three ladies of the play become the three witches they must have provided plenty of food for psychological speculation.

The audiences lapped it up despite the Jeremiahs of the Old Vic, while the informality of the production made it at once more intimate and more contemporary. Sybil wrote to me: 'We've never played to such audiences. None of them move a muscle while we're playing, but at the end they go wild and lift the roof with their clapping. This is the theatre that we like best – getting right in amongst people. Afterwards they all come round and talk to us. How I love those lilting Welsh voices and what darlings they are.'

They were in *King John* together for another Old Vic production with Ernest Milton, towards the end of 1941 and then did another small-town tour of *Medea*, *Candida* and Laurence Housman's *Jacob's Ladder*, about which Lewis wrote to me with great glee. It appeared that, much against Lewis's will, the Old Vic had insisted on their taking *Candida* to lighten the programme. This was the only one of the three plays that didn't go well and Lewis was delighted to be able to cock a snook at the Board once more.

Towards the end of 1940 he had written to me with a most endearing and ingenuous pride to say that he had been elected President of Equity. He was very bucked about this because it would give him, he felt sure, a chance of influencing the theatre through controlling some of the conditions under which actors have to work. And at the end of that year he took on another job which later was to be the major contributory factor in gaining him his knighthood. He became Drama Advisor to the Council for the Encouragement of Music and the Arts. It was the brainchild of Dr Tom Jones, a Welsh compatriot of Lewis's, a former shop-keeper in the Rhondda Valley and later deputy for the Secretary to Lloyd George's Cabinet. He had stated publicly, at the beginning of the war, that without the Arts there would be no point in winning the war because world civilisation would perish. He convened a meeting at the R.A.C., asked for suggestions for promoting the Arts from the interested parties, managed to persuade the Pilgrim Trust of America to put up some money and finally persuaded the government to go half-shares in the project. Lord Macmillan was the first Chairman and the Ministry of Education had a seat on the council.

When Macmillan resigned, Lord Keynes took it on and Lewis became Drama Director. Keynes, for some reason, had a strong detestation of acronyms, so Lewis told me. And so C.E.M.A. became The Arts Council, and Lewis had for the first time two important administrative jobs, for which he was eminently suitable. He had always been intensely public-spirited to a degree that sometimes bordered on eccentricity, if not fanaticism. He had a fierce conscience that not only compelled him to put the community before himself even to his own detriment, but made him impatient of people who didn't do likewise. On the one hand at Equity he could satisfy his social conscience in working for the good of actors and on the other at The Arts Council he could satisfy his artistic conscience by helping to promote the high standards of plays and acting for which he and Sybil had always striven.

I would like to have seen him and Maynard Keynes together. From all accounts they had quite a few jousting matches. And I believe they had one row which reverberated through the building, although I've never been able to find anybody to tell me what it was all about. They were both, however, in their respective fields, giants among men and each appreciated the strength of the other. Lewis always spoke of Keynes afterwards with admiring respect – and even placed him on his own private list of people whom he suspected of being in the British Secret Service. This was almost the highest compliment Lewis could pay anybody whom he admired but couldn't quite understand. Granville Barker was another of his suspects as were Hugh (Binkie) Beaumont, Charles Cochran and Jacob Epstein. It was an odd eccentricity of his, which saved him from being too curious about those activities of certain people that he found mysterious. And their disagreements did not prevent Keynes from strongly recommending Lewis for a knighthood.

Lewis worked like a demon at C.E.M.A./Arts Council, but in spite of it he still managed to find time to play in *The Moon is Down* and to conduct Equity meetings, I have been told, rather in the manner of a very strict football referee at a Celtic v. Rangers match. He had been a member of the Council for years, and indeed there was a story going round before the war of how, at one meeting, they required a decision from Sybil, who was also on the Council. But she was in New York and so they decided to telephone at what was for her seven in the morning. Rather naturally it was considered suitable for Lewis to take the call on behalf of Equity and he took it sitting at the table with the rest of the Council around him. He was very conscious that it was an expensive call and that Equity was paying for it. Sybil was taken completely by surprise. Her delight, however, was clear not only to Lewis but to all the others. Her voice from the telephone went all round the room as though she was declaiming in the Albert Hall. The conversation went something like this, I believe:

Operator: You're through to Dame Sybil.

Lewis: Sybil?

Sybil: Looowis! Darling, how lovely of you to phone. Where are you?

Lewis (very businesslike): At an Equity Council Meeting.

Sybil: Are you? Do give them all my love. How are *you,* Darling?

Lewis (more brusquely): I'm fine. But I'm phoning to ask you . . .

Sybil: Are you really all right, Darling? Are you having proper meals?

Lewis (getting impatient): Sybil! This is an Equity business call and . . .

Sybil: But they can wait a *minute*, can't they? It's so lovely to *hear* you. What time is it for you?

The first lot of 'pips' were well past before Lewis managed to explain the problem and to get her Yea or Nay, by which time the Councillors had given up all hope of remaining businesslike and were openly chuckling at Lewis's dilemma.

Both at Equity and C.E.M.A. this integrity of purpose often led him to do himself down quite considerably rather than run the risk of his being thought in any way partisan. He had quite a tussle when his colleagues at C.E.M.A. wanted to put on Priestley's *They Came to a City*. Lewis thought it an admirable play and just the sort that they should be backing. But he opposed it on the grounds that he was known to be a socialist and that it might appear he was backing a socialistic author's socialistic play for reasons other than the dramatically artistic.

In the meanwhile Sybil had played Constance in *King John* and Rebekah in *Jacob's Ladder*. In this latter she and Lewis both doubled their parts as the two Narrators, or *Chorus One* and *Chorus Two*. But in the middle of the tour I had a letter from Patricia at Bron y Garth to say that Sybil and Russell had turned up to work on the script of a play that Russell had written. He called it *The House of Jeffreys* and it told a partly fictional, partly true, story of a terrifying lady called Georgina Jeffreys, a descendant of the famous hanging judge. The lady was apparently rather more than true to her blood for she was a missionary in Africa with a taste for cannibalism. It was all 'much too much', I gather. Whenever Sybil gets together with Russell they immediately go off into a world of their own, a world compounded of vicarage attic charades, Grand Guignol and 'ham' on such a scale that the sheer effrontery of it makes one believe it. As J. C. Trewin once said, 'When a Thorndike is on the rampage, no one dares to laugh.'

Patricia told me that they all got together in the West Room and sang their way through the missionary hymns with a gusto that shook the rocks from which Bron y Garth (the House of Rock) got its name. They had in fact the time of their lives acting the script rather than working on it. They rolled about the place in helpless giggles that grew farther out of control as the horrors grew more horrifying. But, of course, as well as the outsize, skylarking amateur romp in Sybil, there is also the much stronger, highly skilled and dedicated professional actress. The pro knew very well that you can't go to London in a play built out of family charades, however much fun they might be. And so as well as the giggles Patricia told me of the storms that arose between her and Russell, when it appeared that the only thing that prevented an outbreak of fisticuffs was their vicarage training.

The play did go on in London and Sybil enjoyed the blood, but the public were not so enthusiastic. However, James Agate wrote of it, 'The skill and tact of Sybil's performance are to be gathered from the fact that we did not laugh at Georgina once, not even when she came back from the wine cellar clutching a bottle of Amontillado with which to wash down Roberta.'

After this particular ball was over Sybil went to Dublin early in 1943 to play at the Gate Theatre with Hilton Edwards and Michael MacLiammoir, those two strange theatrical geniuses, who for so long have been the pillars of Irish Theatre. Of course she stayed with Kiff and Kay, not to mention the infant Glynis, at their little flat in Herbert Street. During this time Sybil wrote me a whole string of fascinating letters on the subject of pacifism. Had I been in England, or indeed on the high seas somewhere with the navy, I would have been able to write back intelligently and so discussed it all. But I wasn't in England. I was by now very much in the middle of 'Mittel-Europa' in a prison camp in Silesia, which tended to give one a somewhat biased view of the problems of pacifism in war-time. Most of what she had to say was, of course, backing up Kiff for refusing, on ethical and moral grounds of conscience, to have anything whatever to do with the war. He had, to Sybil's delight, joined the Peace Pledge Union as far back as 1931 and had never wavered in his convictions. Between the lines of her letters, however, ran the thought that the cause of pacifism was not being promoted as effectively as it might be by merely keeping faith with it in Dublin. Rightly or wrongly she has always felt that it isn't enough to hold a strong belief. One must do something positive about it. It isn't enough to *be* a pacifist, one must *do* the work of pacifism. One must stand up somewhere at some time and, if it isn't too paradoxical, be militant about it. It is, of course, the perennial dilemma of any good Christian and so far no one seems to have found an answer to it. At my end in Germany it was difficult not to be rather one-eyed about it. Sybil, however, has this astonishing gift of being multi-eyed at all times and yet being able to hold the resulting paradoxes under a big umbrella of consistency. And so she could agree with, and espouse, Kiff's form of pacifism and at the same time accept my position in the fighting services. Nor did she merely accept our two positions. She openly endorsed them both.

But when I heard from Kiff that he and Sybil had met the German Ambassador at a cocktail party in Dublin, I gave up trying to cope with the problem of finding even the thinnest scarlet thread of consistency in the beliefs of my relatives. After all they were still the same people as before and I felt we had all much better get on with whatever jobs we had to do in the way we thought best. This 'best way' in Sybil's case has always been to redouble her energies, practise more, work more, do more things and see more people, which is exactly what she did. Her pacifism has always been so much a part of her that you cannot but know she is right when you are with her, and it doesn't interfere in the slightest degree with her overwhelmingly ardent patriotism. Indeed, she was delighted to learn at about this time that she was on Hitler's list of important people in England who were too dangerous to be left free when he took over the government. And I think he was probably right. She would have been a great problem for him.

Much of all this I only heard after the war when I got home again. Sybil told me all about everything in her letters, but there must have been a very overworked censor in Whitehall, who had to cope with the blue-pencilling of those letters to me. And so I didn't know till much later about their being bombed out of their flat in Swan Court, nor of their sitting on the stairs with Patricia and our four-year-old Jane during the raid, and of how Jane had kept them all going by singing nursery rhymes in a loud voice till the 'All Clear' sounded. This is why I was so astonished to receive a letter from Patricia in 1944 which said, 'You'll never guess where I am. I'm sitting up in bed in the early morning at *98 Swan Court*! What about that?' 'Well, *what* about it?' thought I, who never imagined they had ever left it. Apparently, by the middle of 1944, the worst of the bomb damage at Swan Court had been repaired and No. 98 had been made habitable again. After living in hostels, flats, digs and pubs, and with all their furniture in store, they were suddenly offered their old home again. The furniture came out of store and they moved back with sighs of delight and relief.

By the end of 1942 in Stalag Luft III we had designed and built for ourselves a compact and efficient little theatre to seat 350 prisoners at a time. From the time we opened it until we were moved out of the camp in January, 1945, we put on a new show roughly every three weeks. We had a council of half a dozen enthusiasts to take care of the artistic direction and our repertoire ranged from Shakespeare and Shaw to farce and revues and from orchestral concerts to band-shows.

My own first production was *Macbeth* and I wrote a post-card to Lewis asking for his advice. He sent me reams of it, and in the event, through me, he did a kind of remote control reproduction of his own 1926 version. I wish I had been able to keep these letters because they would have made a fascinating 'Producer's Guide to Macbeth'. But in any case he was to tell me about it all over again in much more detail when I produced the play in Glasgow in 1949. He would, I think, have approved our prison-camp efforts. Rupert Davies was Macbeth, Kenneth Mackintosh a six-foot-two Lady Macbeth and I played Macduff. Lewis was delighted when I told him of our greatest compliment, which came from an unknown American. At the end of the cavern scene an awed voice was heard to say: 'Gee! That was an eerie son-of-a-bitch.'

'I wish someone had said that when we did it in London,' Lewis wrote back to me.

Later I did *I Have Been Here Before* and *Saint Joan* and once more they both sent me pages and pages of priceless theatrical wisdom. It was only now that I began to realise that what I had thought all my life to be common knowledge about the theatre was in fact highly specialised professional knowledge, which all of us had been unconsciously absorbing at our parents' knees. Everybody, it appeared, did not know the difference between good and bad acting, good and bad production or between good and bad plays. How lucky for those that did. And how lucky to have Lewis and Sybil on call to confirm or deny one's judgement. I had always known they were pretty good, but only now did I begin fully to appreciate how and why. And thus it was now that I began gradually to form the idea of going into the theatre myself as soon as the war was over.

Before all this came about, however, there were two more events in Sybil's wartime life that I remember hearing about. Enid Bagnold had written a play called *Lottie Dundass*, a kind of thriller about a young actress who murders a rival actress. It was a fine dramatic role, and Ann Todd, at that time not nearly as famous as she was later to become, was told she could have the part if she could find a top-ranking star to play the secondary rôle of the girl's mother. The finding of such a star who would be willing to play second fiddle to a relatively unknown actress's lead turned out to be a great deal easier said than done. Several very well-known great actresses read the play and turned it down. And then someone suggested to Ann Todd that she might ask Sybil Thorndike. So she did and Sybil agreed. This very fine actress only needed just one such break. Since then she has never looked back, which is just the very thing to please Sybil.

After that Sybil doubled the White Queen and the Queen of Hearts in Clemence Dane's stage version of Alice's adventures. As the White Queen she was required to strap on the leather harness under her clothes so that she could be hitched on to a wire and lifted into flight over the stage of the Scala. To perform stage-flying is at any age an alarming experience, as Mary can testify after years of Peter Pan aviation. But at the age of 61, Sybil took it in her stride and wrote to tell me that it was exactly the same as the flying she had been doing for years in her dreams. She described it quite simply with her favourite adjective – 'gorgeous'.

But suddenly in the autumn of 1944 all communication between England and prison-camps in Germany seemed to be broken off. The Allies were advancing across Europe and nobody had time to worry very much about prisoners' mail. On 27th January, 1945, in the middle of our dress rehearsal of *The Wind and the Rain*, all ten thousand of us from the five compounds of Stalag Luft III were moved out of the camp to begin a trek to the westward. And after more camps and more marching, a group of us were finally liberated near Lübeck at the end of April.

I arrived home in the middle of VE Day and was sent straight to Portsmouth for an hour or two to be kitted up, vetted and unnecessarily and irritatingly deloused. I had the address of the house near Epsom which Patricia and Mary had bought the year before with considerable help from Lewis. I knew they had been there in September when I had last heard, and hoped they still were. But the spirit of victory had invaded the telephone exchanges and all my attempts to discover their number were met by happy, welcoming messages of joy from all the various operators – but no number. I remembered the number of the Swan Court flat and tried to call Lewis and Sybil. There was no reply.

In the early evening, however, I reached the railway station at Ashtead in Surrey and, feeling much too like Rip Van Winkle, walked and was given a lift up Crampshaw Lane to the house called 'Thirty Trees', named after Lewis's lullaby story. And there the five years came to an end when we all fell into each others' arms like bewildered children and for a while and for once had almost nothing to say.

That evening after much inquiring again from hilarious exchange operators we located Sybil in Manchester, on tour for the Old Vic with Larry Olivier and Ralph Richardson, and I got her on the phone a few minutes before their evening performance. It was a mad, breathless and incoherent conversation in which nothing and everything was said. Then she told me that Lewis was playing at the Bristol Old Vic with Ann. But she must have got her call through to him before I managed it because almost at once he got through to me. We were all emotionally exhausted by the time we went to bed that night and had, of course, entirely failed to exchange any news, views or ideas that made any sense.

Two days later I received a short note from Larry Olivier.

Dear John,
Welcome home! How lovely it must be for you to be with your family again. Your mother's joy since you phoned is a delight to behold. It shines out of her.

Bless you,
Yours,
Larry O.

But it was not till a Sunday a couple of weeks later that the circle was joined again when they and Ann came down from London to spend the day at 'Thirty Trees'. It should have been one of the most joyful of all family occasions, but somehow it wasn't.

There was a strange restraint between us all, as though after five years none of us dared to risk putting a foot wrong. Our only common ground was our lives before the war and we had all travelled a long way from that life. But Lewis, Sybil, Patricia, Mary and Ann had all travelled their ways and I had perforce gone off in another direction entirely. We talked of pre-war things we had shared while we all knew that this world had gone for ever. And so we felt uncomfortable with each other groping around trying in vain to find points of contact. Perhaps we were all too eager to get back to normal again, too eager to say, 'It's

226

all right now. The long nightmare is over.' In ordinary times I suppose we make continuous little adjustments to each other's changing behaviour. It was rather frightening to see how big the adjustments had to be after not just five years, but five such shattering years. We found ourselves looking sideways at each other, almost furtively at times, as though we were talking to strangers whom we felt we ought to know but didn't.

I did go for a walk with Lewis that afternoon and as we had always been able to keep a silence between us without embarrassment, we both rather enjoyed ourselves and were therefore much better company when we got back to tea. During the walk, however, Lewis said:

'I'm rather interested to know exactly what you were doing about the middle of April. Did you have some sort of crisis to face?'

'Yes,' I said, 'I did. The night before we were moved out of a camp near Bremen for our final march, I remember wondering what was going to happen to us and if the Germans would let us go if the country really disintegrated. I walked up and down a corridor in our hut for about an hour doing a sort of conscious willing of – oh I don't know how to put it – a sort of determined hope. I suppose you could call it a sort of prayer that after all these years there would at last be a happy ending.'

'I think I heard you,' said Lewis. 'I was at the theatre and in the middle of the show I said to my self, "John's having trouble. I wonder what it is." '

Later we were able to put accurate dates and times to our experiences, and they corresponded exactly.

But despite my being given three months' 'P.O.W. leave', I didn't see much of Lewis and Sybil that summer. The Old Vic Company was now at the New Theatre with an almost all-star cast headed by Sybil, Larry Olivier and Ralph Richardson. We saw them all. Sybil's Jocasta to Larry's Oedipus, her Mistress Quickly and her Catherine Petkoff in a highly-skilled and hilarious *Arms and the Man*. I remember standing in the wings with Sybil a few days after they opened in *Oedipus*. She, looking magnificent in the clothes of Jocasta, and I incongruously in the uniform of a lieutenant-commander. We were standing quite near to Larry, who was just preparing to make his great entrance as the eyeless king. I hadn't seen Larry since before the war, and Sybil whispered, 'Larry! Here's John.' He just had time to turn, give a full theatrical and delighted wave, whisper, 'Hi John! Lovely! See you in a minute!' when the great doors of the palace swung open and he was on the stage in high tragedy. He came off stage a little later, and before shaking my hand, stood in his costume and gave a naval salute while saying 'Reporting aboard, sir.'

The company went off shortly afterwards to Paris and on into Germany to play for the troops of the victorious British Army. They all hated being ordered on no account to fraternise with the Germans on pain of being sent back home. To Sybil, who if she met Lucifer would soon be chatting to him about his experiences during the Fall, it was downright un-Christian and I have no doubt she ignored the order whenever she thought she could get away with it.

One day I received a rather special letter from her, which by some miracle has survived our many moves and travels. She had written it from Hamburg:

Darling John,
I feel I must write to tell you of a really awful experience to-day – our visit to Belsen. Our *Arms and the Man* company were asked by the Army H.Q. to go to this notorious camp and do a matinée for the staff, who were having a very depressing time with the little children left over from the Camp which was being burnt out. We didn't know what we were in for! After a good long drive from Hamburg we arrived at a quite nice-looking building outside a village, and knowing what we'd heard about Belsen it all looked very nice and clean.

We were met by officials and the head doctor, who hailed me as a friend from Dublin – he was a child doctor. He said, 'I don't care what you're playing or where this afternoon but *you* are coming with *me* Sybil Thorndike and you're going to see the horrors that were children.' So I went off with him, and the others, Larry Olivier, Ralph Richardson, Maggie Leighton, Beau Hannen and Joyce Redman, went off with some other officers. Larry said, 'Don't forget the matinée mind.'

Well, my dear, when we got through the white building, which looked so clean, there crept in on me (and you know my keen nose) the most awful and depressing smell. I said, 'What's that awful smell?' The doctor said, 'That's living children's bodies, that smell is.' Well he took me first to the camp where all the prisoners had been herded together. It was still burning, but the smell was truly awful. He showed me huts where many people, mothers and children, and some old men had been living – no room to *breathe* but it was all being burnt down and it looked *ghastly*. Then he said, 'Now you come and see the children we are saving.' So he took me to the white house and into the wards where these little creatures were lying, mis-shapen, no skin on their bones – one little boy who looked about 8 months old but was really 4 years, all twisted and like an old gnome. Oh John, I can't tell you how awful it was. There was the smell of putrefaction everywhere. He said, 'These children will all recover.' They looked so ghastly, as if they never could walk, but he was hopeful – and he said he was taking some of them back to Ireland with him.

Then, oh it was horrible – he said, 'Now I'll show you the ones who can't recover.' That was the great shock – little creatures with no flesh on them – twisted and contorted. I said, 'I'll never get this sight and smell out of me again.' And the doctor said, 'No, you must remember this all your life. This is what war does – turns human beings into beasts, and the children into sub-human deformities.' I'll never forget the sight and smell – poor little human children – they were none of them moving, just huddled, lying as if petrified. The ones who were going to get well looked nearly as bad, but I suppose the doctor knew what he was talking about as he's a child specialist.

I was called to lunch but felt like being sick. However, my appetite returned and we played the matinée – somehow!

One nurse there had been in the camp with her husband and child, and she told me she'd seen them both killed and she thought she'd go mad, but she was a peasant type and I suppose just screamed like an animal and then mercifully forgot. She was very good with the poor little creatures.

Driving back in the bus to Hamburg, I couldn't stop crying, it was all so fearful and horrible. We played that night at the theatre in Hamburg – *Richard III* – but I was in a haze, a nasty evil-smelling haze. I'll never forget this all my life. Oh, war turns people into monsters – though some heroism comes sometimes, doesn't it? I'll never get over to-day – never.

Your loving,
Mummy

Soon afterwards we turned up at Swan Court one evening to be met by Ann at the door who said, 'Daddy has some marvellous news. But he must tell you himself. He's in the bedroom.' We found him sitting on the bed putting on his shoes. He looked up and in a shaky, incredulous voice, said 'I'm going to be knighted.' We were, of course, sworn to secrecy, and he shouldn't really have told us, but he just couldn't keep it to himself with Sybil away in Europe. And in the June Birthday Honours there it was, 'Lewis Thomas Casson, Knight Bachelor, for services to the theatre.' He felt particularly pleased about it because the Government was still Conservative under Churchill, and so as a socialist he was in a way one up on Sybil, who had received her D.B.E.

under a Labour Government. Patricia and I misquoted Fluellen in *Henry VI* when we said in our telegram to him, 'An it please Your Majesty, the Welshman has done good service.'

Then he and Ann went off together to Germany on an E.N.S.A. tour with Ann as Saint Joan. Just before they left I was able to see Ann in a rehearsal of the trial scene. In some ways she was so like Sybil that I felt I was seeing a *doppelgänger*. In others she had her own highly individual way of playing. Hers was a more intellectual performance, I thought, more apparently controlled, perhaps not quite so warm, and yet it had plenty of Sybil's blazing energy and faith. Ann played her own Joan, but somehow couldn't prevent Sybil from bursting through. Sybil had already seen it at Bristol and was thrilled with it.

In Germany, Lewis not only played the Earl of Warwick but he argued in every camp with the army officers about the ethics of German responsibility for the horrors perpetrated by the SS and the Gestapo.

'Of course the German people must be held individually and personally responsible for the horrors committed in their name at the concentration camps,' one Colonel said to Lewis. 'They all knew what was going on and they could have done something about it if they'd wanted to.'

Lewis looked quizzically at him and asked, 'Must I, as a British subject, be held personally responsible for what you in the British Army are doing in my name?'

'Naturally,' said the Colonel, 'but we are a more humane people than they are.'

'Are we?' asked Lewis. 'Am I to be responsible for the way some of the SS prisoners are being treated by the British guards at one of your camps near here? If you, the Colonel in charge of the area, don't know what's going on, how can I be held responsible?'

The Colonel hotly denied the accusation and was furious. But he caused inquiries to be made, and found that what Lewis had told him was substantially correct. He wrote Lewis a charming letter saying that he was very grateful for what he had learnt. Lewis, of course, was very pleased both at having scored off the Colonel and at finding him a big enough man to admit it.

In August Sybil, Mary, Patricia and I accompanied Lewis to Buckingham Palace where he received his accolade, in company with A. P. Herbert, from the sword of King George VI. We called for them earlier at Swan Court and Patricia went in to say 'Good morning' to Lewis, resplendent, but not altogether comfortable, in his morning suit.

'How do I look?' he asked with his own rather special brand of sad diffidence, which seemed to say, 'I really oughtn't to dress up like this.'

Patricia answered, 'Lovely, Darling, but you've got odd shoes.'

He had been about to go to meet his sovereign with one black and one brown shoe! There must have been something about Buckingham Palace that made him absent-minded, because when they had gone to their first Royal Garden Party in the twenties, he walked up the red-carpeted steps trailing from one shiny boot, a label inscribed 37s. 6d. Sybil had spoiled his entrance by crying, 'Lewis! You've got a price-tag on your boot!' and stooping down to snatch it off. 'If only the price had been six guineas instead of a measly 37s. 6d. I wouldn't have minded!' she told us.

When he had received his Military Cross from the hands of George V, Sybil, her father and I, aged six, had waited outside Buckingham Palace gates. Now, almost thirty years later, we waited again, with Patricia and Mary replacing Canon Thorndike, and I was in uniform instead of Lewis. We watched him cross the courtyard alone and Sybil said, 'Doesn't he look sweet. I bet he hasn't got a handkerchief.' An hour later he came back to us at the gate as Sir Lewis Casson and we showered our congratulations on him. 'Well, come on,' cried Sybil. 'Tell us everything that happened. Was the King nice and jolly?'

'Not very,' said Lewis. 'His father wanted to know all about me when I got my M.C., but to-day I don't think the King had the faintest idea who either A.P.H. or I were, or why we were there. He seemed utterly bored with the whole thing.'

'Oh what a disappointment,' answered Sybil, 'but I expect the poor darling was tired. He has done so much for everybody.'

That evening we all went to the Savoy to celebrate, Sybil thoroughly enjoying being called Lady Casson for the first time. There was a large party of Labour politicians at a nearby table also celebrating their over-whelming win at the polls. We were as thrilled as they were about it. All the Casson family, or nearly all, vote Labour from a mixture of tradition, conviction, compassion, genuine sentiment and a touch of sentimentality. Indeed Patricia and I had worked very hard that summer in supporting the now Lord Shackleton in his gallant, but not quite successful, attempt to wrest the primrose-hearted constituency of Epsom from the entrenched Tories.

On this evening in the Savoy, the jovial enthusiasm of the celebrating socialists had enveloped our table as well, and we all launched into a 'Cassonic' discussion on the future of Great Britain and indeed the world. It was all very gay because we were, I suppose, celebrating not only Lewis's knighthood, not only the Labour victory, but also Great Britain's victory and the blessedness of peace. We toasted Lewis and we toasted Sybil and we all toasted ourselves.

Suddenly Lewis said, 'I'd like to make a speech, not just to you all at this table, but to everyone in the room. I'd like to tell them that at last they've got a Government that can get rid of all the bad things of the past if only they'll back it up and if only they all put their hearts in it. I'd like to tell those Labour politicians over there that they've got a chance no Government has ever had before to make a Britain that we've dreamed of, and fought for. They've been given this huge majority and there's nothing they can't do if they've got the vision to do it and the enthusiasm to inspire the rest of us to follow them.'

Those weren't his exact words but whatever they were he held us in a kind of magic spell of exaltation. When, a few seconds later, he said, 'Shall I get up now and say it all in a loud voice for everyone to hear?' we almost believed that he would. Sybil said, 'Lewis, you can't make a speech like that here, not now, not in this place. Whatever would they think just after you've got your knighthood,' in a voice that sounded as though part of her hoped he would. Lewis half rose in his chair with the mischievous look he had on his face whenever he was pulling Sybil's leg and which she was never quite certain about. He took a slow, long and large actor's breath as though he were about to speak from the Capitol, held it and himself as though poised for action – and then slowly sank back into his chair with a broad smile saying, 'Perhaps I'd better not, it might spoil all our dinners.' The moment passed, leaving us a little disappointed. He was just the sort of person who could have got away with it, though perhaps the Savoy Grill was not the ideal forum.

At the beginning of September I went off on a number of rehabilitation courses. I learnt to fly again, to fly blind, to understand the new world of air-traffic control that had grown up during the war. And in

November I was appointed to be executive officer of the naval air station at Ayr on the west coast of Scotland.

Wherever all this took me I managed to return to Ashtead for most week-ends, and Lewis and Sybil found time to join us whenever they could for Sunday lunch at 'Thirty Trees'. On one such afternoon Lewis and I went for a walk up on to Epsom Downs and for an hour we had that easy relationship of the evenings on the sea wall at Dymchurch.

'What are you going to do with yourself now?' he asked. 'Are you going to stay on in the navy?'

'I don't know,' I said. 'Most of my contemporaries are now commanders and I'm only a two-and-a-half still. And the Fleet Air Arm has grown from being an eccentric Cinderella to become the navy's main arm. I'm only just beginning to realise how out of date I now am, and how much I've got to catch up. The odd thing is that I'm not sure I want to.'

'How long can you stay on?'

'I'm just on 36 now and if I don't get my brass-hat I shall have to retire at 45. That would get me a pension, but not much of one. I wondered if I might not chance my arm in the theatre.'

'I'm not sure I like the sound of that. Of course I'd like to see someone like you coming into the theatre and I've always said that an actor is the better for doing something else first. But you have got a family to look after, haven't you, and the theatre is very insecure – even if you're a success in it. Were you thinking more in terms of acting or producing or managing?'

'I'm afraid I hadn't got as far as that. It's all a bit vague and probably the result of feeling rather out of things in the navy after being cut off for so long.'

'Well I wouldn't do anything about it suddenly or rashly if I were you. After all you are in a job and that means you've got regular money coming in. Don't be too impatient. It'll take you quite a time to settle down.'

Back at the house he told Sybil what we'd talked about and she immediately regarded the whole thing as settled. I was bound to succeed in the theatre whatever I did because she had always known I was a good actor – 'Look at your conjuring, darling, that's acting' – and perhaps I would be a great director into the bargain. 'While you're at Ayr why don't you ring up Matthew Forsyth? He's running the

233

Citizens' Theatre in Glasgow. It was started during the war by the playwright James Bridie. You should go up and see them all.' Which is exactly what I did just before Christmas.

Two months later my resignation from the navy had been accepted and I was given my last free ride in a service car. I left the naval air station, where I had been more or less in charge of the airfield and five or six hundred officers and men, and was driven to the stage-door of the Citizens' Theatre in the Gorbals, where I was under the orders of a girl of 25.

Another chapter was about to begin. I was now in the family profession and would be judged professionally by Lewis and Sybil. I would also learn from them and about them as a fellow-worker rather than an onlooker.

On the day I retired from the navy, Lewis was in Bristol and I told him the news by telegram. Within an hour or two back came a telegram from him to me. Once again he found the right quotation: 'The Lord be with you. And with thy spirit.'

Chapter 12

VIEW FROM WITHIN

In February of 1946 in some rather squalid theatrical digs off Sauchie-hall Street in Glasgow I had a long letter from Sybil telling me about the plays she, Lewis and Ann were rehearsing for a season at the King's, Hammersmith. The company was known as the Travelling Repertory Theatre and was run by Basil Langton, who played some of the leads and shared the production with Lewis. They had a large and interesting repertoire consisting of *Romeo and Juliet*, with which they opened in March, *The Wise have not Spoken*, *Saint Joan*, *Electra* and a play about President Woodrow Wilson called *In Time to Come*. All three of them should have been if not in their seventh heaven then in at least a sixth. Lewis and Sybil have always believed that repertory theatre is the one true theatrical faith and here they were starting out in the post-war world with a set of plays which gave them all the scope they could want for large-scale acting and for theatrical evangelism. But it didn't seem to work out that way. I got a strong feeling of tension and frustration from their letters. I don't think any of them were as happy as they had hoped to be. Lewis kept writing blistering comments to me on what was to him an almost complete inability to speak properly on the stage on the part of most of the actors. He, Sybil and Ann probably enjoyed the *Electra* more than anything else because they always enjoy 'The Greeks' more than anything else. I am still not absolutely sure myself that 'The Greeks' are as much everybody's theatrical fare as they have always believed. That the plays are superb and that the poetry of Gilbert Murray's translations is equally so no one who loves the drama can deny. Nor can it be denied that they provide the best possible acting parts for actors who are not afraid of acting on the grandest scale. And yet I wonder if this latter isn't the main reason why the plays are produced. If, as has been said, people don't know how tall they are till they stretch, 'The Greeks' above all others make actors feel like giants. But they may very easily grow too big for their audiences in the process.

Lewis always believed, and so does Sybil, that in playing the great dramatic rôles it is not the job of an actor to come down to the level of everyday life but rather to lift everyday life up to the heroic level. Once, when we had all been to see a very famous actor playing Lear, Lewis said afterwards, 'Yes it was a very capable, very professional and very natural performance. It wouldn't have disturbed anyone. We have merely been told that everything will always come right in the end if only we let things take their course. We have just seen a Lear who in effect said to us, "Don't worry about King Lear. The play is only about ordinary people like you. There's nothing to be frightened of. Just relax and I'll come down and introduce you to some nice ordinary people." Instead of that he ought to have been saying, "Hold on tight! Fasten your seat belts! For the next three hours I'm going to take you to heights you wouldn't even have dreamt of on your own. You'll have to work hard to keep up with me, but when you come back to earth you'll be three feet taller than before. Are you coming? Right! We're off!" That's really what every artist ought to be doing – lifting people up, making them bigger.'

As one of those who normally has to be lifted up rather than to do the lifting, I am all for artists behaving like this. Sometimes, however, it seems to me that the artist forgets that some heights are too high for a lot of people. The 'passengers' then either become dizzy and frightened by vertigo or else get a crick in the neck from looking up too far and too long. This to my mind is what nearly always happens to audiences watching 'The Greeks'. There is a fairly large, but nonetheless esoteric, group of theatregoers who are moved not just by the human individual tragedies ('ain't we bin in the bloody war?') but also by the Olympian tragedies, tragedies of Man rather than men, who can understand Goethe's *Hier bin ich Mensch* as well as *Hier bin ich ein Mann*. These people will queue up again and again to see *The Medea* or *The Trojan Women*. But they are not the public, they are a special public with at least some experience of 'Olympian flights', even though the crowds for Sybil's original *Medea* stopped the traffic outside the Holborn Empire one afternoon in 1919.

When Sybil played Joan a very special thing happened. Shaw wrote a play and Sybil played a part both of which took every kind of person in the audience up to the heights. She didn't invite us to live with heroes. She made us all feel heroic. For once the large-scale hero, or heroine, was human and therefore she uplifted us mortals to heroic stature. Shakespeare has the same effect when he is played humanly rather than holily, and gutsily rather than intellectually. But it doesn't always happen. Artists, and especially humble ones like Lewis and Sybil, often tend to forget that the rest of us can't always become co-pilots and sometimes are very scared of being merely passengers. To extend the aeronautical analogy, I have a notion that a lot of big-scale drama should be to an actor what doing aerobatics is to the fighter pilot, a means of extending the knowledge and operation of his craft. But the good pilot rarely performs his aerobatics in action, even though without doing them he can't get into action at all.

I don't want to make too much of it, but as well as giving Lewis and Sybil their 'take-off' as it were, 'The Greeks' have often caused their followers to be left behind – to the bewilderment of the followers and the disappointment of Lewis and Sybil. And I think this is what happened to some extent at the King's, Hammersmith season. They all had on the whole good notices but the public didn't come in the numbers that these excellent productions deserved.

Lewis had one particular personal blow to suffer when he played President Woodrow Wilson. He loved the part and saw it as a justification for the idealism for which Wilson was never given full credit. He took immense pains with the characterisation, with his make-up and with the skilled playing of the rôle. It was not only a very fine performance by many accounts but also one of those rare occasions when he played the lead with Sybil in the supporting rôle.

After the first night his old friend James Agate came back stage and congratulated him for what he described, with unashamed enthusiasm, as a great and moving performance in a significant play. Agate made no bones about it. This was fine. This was important. Lewis went home immensely cheered by such praise from a critic who was not renowned for giving it without stint. He was therefore terribly depressed next morning to discover that Agate had written a scathing attack on both the play and his own performance. Never one to expect, or want, thoughtless and uninformed eulogies, this attack after such apparently sincere appreciation was like a blow in the face. For a while it completely knocked the stuffing out of him.

At about this time I wrote to him to say that although I'd watched the whole family acting for as long as I could remember, I didn't really

Lewis and Sybil

know what was the essence of it. 'What is acting?' I asked. 'What must I get my teeth into mainly?' He wrote back enclosing a short article, which he said he had used as the basis of a lecture he had given a few months earlier to a group of students:

The basis of acting is an imaginative sympathy with all forms of life; a power to imagine oneself incarnated in another person or living thing, and to live, think and feel *as* that other person or thing, in imagination, or in impersonation, or both.

This imaginative sympathy is closely allied with auto-suggestion and daydreaming, and is present in some degree in every human being. One of the chief values of the Theatre is the widening and deepening of our emotions by cultivating it, and disciplining it, to the highest degree.

In the dramatic artist it must be both inborn, and cultivated, in a high degree. In whatever degree it is present, it can be developed by keen observation of life (either directly, or indirectly by reading) and by the study and practice of acting. And these can be greatly stimulated and guided by expert criticism and teaching, and the results can be judged.

The dramatic artist must have strong vitality and a marked personality of his own, with which to impress others and attract their interest and attention. These attributes cannot be implanted by teaching, but by the study and practice of relaxation, acting, singing, public speaking, etc., and, under expert tuition and criticism, the power of projecting that personality and generously giving it can be developed, and the results assessed.

The art of acting consists in the skilled use of these powers and of the technical means of expressing them so as:

1) To invent a character appropriate to the dramatist's design and to the mood and period of the play.

2) To present that character to an audience on a scale commensurate to the size of the building, so as to create the illusion that the character is an autonomous living being, making manifest to the audience its thoughts and emotions, spoken or unspoken, and compelling the audience to think and feel with it.

3) To co-operate with others in the creation of the emotional tension, atmosphere and shape of the play, subordinating, as far as is necessary, the individual to the whole, and personally seizing and holding the audience's attention whenever the action requires it.

4) To set a standard of clear, lucid speech, and to show forth in rhythm, tone, melody and movement, the beauty of form latent in the written play.

The mastery of all these is greatly assisted by the tuition and criticism of those who have studied and practised the art, and are familiar with its traditions, conventions and difficulties. The technical skill can be judged, and the results assessed.

During the autumn Matthew Forsyth invited Lewis to play Dr Marshall in James Bridie's *The Sleeping Clergyman* and I was able to watch him putting these ideas into practice. The Citizens' Company opened on 9th December, for a season of one week in Perth and Lewis came up and joined us to begin rehearsals for the *Clergyman*. By now I had become Matthew's deputy producer and had already done *Gaslight* as my first solo professional production. Lewis and I had long walks beside the River Tay in between shows and rehearsals and I hung on his every word while he told me about acting and producing. His advice on acting was very much on the lines of his article, but that November he had written another short article for *The Prompter*, the Citizens' Theatre Society's monthly magazine, which he called 'Is the Art of Acting Decaying?' It is really complementary to the earlier one so that together they give a very good summary of Lewis's philosophy of acting:

I am putting forward the thesis that the art of acting is decaying; but first I want to distinguish between the art of acting and the art of the theatre. Acting is an individual personal art. Its essence is the assertion of individuality. The theatre is a co-operative art, to which many individuals contribute. It may be that the art of the theatre is advancing, but the art of acting is decaying, for the theatre tends to depend less and less on the actor, and more and more on externals – the dramatist, the producer, scenery, lighting, music, and finally the microphone, the film and the machine generally. The actor is tending to hide behind all these things and to leave the responsibility to them; while the film-fed audience desires absolute naturalness, even at the expense of effectiveness, beauty and style.

The point I want to make is that the actor is tending to shirk his responsibility and become a personal marionette. He is tending more and more merely to walk on the stage and behave in a way that people do normally, AND THIS IS NOT ACTING. In a little theatre or on the films he more or less gets away with it, though much is lost even there. In a big theatre he doesn't get away with it at all.

All stage speaking, however natural it may *sound*, should be rhetorical, that is, it should be the result of studied skilled *art*, as distinct from nature as opera and ballet. It is not a matter of loudness, but of making the speech significant by tune, phrasing and accent proportional to the size of the theatre. Audiences now have to expend too much effort on hearing and understanding what is said. It is the actor's job to make that easy, so that the audience is free to expend its efforts on understanding and imagining the unsaid things behind the dialogue.

It has become the old vicious circle. The dramatists and public see so little big-scale acting that they no longer expect it or demand it; the actor no longer desires it, for he is in far greater fear of being thought 'ham' than of being thought ineffective. At all costs, and in all crises he must remain an English gentleman with a firm chin and an unsullied crease down his trousers. But I should say that a 'ham' actor is an audible bad actor, which I claim is at least one degree better than the inaudible bad actor.

Merely being an actor is not enough. The actor must imagine and create more vividly, more significantly than life. The modern actor suffers from this fear of overdoing it more than anything else. Actors, producers and audiences are all too frightened of life. The modern actor playing a heroic part often prefers to bring it down to his own level rather than pull himself up to the heroic level.

The good actor's duty is to hold the concentrated attention of the audience and make them feel what he wants them to feel – to stimulate their creative imagination by every device, and by dramatic suspense. To do this, he must imagine and impersonate a character other than himself, and create an illusion of the real presence of that person in a chosen time and place. Finally he must project the thoughts and emotions of the assumed character in such a significant form as to arouse in the audience a recognition of truth and beauty, and sympathetic emotion.

These are all the actor's jobs, and I complain he is letting them slip out of his hands.

He was also getting his first chance of seeing me act professionally as I had the small part of old Eckman in *The Wild Duck* of Ibsen. To my chagrin he didn't think much of it and told me so. 'You're still an amateur, John. You've got a good voice and you know how to use it, but you're not really thinking through the part. It's only a small part so it doesn't really affect the play. But you'll have to do better than this to be a professional.' All of which was very salutary if somewhat depressing at the end of my first year in the theatre. What was not so much depressing as, I fear, irritating was Lewis's depression that I wasn't at once a first-class actor – and, as it turned out, never likely to be one. His great concern for the welfare not only of his close family but for all his relations was very endearing, but his concern at times came near to a kind of despair for the burdens that he felt we had to carry. Where he and I got across each other was in my irritation of having to cope with his depressions about the dangers of my being depressed!

Later on Sybil saw me in *The Wild Duck* and she was very critical too.

In fact this was the first time in my life that I had met Sybil as a critic.
I had become accustomed to her determination and ability to make all
of us out to be better than our wildest dreams and even our intentions,
and so to find her saying, 'This won't do,' was quite a shock. 'Your
speech and your make-up are fine,' she said, 'but you don't move or
walk like an old man. You make us aware of your muscles. Old people
walk with their legs apart as though they had sores. Have a look at some
of them. Keep on looking at them in the street and imagine that you
are them. They can't move quickly and they're always afraid of falling
over.'

At this time Sybil was 65 and Lewis was 72 but when she spoke of
'old people' she was clearly not talking about themselves. By 'old
people' she meant 'really old people, not like Lewis and me.' And of
course she was quite right. When Lewis opened at the Citizens' after
Christmas as Dr Marshall he had to play the first scene as a man of
about 30 and he got away with it by a display of vigour that put the rest
of the cast to shame.

In the last weeks of rehearsal, however, I saw another side of Lewis
at work which did not always endear him to others in his company.
Several times Matthew gave him corrections for his performance and
in every case Lewis put on the 'Look' and fought back with no small
vehemence. His resistance took the form of either arguing in a fierce
and, I'm afraid, scornful voice, or else he so overdid the correction
that it became sarcastically farcical. Poor Matthew! He was one of
Lewis's most devoted fans, but he was also the producer and had to be
in command. As his deputy I was beside him through most of the
rehearsals, and at the back of the stalls one day he said, 'I love your
father, John, but God Almighty, he can be irritating. I think I'll take
him out to lunch and tell him off privately.' And tell him off he did.
Said Matthew to me afterwards, 'I was in fear and trembling about our
lunch because after all he is Lewis Casson. But he completely disarmed
me by saying he knew he'd been very naughty and was very sorry and
oughtn't to try and produce when he was engaged as an actor. And I'll
bet he'll do it again to-morrow.'

On New Year's Day Sybil was in Glasgow as well as Lewis and that
evening we were all having a drink together in our tiny little flat.
Suddenly the phone rang and when I answered it Ann's voice came
through from London. 'Douglas and I have just got engaged,' she said.

'How splendid!' said I. 'Congratulations to you both and . . .' but Sybil had now grabbed the phone and seconds later in a voice that was exactly that of Constance mourning Prince Arthur she cried, 'Oh *Ann*! You're not! Oh dear!' Then Lewis took the phone and said his love and congratulations in the most diplomatic tone I ever heard him use. We calmed Sybil down and got her back on the phone to give her blessing, but somehow she felt compelled to give a very fine performance of her own mother's reaction to her engagement to Lewis. You'd have thought it was the end of the world. By the time we went to bed, however, she was already Douglas's doting mother-in-law. 'After all,' she told us, as though we had been dead against it, 'Douglas is a very good actor, you must remember. You said so yourself, Lewis. And of course he's a socialist and very left. He's a pacifist too *and* a vegetarian. Oh I wonder what Ann will do about that. She can have fish, can't she, because fish doesn't count.'

Douglas Campbell had been a member of the Citizens' company when I joined it and had been one of the first to greet me on my first day with the words, 'Hello, I know Ann.' He was very much my sort of actor, vigorous, gutsy and intensely individualistic. 'He'd be difficult to produce,' I had thought and when, later on, I did, I discovered that I was wrong. At all events he seemed to Patricia and me to be just the fellow for Ann.

Once Sybil accepted the idea she rushed back to London with all sails set and all guns firing. The wedding was five weeks later in Chelsea, and Patricia, Lewis and I all travelled down by night-train from Glasgow. The reception for about thirty people was at Swan Court in the tiny sitting-room, but there was plenty of champagne; we all got much too raucous and by the time the three of us caught the night-train back again to Glasgow we certainly didn't need any sleeping draughts.

After *The Sleeping Clergyman* Lewis played the lead in *The Righteous are Bold*, a strange play set in Ireland about an old priest who has to cast out the devils from a young woman who had somehow contracted them in England. As the priest Lewis had to learn most of the Catholic exorcism in Latin and I must say that if I had been a devil Lewis's rendering of it would certainly have cast me out. I had to play the part myself in a revival the following year and found them such marvellous words to speak that I still remember them. I also remember very well using the whole speech with most gratifying results in reply to a taxi driver who had sworn at me!

During the run of the *Righteous* the company were rehearsing a play about James VI of Scotland called *Jamie the Saxt*. It was a vigorous and exciting drama by Robert McLelland who had written it in Lallans Scots – a language almost incomprehensible to the Sassenachs – and that wonderful actor Duncan Macrae was playing Jamie. I was playing Sir Robert Bowes, Queen Elizabeth's ambassador to the court at Holyrood. It was a small but lovely part and the only one written in English. Sir Robert was a disdainful man who regarded the Scots as a collection of barbarians, and I had that enjoyable experience of having a three-minute real scene-stealer at the end of the second act. Furthermore, I felt it was a complete sinecure of a part, an absolute snip in fact.

Lewis was staying with us in Glasgow and one morning I asked him if he would run me through my scene, which was only three pages of dialogue. I am ashamed to say that I made the request more to please him than to benefit myself, because after all I was pretty good at it, I thought. Lewis agreed to work on it with a smiling gentleness that belied what was to come. We began work at nine o'clock and by eleven we had only reached the bottom of the first page. By lunch-time we still hadn't finished. I was at my last gasp and Lewis was just getting his second wind. I don't think I've ever spent such an exhausting or such a rewarding morning. Not only did he not pass a single sentence, he didn't pass a single word. When he asked me to begin I drew a deep breath and he at once said, 'Hold it! Your breath's all wrong,' and we spent ten minutes on that. Then I managed to get out a couple of words and he stopped me again to inquire what I was thinking. My thoughts were wrong, of course, and had to be put right. I began again but though the thoughts were right, the inflection was wrong, then the inflection was not marked enough and then I got the line itself wrong and we began all over again. Half-way down the page he said, 'What on earth are you doing with your hands? Try doing the first page without saying any words and only using your hands.' This exercise was like trying to communicate to a deaf mute with one's head in a bag, but it got my hands moving and 'talking' in a way they never had before.

When over lunch Lewis said, 'Well we've made a start, and it's a little better. We must find time to do some real work on it later on,' I could cheerfully have clobbered him.

I don't know if his method of never being satisfied with anybody's performance was intentional, but I do know that it got results if one was not flattened and made to feel suicidal by it. In fact this desire to clobber him quite often did the trick by making one double one's efforts if only to win the battle. Soon after I joined the Citizens' Theatre Douglas Campbell told me that Lewis had once rehearsed him in the part of Orestes in a room the size of a lavatory. The more Douglas 'pulled the stops out' the more Lewis groaned. 'There was Lewis,' said Douglas, 'with his face only a couple of feet from mine, muttering away that I was no good and ought to give up acting. He had me there for a whole hour and never said anything but "Oh my *God*! No! Do it again!" During my lunch I worked myself into a fury and said to myself, "I'll murder him when I go back." And when I did go back I yelled and ranted my words like a lunatic. All he said when I'd finished was "Why the hell didn't you do it like that this morning?"'

At about the time of the *Righteous* Sybil was in a play of Clemence Dane's, *Call Home the Heart*, which had been written in one of the author's rare lapses into sentimental whimsy. None of us liked it very much except, of course, Sybil, who, as ever, was able to turn a not very exciting part into part of herself, and so gave it her own inimitable lustre. But it was during the run of it that J. B. Priestley sent her the script of *The Linden Tree* to read and she was absolutely delighted with it. The part of Professor Linden was so exactly Lewis that she couldn't wait to tell Jack Priestley so. And when Lewis read it he thought so too. Her part of Mrs Linden was not so exciting but they were both so anxious to do the play that Sybil was quite happy to let Lewis have the lead. Once again, however, Sybil brought the whole of herself to a small part and made it a memorable one. I have seen several productions of *The Linden Tree* since then, amateur and professional, and the Mrs Lindens have been entirely unnoticeable.

As Professor Linden Lewis focused all his experience as an actor that he had been accumulating in his nearly fifty years on the stage. When the play opened in August 1947 at the Duchess Theatre I remember so many people, including critics, saying, 'How good to see this straightforward natural acting by Sir Lewis.' But I had the pleasure of hearing him through his words in the Swan Court flat, and I know that if anyone had spoken like that in real life one would have sent for the police! He spoke his words on the largest scale with the skill of a rhetorician and made them seem natural to the audience by his skill as an actor. I was not at the opening myself because that autumn I had just taken on the job of Director of Productions at the Citizens' and had my hands pretty full. But I had to spend a few days in London to hold some auditions just before Christmas and was given one of the house-seats in a packed theatre. It was a most beautiful production by Michael MacOwan and, as is Priestley's wont, it completely captured the mood of the moment, the mood of post-war England. As Micky MacOwan said himself, it is a play that expresses both hope and sadness – hope for the future and sadness for the passing of the past. The whole message was instilled into a speech of Professor Linden at the end of the play when he talks about the meaning of the Elgar Concerto as 'a kind of long farewell' to the world of gentle civilised living before 1914. Professor Linden makes us feel the nostalgia and then suddenly hurls us into the future by saying, '. . . what happens? Why a little miracle. You heard it. . . . Young Dinah Linden, all youth, all eagerness, saying hello and not farewell to anything, who knows and cares nothing about Bavaria in the nineties or the secure and golden Edwardian afternoons, here in Burmanley, this very afternoon, the moment we stop shouting at each other, unseals for us the precious distillation, uncovers the tenderness and regret, which are ours now as well as his, and our lives and Elgar's, Burmanley to-day and the Malvern Hills in a lost sunlight, are all magically intertwined. . . .'

This is what, it seems to me, is so exactly what Lewis and Sybil have spent the latter part of their lives doing – using the best of what is past and instilling it into the present for use in the future. They know how to use sentiment without falling into the mush of sentimentality. In *The Linden Tree* Lewis could say all those things that he had wanted to say that night at the Savoy. Moreover he could say them with his deep and gentle sincerity, which was almost more effective than the fierce fire of his evangelism. And Sybil kept her own fires banked and dampened so that she could be the loving wife helping her husband to do something that they both believed in.

That was how it turned out, but I gathered from Micky MacOwan that the path to its success was at times a fairly thorny one. Lewis wanted not only his own way with his own part, but with all the other parts as well, and they had quite a few fights. Sybil has always needed a strong producer to prevent her energy from exploding into charades.

She has nearly always had Lewis to do this for her and it worked mostly because in the end she nearly always did what he said. This time she had a smaller part, with Micky to keep her on the rails and to use her as an ally in the much more difficult job of keeping Lewis on the rails. Thank God he did, because the result was the best performance of Lewis's life, and incidentally it saved me a lot of trouble later on in Glasgow.

The play ran for a year at the Duchess Theatre, and when it was finished I persuaded them to come to Glasgow to play their parts all over again in a new production with my company at the Citizens'. This meant that they had to go right through the whole business of re-hearsals again, but even that didn't mean there were no fights. Lewis simply couldn't resist producing all the other members of the cast and I'm afraid didn't feel that he had to be so tactful about it, knowing that his son was the actual producer. He did, in fact, try to ride rough-shod over me once or twice. One afternoon I was rehearsing Sybil and another actor in a rather quiet scene when I heard a rumbling voice from the wings, which I recognised as Lewis, telling a young actress how to speak her lines. I called out, 'Quiet please!' The rumbling continued unabated. So I called again, this time in a quarterdeck voice. 'Can I have quiet, please?' I might as well have tried to stop an ar-moured division for all the good it did. Then I shouted, 'Lewis! Will you for Christ's sake shut *up*?' And silence fell on the stage. I waited for the explosion, but he suddenly became as meek as a lamb with a muttered 'sorry'. Sybil was delighted, of course. 'About time too,' she whispered to me, 'he gets very naughty at times.'

Later that evening in our flat I gave him a whisky and soda and said, 'Look, Pop. You've forgotten more of all this than I shall ever learn, and I want to learn all I can while you're here. But I have to run this company for the whole year, and I've got to be the boss in the theatre. In fact you're my employee at the moment. When we are home here I'll be your son and you can tell me anything you like.' He grumbled a bit at that – something about 'Why don't *you* tell them then? They've got to learn.' But before long we had worked it all out and from then on all was well.

Sybil was sheer delight to direct, because she would try anything I suggested and always seemed grateful for it. She has never had the slightest concern about her own dignity and therefore has never been known to stand on it. She doesn't mind running the risk of looking foolish because she simply can't believe that looking foolish matters as long as it's all part of finding new ways of doing things. She would take an idea of mine, try it out and then add her own ideas, finally transforming it all into something much more exciting. No other actor that I ever directed made me feel less of a director and more of a catalyst. I never had to do more than start her off, and then keep what was started under some sort of control. At the same time I noticed that she kept finding time to say encouraging things to each member of the cast, so that they all felt individually that they were doing something very special in this play.

Lewis went his own way, and wanted the rest of the cast to follow it. If I wanted to change any of it I knew I was in for a scrap. That is why I blessed the name of MacOwan for having held Lewis on a rein until the performance was soundly and beautifully set, so that I was able to avoid an awful lot of argument in the reproduction.

We had a very successful three weeks run and then I took them and the company off to Ayr for a week. Just before Christmas each year we used to take part of the Citizens' company for a six-weeks' weekly-rep at the Gaiety Theatre, Ayr. It was run as a very successful music-hall for the entire year, but our six-week season gave them time to breathe before their pantomime season, and it gave us a chance to expand our audiences. I had wondered whether Lewis and Sybil would be prepared to play in this small town, which although very pleasant was a bit off the main theatrical track. I needn't and shouldn't have worried. They wouldn't have missed the extra week for worlds and we had a fine time breathing the sea air and wandering around the Burns country whenever we could spare the time.

Each afternoon, however, Lewis and I worked. The production after our Christmas play was to be *Macbeth* and I wasn't going to miss the chance of picking Lewis's brains. He and I sat in their hotel bedroom and read through the play together. Or to be correct, I read through it and he told me what was wrong. If he himself had read it I know I would have enjoyed listening but would not have known why it was good. With me doing the speaking he could do the producing and so had to give me reasons for doing it. The script we used was the very same pocket edition that Henry Ainley had used in the 1926 production, and Lewis had marked the phrasing and the inflections of every speech.

He began by saying, 'Keep the idea of a St Andrew's cross in your mind. Macbeth begins without being over-ambitious at the lower end of the diagonal. Lady Macbeth is the driving power and she is at the top of the other diagonal. As the play progresses her power decreases and his moves up. They pass somewhere just before the Banquet Scene when she suddenly realises she has lost her "command". She goes on downwards till her soul disintegrates in the sleep-walking scene, and he rises to heroic tragic stature when he goes out to face his destiny in the fight with Macduff.'

The odd thing was that during these sessions he had none of his usual fierce impatience that was always in evidence at rehearsals. I think that as I was going to be producing it rather than playing it he didn't have any feeling of urgency about it, nor of worry that the performance was going to be bad. He was helping me to help other actors and we could look at the problems calmly and enjoyably together rather in the manner of a university tutor and a favourite student for whom he had high hopes.

At one point I was reading Lady Macbeth's lines and thought I was giving a quite passable imitation of Sybil's performance. Half-way through the speech he stopped me with the words, 'No, no, no. She's not like that at all.'

'Didn't you agree with Mama's way of doing it then?' I asked in my own defence.

'Good heavens, no!' he shot out. 'She was very good, of course, but we had quite a tussle about how she saw it. And she got her own way for once!'

A month or two later we opened with Duncan Macrae as Macbeth, Margaretta Scott as Lady Macbeth and Douglas as Macduff. At the last performance of the previous show Duncan broke a bone in his ankle. He gallantly played the dress rehearsal and the first three performances and then just had to stop. In a repertory you usually can't afford under-studies and so there was nothing for it but to play it myself. As the producer, I knew the words and so I got Douglas to produce me all through a week-end. He was one of Lewis's disciples and so the two of us saw eye to eye about it. Both of us were also keen fencers and so enjoyed ourselves enormously in the fight. He and Peggy Scott got me through the first performance, with Patricia in the wings to keep me calm. That evening we telephoned Sybil and Lewis at Swan Court and told them all about it. 'Splendid,' said Lewis, 'I told you it would play itself if only you let it.' And ever since I have been wondering just what he meant!

They had either just opened or were about to open in Margery Sharp's play *The Foolish Gentlewoman*. *The Linden Tree* was the first of many plays that they were now going to do together as actors and employees. *The Foolish Gentlewoman* followed it and was the first of a series of successes for them under the management of Binkie Beaumont of H. M. Tennent. It was the beginning of a most happy association. In the middle of the thirties Tennents had asked Lewis to do a rescue job on a production of a play in which Douglas Fairbanks Junior and Gertrude Lawrence were the stars. The try-out tour was not going well and they asked Lewis to see it and re-produce it. He saw the play and told Tennents, 'I think it's a thoroughly bad play and if you bring it to London it'll be a ghastly flop, even with Fairbanks and Gertie Lawrence. There's a lot I could do to it but I don't think it's worth it. And I'll bet if I do re-direct it I shall make myself so unpopular with you and the cast that you'll never again ask me to produce a play for you.'

But they persuaded him against his will, and with many reassurances, to take it on. The play did flop and Lewis persuaded Clemence Dane to write another one for them. She wrote *Moonlight is Silver* in just under a couple of weeks and Lewis produced it. This, too, was a flop and Tennents never again asked Lewis to produce a play for them.

Frankly, however, I can't believe that this would be Binkie's view of the situation. He has always been much too shrewd a man of the theatre to let one, or even two, flops stand in the way of his using a good producer. But I do think that Lewis demonstrated in these two productions that he was not altogether the most suitable man to direct plays in the way that he himself called 'the wishy-washy naturalism of the West End'. In order to stay in business commercial managements have to be something more (or perhaps the word should be 'less') than promoters of artistic explorations, and Lewis was always unequivocally an explorer. As happens with most explorers, however, Lewis's explorations were not always to his own personal advantage.

Sybil, on the other hand, by the end of the thirties had already begun to come to terms with the London commercial theatre. Paradoxically she has been able to do it without having recourse to compromise by the simple expedient of turning every part she plays into a kind of crusade for herself. She learns something from everything and so is able to turn even utter triviality or foolishness into memorable flashes of insight for her audiences. When the Second World War came she had grown out of the need to spend her life finding one Joan after another. She had begun to realise that you don't really have to go on repeating artistic peak experiences in order to be able to use them to illuminate the lower and less vertiginous foothills. Miss Moffat in *The Corn is Green* was the first sign of it. She began by trying to turn Miss Moffat into Joan. She ended by making us see Miss Moffat as a remarkable woman.

This, I am certain, is what Binkie suddenly saw, with what I can only call managerial genius, and he set the stage for a whole series of his and her successes. Furthermore, he knew that if he had Lewis in the cast as well he would have access to his knowledge and skill and at the same time be assured that Sybil would be kept under control, but never under restraint. She had always been an actress of astonishing power and invention, but there had also been a kind of 'hockey-girl heartiness' in her, which Lewis had had to contain. Without losing any of her power and originality she now seemed to get rid of the 'hockey-girl' to take on a kind of warm-hearted twinkling dignity. She moved with a new and confident gracefulness, and her presence on a stage had the sparkle, warmth and welcome of a family room on Christmas morning.

When they followed *The Foolish Gentlewoman* with *Treasure Hunt*, her performance of the dotty Aunt Anna Rose made one feel sorry for anyone who was silly enough to be sane, and to wish that more of us had an Aunt Anna Rose in our family. But of course we Cassons always have had Sybil's Aunt Anna Rose in our family. Now she let other people see it and they fairly gobbled it up.

They were rehearsing it very hard towards the end of the summer when Patricia and I took Mary with us for a week's holiday in Brittany. While we were away we parked our respective children with some friends of ours. In London it so happened that Sybil had gathered the Campbells, Ann, Douglas and their two very small children, to her bosom, or to be accurate into the one small spare room at Swan Court. It must have been like a mad-house with them all rehearsing parts within earshot of each other to the accompaniment of the howling of babies.

On one day Lewis was found sitting on the edge of the bath saying his lines because there was nowhere else for him to be in private.

With all this going on Lewis had a letter from a wealthy laundry-owner in Portmadoc making him an offer for Bron y Garth, which was so low as to be laughable. But when we returned from Brittany we found to our horror that Lewis, without even the mildest piece of haggling, had accepted the offer as it stood. No one, I am sure, could have been more surprised than Sam Beer, the laundry-owner, who probably made a low offer as a start to the negotiations. And so he got a bargain and the family lost Bron y Garth. The fact that we were going to France for holidays, that our children were on holiday in the south-west and that the Campbells were at Swan Court, made Lewis suddenly get fed up with the whole outfit. 'What the hell's the good of spending all this money on Bron y Garth when none of the family go there? I'll sell the damn place.' Once more he took one of his very over-quick actions and went ahead regardless. We only just prevented his selling the place lock, stock and barrel, but he listened to Patricia just in time and gave her the job of dealing with the contents. And so, although most of the effects were sold, she managed to save a lot of family heirlooms and pieces of furniture. She took charge of the sale that autumn and was able to hand Lewis a sizeable cheque at the end of it.

Early in the New Year Lewis bought Cedar Cottage, a charming little seventeenth century farmhouse near Wrotham in Kent, which he intended to be a substitute 'family home' in place of Bron y Garth. He paid quite a high price for it and spent a good deal more in renovating it. Ten years later he sold it, and once again he accepted the first and absurdly low offer that was made. 'When in doubt, take action – fast!' was as ever his motto when monetary decisions had to be made. He saw himself as a shrewd and decisive man of affairs who knew the ins and outs of financial transactions. Or rather he hoped other people would see him as a shrewd and decisive man of affairs and so tried to live up 'to what he hoped other people thought he was.' In the theatre and in almost every other area where he had to deal with people, he was indeed shrewd and decisive. But in his heart he hated everything to do with money. It made him feel unsure of himself and he was always worried by it. When he had to cope with it he made rapid and un-considered decisions just to demonstrate decisiveness and to get the whole horrid business out of his hair as quickly as possible. Furthermore, he didn't approve of what he took to be the profit-motivated business philosophy, and yet he was also aware that to be businesslike was to be efficient and competent in a way that he was not, and wished he was. Where people or really 'good works' needed help and encouragement he was generous to a most lovable and occasionally infuriating fault, but he then had to justify it by grossly overplaying, sometimes to the point of burlesque, the rôle of the eagle-eyed, confident, quick-acting and largely imaginary 'business executive'.

When Patricia had at last tidied up everything at Bron y Garth her last act was to donate most of the large number of books to the Portmadoc Town Council on condition they would use them as a nucleus from which to start a public library. She was a little fearful of Lewis's possible reaction until she got this letter from him:

15th Feb. 1950

My dear Patricia,

Your idea for the books was an inspiration, and we're both delighted with the Council's acceptance. Anyway why should you have been afraid of my wrath? I really meant it literally when I put the whole thing in your hands and said that your decisions should be final. I shall never be grateful enough for all you have done and are doing. Judging by the worry and depression I got in dealing with the infinitely easier decisions and work at Cedar Cottage, dealing with Bron y Garth would have killed me off! So I owe you what remains of my life!

Love,
Lewis

All these goings-on made the rehearsals and run of *Treasure Hunt* an emotionally turbulent time for the family. It ran for nearly a year and then they came to Glasgow again to play with my Citizens' company at the 1950 Edinburgh Festival. We were the main 'Drama' that year and Tyrone Guthrie came as guest producer. We did three plays, the première of Bridie's *The Queen's Comedy*, which Tony Guthrie and I directed together, the première of Eric Linklater's *The Atom Doctor* (later called *The Mortimer Touch*), which Tony directed, and the old classic Scottish melodrama by John Home, *Douglas*, which I directed and for which we engaged Lewis and Sybil. The play is some two hundred years old and is the story of Lady Randolph, who recognises in a shepherd boy her long-lost son, only to lose him again in a classically tragic manner. It is not a great play, but the year before my boss, James

Bridie, had come to me at the theatre and said, 'John, let's do *Douglas* at next year's Festival. It's not very good writing but it's marvellous acting stuff for large-scale actors. See if you can persuade Sybil and Lewis to play it for us, and you produce it.'

It had been first produced in Edinburgh in the middle of the eighteenth century and when the curtain fell an ardent Scottish patriot had called from the gallery, 'Whaur's your Wullie Shakespeare noo?' But when I first read the script I'm afraid I was not quite so enthusiastic. I sent it off to Lewis, however, and a few days later he wrote back to say that he thought they could do something with it. 'It's a bit hammy,' he said, 'but I don't think that matters. There's some splendid stuff for acting. I'm making a few amendments to the script and then I'll send it back.' Mrs Siddons played Lady Randolph at Drury Lane in 1815 and we (Lewis, Sybil and I) decided we would do it in the convention of Mrs Siddons' day when all plays were done in a very flamboyant form of their own modern dress. And so we had vivid tartans and plaids at their eighteenth century best, and for scenery we used back-drops and wings painted strongly and realistically, which gave them all lots of room for huge sweeping dramatic movement. 'Enlarged twopence coloured' would have described it.

Ann and Douglas had been in my company for the year leading up to the Festival, and Douglas stayed on to play the heroic Young ('Upon the Grampian Hills my father feeds his flocks') Norval, the long-lost son. Laurence Hardy was the villainous Glenalvon and the supporting cast were well-tried professional repertory actors, among whom was Stanley Baxter. We rehearsed in Glasgow and an explosive time was had by all. Lewis, however, seemed to have learnt the lesson of *The Linden Tree* and this time was a tower of strength.

When we went to Edinburgh we discovered that everyone was expecting us to guy it in the manner of a kind of classical *East Lynne*, and it was a great thrill to confound them all. In his book about Sybil, J. C. Trewin wrote of her performance:

. . . many of us had thought of John Home's tragedy of *Douglas* – if we had thought of it at all – as a forgotten rattle-trap. . . . So we said, comfortable, mocking wiseacres, as we sat in the Lyceum Theatre at Edinburgh. Presently, after the prologue that Burns had written for a Mr Sutherland's benefit night at Dumfries, the curtain rose upon 'the court of a castle surrounded by woods' and upon the figure of Lady Randolph in melancholy meditation.

Dame Sybil Thorndike stood there, contriving in poised, sculptural dignity to suggest that she had been framed in the heroic mould. Without stirring she swept us off on a vocal tide of emotion as a quick-running but quietly pouring flood fills a sandy bay upon a night of autumn. Dame Sybil did not flick at the verse. As we listened to the searching utterance that pursues every word, lets no vowel escape it, slurs nothing, flashes up the sense, we heard indeed what Lady Randolph calls, 'the voice of sorrow from my bursting heart.' We are told often of the grand manner. Here it was, without excessive striving, forced passion. Dame Sybil, speaking and acting as if *Douglas* were new, governed the stage in attitudes beside which a picture of Siddons waned to a hardboard cut-out. Genuine tragedy ennobled Home's melodramatic anecdote; tinsel shone like gold.

Lewis and Sybil had hoped that some high-minded theatrical promoter would see this Edinburgh production and be prepared to risk taking it to London, and of course I had hoped so too. But I am also bound to say that if I had invested my life's savings with a theatrical promoter I don't think I would have been too happy if he had decided to promote *Douglas*. It was great stuff, it did us all a lot of good and I am sure made all the actors better able to act whatever plays they might later be engaged upon. At the Festival, as was to be expected, we played to packed houses. But when we later took all three of our Festival productions for a week each in Glasgow, it was *The Queen's Comedy* and *The Atom Doctor* that the public preferred. High Tragedy in the grand manner is no longer, it seems, the popular fare that it used to be even as late as the early twenties. We were all immensely glad to have been able to do it, and the perspicacious theatre-goers enjoyed, even if a little nostalgically, being swept away in a torrent of emotional drama. But in 1950 the theatre-going public had already moved away from this sort of theatre. As Lewis said to me just before they left Glasgow to return to London, 'People nowadays don't want the theatre for large-scale feeling and imagination. They'd rather go to the ballet and opera for it. They know that it's unreal and so aren't afraid of it. We see straight acting realistically on film and television and so people expect, and actors are trained to give, plain naturalistic realism on the stage. The trouble is actors aren't trained to act any more and the naturalistic realism is too damned plain. In fact it's bloody dull.'

What appears to have been lost in the move to naturalism in acting, Lewis maintained, was not only the ability to project a performance to an audience, but the ability even to be heard at all in any building bigger than a village hall. When he and Sybil had been with us in Glasgow, I think during *The Linden Tree* rather than *Douglas*, Michael MacOwan's production of Priestley's *Summer Madness* appeared on its pre-London tour. Lewis, Sybil, Patricia and I had all gone to see a matinée. The next day Lewis, mainly because he felt he had to help, but partly I can't help feeling to get a little of his own back after *The Linden Tree*, wrote this letter to Michael MacOwan:

21st October, 1948

My Dear Michael,

I didn't have a chance of talking much to you yesterday so may I write instead? The play is so good and so important, and you have done such fine work on it that I am most anxious to help if I can.

I do feel that the whole play suffers from the fact that all the men, including Leslie [Banks] are still in the stage (which is permanent with many actors) where they are more interested in *being* the people and interpreting to themselves their characters, than in projecting, on a scale proportionate to the building, the thought and emotion the dramatist has devised for them. Surely this is only the *rehearsal* stage of acting. The whole business of naturalism is only a means to an end. The play is packed with thought, but it is all presented, quite beautifully, much more in the 'Take it or leave it' style than in the 'Have you got that?' style. I know Priestley likes it so, though he takes jolly good care not to use it in his public speaking; but it will wreck the play if it is used at the Cambridge. It will be no use then just telling the actors to 'speak up'. All actors know that in the cheapest farce the most venerable mother-in-law joke must be not only heard, but planted, if it is to get the laugh that shows it has achieved significance, though the skilled actor may completely disguise the fact. It is just as absolutely necessary to achieve significance in projecting every emotion of philosophic and political thought, though it is now considered ham even to attempt it. In the old melodramatic school effectiveness and significance may have counted too much and naturalism too little, but actors still in touch with the old tradition like Hodges, Calvert, Beveridge and James Welch had no difficulty in combining both to perfection even in the largest theatres. But two wars seem to have completely broken the old tradition; leaving the actor happily indifferent to the real and conscious *holding* of the attention of the audience, so long as he is 'in the part'.

I know I am in danger of becoming a crank on this question but I am convinced that if really serious plays are to be effective in theatres like the Royal and the Cambridge, actors will have to be taught all over again to analyse quite consciously the naturalistic speech their imagination suggests as appropriate, and reconstruct it artificially (i.e. with art) into a rhythmical musical pattern, enlarging the phrasing, resonance, emphasis, volume, tune and range of pitch and *silences* of every speech sufficiently to make it significant in the particular building; and be free enough to vary any one of these items to hold every individual audience. And all this while giving the illusion of naturalism. *This is the actor's job* (not even the producer's if the actors know theirs) and few dramatists now know anything whatever about it though they may see play after play collapse for lack of it. The audience must, *without effort*, hear and appreciate significance; so that the actor can stimulate them to use their energies and faculties in imaginative and creative effort of their own.

Yours ever,
Lewis

The year after *Douglas* he wrote on similar lines to Hugh Hunt, the Director of the Old Vic, before the production of *Romeo and Juliet* in the Assembly Halls, Edinburgh, for the 1951 Festival:

6th August, 1951

My Dear Hugh,

I am writing this at the risk of appearing an interfering busybody. I do not know how much experience you have of producing for a large difficult building like the Assembly Hall. I have found that audibility in such buildings depends (in *increasing* order of importance) on:

1. Volume
2. Clearly differentiated vowels
3. Resonance in low-volume speaking
4. Wide range of pitch in intonation
5. *Phrasing.*

1, 2 and 3, even 4, are now reasonably attended to by good actors, but I know hardly any who know enough about 5, even to realise the necessity of consciously working it out when studying a part.

Ideas are conveyed in the form of *phrases* rather than words (though a phrase may consist of a single word) and each phrase should be wrapped up in a separate parcel, cut off from the next by a silence (definite even if microscopic) long enough for the idea to be absorbed, before passing on to the next. The better the phrasing the higher can be the speed, and the lesser the volume, of the speech. The length of the phrasing pause should depend on:

1. The importance of the preceding phrase
2. The difficulty of grasping its idea or seeing its picture
3. The general speed and volume of the whole speech
4. The position of the key word of the phrase (the later, the longer the pause)
5. The size, echo and resonance of the building.

Such positive conscious phrasing affects only the sense and syntax, and once learnt allows of any emotional content in tone, rhythm or tune.

The chief trouble is that few actors can make a definite stop without letting down tension either by drooping the final word or by taking a breath. Personally I have found it saves time to devote the whole of the first rehearsal to settling the phrasing and marking it in the actors' books, so that the part is learnt in phrases. If it is not, it will have to be corrected later, or inaudibility cured by loudness or slowness.

'Now/ / / ere the Sun/ / advance/ his burning eye.'
I always actually write out my part in phrases set vertically,

'*Now*
Ere the *Sun*
Advance/ his burning eye
The world/ to *cheer*
And night's dark *dew*
To *dry*'

Some day I'll write you a similar treatise on melody. I'll spare you now!

Yours,

Lewis Casson

P.S. I'll bet whoever plays the Prologue, if left to himself, will puzzle the audience with the strange words, 'botha likin dignity'!

As it transpired the production of *Douglas* was to be the last time that either of them would have the chance of acting rhetorical, poetic drama. Nevertheless when they went back to London they were full of plans for a production in which Sybil would play a part which she has always longed for as much as Joan – Queen Elizabeth I. The play was Clemence Dane's *The Lion and the Unicorn* and it is one of the best plays she ever wrote. Lewis and Sybil had been wanting to do it for years but had been quite unable to find a sponsor. However, the great Charles B. Cochran had been to see *Douglas* during its Glasgow run and although not quite enthusiastic enough about the play, had suddenly renewed his old enthusiasm for Sybil. Had they got a play, he wondered. Indeed they had, *The Lion and the Unicorn*. And when C.B. read it he said he would be delighted to put it on. It was to be his final spectacular swan song and they would do it early in the New Year, 1951.

In high spirits Lewis and Sybil got down to plans with Clemence Dane, who as usual turned out to be as totally intractable as she always was about even the change of a preposition in her play. She was a superb writer, but her sense of theatre was occasionally swamped by her absolute conviction that her writing was always dramatically unimpeachable. Like many others before her, she confused a long experience of play-writing, working in the theatre and watching plays with knowledge of the art of acting as professional actors know it. She could not bring herself to see that Lewis and Sybil knew more about what was dramatically effective on the stage than she did. And they argued for weeks about acting and production technicalities. The result was that they were not ready to go to Cochran with completed plans until the middle of January. After discussing it all with him they went off to St Jean de Luz on a long-delayed and much-needed holiday, so as to be fit and fresh for yet another great task when they returned in February.

But while they were away disaster struck. A worn-out washer on a bath-tap caused Charles Cochran to be so badly scalded that he died in hospital a few days later. They were heart-broken that their old friend, who had given Sybil her first part in the West End, should have died in so horrible an accident. And of course it meant the end of their plans for *The Lion and the Unicorn*.

At almost exactly the same time as they were writing to me about this, our beloved Osborne Mavor, James Bridie, chairman of the Citizens', had a brain haemorrhage and died in hospital in Edinburgh. He was 63. During my five years in Glasgow he had become not merely my boss, but my guide, my mentor and my friend. And so while Lewis and Sybil were writing to us about the tragedy of Cochran's death, I was writing to them about the tragedy to me of Bridie's. In fact I had a letter from Lewis written at St Jean de Luz saying, 'Your heartbroken letter about Bridie reached us almost at the same moment as we heard about Cochran.' And indeed heartbroken I was. From the moment I first met him before I left the navy, Bridie and I somehow struck chords in each other, though it was more a father and son relationship than one of equals. To this day I find myself mentally referring to his judgement whenever I have to face a problem of human relationships. He had been a consulting physician of some eminence in Scotland until he decided to be a playwright instead, and during the war he had done a great deal of work with mental patients. Thus it was that although I had learnt from Lewis whatever I knew about moral principles, duty, integrity, responsibility, singleness of purpose; and from Sybil about unrestrained generosity, enjoyment of the company of people, warmth of personality, star quality; and from them both enthusiasm for living, tolerance, courtesy, laughter; it was from Bridie that I learnt to regard people not as 'them' but 'us'. To him this was not a matter of morality but of plain common sense. He used to say, 'I'm not a playwright. I'm a writer of librettos for stage performances. I'm not saying that this or that is the answer, but rather "Have you ever looked at people like this? I don't know the answers. But by looking at people together we may find out a bit more about all of us." ' He taught me to believe that you can't ever change people. You can only learn to live with them, and so help them to see things differently and to change themselves – 'if you're worthy of it' as he said.

These are the things we don't really learn from our parents. We're too close to them and they are bound to have dominated us at some time or another. Only when Lewis was a very old man did I realise that in an odd way he had been disturbed by my having taken Bridie for my mentor. There was no parental jealousy about it because Lewis wasn't like that, but it made him feel depressed that I was looking to someone else as an authority on some things instead of to him. It never made any sort of barrier between us, but I know he was wistful about it, not to say sad, at times. If I had been a little wiser perhaps I could have shown him in good time that it was nothing against him if I found someone to advise me who, sometimes in some areas, was wiser than he. If only all of us who are parents could think of ourselves as privileged guardians of our children for fifteen or so years and not as 'owners', a lot of our parental/filial relationships would be a great deal easier.

Be this as it may, however, Lewis and Sybil lost the chance of playing in *The Lion and the Unicorn*. The project was to come up again later, but again they were to be disappointed. And so we never saw Sybil as Gloriana, nor Lewis as her faithful counsellor, Lord Burleigh. Later on they were to do extracts from the play in recitals, which only made anyone who heard them regret that they had not done the whole play. This was one of Sybil's bitterest disappointments for she had set her heart on Elizabeth, while Lewis had been looking forward to staging one more big production. They came back to London from their holiday as two very sad people. And I'm afraid that a week or two later I came down to London about something which made them sadder still.

At the beginning of January I had received a letter from the firm of J. C. Williamson Theatres, who at that time owned and ran nearly all the theatres of Australia and New Zealand. They offered me a two-year contract to be their resident producer in Australia at just on three times my salary at the Citizens'. Of course I took the letter to Bridie, and he said, 'Oh John, don't be such a bloody fool. You don't want to go to Australia!' 'No,' I answered, 'but I can't see how the Citizens' is going to be able to pay me more than £20 a week in the foreseeable future and my family is getting to an expensive age.' The upshot of this was that he persuaded me to stay another year with the promise of being the producer for his next London production. Then at the end of January he died, and a few weeks later I accepted the Australian offer.

Lewis and Sybil took the news very phlegmatically as I would have expected. I had given them no warning that anything was in the air because before it was settled we didn't want a lot of wildly speculative family 'PLANS'. But of course it did mean that Patricia and I with the children would be away for at least two years. Lewis and Sybil were then 76 and 69 respectively, which for most people would have been an age at which trips to Australia by relations would have been viewed with great alarm. But the danger of our not seeing them again wasn't mentioned at all and I doubt if they gave it more than a whisker of a thought. We are, however, a very 'family' family and while being glad that adventure, promotion and indeed more money were all in the offing (and Lewis was particularly pleased about the latter!) they were sad about our going off.

I was to leave London in July of 1951, and Patricia would follow with the children in November when I had found somewhere in Melbourne for us to live. In the meantime there was lots to be done and lots being done.

During February of this year, Sybil had been sent a play by Binkie Beaumont in which Edith Evans was to play the lead. The part he had in mind for Sybil was a much smaller one, but he wanted her to be in it to give some weight to the rest of the cast. We all read the play and all, including Lewis, were against her playing the part. 'It's nothing!' we all said. 'Edith will be able to swamp you. Don't do it!' And Sybil put on her kind of ham-Mona Lisa look, as she always does when she is about to do the opposite of what everyone is advising her, and said, 'I think I can do something rather interesting with it. It's rather a good part and she has to play Schumann, which will be fun. I think I'll do it.' And do it she did in the play *Waters of the Moon* by N. C. Hunter.

There may have been a few fireworks years before when Sybil was in

As the Spirit of Industry in a morally improving Industrial Pageant

Lewis about the age of 70

the same play as Marie Tempest, but we all expected there to be a veritable Vauxhall Gardens' Grand Spectacular when she and Edith played together. Sybil has always been an apparently guileless and innocent-looking scene-stealer whatever the size of her part. After all the ability to be the one person in a crowd that everybody notices at the expense of all the others is the main part of what we call star-quality. And when you have two people who both in their different ways have this quality on a stage together, something has to give.

Edith had the leading part of an extravagantly flamboyant lady that suited her skills and personality not only like a pair of gloves but like her own skin inside them. Sybil had the part of a faded, bitter widow whose life was over, and she faded into the background rather like a trombone in a string quartet. I know of no one who can steal a scene so quickly and effectively by doing nothing with panache. When she knitted quietly on the sofa you had to watch her because knitting suddenly became to you the most important thing in the world; when she played Schumann in the background, Wendy Hiller's speech grew into poetry and I'm afraid you remembered the Schumann; and when anyone was doing anything Sybil had only to blow her nose for everyone else to become the background to it. I've had experience of this myself not so long ago. When Lewis's sight grew too bad to read, and again after his death, I have partnered Sybil in several poetry recitals. During the time I was reading she sat as still as a statue, but it was such a beautiful statue of a mother enraptured by her son that I am sure no one paid any attention to the son. In my case it obviously didn't matter because anyway the audience had come to see her and not me. But when the 'partner' (and in this play the 'senior partner') was Edith Evans it was a very different kettle of fish.

Edith herself is, of course, a not inconsiderable exponent of the art of capturing the riveted attention of an audience by making of the most trivial action a vision of delight. I know when she played Rosalind at the age of 48, there was not a man in the audience between the ages of 15 and 90 who was not head over heels in love with her, and when she walked across 'the Pit' in *Daphne Laureola* she turned an apparent piece of genuine levitation into a symphony of floating movement.

And so *Waters of the Moon* was a meeting of giants. Only quite recently Patricia and I dined with Frith Banbury, who had the not altogether enviable task of directing the play. It must have been rather like having Circe and Brunnhilde in the same cast. We asked Frith if he would tell us what happened and he said that during rehearsals there had been no more than the usual frictions involved in putting on a play. He went on to tell us what happened after the play had got under way. One anecdote delighted us so much that I asked him to write it all down for me. This is what he wrote:

After the play *Waters of the Moon* had been running several months I was rung up by the stage manager who said, 'Mr Banbury, Dame Edith has been in tears at both performances to-day. I'm sorry to worry you when you're rehearsing another play, but I thought I'd better let you know.' 'What's up?' I said. 'Well, Mr Banbury . . .' and she tactfully cleared her throat . . . 'it's Dame Sybil's overacting!' I had watched the performance from in front a few days before, so I sat down and wrote two notes:

1) 'My dear Edith,
   I was in front the other afternoon and thought that Sybil was giving the customers rather too much for their money. However, I know that you will realise that it is only ebullience and *joie de vivre* that makes her do this, and that you will make the necessary allowances.

                                                                      Yours ever,'

2) 'My dear Sybil,
   I was in front the other afternoon and thought that there was rather too much general over-emphasis on your part. It is such a pity to spoil such a beautiful performance by pulling faces. I know that I only have to mention this to have it put right.

                                                                      Yours ever,'

'My dear Frithy,
   It is only your constant vigilance that keeps the production in any sort of shape at all. As for peoples' *motives* for over-playing, I can only say that I have not yet attained your degree of Christian charity. However, I'm progressing.

                                                                      Yours ever,
                                                                      Edith'

Next morning came one from Dame Sybil.

'My dear Frith,
   Yes! I *was* rather naughty on Saturday afternoon, but I had two grandchildren in front and was determined that they should know *exactly* what the play was about. Consequently, much underlining . . . However, I've pulled myself together now, and, if you come again, I think you'll find all is in order.
   Have a good time in America.

                                                                      Yours affec,
                                                                      Sybil'

In the event they both gave exquisite performances held in delicate balance by some alchemy of Frith Banbury. When Patricia and I, with our family, came to London in June at the end of my last Glasgow season, it was the first play we all went to see. The production had a sad and wistful magic about it that was as memorable for Sybil's tiny part as it was for Edith's bigger one. I remember our coming out of the Haymarket Theatre feeling we knew much more about all those unhappy people lost in obscure, lonely backwaters. It was a lovely show and we saw it quite a few times.

We also went to the Phoenix to see Lewis playing Antigonus in *The Winter's Tale* with John Gielgud as Leontes and Diana Wynyard as Hermione. Once again we watched Lewis contain and control his acting powers into a moving gentleness that somehow gave more meaning to the other stronger characters.

That summer was the year of the Festival of Britain, and so our valedictory holiday in London was a round of splendid gallivanting. We were allowed to use Cedar Cottage as our base and Lewis's old Rover for our transportation on our daily excursions to theatres, expeditions and, of course, the fun fair at Battersea Park. London, beflagged and gay, seemed to be specially dressed up for us so that we would have a vivid picture to take with us to Australia. 'After all these tiresome years,' said Sybil, 'London has put on its best clothes to cheer us all up. Isn't it all lovely?' And the fact that Cousin Hugh was the co-ordinating architect for the South Bank Exhibition and responsible for much of London's light-hearted and witty decoration made us feel even more that we belonged to London and London belonged to us.

At the end of the month Nevin Tait, one of the three brothers who owned J. C. Williamson's, and the one who ran the London end of 'The Firm', gave a lunch with his daughter at the Café Royal for the entire Casson family, which Sybil in her inimitable way took over completely. She held forth about the glories of the Australia she had known nearly twenty years before in a way that must have astonished the Australians. Those at the lunch not only learnt things about their country that they had never heard of before, but what is more, thanks to Sybil, they actually believed them.

We ran in and out of Swan Court, we ate meals with them at all hours, and we talked and talked even more than usual because I suppose we felt we were soon going to be starved of it all.

After lunch at Swan Court on 7th July I said my farewells to Lewis and Sybil. We were all a bit emotional with a mixture of excitement and depression. None of us knew what was going to happen but here we were again at the end of one of Lewis's chapters, or the beginning of a new one, and as always with them it was the adventure of the new one that mattered rather than the nostalgia for the old.

A fortnight later after a somewhat euphoric stopover in New York and a shorter one in San Francisco I landed in Sydney. There was, of course, a pile of letters waiting for me, not only from my own family. Sybil has always been a compulsive letter writer and during the next seventeen years was going to write between fifteen hundred and two thousand letters to us in Australia.

But to begin with Lewis was going to be a good correspondent too. So while I buckled down to work in Sydney and Melbourne, to be joined by Patricia and our three at the end of November, it was mostly by letter that we kept in touch with Lewis and Sybil, and through them with England and home. Their story must now therefore be told through their letters.

Chapter *13*

LETTERS AND VISITS
TO AUSTRALIA

As I flew westward over America and the Pacific, Lewis and Sybil were already sending off letters eastward. 'We there before thee, in the country that well we knowest, already arrived are inhaling the odorous air' they might have said, misquoting Robert Bridges. Sybil wrote first while I was still in New York. It was a short note and only said:

Darling John,

How we're all wondering what you're doing and what you'll think of New York. Pat and the girls came up yesterday to do the Festival Gardens again. They all looked so sweet when we came in from the Buckingham Palace Ball. Saw Douglas Fairbanks and he said, 'How's John?' and sent his love to Pat and the girls and wished he were in N.Y. to show you round. I had a long dance with Herbert Morrison and settled the Labour Policy!! Long talk with Princess Alice – she came up to me – not me to her!! and talked to Osbert Sitwell – it was all most enjoyable.

They seem to have been well in with royalty at this time because her next letter said:

We had a wonderful time at the laying of the foundation stone of the National Theatre yesterday – by the Queen – the King not being well enough yet for public functions. I 'delivered' the Ode after the Queen's lovely speech. Then before the stone was laid about 20 of us went with Her Maj. and Princess M. to have drinks and be presented. I had quite a nice talk with the Queen with Lewis, and then Princess Elizabeth said, 'Didn't I meet your son at the Perth Drama Festival this spring?' So we said together, 'Yes, Ma'am,' and she said, 'Has he gone to Australia yet – and is he taking his wife and – 3 children, isn't it?' We had quite a talk about you. What a marvellous memory she must have! . . . We've had your p.c. from up in the air over the Pacific. Oh! I thought you'd be thrilled with Frisco – Oh! the feelings, feelings, it gives me. Just the sound of the name, I can smell it! Sounds and smells do something to one. Oh! How you must long for Patricia. Sharing it is everything. I never really enjoy things alone. 'If only Lewis were here.' But that's marriage and more important than anything. It's very interesting your comments on the new

265

form of musical. *I* think the new form of drama *is* the musical – only in that way will the audience accept big-scale and in a way something bigger than realism. *The Consul* as a tragedy was the modern version of Greek tragedy, We *must* come out and I'm more inclined to fly out and get to you quickly. Let's find a good play. I'm weary of *Waters of the Moon* – feel like screaming! 'I am aweary of this Moon – would it would change.'

And there was one from Lewis as well:

You seem to have made good use of your time in N.Y. and I'm very glad to find you think the standard nothing to alarm you. They are certainly way ahead of us in the musical show, partly I suppose because they have more joy in life of a sort than we have at the moment, and partly because they don't keep their musicals and their straight drama in such separate compartments as we do. . . . How thrilling getting your first look at Frisco from the air. I hope you remembered all the folklore about my mother's father investing all his savings in sites on the waterfront about 1825–30 and losing the lot in the first fire. And now you're safely in Sydney where the harbour 'has a pretty view' according to further family folklore. Your N.Y. letter to me was lovely. Yes we *are* close together, you and I, and talking doesn't matter one way or the other. We do know.

I was now indeed in Sydney, but whether 'safely' was the appropriate word was a question open to doubt. There would be four months on my own before my family arrived and by then I would have had to produce one comedy and be well into rehearsal for my first musical. This was *Kiss Me Kate*, which the whole family had been to see in London. The kaleidoscope of our lives began to turn faster and faster and we became almost entirely concerned with finding our feet in the bright, unrationed, sunlit land of Australia.

My own family sailed on 27th October the day after Lewis's birthday, three days after Sybil's and the day before mine, and they reached Melbourne a month later. Sybil wrote to me on the day after their arrival with her usual relish:

London, 28th November
Darlings John and Patricia,
How lovely to write to you together! When we got in last night Jerry, the porter, said 'They'll be there.' I said, 'Silly, it's only 27th. They don't get there till to-morrow.' 'It's to-morrow there *now*,' he said very knowingly being nearly a Melburnian! How we've been thinking of the arrival, and if, John, you saw them first or, Patricia, you spotted John. Anthony's letter was so graphic about Colombo and Cocos.
We are having such a hectic time and after next week 'I really mean to rest'

(!) (Patricia I hope when I say this *you* take warning!!) but how difficult it is – people and causes just swarm on one. Lewis is fine and Much Adoing hard.

Lewis was to open in *Much Ado* in January of 1952 while Sybil, despite being 'weary of the moon' was to go on playing in it for another eighteen months, till she would really be at screaming point. In February she wrote to us about King George VI's funeral. They had been taken into Westminster Hall privately with Clemence Dane to see the Lying in State and then the next day, both in their seventies, Lewis 77 and Sybil 70, they had stood in the crowd in the Mall.

To-day we left home, Lewis and I, at five to eight, got to the Mall [on foot from Chelsea!] where it turns in to St James's Palace at 8.20. Very cold, but we got a good place at the corner with a grass plot in front of us so we could see through. At 9.30 the gun went off and he was 'piped' out of Westminster Hall – we heard the Funeral March in the distance – we were so turned over with emotion when the airmen's band came first – and oh! all marching so beautifully – very long procession and the bands kept replacing one another as they moved on. Then the Dead March in Saul came by the Guards, and then the Life Guards about eight abreast, then Heralds all in gold, then the bluejackets and the gun-carriage – looking somehow so simple – we were all sobbing – Lewis *is* such a comfort he is so full of emotion at these times – then the great gold and glass coach with the two queens and Margaret and Princess Royal all veiled – they looked like Mutes – and the coachman in scarlet cape on cape and postilions – oh! we were bouleversés. We walked home – it took half-an-hour to pass – and we were frozen but got warm walking fast, and I gave Lewis brandy and hot milk and I had sherry and hot milk!!! Then Lewis stayed quiet while I went to see Ann and tell *her* – then I lunched with Mary. Ian was there too [they were engaged at this time]. They had been going to take Diana to see the Lying in State but it was such terribly bitter weather and the queue was over a mile long and Mary wouldn't risk it. I should think there'd be a lot of deaths from the queue! Then at Mary's I heard the wireless of the Paddington ceremony – the pipers played 'Speed Bonnie Boat – over the sea to Skye' it finished me! And as the train went out the pibroch played the Piper's Dirge. Then I raced back to Lewis and we heard all the Windsor bit and saw it on T.V., saw the coffin go up the steps of the lovely St George's, and he was 'piped' up there – three times he was piped – that shrill sound was so touching. We then heard the whole service, so simple and short and beautiful. Oh! we were so proud of England – the discipline – the magnificence of it all.

That letter is almost the only one we have of hers in 1952. Mary married Ian Haines in April of that year. Her marriage to William

Devlin was one of the casualties of the long separation of wartime, and in 1951 she had met the form master of her eleven-year-old daughter Diana. Her marriage to Ian was a most popular move and I remember Sybil wrote ecstatically about it. Like most mothers Sybil has always been determined to have all her young 'living happily ever after', only she is better than most mothers in mentally rewriting real life so that come what may life is seen to be lived happily ever after. I've often wondered how much of all our lives is geared unconsciously to proving that she's right. At all events Mary and Ian were married and they became the members of our generation in the family who would watch over Lewis and Sybil during the next fifteen years. The rest of us were going to be spread over the entire globe.

At the beginning of '53 Sybil was offered the lead in *The Living Room* by Graham Greene, which would have meant being released from *Waters of the Moon*. This is what she said about the machinations that went on:

19.2.53

Really life in the theatre is almost an absurdity. Lewis and I sit back and say, 'Mad – the whole thing!' But if you could see the ridiculous comings and goings of Binkie against Donald Albery and Graham Greene to get me into G.G.'s play. It's like a farce – being rung up by one or the other all the time. I'm bound by contract to Binkie till this play ends, and then to do suburban dates. If he wants to be nice he'll release me and let me open in town with *The Living Room* in April. I say nothing – Donald is doing the talking and I sit back and go on with my old *Moonface* here. I'd so like to do it too. I've just now had a ring from John Perry (of Tennents) – will I go to tea to-morrow and talk over a plan? I bet he's got an alternative for me to prevent me doing the G.G., and he'll probably use Lewis as a bait in some machiavellian way. But I *don't care*. What comes, comes, and I'll be running off to Australia and seeing you all, and with Lewis have a lovely change and see some new country.

Right from the moment we arrived in Australia Sybil was working away at finding a means whereby she and Lewis could work their way there too. It is significant that despite their determination and their enthusiasm about it, they never gave a second's thought to the idea of going for a holiday. If you go to a place you must go with a working purpose, otherwise you're being idle.

John Perry's tea-party did start something, however, because her next letter said:

25.2.53

Quandaries and quandaries in the Valley of Decision!! Really what a life the

Sybil (centre) with Kathleen Harrison (right) and Estelle Winwood (left)
in the film comedy *Alive and Kicking*

Sybil and her grand-daughter Jane in *The Chalk Garden*, Australia 1958

As Mrs Railton Bell in Terence Rattigan's *Separate Tables*

A recital with Lewis

theatre is! One never knows where or what or who and certainly not why! I told you I saw Binkie and John Perry. Well then I go to lunch with Stephen Thomas of the British Council. Very thrilled that sometime or other we'll do recitals in Antipodes. . . . but en route will we do the National Theatre of Nairobi – the only National Theatre in the Commonwealth and acted in by amateurs!! Also to New Delhi and a few places thereabouts – all very nice – then Perth and quite a strenuous Australian and N.Z. recital tour. Well, Lewis funks his strength for the strenuosity. He *does* get very tired and I do know what air travel and racket can do to us from previous experience. Binkie (this is *private absolute* for you two) wants us both to do an enchanting play with John Gielgud, both parts absolutely right for us, and a jolly good play for Australia by the way. It's by the same author as *W's of the Moon* and is twice as good. That would mean August till spring when John G goes to U.S.A. So what? Do you not think we'd better do it – very well paid and save a bit – then do Australia directly it finishes – then India and Nairobi – or India alone? They could fly me there and leave Lewis with you, and then I'd come back to you and stay longer. India must be between Nov. & Jan. or *trop chaud*. Well! Well! I get a little anxious about darling old Lewis – he gets so tired – though no one outside the home would notice! His Gloucester is beautiful. I was moved beyond words. Wolfit is packing the King's Hammersmith and Lewis is staying with them, but has plenty of breaks as he only plays in *Lear* and *Oedipus*.

Apparently John Perry's 'bait' was sufficiently strong for in September they began rehearsals for *A Day by the Sea* and opened in Liverpool early in November. First of all, however, Sybil went on tour with *Waters of the Moon*. In Edinburgh she watched the Queen's Coronation on T.V. and told us about it in another letter:

What a day of emotion! That ancient ritual and the grace of the Queen, and the calm and assured way it was all done – there is no country like ours. I felt so proud that the foreigners should see it all and our crowds and our democracy and our friendliness and those darling two – Elizabeth and Philip kneeling at the altar like two children. The Archbishop was wonderful – his voice so good. And what about Everest?!! What a gift for her.

Then a few weeks later from the home of Esmé Church near Leeds she wrote:

. . . I get a bit down – quite unscientifically – quite faithlessly – about theatre here – the only ones pushing out into anything seem to be the amateurs (not the ghastly sort, but the real earnest strivers) and yet they've not got the sheer accomplishment to be able to do it. *Where* are our Picassos – our Matisse or

Nashes – our equivalents in the Theatre? The leaders like John G and Larry don't seem to do anything *NEW*. I suppose because all interpretive arts have got to *pay* now. I don't think from what you say that Australia differs greatly from here. Taits and Littlers are akin. Binkie is better but still kept in the safe circle. However, to do a job well is the first thing! . . .

On Sybil's birthday, 24th October, Lewis wrote a letter from Swan Court, in which he said:

Our excitement about the new play has been terribly complicated by this unfortunate Gielgud business. I think Sybil has told you something of it. Rather foolishly he took on the job of producing and playing a very long part. Got very strained and tired – and there you are. . . . We were all in fits as to what would happen, but Tennents and he decided to go on. But we don't know yet what the results will be either when we produce in Liverpool or still more in London. Personally I think it's quite likely to be to some extent a plant by the authorities. It's all a great pity.

In the event their fears of disaster for the new play proved to be if not groundless at least unjustified. But this was mainly thanks to Lewis and, even more, to Sybil, who had the larger part in the show. Lewis told me later that when she made her entrance on to the stage at Liverpool she fixed the audience with a look as though she were saying, 'I don't think it matters. Do any of you?' and daring anyone to think otherwise. Apparently nobody dared.

During all this time I had been producing plays and musicals in Melbourne and taking them later to Sydney and the other Australian cities. I had even been to New Zealand to open my production of *Seagulls over Sorrento*. We were all loving Australia and loving its warm friendly people even more than its warm climate. But I'm bound to say I was not loving working in the theatre in Australia. It was largely my own fault, I'm sure, but the contrast from working under Bridie in Glasgow in a theatre where artistic quality was the aim rather than commercial success was too big a jump for me to take after such a relatively short time in the professional theatre. In Australia the theatre under J. C. Williamsons, 'The Firm', was unashamedly commercial, not to say capitalistic. Not that there is anything the matter with that. But like my parents I have never been able to operate on the philosophy that employees are no more than expendable raw material. It is regrettably a theory held by many theatrical managements that actors are merely a form of potential wealth which can and must be exploited at will. Actors, in the view of 'The Firm's' management, were tiresome necessities that would be dispensed with if it were possible, but should certainly never be pandered to, and only treated as human beings if they were stars, and only then if they were successful stars.

And so although we always remained on the friendliest terms with the Tait Brothers, by October, the Australian spring, of 1953 it became very clear that one two-and-a-half year contract was going to be mutually sufficient. That was the end of my dreams of becoming an antipodean entrepreneur, and I wrote about it to Lewis. On the 18th November he wrote back to me:

So you've made the big decision and I don't think any decision can be as bad as the indecision before it. Now at any rate you can plan definitely. You mustn't take it too seriously. After all if you'd been still navy people you'd have had to put up with the same upheavals, and in the theatre most of us have had, and will have, periodic upheavals like this, and much uncertainty about the future. The main thing is for you both to hold on to your belief in yourselves and your children. It is a big disappointment to you both, of course, but so often these upheavals lead to something better. All very platitudinous, but perhaps all the truer for that. Now as to planning. I suppose you'll stick to your idea of coming for a look round as soon as Perth is over?

I had been over in Western Australia to direct a production of *Pygmalion* and to play Doolittle. When it was over I returned to Melbourne and earned an honest shilling or two by giving a poetry reading recital on the theme of 'Royalty', cashing in, I suppose, on the impending visit of Her Majesty and Prince Philip to the Commonwealth.

On 7th March I sailed for England on my own in the *Oronsay*. We couldn't afford more than one passage at that time and I had to have my 'look round' for some sort of job. I left the ship at Naples and flew on to London, arriving there on 23rd March. The excitement of being back in England was tempered more than I cared to admit at that time with a great deal of anxiety about our future. Lewis and Sybil were, I am sure, just as anxious but they covered it up very well. They had lots of suggestions and got me introductions to all sorts of people in both the theatre and the still adolescent television industry. Thanks to them I even spent a couple of days at Denham Studios with Douglas Fairbanks, who was most helpful. The fact, however, remained that there wasn't going to be much in the way of a job for a director with only five years' experience of a Scottish repertory and two years in what most English people thought of as the wild outback of Australia.

A Day by the Sea was playing to packed houses at the Haymarket and, of course, it was the first show I saw. All I remember of it now is that I enjoyed it, and that Lewis, now 78, put on a very heavy character make-up to play an old man of 75. In fact to the day of his death fifteen years later I don't think he ever saw himself as older than a fairly healthy 65, who unfortunately was having a few minor, though tiresome, set-backs. Other people might think it was age, but he didn't agree. He was in his view not unjustifiably irritated and annoyed with himself for getting run down and tired more often than he used to.

We went down to Cedar Cottage a lot and they introduced me to their somewhat eccentric neighbour and his wife. This was Colonel Alfred Wintle who made a name for himself later for de-bagging at gun-point a solicitor whom he believed had swindled an elderly relative. To me it was very interesting that Lewis and Sybil enjoyed his company and indeed admired him so much. There was a side of Lewis which never grew out of hero-worshipping any reasonably competent swashbuckler, perhaps the Rudolf Rassendyl in him that he had never had the chance or money to indulge. Alf Wintle represented to Lewis the Man of Decisive Action who snapped his fingers in the face of Red-taped Authority and took the consequences in the certain knowledge that under no conceivable circumstances could he himself be wrong. It is of course an attitude that leads to sainthood or fascism, depending on the circumstances. Lewis could admire the decisiveness, even envy it, but his own deep humility could never have allowed him to have the certainty of the fanatic.

On the evening of Easter Sunday we were all three summoned to the house of Sybil's sister Eileen by her son Stephen. She had suddenly and unexpectedly become unconscious and a doctor had been summoned. Lewis and Sybil and I had gone to the hospital with her in a hastily summoned ambulance. After about an hour the doctor came and told us that Eileen had suffered a brain haemorrhage and was unlikely to recover consciousness. She died the next afternoon and Sybil was heartbroken. To add to the worries Eileen had not been very well off and her family were likely to be even more hard up. Lewis at once took over the mortgage of their house and presented it to them, without as far as I know ever seriously considering any other course of action.

Three weeks later came another family upheaval. Douglas and Ann had signed up with Tyrone Guthrie to go to Canada and work at the newly formed Festival Theatre in Stratford, Ontario. They sailed from Southampton on 2nd May and Sybil wrote about it to Patricia in Australia:

Darling Pat,
We saw off the Campbells yesterday and it felt like you going to Australia all over again. The children were completely self-contained . . . went off in a carriage to themselves. There was a big wind yesterday so getting by tender down Southampton Water must have been quite a 'do'. We'd had an agonising time the day before because Don Harron and his wife and child, Don playing in Guthrie's Co. with Douglas – they were all going together when on Friday night – no Sat. – the child of three woke up covered in spots – chickenpox! The line wouldn't hear of her being taken on board but oh! the scare about little Thomas because they'd all been playing together. Dirk and Teresa both have had c.p. but not Tom. Ann kept waking in the night to see if he'd come out spotty – it would have been a ghastly fiasco. However, by prayer and meditation all went well. I shall miss them horribly as I see them daily and they've grown into my life so. . . .

Lewis and Sybil had by now agreed to tour Australia and New Zealand under the joint auspices of the British Council and a most enterprising, if somewhat mysterious, New Zealand entrepreneur called Dan O'Connor. He is one of those extraordinary people who appear to spend the absolute minimum of effort on their affairs and yet for whom the affairs always seem to become highly successful. He had signed them up in London and we were all to sail together via the Cape at the end of June.

I very nearly didn't sail with them, which would really have put the cat among the pigeons. I had spent a week, to Lewis's secret delight, working in the John Lewis Partnership, at the invitation of their chairman, the late Spedan Lewis. He had been for years a tremendous fan of Sybil's from as far back as the early twenties, when he had suddenly out of the blue asked her to lunch with him. During the meal he asked her, 'Are you married?' She said, 'Yes, I have a husband and four children,' to which he had quite simply replied, 'Damn!' At all events I had a very interesting week in his various shops and might well have become what they call a 'partner'. It would have been rather ironic if I had waved Lewis and Sybil off to Australia while I had proceeded to bring my family back to England. What it did do was to sow in my mind the seed of an idea that there was a by no means unpleasant nor unrewarding life yet to be explored in the world of industry and commerce.

What prevented me was an event in Australia which during the coming months was to have a considerable bearing on all our thoughts. The Prime Minister of Australia, Mr Robert Menzies, in March of this year had given his blessing in the form of £100,000 of Government money to the formation of what was to be called 'The Australian Elizabethan Theatre Trust'. Its chairman was to be the Governor of the Bank of Australia, Dr Coombs, and its purpose was to promote the performing arts of drama, opera and ballet in Australia. In April they advertised throughout the world for an executive director. Patricia had cabled me the news and I had at once applied for the job, while pulling every conceivable string that I could get my hands on in London. In the event I was to be pipped at the post by Hugh Hunt, and ever since have never ceased to praise the Lord that he got it instead of me. At this time in London, however, I could think of no one more suitable than me for the job nor any job more suitable than this for me. And so back to Australia I went, with Spedan Lewis's promise that the job with them would be open till September.

The previous November there had been an article in *The Times* paying tribute to Lewis's fifty years in the theatre. He wrote to us saying that he had been inundated with telegrams and that it had all come as a complete surprise to him. 'I don't know why they chose 7th November, 1903, as my first professional appearance. I put it about 1900 generally.' Now in June 1954 a big charity matinée had been organised at Her Majesty's Theatre to celebrate Sybil's golden jubilee. Like Lewis she had no idea why June of 1904 had been selected as her starting date, but the jubilee was a great occasion attended by the Queen Mother. Lewis and Sybil for their contribution to the matinee allowed me to direct them in one of the scenes from *The Lion and the Unicorn* and so Sybil got the chance of fulfilling at least a tiny part of her ambition to play Elizabeth I.

Just before we sailed we all three flew up to Glasgow where, at the University, Lewis was made an Honorary LL.D. in the company, to his delight, of their old friend Krishna Menon. When they introduced me to him it was clear that they all three held each other in an affection that was nearer that of a family than mere friendship.

We sailed from Southampton in the *Dominion Monarch* on 25th June to go round the Cape of Good Hope to Perth. This was, I believe, more than a mere sailing to Australia, which at their age should have been a quite big enough event on its own. But it was also the beginning of another exploration for them into a new world of theatrical endeavour. They were off on their first Recital Tour. On the face of it here were two old people setting off to hold audiences for a couple of hours at a time by reading poetry to them. Furthermore, they were not going to pander to those audiences. They were going to read Shakespeare and the Greeks, Milton and Chaucer, Shaw and Browning, Gerard Manley Hopkins, T. S. Eliot and Edith Sitwell, and they were proposing to pay their way and their salaries in so doing. There was to be no scenery but a simple platform, two chairs and a table. He would wear a dinner jacket and she would wear a full classical evening gown with a long Indian silk shawl over her shoulders, and which incidentally she was going to wield and use rather like one of the crusaders wielding his sword.

Every day on the voyage out they rehearsed their several programmes for at least three hours and sometimes more. But that didn't prevent their being the life and soul of the ship, whether in taking over the conversation at the captain's table or giving their presence and support to the balls, routs and assemblies that make up the routine of a passenger liner on passage. We went ashore and up into the hills at Las Palmas, we went ashore as guests of the theatre director John Roberts at Cape Town and we all had a gay old time till we arrived at Fremantle on 15th July. Their opening recital was on the 16th in Perth.

Dan O'Connor had somehow managed to hire the ballroom at Government House for their auditorium and I shall never forget their despair when they tried it out for sound that first afternoon. It was an oval room with a hard parquet floor and not very high ceiling and the echo was devastating. You could not hear a single word that either of them said whether their speech was loud or soft, fast or slow. For sixpence we would all have cut our throats. However, for once I had an advantage over them. From having done concerts and shows in the Navy, in aircraft-carriers' hangars, in coal-sheds, in canteens and even in a prison-camp shower-house, I had faced the problem of lamentable acoustics perhaps more often than they. And so I said, 'Let's not worry about this. Let me fix up the lighting (for which incidentally no provision whatever had been made) and you can come and look it all over in the morning when the seats are in place.' This is exactly what they did and the acoustics were as bad as ever. I did remember, however, that people on chairs covering a floor do have an astonishing effect on improving audibility. I tried to cheer them up with this, but even Sybil seemed convinced that they would get the bird.

As the time drew near Lewis looked more and more like Boris Karloff, Sybil paced up and down muttering her lines of Medea's speech, 'Ye women of Corinth' – and I thought, 'It's "Ye women of Perth" that had better look out' – and Dan O'Connor put on a face like Stonehenge on a February morning. But the ballroom was packed and the Governor and his Lady were in the front row and suddenly they were off after a simple opening ceremony of Lewis's invention, which began by his saying: 'If you will be upstanding, Dame Sybil will pray for the Queen's Majesty in the words of the National Anthem' and then Sybil spoke the words beginning 'God Save Our Gracious Queen . . .' and we could hear every word.

I think even they were astonished at the success of this recital. The audience never moved until the end when the applause was tumultuous. And then after only the briefest of pauses they were swept into a reception given by the Governor, and the two of them went on till after midnight. At least that is what they told me later, for at midnight I boarded a plane at Perth airport to make the overnight flight to Melbourne to rejoin my family, prepare the way for Lewis and Sybil and to set about earning some money as quickly as possible.

Lewis and Sybil flew to Adelaide at the end of July where Patricia met them after driving the 500 miles from Melbourne with, of all people, the little stage-manager Tommy Hudson, who had emigrated to Australia. They did, I think, two recitals in Adelaide and then drove on to Melbourne with Patricia and spent a night with enormous enthusiasm on a sheep station owned by some friends of ours. Here it was that Sybil made the day memorable for their hosts by describing a clutch of emus as 'a lot of desiccated ballerinas'.

They reached our Melbourne home just before dark on 4th August to be tempestuously welcomed by their three grandchildren, whom they hadn't seen for nearly three years. 'Now Iona Avenue is no longer just an address for letters, it's a real place and a lovely place too,' Sybil cried, as she inspected the house – at once of course, before taking off her coat. Lewis followed her, beaming and approving, and we were a very happy family.

The following day Patricia had arranged a lunch-time press reception for them, and we had invited something like twenty fairly hard-bitten Australian journalists to meet them and eat and drink with them in our garden. Despite the racketing about since their arrival in Perth, the sea voyage had done them both a lot of good and they captivated the ladies and gentlemen of the press. Before long they were talking and arguing with everybody on subjects ranging from politics to gardening, from Australian wine to the price of wool. One never knew when Lewis did all his reading. One was just continuously astonished that he had done more homework than anyone else about what was in the news. Sybil talked about both what was in the news and what was not and certainly more fluently than anyone else.

They performed each of their recital programmes three times in the next two weeks and on every day Sybil had some bazaar to open, some ladies' tea-party to address or some function to electrify with her ebullient spirits. The two 'old dears' commandeered the Melbourne headlines and captivated the public. And by the end of August we had all seen their recitals over and over again.

Looking back on this creation of theirs fifteen or so years later, and out of the immediate and undoubted glamour of it, one can now begin to make some sort of sensible assessment of it. All of it was on a level that would have been beyond the reach of any actors that I know. But what one can now see is that their greatest successes were those items which they treated strictly as readings or as 'readings by heart' (Sybil actually read very little, except in the 'book' of her prodigious memory). They had naturally included scenes from *Medea*, *The Trojan Women* and *Hippolytus* as well as scenes from Shakespeare and Shaw. Whether from nostalgia or from a sense of dramatic duty I don't know, but they often 'played' these scenes as it were, for real. The audience was then asked to accept the reality of Lewis's 78-year-old Benedick wooing Sybil's 71-year-old Beatrice, which it manifestly found very difficult to do. When they read or recited and only acted vocally they gave performances of such virtuosity that the audiences were completely carried away. Their voices were ageless and the artistry with which they used them made the highly-skilled, highly inflected speech appear entirely natural. As a listener one could only wish that one's own voice sounded as well and commanded such attention.

Three weeks after they arrived in Melbourne they were off again. Patricia had done such an excellent job of publicity and general management for them that Dan O'Connor asked her to go along with them to Canberra and Sydney. She even managed to talk the Public Relations Manager of General Motors Holden into lending them a Holden car to tour around in. And so Patricia drove them to Canberra. That evening I got a telegram to say, 'No spotlights in hall stop get some and bring Canberra. Love Patricia.'

Next morning I managed to hire three spots and after lunch took the plane to the Australian capital city. We fitted the spots all right and then discovered that despite Patricia's careful instructions that Sybil was to be wearing a gown of gold, they had hung drapes all over the stage of exactly the same gold colour. She would have entirely disappeared in front of them. The caretaker told me that the curtains were a matter for the Department of the Interior and no one else had authority to change them. 'Let's get their authority then,' I said rather tetchily. 'Office is closed now till to-morrow morning. Anyway there's no one here to do the work.' By now it was 5.30 p.m. Lewis, Sybil, Patricia and I were supposed to be dining at the house of the U.K. High Commissioner, Sir Stephen and Lady Holmes, where we were all to spend the night, and at 7.30 p.m. the recital was due to start in the presence of Their Excellencies the Governor-General and his wife, Lord and Lady Sim. It took me half an hour to persuade the caretaker to pull out some black velvet drapes and let me hang them myself in place of the gold. In the end we had to hold off opening the doors for ten minutes while I, perched precariously on the top of a fifteen-foot step-ladder, finished off hanging the drapes. I missed a very nice dinner at the Holmes' and changed into my dinner jacket, brought by Patricia to the hall with some ham sandwiches. I changed and munched among a collection of musical instruments under the stage. But Sybil's gold shone like a star in front of the black, and fortunately Lewis's dinner jacket was midnight blue.

We had all been asked to stay a night at Government House and next morning moved over from the Holmes' in time for lunch at Yamala. As long as they don't have to do it every day Lewis and Sybil have always rather enjoyed taking part in a life of formality and ritual, and at Canberra they got it in full. In the afternoon we were taken as guests of the Prime Minister to listen to some of the speeches in the House of Representatives, much to our interest if not to our edification, and in the evening there was a splendidly formal dinner at Government House. Of all things, after dinner we had a sing-song in the Governor-General's drawing-room with Their Excellencies, Mr Robert Menzies and his wife Dame Pattie and Lewis and Sybil as an enthusiastic audience. The 'conductor' was the Military Secretary, Colonel Martin Gilliatt, and the *pièce de résistance* a version of 'The Twelve Days of Christmas', with actions invented by Patricia for our children during the war.

In the morning Patricia departed in the Holden for Sydney at 7.45 a.m., but not too early to be seen off on the steps of Government House by His Excellency himself. Later on Lewis, Sybil and I were flown with Lady Slim to Sydney in the Governor-General's plane. Lewis and Sybil went straight to their recital hall where Patricia was already waiting to launch them into their performance.

Within a couple of days of their arrival in Sydney the announcement was made of Hugh Hunt's appointment as executive director of the Elizabethan Theatre Trust. Lewis wrote to me, 'I know it must have been a considerable disappointment to you, but I boldly confess that I am on the whole relieved! The more I see of the people concerned the more doubtful I am that the job would be anything but a torment ending in your being a scapegoat!' He then immediately plunged into details of a scheme we had already discussed of my forming a company to produce *The Lion and the Unicorn* and getting J. C. Williamsons to back it. It almost came off too, but away in England the theatrical powers-that-be were beginning to stir their stumps. Everybody was joining in the game of 'What to do with the Cassons in Australia'. Schemes from Binkie Beaumont, the British Council, Williamsons and their smaller rival Garnett Carroll came pouring in while Dan O'Connor agreed with them all but made no decision.

By now Lewis and Sybil on their own, or rather with the O'Connors, had flown across the Tasman Sea to New Zealand. Again it was Sybil who, despite all the family worries, was able to write of the joys of aviation.

This letter was posted in Queenstown, South Island, on 3rd October:

Here we are in Queenstown in the middle of the Southern Alps. We came in a small specially chartered plane that just held Dan, Shirley, Lewis and me. Very nice and very good pilot and the trip was fantastic. We went through the mountains called 'The Remarkables' and they *were*. All peaks and no gradual anything, terrific precipices and needle-points. I got the most awful quirks but pleasurable ones. We saw the big lake Te anua but couldn't see Milford Sound as the clouds were down. The peaks were a glory! And then over this lake that Queenstown is on – it's wonderful. We came down low and went into each bay rather like our launch trip in Sydney Harbour. And after a huge lunch Lewis and I climbed nearly to the top of Ben Lomond and now I'm dropping – 2 hours up and 1¼ hours down and my legs are nearly *off*. To-morrow if it's fine we go to the Franz Josef Glacier and Mt. Cook. Fancy our meeting Hillary last week! He's a darling.

But in the middle of October after frantic cables, letters, phonings, worries about me, they finally agreed to join forces with Ralph Richardson and his wife Meriel Forbes and to do the two Rattigan plays *The Sleeping Prince* and *Separate Tables* in an Australian season to open in Perth. As Sybil wrote from Townsville by now in Queensland, 'It's all settled. Ralph and Mu open 20th April, not with Taits with Carroll – which also includes Dan! Binkie is sending a producer ahead. He seemed to think we should do the Ralph thing but we feel awfully perplexed and worried about you.'

As things turned out they needn't have worried because when they returned to Melbourne for a family Christmas after touring Tasmania, I had only a few more weeks to run as a professional man of the theatre. In fact I think my last job as a producer was to direct them both in a radio version of *Medea* for the Australian Broadcasting Commission.

In December I had given a talk to a luncheon club on 'Applying theatrical principles to business'. As a result I was offered a very pleasant job in a firm of management consultants with whom I was to remain for fifteen very rewarding years. Thus, when Lewis and Sybil set off early in January for a tour of India, I was literally 'in business' to the considerable relief of us all.

On Boxing Day Patricia and our daughter Penny had taken off for Hong Kong to be the guests of our very dear friends Mike and Wendy Turner. Patricia was combining the holiday with being Advance Manager for Sybil and Lewis to arrange recitals for them in both Hong Kong and Singapore when they had finished with India. And so it came about that as well as visiting their antipodean family, as well as beginning a new sort of theatrical career and as well as endearing themselves to a whole new continent, they fulfilled two more of their ambitions – to visit India and to visit the Far East.

Both of them had been deeply involved with the people of India ever since the twenties when they had been introduced to the poet Rabindranath Tagore. Lewis had met Gandhi and they both knew Nehru and his sister Mrs Pandit. They had often visited the Indian Settlement in London's East End run by their friend Muriel Lester. Now they were going to see this mysterious and magical country for themselves. Patricia had written to the British Council representative and his wife, the Clutterbucks, with strict injunctions about not over-tiring them and not involving them in too many social activities that Lewis and Sybil were at one point slightly aggrieved at 'being treated like Dresden china'. Her letter from Delhi to Patricia in Hong Kong written on 21st January gives one some idea what they were up to:

. . . No time to write – life is too full (just getting dressed now for a Gala Performance). We saw the Taj Mahal yesterday. I can't find words to say what we felt. We went with my old friend Raj Kumari Amrit Kaur – she's Minister of Health – in Nehru's private plane and it was one of *the* days of our life. Lewis is ecstatic about it all here! The recitals have been a huge go. We were told the Indian audiences would be fidgetty – it's their custom to chat and move about – but the silence was lovely, not a sound and then terrific applause. Such gratitude from all the Indian people – such a quick audience – comedy as quick as any in Australia. Nehru is arranging for us to see Everest and Kanchenjunga!! We are in a *dream* – and both so fit and well and happy.

And they did go to Darjeeling and Nehru did arrange for them to see Everest and Kanchenjunga. But even he could not have arranged for the totally clear sky on the morning when the two of them stood hand in hand and watched the dawn come up over the range of the Himalayas. That, Sybil has always been convinced, was a very special dispensation by the Almighty. The next morning they flew to Hong Kong from where I had the only letter Lewis wrote on the trip:

We had a wonderful time in India but Sybil will have given you so much detail that it's no use trying to compete now! But the flying visit to Darjeeling and Kalimpong put the cap on the lot and now Hong Kong! which just as much surpasses what we imagined as the Himalayas did. Yesterday we drove out to the China border, which was quite thrilling and the drive back by a new military road over the mountains was like the foothills of the Himalayas again. The road went through all the country Patricia used to ride over and where you and she used to picnic when you were engaged all those years ago. The whole place is full of your memories! We've only two more whole days and we don't want to go a bit, though I think deep down we're both getting a bit tired of the continual racket! There's too much to take in so quickly in beauty and interest and new people and different peoples. But we both feel we must do India and Hong Kong again, though *when* God knows. It's not really seemly for us to contemplate such things at my age or even Sybil's! Patricia is looking very well and seems to have grown! Or we've shrunk!!

And Sybil still talks of their looking down on Hong Kong harbour from the Turners' house on the Peak where they stayed. It is one of the most magical views in the world whether seen by day with range after range of mountains or by night with the fairyland of lights in the harbour below.

The 'continual racket' did, however, continue (would they ever have let it stop?). After a brief visit and recital in Singapore they came back to Melbourne again for a week or two before beginning rehearsals with the Richardsons. Our youngest, Jane, went off one afternoon on her own at the age of 15, saw the director of *The Sleeping Prince* and *Separate Tables*, Lionel Harris, and got herself the job of the young Princess in the first of the plays. And so when they went off to Perth at the end of March they took Jane with them.

They opened on 20th April in Perth and the very next day I telephoned Lewis to borrow £2,000 for the deposit on the house which was to be our Melbourne home for the next fourteen years. It was typical of Lewis that he never turned a hair and arranged for the money to be sent at once, for which we all thanked him and the Lord in that order.

When they came back to Melbourne and opened the two plays early in May I had one of my few rows with Sybil. It so happened that I had kept one link with the theatre when I went into business and that was by being a radio dramatic critic. I had a monthly programme called 'Theatre Review'. I had acted with Lewis and Sybil, I had directed them, now I had to criticise them! The first play, *The Sleeping Prince*, was easy. The acting and the direction were superb, and Sybil had a ball as the outrageous and bombastic Grand Duchess and for once her part could not be over-exaggerated. But in *Separate Tables* she played Mrs

Railton-Bell, a most unpleasant, snobbish, ultra-conservative, well-off widow in a seaside resort. When I saw it I knew from her performance that Sybil didn't like Mrs Railton-Bell as a person, and was using the part to have a crack at all the Mrs Railton-Bells, and to show her disapproval. In my broadcast I said that for once she was going against all her own oft-stated principles of acting, the main one of which was never, never, never to dislike the character you are playing. Her theatrical approach to every part from Lady Macbeth to a red-nosed slut has always been 'There but for the Grace of God go I' or if playing a saint 'There had I only used the Grace of God properly I might have gone.'

When I got home from doing the broadcast we had a high old dust-up and much temper whirling around. Sybil said, 'I loathe Mrs Railton-Bell!' And I said, 'Yes, I know. That's what I'm complaining about. Of course she's awful, but *she* doesn't think so and so you mustn't think so when you're playing her.' It soon became clear that Sybil thought she had really understood her when really she had only recognised her. Of course we ended up the best of friends and vowed undying love and affection before we went to bed, but I also noticed that thereafter with great skill and subtlety she changed her performance of Mrs Railton-Bell.

One night when we were all preparing for bed Sybil suddenly screamed from her room, 'John! Come quickly.' I dashed into her room and there she was in her nightgown standing in the middle of the room with a look of horror on her face and pointing at a large white chamber-pot in the middle of the room. 'Look in there! It's an enormous tarantula.' And there was indeed a huge spider lying spread out in the bottom of the pot. Lewis was already in bed and appeared to be quite unperturbed. I flung a towel over the utensil and carried it with mock ceremonial out into the garden. Having got rid of the intruder I returned to Sybil and with a flourish replaced the object under the bed. I then turned to Sybil and said, 'The spider must have been called Donalbain.'

'Why on earth Donalbain?'

'You know – in *Macbeth*, "Who lies in the second chamber? Donalbain!"'

After that the whole episode became hilarious and just as we were going to turn out our lights Sybil put her head round the door and cried, again from *Macbeth*, 'Methinks the time is near at hand when chambers will be safe.' She had taken out her teeth and was giving an imitation of an old charlady we all knew. It took us another half an hour after that before we could stop laughing and go to bed.

We had quite a crowded house at this time because my mother-in-law, Betty Chester Master, had come to Australia to stay with us after the death of my father-in-law to see if she liked Australia well enough to live there permanently. She and Sybil were almost the same age though Betty was lucky enough not to be wracked with the arthritis that has been the bane of Sybil's life for many years. What used to keep us all in fits of laughter was the unconscious competition that was waged between the two of them. Sybil might say, 'Oh dash it! I haven't got a handkerchief,' and would begin to struggle out of her chair.

'I'll get it for you, dear,' Betty would answer bounding up like a gazelle and would be out of the door at the run. A slight cloud would pass over Sybil's face, and then when Betty returned saying, 'Here you are, dear. You mustn't tire yourself,' she would find Sybil in full flood at the piano playing an elaborate, difficult and energetic Bach fugue. Little ploys like this went on all the time with great charm and sweetness. They were very fond of each other but each had to keep her individual feminine end up.

On Sunday 24th July we moved house to our newly acquired property. As it was only half a mile away we did the work ourselves and the whole family joined in. Our Australian neighbours were thrilled and delighted to observe the famous Sybil Thorndike and Lewis Casson riding in a borrowed truck with the furniture. When the last load came Lewis in his shirtsleeves sat balanced uncertainly in the back on the top of a large chest of drawers. With the wind blowing in what was left of his hair he beamed and waved at all the local inhabitants out for their Sunday afternoon walks. He had the time of his life that evening with a hammer, nails and screwdriver effecting first-aid repairs to the fittings and hanging pictures, mostly in the wrong places, while Sybil helped make the beds and arrange the furniture. By bed time we felt we were properly in and we opened a bottle of champagne to celebrate the proper establishing of a Casson home in Australia. First thing next morning they flew off to Sydney.

The Elizabethan Theatre Trust had recently taken over a large suburban theatre in Sydney, I suppose with the idea of making a kind of

Australian Old Vic of it. Hugh Hunt had the splendid idea of using the Sydney opening of *The Sleeping Prince* for the opening of his Elizabethan Theatre, as it was called. Lewis wrote to me rather sourly about the whole business of the Theatre Trust a few days after they opened:

We met the chief Sydney members of the Board at a very dull on-the-stage party after the show. Very badly run, nobody introduced to anybody, and I thought the Board members quite nightmarish in their towering ponderous dullness. I don't think they have an idea what they're up to. Dr Coombs (chairman) again didn't show up and I am starting a rumour that he doesn't really exist, but is only a Jung myth symbolising fatherhood! Elsie Beyer was there, thoroughly frightened at the Frankenstein they have created! I shall be greatly surprised if it ever comes to life or if it does that it will survive long.

Towards the end of the year the company went over to New Zealand and in Auckland Lewis celebrated his eightieth birthday. For Sybil's birthday, her seventy-third, two days before, we had sent her a minute chamber-pot with a cardboard spider labelled Donalbain and she wrote to us on 26th:

The Buffday! I *adore* my potty, we simply yelled when we saw Donalbain. But what a love of a thing. The company adored it, especially Mu! I can't tell you how touched Lewis was by your letters. He felt so proud to have said to him what you both said. The party for us both at the theatre was a riotous success last night. They did it beautifully for us. Lovely eats and every sort of good drink. Lovely cake and masses of flowers. At 12 o'c it became Lewis's birthday so we all sang and we both made speeches and we stood in the middle while they sang Auld Lang Syne – very gay – and Lewis kissed me there and then to cheers from the stage-hands. Apparently the stage-hands had never been invited to a party before and they were so bucked. Off to Christchurch to-morrow. We finished the cake with the hotel chambermaids at 11 o'c this morning!

They got back to Melbourne at the end of November, but before we had our family Christmas the Trust put on a production of *Medea* in a modern and, we thought, rather banal translation, with Australian-born Dame Judith Anderson brought over from the States to play the lead. The opening night at the Comedy Theatre was a gala occasion. In fact Australian opening nights are nearly always 'gala'. The men sometimes even put on tails and the ladies put on (or nearly take off!) the lot. This one was a very special splurge for the opening of the Trust's first big dramatic venture. The Casson family were given one of the dress circle boxes – the royal box – and when Lewis and Sybil came in to take their places the whole audience stood up and applauded. All eyes were on them, and I fear that when the curtain went up a good many eyes remained on them rather than on the stage.

I've already said quite a lot about Lewis's views on dramatic speaking even when the words are by a great poet. This time it was one of his beloved Greeks. He didn't like the words of this translation at all, and he hated the ultra-naturalistic speech of all the actors. There he sat leaning over the edge of the box with his head in his hands and not just muttering but audibly groaning. At one point the whole house must have heard him say, 'Oh God, I can't stand much more of this!' Sybil kept nudging him and hissing, 'Lewis! Behave yourself. Everybody's looking at us!' He hissed back, 'They've got nothing else to look at.' He was absolutely seething by the end of the evening.

But such was his charm that when Judith Anderson came to lunch with us all a few days later he told her exactly what he thought of the play and she smilingly agreed with him.

Our dear friend Paddy Wilkinson and her mother gave their usual lovely Christmas morning party in the warm sunshine of their garden, only this time it was a very special one for Lewis and Sybil. They were coming to the end of an eighteen months' stay in Australia and there was a great deal of love and affection in the garden that morning. The cold champagne flowed, the hot sun poured down and toasts were drunk. We had all been to the Christmas Eve midnight service, and Lewis and Sybil had each read one of the lessons, and on Christmas Day itself there was a clear cloudless sky with the temperature in the eighties. Our Christmas dinner that night was one of the happiest we ever had.

And then suddenly the next few weeks, which included a fortnight's holiday together by the sea, flashed by until on the evening of 25th January we all found ourselves crowded into one of the cabins of the *Southern Cross* having a rather overplayed, rather tearful and very emotional farewell party. They sailed early next morning and we knew that from Melbourne Pier to the entrance of Port Philip Bay is a three-hour passage. So we piled into our car, Patricia, Anthony, Penny, Jane and I and drove the sixty miles to 'The Heads'. And there through binoculars we all saw each other clearly again and waved and waved till we were all little dark blobs in our respective lenses.

Their time in Australia could be described as a period of astonished excitement for them both. They hadn't just observed things from the sidelines, like honoured guests who don't belong in a place being shown round by the locals. From the moment they arrived they plunged themselves into Australia. They steeped themselves in its energetic and bustling life, and they did almost everything it was possible to do. The way in which they flung themselves at Australia and in which Australia opened its arms to them had almost something of the violence of a love affair. Right at the beginning when Patricia had taken them to spend the night at that big sheep station, and Sybil had drawn back the curtains in the morning to look out on to the endless rolling bush country to see a mob of twenty or thirty kangaroos leaping over the land, they had grasped and accepted the 'otherness' of Australia. This wasn't Europe in the South Pacific. This was a new land that they wanted to embrace and make part of themselves. Later that morning the short, gentle, almost monosyllabic elderly property owner had quite calmly killed a deadly snake in the middle of the lawn with an apparently casual flick of his stock-whip. Over breakfast they had talked about, shared and accepted each other's wildly different expertise and had established a mutually respecting unbreakable friendship. They didn't just become part of Australian life, they enriched and enlivened the people they met and talked with. They made, as they have always made, ordinary people feel that their lives and what they did with them really mattered. And as they made people grow, they grew themselves from what was returned to them in warmth of affection and delight in their company. They arrived at another sheep station in the middle of a shearing. Australian sheepshearers are a highly skilled, very tough, hard-bitten body of men. They are paid by the number of fleeces they shear, work at high speed and make very good money if they keep up the pressure. And yet on this day the whole gang broke off their rhythmic working to demonstrate to Lewis and Sybil, as a kind of dramatic presentation, the whole process of rounding up sheep, shearing them, classifying the wool and compressing it into bales, so that these two people from England would know how it was done. 'Well they were so enthusiastic about it,' said a shearer afterwards, 'we had to show 'em the whole thing.' And they had astonished the inhabitants of our respectable Melbourne suburb by rehearsing their recitals and plays in loud voices while perambulating along the tree-lined streets. But it didn't matter what they were doing, visiting a university, having a picnic, seeing over a steelworks, lunching with a bishop or shopping in Collins Street, they devoured Australia and Australia devoured them to their several and mutual advantages.

Although theatrical people like, and indeed demand, a good curtain, a good rounding off to a chapter, with these two there is a difficulty. Long before one chapter closes they are already partly involved in the next. We waved them farewell as the ship sailed seaward from Port Philip Heads, but they had already started their next adventure. They landed at Durban on 8th February and in a whirlwind tour of about ten weeks went to Johannesburg, the Kruger Park, East London, Cape-town, Nairobi, Northern Rhodesia, Istanbul and Tel Aviv. They got close to a pride of lions, watched a cheetah stalk a herd of gnus in the Nairobi National Game Reserve, while Lewis discussed the philoso-phical implications of hunting with the ranger; they played to all-African and coloured audiences as well as South Africans in Capetown and they flew round Kilimanjaro, flew through Cairo to Turkey, recited at Ankara and took Israel by storm and in their stride.

On 28th April Sybil wrote from London to say, 'Well here we are and it feels as though we've never been away except for a gnawing longing for Melbourne . . .' and a few days later,

. . . we went to Alec Guinness' first night of a French farce (done beautifully) with Binkie last night and the whole theatre clapped us and we held a kissing reception in the stalls!! Great fun and very exhausting. I'm going to be in Larry's film with Marilyn Monroe – the old girl I played in Australia only now she's the Prince's mother-in-law, as being his wife, and him off with Marilyn, isn't respectable for the puritan American public! Crumbs! We do this in July and August, but before that and during it we're both going to be in *Family Reunion*. After that we're going to America, but opening in Canada and Binkie says we can have a week free '(*sic!*)' to stay with Ann!

And that's exactly what they did, in Graham Greene's *The Potting Shed*, and came back to London the following summer to find Patricia there on her first holiday out of Australia, signed a contract with the Tait brothers to return to Australia in *The Chalk Garden*, with Jane to play the young girl and by the end of July 1958 were back in Australia after a two-day stopover at Honolulu lying on Waikiki Beach learning the lines for *The Chalk Garden*, and which they laughingly called their holiday, to plunge straight into rehearsals, temporarily without Jane, who had had an emergency appendix operation a couple of days after their arrival. All that had to be written as one sentence in the hope that it will convey a small part of the feeling of breathless rush of their lives at this time, with Lewis now nearly 83 and Sybil nearly 76. *Presto agitato* ought to be inserted in the margin! It was only eighteen months since they had left us and here they were back again saying they had come 'back home' to Australia where they felt they really belonged.

But there was a difference from last time. First of all since we had last seen him Lewis had decided that in his eighty-third year he had every right to be a bit of an eccentric if he wanted to be – and he did want to be. When the weather got warm he became a familiar figure in our shopping centre wearing a collarless shirt undone at the neck, bright scarlet braces holding up his unpressed trousers and a pair of old and battered checkered carpet slippers on his feet. He also felt he could say what he liked in a loud voice at any social gathering and as we shall see he did.

After *Chalk Garden* opened at the end of August, when the weather was beginning to get warm, he announced that we needed a tool shed in the garden and that he was going to build one. This would have been lovely for us if only he hadn't also been determined to build it in a couple of days. And so here was the sturdy octogenarian going flat out in the blazing sun for two long working days, and then, of course, playing his part in the theatre at night. We never discovered what the hurry was, but we all believed that some sort of demon was driving him on. As far as I know the shed is still standing twelve years later.

When it was finished he started a class in speaking Shakespeare and poetry for any member of the cast of *Chalk Garden* who wanted to join in, and he worked these volunteers like slaves for three mornings a week. One Sunday we had all gone down to the bay to have lunch at Frankston with our friends Jim and Edna Hunt. Their huge garden was at the top of a fifty-foot cliff with a little winding set of steps down to the beach. After lunch we were all going off for a swim and Lewis was bringing up the rear of the procession. Suddenly he tripped and fell headlong on the steps hitting his head a very nasty crack. He was lucky not to have broken his neck, but all the same he was badly shaken. After he had recovered a little we helped him back to the house, put him on a bed and sent for the doctor. The doctor's verdict was, 'Well you're very lucky. If you stay here absolutely quiet for to-night and don't move, you'll be all right. You've got a slight concussion.' When the doctor went out Lewis said crossly, 'A lot of damned nonsense. I'm perfectly all right. He doesn't realise that actors know how to fall without hurting themselves. I *must* go back to-night because the class is expecting me in the theatre to-morrow morning.' We pleaded, we wheedled, we implored, we ranted and in my innocence I thought that I had finally persuaded him to stay. Our host and hostess were delighted to have him and we left him on the bed and went to have a drink before driving back to Melbourne. Five minutes later the door opened and a rather furtive Lewis came into the room saying, 'I think I'd like a whisky and soda.' Sybil said, 'Lewis, you're impossible. Why can't you do what you're told for once?' But he didn't, of course, because he *knew* that actors know how to fall. Some months later he began to have trouble with his eyes. There was a growing black blob in the middle of his field of vision. When he had them looked at, the specialist said, 'Have you had some sort of fall lately?' Yes he had, but he had 'known how to fall'. Very soon he was nearly blind, being able only to 'see sideways', having only peripheral vision. It was a very special tragedy for him because it meant that for the last ten years of his life he would be unable to read, and he had always been a voracious reader. His blindness and increasing deafness made him feel desperately isolated and frustrated. However, all this was later and in the meantime they were both their energetic selves.

I remember another Sunday when we invited some of my new business colleagues with their wives to come and meet them both over forenoon drinks. I saw one young man, a highly intelligent civil engineer by trade, looking across at Lewis with an expression which said, 'I'd better go and talk to the old chap,' which he did. Five minutes later I looked again and there was the engineer fighting for his life pinned in a corner by Lewis and involved in a fierce argument on his own subject.

Lewis was, however, not the only one who was sometimes a little eccentric. Sybil spoke at a luncheon in Melbourne one day to a vast gathering of society hostesses. She began by saying what a pleasure it was to be there and went on, '. . . you all look so charming in your pretty frocks. And it's absolutely wonderful when I think of what you all came from.' There was a stunned silence during which Patricia hissed, 'Sybil!' and kicked her under the table. Unperturbed Sybil continued. '. . . when I think that you've all come from your kitchens and your housework I admire you all so much!'

The play had a three-month run in Melbourne and Sybil was gorgeous in it from the moment of her first splendid line spoken off-stage, 'Has anybody seen my teeth?' I never saw either Edith Evans or Gladys Cooper in this fascinating rôle but I'm jolly sure they didn't find the wisdom and the understanding in it that Sybil did. In some ways it was a wonderful thing for Jane to be playing with them and I'm sure she learnt an immeasurable amount of acting skill from them, especially from Lewis, and she was very good in the part. But between her and Sybil there was, however, a certain amount of rivalry, which I am fairly sure neither of them was aware of consciously. It led to several minor passages of arms on the tour. We got something of it from phone calls and letters and more from the knowledge that the sweeter Sybil's words are in her letters the more she is finding it difficult to be sweet.

They had a not very happy Christmas on their own in Sydney (Jane flew to Melbourne for the day, but it was thought to be a bit too much for them). Later in the tour, after Brisbane, Patricia accompanied them to New Zealand as their personal assistant-cum-managerial secretary. From her I heard about Lewis's growing naughtiness and eccentricities. One day Sybil was talking to a large audience of ladies consisting ostensibly of those who wanted to show an interest in the arts, but actually of those interested in showing off their astonishing collection of confectionary hats. At the end of her talk Sybil said, as she often does, 'Come on Lewis you say something now.' Lewis got slowly to his feet beaming at them all, and began to speak: 'Ladies, I'm sure you can realise how difficult it is for me to find anything to say after Sybil has been speaking for half an hour. As always, she has said it all. I've been sitting here while she was talking looking at you all with your lovely hats – like a garden of flowers' – much tittering and smiling from the ladies – 'and yet for some reason, as I sat there all I could think of was – Sodom and Gomorrah!' All the hats rose and hit the roof. But the gentle smile stayed on his face as he went on after a long pause. 'But that must be me because you've been such a charming audience and I'm lucky to be the only man here to see you all.' And as quickly he had charmed them back again. What he was up to Lord knows, but it wouldn't have surprised any of us if we'd discovered that he'd been conducting a private investigation into audience reactions.

Later in the tour at a mayoral reception in Dunedin, Patricia saw Lewis at the other end of the room talking his head off to a very bewildered looking civic dignitary. She crept up close behind him and listened. To her astonishment she found Lewis was talking complete gibberish in an exaggerated Welsh musical tone, while the dignitary looked round desperately for help. Patricia managed to extract Lewis from the 'conversation', and then asked him what on earth he was doing. 'Oh nothing much,' he smiled at her. 'That fellow didn't understand anything anyway so I thought I'd practise some new speech tunes.'

At the beginning of June their tour was over and after a valedictory week in Melbourne they flew off over the Pacific so as to have a short holiday with the Campbells in Canada. They were back in London early in July and Sybil was off into a film, on location in Scotland, almost at once. But she wrote to us about Cedar Cottage in a so atypical melancholy vein that we began to worry about them. Incredibly there seemed to be a sign of age beginning to show itself.

Your letter made us miss you all and the Mathoura Road house – and all the friends – desperately. More particularly did we feel it yesterday, our first visit to Cedar Cottage since we got back, and which left us both suicidal. I have not had such a depression for years and I wanted to pack up and go off on the boat to Australia, where we never felt that sort of depression. The garden was a wilderness and the house looked dark and boring, and as Lewis and I had come down by the most crawling train and so we were tired before we got there. The Williamsons [a couple whom they had employed to look after the place and who noticeably hadn't] and their three children and another coming, I *like* them *all*, but I must say it got me down, and as for Lewis – he was in Hell's *own* depression. I don't think we *can* cope with it now with no car, for Lewis's eyes are too bad to risk driving, besides his deafness and age. In his own work he is only 60 and alert at that, but cars, cottages, any sort of responsibility and he's 83 at once. And he's such a *darling*, but he just can't cope with all that the cottage entails, and gets no kick out of it in the finish. I don't think he likes being in the country, not to live in! I think we may possibly get a smallish house in London – in Chelsea somewhere. What do you think of the idea? It would be central for any of the children and for yours when we conk out.

We wrote back and said, 'Why don't you sell Cedar Cottage and just enjoy living at Swan Court?' This is just what they did, a year later, and felt much happier as a result. I think both of them in an odd way would have been delighted to get rid of every possession they ever had. A really comfortable suite in a hotel with everything found would have suited them much better than having a home to run and look after. Once their family was grown up there was really nothing in the way of material possessions that mattered to either of them. They just didn't want 'things', or 'hoards' as we have always called them in the family. There is one picture, 'The Man with a Glove', that they rashly and gloriously bought for £15 when they were first married and hadn't got a bean and an exquisitely shaped plain blue vase which Lewis gave to Sybil as a present for my being on the way. I can't think of any other possessions that have ever mattered to either of them. They had only been worried about Cedar Cottage because they had thought that we all wanted it as a 'family home'. I found it very difficult to explain to Sybil that the idea of their four grown-up children and their wives, husbands and families all sharing together one family home did not altogether commend itself to any of us.

Appropriately enough at the end of this year Clemence Dane presented them with her latest play *Eighty in the Shade*, which went off on tour in November. Sybil wrote from Edinburgh on 2nd December:

. . . Edinburgh is at its most magical – cold – sun and slight mist must make it *the* most lovely city in the world – it's better than Athens. Play went with a Bang-Bangest last night – our ending isn't right yet, and Clemmy [Clemence Dane] is as obstinate as five mules. She *exhausts* us! So many dear friends here, it's lovely. Cathy Honeyman not well. Lovely flowers from Rona Mavor, but all have colds – *so* peculiar. Lewis and I must be immune!

They were playing in Brighton during the week before Christmas, and it was in Brighton therefore on the 22nd December that they celebrated having been married for fifty years. It was, I believe, Ian's idea that, because their four children with respective wives and husbands were scattered all over the globe, we should all club together and present them with a large globe for their Golden Wedding. Ian went off and bought it, wrote the inscription on it and delivered it to them at Swan Court from where they were commuting to Brighton each night. Her letter to us about it was written on Christmas Eve:

Darlings,
I've not had one second free since last Sunday morning leaving Blackpool –

literally, not a second. Oh the Golden Wedding! Lewis and I said it would have been better to live in sin, then there wouldn't have been such a fuss! But it was a *lovely* fuss. Your telegram came and greeted us when we got to 98 on Sunday. Then Mary and Ian came in and we were told to hide till they said 'Look' – and there it was on the grand piano – The Globe of Globes. We nearly fainted at the beauty – never had we imagined such a glory – mountains all in relief and it's huge and heavy and solid – in metal and a stand of lovely wood. You never saw such a thing! We don't know how to thank you all, it's the most perfect present we have ever had. This isn't a proper letter. I'll write on Boxing Day, a real one. We left home on Monday at 10 o'c and did a T.V. then 12 o'c train to Brighton, photographers *en masse* – and two even travelled down with us – tho' we both refused to speak, thinking of our important first night at Brighton when Tennents etc. were to be there. The telegrams were such as were never seen – hundreds and hundreds – bottles of champagne – a Jeroboam from Binkie – and presents galore. The company gave us steak knives and forks in a case. I've never had a knife that would cut a steak!! I tried to keep calm – tho' the day had been a little hectic – photographers all day till we were nearly dead. But best of all was your joint letter. We've never had a more wonderful letter. Thank you dear John and Pat for agreeing! The play went over huge. Everyone bucked to bits. Binkie thrilled and we open at the Globe on 8th Jan. We drive to London after the show to-night just in time for Midnight Service. I must now write to Kiff and Ann about the Globe – Oh what a glorious present! Lewis and I gave each other rings and we bought them in Leeds at the shop where we'd bought our engagement ring fifty years ago!

Lewis also wrote that evening in one letter to all five of us in Melbourne:

I am writing this in my *very* long wait in the new play. I *almost* begin it with a scene of about six minutes and then disappear till well on in Act III when everybody has completely forgotten me. People seem to like the play but the critics won't. They will expect something better from Clemmy and won't find it! If it succeeds it will be purely on Sybil's performance. But enough of that!

Thank you all for the magnificent globe. It will become the centre-piece and shrine of our flat when we daily commemorate the scattered family by a sacramental turning of the globular prayer-wheel! All of the vast tribe of Golden Wedding Press Photographers took our pictures including it and we'll send you copies.

Now finally (for John and Patricia) how can I thank you (possibly Sybil can) for your wonderful Golden Wedding letter. We shall both treasure it and try to live up to it, and will take it out and read it again whenever we feel down and I will wish it were all true. Happy Christmas to you and of course 'all old friends round Walla Burra Crag.'

It has been said by some cynic that a married couple should have a double bed for their first ten years of married life, separate beds for the second ten, separate rooms for the third and separate houses thereafter. After fifty years Lewis and Sybil still shared the double bed they bought in 1908, and only bought a spring mattress for it some forty years later. It is no mean achievement to be happily married for fifty years, and anyone could be excused for sitting back when they had achieved it. Lewis and Sybil were not going to sit back at all. They were going to go on acting in plays together for almost another ten years. And they were even going to make one more trip to Australia before we came back to live permanently in England.

Chapter *14*

'WHEN WE ARE OLD, ARE OLD'

NEITHER Lewis nor Sybil ever really liked working in films. They have always felt that acting in films, and therefore also television, was not really acting. To them acting has to involve direct and immediate contact with an audience, which in its turn means 'projecting on a scale commensurate with the size of the building' the thoughts and emotions of the playwright. If you project your personality on a film in the way a stage actor should project, you come right out through the screen and all realism is lost. In any event when watching a play the audience is actually taking part in the creation of an event, here and now, while the play is going on. Watching a film the audience is asked on the whole to accept the camera as an eye-witness of events that are past. Furthermore, whatever may happen on the screen the audience's reaction can have no effect on it. The audience only observes. It cannot participate. At least that was their feeling about it and so, although they both acted in films, neither of them ever accepted it as a medium for themselves. And because they didn't awfully like it, they never really mastered the technique of film acting. It was a pity, because I feel sure they could have made as big an impact on film audiences and on the makers of films as they have on those of the theatre. That they had what amounted to a kink about it cannot be denied.

In 1921 we were all taken to see a trade show of Sybil appearing in a number of silent short films, which apparently the trade decided not to show. Looking back on it now, I can't say I'm altogether surprised, though we were very impressed at the time. She played a rather hearty, somewhat uncertain Esmeralda in a version of *The Hunchback of Notre Dame*. After all Esmeralda is a sexy little creature whatever other attractions she might have and somehow this seemed to embarrass Sybil. Her performance, as it were, apologised for having to be just a girl who aroused the passions of men, and so she played it as a charade. She was also cast as Jane Shore, the lady who got into trouble with King John. This was much more her cup of tea, but her rather holy death in a ditch by stoning in an immaculate white robe and unruffled coiffure must have tried the imagination of the viewers beyond all reasonable endurance.

But when, in 1928, Herbert Wilcox asked her to play Nurse Cavell in his quite beautiful film *Dawn*, one of the last of the silents, we all thought that we had a new film star on our hands. The physical likeness to Edith Cavell that she managed to achieve was not just a matter of make-up. She really did become the person, and as with 'Joan', it was a case of 'There had I used the grace of God properly . . .'. Of course this was very much in the middle of the Joan era, and Shaw himself had compared Joan with Cavell in his preface to *Saint Joan*. Thus she could even put Joan on celluloid as well as on stage and persuade Joan to perform a part in a film.

But her success in this rôle was, I believe, in a great measure due to the film's being a silent one. She had to do without the one faculty that above all her many others puts her on the Olympian scale – her voice. Because the medium was new to her, she was a little nervous of it and therefore allowed herself to be technically controlled by the artistry of Wilcox. I remember very well being allowed to go to the studio when I was a midshipman on leave, and watching Wilcox and Sybil working together. I don't remember ever being so emotionally moved by a film and have often wondered if it would have been so impressive if Sybil had been able to talk in it. To this day I can still see the figure of Edith Cavell with the wind rustling her skirt as she stood, a small, erect, lonely figure, facing the firing-squad. Sybil had a look at that moment that in some extraordinary way showed both fear and courage. No one could face that sort of death without fear, but Sybil showed that you can have the fear and yet face it with triumphant dignity as Edith Cavell undoubtedly did.

The following year she was in one of the first talkies, a highly melodramatic number called *To What Red Hell*, and we went to see the preview. It was indeed hell! The story was about a mother's agony when her son has been wrongfully condemned to death for a murder he did not commit, and Sybil was allowed to do the lot. She gave it her full dramatic treatment of Hecuba, Medea, Judith of Israel and Joan all rolled into one and she jolly nearly bounced clean out of the screen.

Two years later she played the Lancashire mother in the film version of *Hindle Wakes*, the play that had shocked Manchester audiences nearly twenty years earlier. Victor Saville was the director and I watched him on the set one day admirably damping down Sybil's stage acting. But this time she was a grim Lancashire mother, and the dry caustic Lancashire accent did not lend itself to much in the way of histrionics.

She was in quite a few more films in the thirties and during the war was in *Major Barbara* with Wendy Hiller. In 1948, however, she got a part that she adored because it involved her being villainous. She played the blackmailer The Sow in *Britannia Mews*. The old creature could have been a much more horrifying character than Sybil was allowed to play her. When she first went to the studio she got into cahoots with the make-up people and between them they designed a face that would have scared the daylights out of anyone. When it was finished she walked on to the set and the whole place was hushed by it. The director said 'It's wonderful. It's superb. But of course you can't use it. It's much too terrifying.' Fortunately for posterity, however, someone took a photo of her in it and for years we had it on our mantelpiece. When strangers came to the house they would say, 'Good God, who is that?' and Patricia would answer quite casually, 'Oh, that's my mother-in-law,' and change the subject.

She didn't much enjoy doing *Gone to Earth* directed by Michael Powell. From what we could gather, Mr Powell made the mistake of thinking that he could use autocratic methods with Sybil. Anyone who knows her could have told him to save himself the trouble. According to her story he made her do some piece of business over and over again, only each time he told her to do it differently. Looking back now she thinks he was trying to exasperate her to the point of having a fight with him, which as the director he would be able to win, and so demonstrate his authority. Sybil did what he wanted each time, meticulously and very professionally. Finally, however, she said quietly, 'Mr Powell, I will do it in any way you want. But you don't seem to be able to make up your mind what you *do* want.'

Whatever else people do to Sybil, nobody has ever succeeded in making her look foolish or embarrassed, mainly because it never seems to occur to her that anyone would want to try. Why would anyone want to? It's such a waste of time! When she was in America she agreed, rashly as many people thought, to appear on the famous Mike Wallace Show. Mr Wallace was, I'm told, a barrister. His show took the form of two interviews of fifteen minutes each with some famous person. When the person agreed to appear, and it was always at least a month in advance, Mr Wallace's 'investigators' would go to work. Their job was to dig out things that the VIP had done or said in the past that he or she had forgotten, or hoped had been forgotten. By clever questioning, or cross-examination, the person would be led to say very firmly before the camera all sorts of things that could be and were contradicted by the past. Strong men were sometimes reduced to stammering in-coherence, and it was not uncommon for a lady interviewee to end in floods of tears. There was an enormous viewing audience of millions and so the VIP was torn between the publicity and the money on the one hand, and the danger of being publicly humiliated on the other. Most of them thought they could win, and most of them only won the humiliation.

Sybil's friends all said, 'You mustn't do it. He'll slaughter you. It'll finish you in America.' But she smiled and said, 'He seems a very nice man. I think it will be rather fun.' And so she went ahead with it in the sure knowledge that the nice Mr Wallace wouldn't say anything un-friendly. His investigators had the time of their lives looking into her background. With Lewis she has always been a socialist. They had stood in a crowd of miners during the depression and sung the 'Red Flag' with them, she was a subscriber to *The Daily Worker*, she had sat next to Mr Maisky at a dinner and called him a 'dear man', she has always said, in company with the Red Dean, 'Christianity and Com-munism have the same purposes,' she is a confirmed and convinced pacifist and said so with great force even during the war, she has been on platforms with unorthodox and unpopular people like communist politicians, spiritualistic faith-healers, atheists, Indian mystics, Euro-pean revolutionaries, and once argued with Mr Jinnah at a dinner as a protagonist for the imperialism of Rudyard Kipling. Mr Wallace had in fact a great deal of valuable ammunition.

He began with great warmth and charm and soon had Sybil in an expansive mood. She aired her views on everything – acting, art, religion and politics. Then he began to move in. He got her to state categorically some opinion which was completely in contradiction to a quote of something politically revolutionary that she had said publicly in the nineteen-twenties. I'm told that Wallace said something like: 'That is your opinion to-day?'

'Absolutely.'

'Have you always felt this?'

'Of course.'

'Dame Sybil, in nineteen-twenty-five (he gave an actual date) you said . . . such and such.'

'Oh, no I'm sure I didn't.'

'But I'm afraid you did,' and he quoted her words verbatim.

Sybil then began to look worried. Consternation grew on her face, and Wallace began triumphantly to press home his case.

'So you must admit that you did hold this opinion.'

'Yes, I suppose I must have.'

'What have you to say about that?'

There was a long pause with Sybil looking very serious. Suddenly she roared with laughter and answered: 'Well I must have been a perfect fool, mustn't I?'

From then on Sybil had charge of the interview. She even invented a kind of ghostly ally out of sight of the camera to whom she kept turning and giggling as though the 'ghost' and she shared some secret joke at the expense of the interviewer. What 'poor Mr Wallace', as she called him, didn't realise was that she played the whole interview as a kind of farce, very serious face when the interviewer was serious, charming when he was charming but with just that skilful and subtle actors' edge on it that allowed all the viewers to see that she was pulling the interviewer's leg. The show was a triumph for Sybil and for days afterwards she was accosted by complete strangers on the streets of New York and congratulated on 'fixing that interviewer'. When I heard the story and asked her, 'Did you see him after the show?' she replied, 'Yes, he came round to say good-night to me. Poor man he looked rather peaky, I thought – a little pi-ano?'

This wasn't the first time Sybil had been interviewed on television, of course. But as far as I know it was the first time she had taken part in one of these popular competitive interviews where the aim is to show up the interviewee. Whether somebody in London saw the programme or not I don't know, but her reputation as one of England's important institutions was to become known throughout the country through her television interviews in the sixties. She talked with pop-singers, with hippies, with writers, broadcasters and other actors, with politicians and parsons, until nearly everybody came to know those eyes that

somehow manage to sparkle with shrewdness, wit, kindliness and a
kind of innocent naïvety all at the same time. I'm sure that it is through
television talking that she has come to be regarded in recent years as
one of the leading ladies of England, rather than as the leading lady of
the theatre. When she is talking with people instead of acting for them,
as she found she could do with a television audience, she could be a
large-scale exciting person of great enthusiasm and charm, and in effect
the darling of the viewers most of whom now have never seen her play
Saint Joan. Her interviews have been seen all over the English-speaking
world.

Lewis quite enjoyed acting in television because in the earlier times
it was done live. He felt that this involved 'the risk of being wrong'
that every actor needs if he is to be kept on his toes. In this way he felt
that the viewers had at least something of the theatre audience about
them in that even in a small way they had some effect on the performance. When a play or a show is to be 'put in the can' to be shown later
the risk is absent. This is the main reason for having television audiences
in the studio at the time of recording. It is also the reason why Lewis
did not enjoy being a film actor.

He not only disliked filming, he actively hated it. The whole business
of hanging about for hours in a studio, the apparent prodigal waste of
time, money and materials were to him something like a nightmare.
While Sybil was hard at work in the studio making *Alive and Kicking*
after getting back from Australia in 1958, he used to go with her from
time to time and sit around, feeling all too often rather out of it and
obviously wishing he could get his hands on the stage management.
Towards the end of August I got a letter from Sybil saying:

Fri. 22nd. Finished my film yesterday. Lewis suddenly was whisked off by
plane last evening to Rome to do Tiberius in the Ben Hur film. Rang him in
the studio at Elstree in the morning and said could he do it? He was thrilled
as a schoolboy and I really believe enjoyed going off on his own without me to
fuss around. He plays his one scene with Jack Hawkins (who will take great
care of him) and flies home Tuesday – and in two weeks goes again to do
another scene – return fare £78. They don't care what they spend these film
people. They pay him for the two weeks he does nothing and the fee for the
two scenes is fabulous! We couldn't stop laughing when we discussed it.
Darling old Lewis, he went off in a special grand car they sent to the airport

looking about 10 years old and very naughty!! I felt utterly left behind, but after he'd gone I couldn't stop laughing – he was so killing.

Five days later Lewis wrote to me himself about his adventures:

My dear John,

Since I last wrote to you I have been to the moon! Well at least I have been on such a completely lunatic expedition that that is what I feel. On Thursday last I was at the Elstree studios with Sybil and at lunchtime Aubrey Blackburn [their film agent] rang me up there to ask if I could fly that day to Rome to play the Emperor Tiberius in *Ben Hur* the next morning (Friday) in a scene with a crowd of 2,000 people in a great emergency, through an actor falling out. Anything for a lark! I said I'd see Mr Zimbalist, the producer, at Claridges at 3.30 (he had flown from Rome that morning). When we met I told him I had several engagements this week and must be back on Monday or Tuesday at the latest. I told him I must have the lines to see if I could do it in the time. He told me the script was by Christopher Fry and gave me a scrap of paper of about three speeches. I took it on! Rushed home and packed and caught the 8 p.m. plane. (By this time I knew there was another scene to be shot a fortnight later.) Arrived Rome (Britannia machine for the flight. Thunderstorm over the Alps.) Arrived 11.20 only passenger to get off at Rome. No BEA officer in the office. Nobody apparently to meet me as promised. Eventually found both and car. Italian boy with a little English. Labyrinthine hotel all over lifts and passages like Larry's Elsinore. [Olivier's *Hamlet* film] Bed at 12.15. Knock. Enter Frank Thring! [the Australian actor]. He's Pontius Pilate. Living on the fat of the land since April. Tells me George Relph was engaged for Tiberius but he was so fed up and badly treated that he had chucked it. Next morning at studio at 10 a.m. for dress and make-up. Met Wyler the American director. He wants Tiberius to look 102 (he was actually 71). Make-up room. Wonderful artist. Entire face built up by something dissolved in acetone. Dries hard in thousands of wrinkles. It took 2 hours, and ½ hour for the wig. Then dress fitted. Very elaborate. Driven by car to lot. (Vast crowd. Jaffa gate shot. Camels, horses, Roman soldiers, thousands.) I had to walk over dirty lot in gorgeous costume to be inspected by the director. He at once condemned the make-up as too extreme. Back and removed make-up. Took an hour! Sandwich lunch. Now 2 o'clock. Spent the rest of afternoon in and out of dressing-room hunting for and waiting for the script director to settle the lines I was to say. Hopeless – no script. Car back to hotel (10 miles). Dinner. In walks George Relph! He told me the whole story. They had released him but wouldn't give him a plane ticket – evidently wanting to be sure of me! Sent for the lady liaison officer in the hotel and told her what I thought of it. Still no final script. Another bad night. Back to studio and wasted all morning trying to find the script man. Lunch.

In he walked. Said my script was definitely not to be used. Wouldn't hear of my writing it myself. Could not get it now till Monday morning. I decided to see the Producer (now back in Rome) and put an ultimatum that I would write my own lines, learn them on Sunday and use them at the shot on Monday or I would go home, whichever they preferred. They preferred my going home! And were then most charming. Car at once back to hotel to pack and on to aerodrome. Caught a plane at 5.30. Swan Court at 10.30, much to Sybil's astonishment, about 52 hours from leaving Swan Court on Thursday. The whole place is like a maelstrom. Vast buildings, an area of about a square mile. Thousands of American and Italian employees. You drive everywhere from one building to another. Hopeless confusion, broken English, no one responsible for anything. Mad! Mad!

He never had more than little parts in films. I wish he had done more, because his ability to be still combined with an intensely visual imagination could have given him the kind of mantle that was worn by Sir Cedric Hardwicke. Lewis, in my not unbiased view, would have worn it better, and I think he would have been better in films than Sybil, who as it happened, got the film parts. Oddly enough Sybil's forte in films was in comedy rather than in drama. In comedy she could be much more outrageous because comedy so often needs her sort of outrageousness. But in drama and tragedy you can only be outrageous on the stage. On a film it appears as ham.

Just before the sixties got under way Lewis was very thrilled to be given an honorary LL.D. at the University of Aberystwyth. He had written in April while playing in *Eighty in the Shade* to say:

We are lunching with Binkie and John Perry on Thursday and I'm hoping to get leave to go to Aberystwyth for my Doctorate on July 15. But it would mean three shows off as it is matinée day and it takes a whole day to get there. My Fellowship isn't till Oct. 22nd (at the Albert Hall). I don't think the play will last till then, but where we shall be I have no idea!

He did go to Aberystwyth and the play didn't last till October and so he was able to go to the Albert Hall as well for his Fellowship, which was of the College of Science and Technology. He was particularly pleased about the Fellowship because it meant that someone had remembered his early engineering and organ-building. The citation read:

Sir Lewis Casson

It can truthfully be said of Sir Lewis Casson that he is a man of parts. Even he must by now have forgotten how many parts he has played and in how many parts of the world. Student of engineering, organ builder, schoolmaster, soldier, actor, producer, manager, lecturer, critic, he has expressed himself with gusto and delighted his public.

His great gifts as an actor are dimmed only by his pre-eminence as a producer of plays, and he can claim an enviable list of first productions that have set a pattern for all subsequent producers. He has been equally as successful with Shakespeare as with Shaw.

He has a love of music; this and an analytical mind perhaps give the clue to his outstanding success as a producer.

The same gifts are displayed in his pastimes of bookbinding, mending china and constructing old cars out of odd components. Anxious Annie was as famous in the theatrical world as Boanerges in South Kensington.

He has been President of the British Actors Equity, Drama Director of C.E.M.A. and a member of the British Council Drama Committee.

Finally, it may be related that not only has Sir Lewis, like many other old students, become a leading man. He has also demonstrated that a member of the College may marry a leading lady.

It is a matter of pride and interest to record that he was a student of the City and Guilds College from 1892 to 1894.

In September our Penny, having qualified as a nursing sister in Melbourne, came to England to learn and practise midwifery. She was followed by Anthony, who with a Master's Degree in Metallurgy had also decided to try his fortune in England. That left Jane with us in Melbourne but only for a few months until, in the next August, she and Patricia got on a boat for Europe. Sybil went off on tour in *Sea-Shell* in October, a play that Lewis didn't like. But he wished he had been in it for he had written to me: 'It's rather sad not being in Sybil's play as we've managed to be together since *Waters of the Moon*, and I'm feeling a bit out of it and somewhat depressed.' And the months that followed continued to be more depressing. *Sea-Shell* didn't go and Lewis had only a few television plays to do to keep him busy.

The accumulation of this depression finally made him sell Cedar Cottage in the middle of 1960, but by then they were rehearsing Noel Coward's *Waiting in the Wings*, a play about a home for old actors, and they were together again. During the run of the play, however, Eammon Andrews did a *This is Your Life* programme of Sybil. It was bad luck for me that of the two of her children who were away over the ocean, and could therefore be brought into the programme as a shock surprise, Ann in Canada and I in Australia, Ann was the nearer. I don't think it is always realised what a shock such appearances can be, especially to older people. They showed her shots of Ann in Canada. Suddenly Ann walked in and Sybil said afterwards she thought it was some new form of three-dimensional projection. I must say I felt a long way away when I was asked to record a two-minute message on a tape knowing that the rest of the family were all having a surprise meeting together. Sybil of course carried it off superbly, but somehow they both felt awful, in different ways, that Lewis had known about it and had had to keep it a secret from her. They have always hated secrets from each other. Lewis had quite a bad feeling of guilt about it, which added to his more and more frequent bouts of depression.

He worried about Jane, who was not having much luck with the start of her theatrical career in England. He worried about Anthony, who wasn't too happy in his job. He got fussed by Ann and Douglas with their children, all of whom at Sybil's insistence lived in the flat for a time, and above all he worried about money and their future.

Patricia returned to Australia after Christmas, and in the spring they knew they were going to do the play by Hugh Ross Williamson, *Saint Teresa of Avila*. Lewis wrote to me quite pleased about it. As always he had reservations, albeit sound ones. This was dated 8th March 1961:

I think the children's affairs seem straightened out and Anthony and Jane seem very happy and jolly. Penny always was and is! Patricia did a marvellous job over it, and we feel rather ashamed we had got in such a flap about Jane's future. Yes I am too much bothered about money. I always have been and I'm afraid I always shall be. It's part of my childhood, I know. So is Sybil's vicarage training that the money always will be there, provided by God or the Ecclesiastical Commissioners!

It's quite exciting that the Teresa play is really going to be done, and now we are all bombarding one another about revising it! He has been much too complacent and self-satisfied, but nearly always agrees readily to any suggestions that he ought to have thought of himself. I think he started off on the wrong foot by being obsessed by Teresa's *obedience*, which of course she herself keeps harping on in her own writings, but I think she was obsessed by it because she was really a rebel and there was always the fight between the rebel genius and the rule of obedience, for which among other things, she was fighting. And the *clash* is the essence of the play. I think the same thing has happened with Hugh Ross Williamson. Now he – always a rebel – has gone over to Rome he finds the obedience chafing and by a reverse process has to emphasise it. It's to some extent the same problem as Saint Joan's – genius v.

the *status quo*, and unfortunately he has written the *status quo* part – mine as the Father General – better than the rebel Teresa.

A couple of weeks later Sybil wrote:

. . . Lewis had a nasty time with the specialist this week over his eyes, which has got him down. No spectacles other than those he has can do any good. It's apparently permanent bad sight but the specialist said, 'There's no indication that you'll go blind and it even might improve.' But he had hoped new glasses would help, and it's very frustrating for him, John. I'm taking him with me to Wales next week. The sight of the Moelwyns will do him good. He is so keen on playing the Father General in the Teresa play and yet gets in a funk, 'in case I let you down,' he says to me. As if he *could*! And the moment he starts rehearsing with me and rehearsing *me* he sheds 25 years – and he's so wonderful in the part. I asked him if he'd like to give up the part and he said, 'If I give up the Father General I'll not care to go on at all.' So he'll play it and after-wards we won't bother to do any more but just live, John, and I think that's what you would advise.

I might indeed have advised it but I don't think there would have been the slightest chance of their taking the advice. But her saying it seems to me to indicate that she saw Teresa as perhaps a sort of final peak from which she would need to go on no farther. If Lewis saw the similarity between Teresa's problem and Joan, Sybil saw the chance of another Joan in Teresa. But, as Lewis also clearly saw, Hugh Ross Williamson was not Bernard Shaw. It did not, however, matter a fig to Sybil. Once again she could play the part of a deeply devout, re-ligious rebel. Once again she had a part which she could play not merely with energy, but with sacramental energy.

Although the play didn't open till the middle of September in Dublin they were already working on it, according to Sybil's letter, as early as the beginning of March. Sybil began to live Saint Teresa. In July the saint got mixed up in the same letter with a cosmonaut.

Darlings, Had such an exciting party at the USSR Cultural Relations house meeting Yuri Gagarin the space man. He was adorable, so young, like Anthony and about his height, quiet and with the same ravishing smile as Anthony. We hear he's lunching with the Queen. *That* makes for friendship between nations. Seeing that nice, quiet, friendly boy made us both feel weepy and we thought what nonsense wars are. We're both off to-morrow to stay at the Stanbrook Convent of the Benedictines. We shall see the Lady Abbess through a grille, we think, but she's going to tell us about Teresa of Avila. They are a very learned community but of course it's an enclosed order.'

She wrote again a few days later to tell us about the convent:

We got back last night from our wonderful week-end at Stanbrook Abbey. We stayed at a charming, very simple guest-house in the grounds and were up in the Abbey at all hours – talking through the grille to the Rev. Lady Abbess and other nuns. They never mix with outside at all, but a happier-looking lot of women we never have seen. The Rev. L.A. asked if we would read the Teresa play (or 1¼ hours of it) to the whole community, so we did. We were on one side of a large room, with a grille stretching the whole width, and about 50 to 60 nuns the other side. You should have heard the laughs – hope ordinary audiences get the comedy the way the nuns did. Our side of the grille were the extern nuns, who cope with the outside world – visitors, etc. – and three priests, two of them abbots. They all loved it and we were thrilled. One nun, Dame Felicitas, does all the music and she is helping us with the music for Teresa – they are all called Dame! Lewis went to Mass with me every morning, and to vespers and to Benediction in the afternoon. He thoroughly enjoyed himself, and we gave them a talk on speech (asked for by the Rev. L.A.) and poems. They fired questions at us and it was all enormous fun. We have come home refreshed and stimulated.

But at the end of August she was saying, 'We had our first rehearsal yesterday and so of course I feel in despair. I just can't *act*! I really find the Theatre exhausting. Anyway I'm bad with rheumatism, sciatica, the palsy and all other sorts of music, so a bit groggy on me pins. But never mind I only hope the play will be a go. I really feel it should.'

But it wasn't going to go all that well as her letter from Dublin shows:

Darlings, Just a line to say all went well. We see what Teresa of Avila can be. The author had *not* done his homework, which gets me mad. The Devil [Sybil always gives him a capital letter] did all he could to bitch everything up. My voice nearly gone, very bad sciatica in one leg and the other with a slipped bone, Lewis on the verge of a nervous breakdown, a strike of dockers so no scenery or props or lights till the actual show. But Teresa's own method worked! I made a long nose at the Devil and jeered at him and I could hear the Lord laughing and saying 'Go it, Syb and Lew – see how much you can stand, and I'll be there to give you a push!' And it all went wonderfully. Lewis improving, my voice returned, my legs both hell but capable, audiences wonderful and life holds out hope! I believe in God, and shame the Devil.

After a tour of packed theatres round England the play opened in October in London. Her letter to us about it gives not only her own feelings about the play and the critics, but the way in which she uses everything, even disappointments, to advantage.

The play is going wonderfully with a new sort of audience, not a bit typical West End. But the notices for the play are *all* bad – the acting commended. The critics have a different standard and it's *not* always what the public deeply want that the critics praise. Our first night was a riot – yells and bravos and curtain after curtain – and then stinkers of notices. But last night was just as big and people loving it. Most odd. It is *not* a first-class play but if one waits for that one would never act at all or just do the classics which isn't what one wants at all. *Acting* is something apart from just plays. It's another art.

Saint Teresa of Avila however, did not fulfil the promise of those first enthusiastic audiences. Perhaps Sybil's belief in it was partly her own wishful thinking, perhaps unconsciously she was worrying about Lewis, perhaps the critics were right or, more likely, that there was only a very limited, even if enthusiastic, audience for a religious play. It ran only until 2nd December, when she wrote:

To-night is our last night of *Teresa*. It has been worth it for Lewis's beautiful performance, and for my Teresa. I've never had so many letters from people moved by it. It should have been done like a Morality Play almost as if in a church, and all the comedy is like the old Moralities. Ah well!'

In the meantime they had been planning for one last trip to Australia with another recital programme. This time it was to be sponsored by the Australian Elizabethan Theatre Trust (much to Lewis's surprise) mainly owing to the encouragement and insistence of their new executive director Neil Hutchison. There had been a lot of haggling over who was to pay for what and a lot of niggardly thinking on the part of the financial men of the Trust, to Neil Hutchison's fury, to Lewis's despair and to Sybil's shrugging of shoulders. But by the end of November it had all been arranged and they were to sail in the *Canberra* towards the end of January.

But just before they sailed we had one very alarming letter from Sybil:

I am in a blue funk about Lewis. I don't know what to do. When Lewis saw the itinerary for the tour he went all to pieces. I'm beginning to wonder if he can do it. I do feel the sea voyage and seeing you, John, will be good for him, but he isn't fit and his nerves are too awful and he seems to funk everything. I'd feel happier to do the show by myself. I'm doing one on my own on Sunday in spite of a node on my vocal cord, which will go when I can rest a bit. We do so want to come and I would fit in with anything Neil suggested as I'm very fit (apart from a few stupid things which won't worry me anyway). It would be too disappointing not to be able to come (tho' that has entered my head). Lewis is in a poor way nervously, just wants to give up. I think it's partly the misery of not seeing properly, can't read with any sort of comfort and you know how he loves reading.

But they did come. They had Christmas in London at Ian and Mary's home with our three and Diana. Sybil had had a minor operation by the leading throat specialist, who had 'chopped off the node', according to Sybil. Jane was off to Hong Kong the following week on a Christmas present trip from her godfather and his wife, the Turners, with whom she stayed, Penny was now a hostess in BOAC, while Anthony was shortly going to join a computer firm, which oddly enough Lewis had suggested in a letter to me at least a year earlier. Lewis ended the year with a postscript to a letter of Sybil's which read: 'I still can't believe that we shall follow this letter soon to Australia. Here's to all old friends round Walla Burra Crag.'

Patricia was engaged by the Trust to be their manager and general organiser for the tour and she flew across to meet them when they disembarked at Perth. Sybil's letters and one or two other reports from London had made us rather anxious. After all it is not easy to do a fairly rackety and strenuous tour of Australian townships when you are in your eighties as both of them were by now. There were twenty-five recitals to perform in a little under three months, and it was the Australian summer. In Perth the temperature averaged 104° while they were there. Patricia went to meet them full of apprehension. But we needn't have worried. As Patricia wrote to me, 'There they were on the ship absolutely bursting with joy and saying farewell to everybody from Lord Chandos to dear little mothers with their babies. I said I hoped they wouldn't find the theatre too dreadfully hot, and Sybil said, "No, Darling, of course not. We simply love the heat." ' It really was a bit much in Perth, however, and after each of their four performances their clothes were wringing wet. But when they reached Melbourne they were as radiant as ever and ready for anything. They performed in Melbourne, Sydney, Adelaide and countless little country towns in Victoria and New South Wales. They coped with it wonderfully, although there were times when even Sybil wilted a bit.

One evening they arrived at a hotel in Newcastle, New South Wales, after a tiring journey. They went to their rooms and undressed for an early bed. After helping them to unpack Patricia went down to order a meal for them and found a deputation in the foyer. Someone had blundered and they were expected at a reception in the town. When she went upstairs to tell them Lewis was already in bed and Sybil in her dressing-gown. Sybil burst into tears and said, 'Patricia, I simply can't do it.' But she did. She got dressed again and with Patricia beside her went off to the function, gave a superb off-the-cuff speech and was charming and gracious to everyone.

The next evening they found that the dressing-room at the theatre was at the top of a long flight of stairs. Sybil's arthritis was very bad and it took Patricia ten minutes to help her down to the stage. Again I heard about it in a letter. 'As we stood in the wings I looked at this little stooping figure, a very old lady in pain leaning on a stick, I wondered if she could get through the show. Lewis standing beside us had the same thought. "Will you be all right, Sybil?" I whispered. "It's time for you to go on." "I'm fine, dear," she answered, "Here, take my stick." As I took it she suddenly and miraculously seemed to grow tall. Her bowed back straightened, her head came up proudly and twenty or thirty years fell off her. She strode on to the stage as only she can do it with all her old style and blazing energy.'

One last little incident must be recalled. At a lunch in the town of Traralgon in Gippsland Patricia asked the Mayor if he would be coming to the recital. 'Too right I'm coming,' he replied. 'I wasn't going to, but after meeting them, well I mean to say I can't see how these two old ones can do a recital and I've gotta find out.' And afterwards he came back stage rubbing his hands and greeted Patricia at their door with, 'Terrific! That's what they are. Terrific! And look, I never went to sleep, not once, and I always do.'

By April they had been up and down the land by car, train and aircraft and were still as bright as buttons. It seemed to us that they had only just stepped ashore at Perth when they were re-embarking on a liner for home. The three months were 'like an evening gone'. When they had left us in 1956 their send-off had been tearful and emotional. We all felt something final about it. Now, oddly enough, even though they were without any doubt very much older, which makes eleven thousand miles a very long distance, their farewell party took on the mood of a celebration. There is no doubt that their depressions and their feeling old and tired had somehow disappeared into the Australian sunshine or, to quote the hymn again, they flew 'forgotten as a dream dies at the opening day.'

Sybil wrote almost every day from the ship and so we heard of their doings from Perth, Bombay, Aden, Port Said and Marseilles. The change of tone from that of the outward voyage was remarkable. At the Captain's table with them were Sir James Darling, the famous head-master of Geelong Grammar, and his wife. Sybil's letters were filled with the lively discussion ranging from education to philosophy and from Australian morals to modern painting, and they all loved each other's company. Jim Darling told me when they returned to Australia that they had never had such a stimulating and enchanted voyage. Lewis and Sybil gave a cocktail party, several dinners and even danced together. They went ashore together at Bombay, which was too hot, and at Marseilles, which had too many steps, but none of it stopped them enjoying it all. During the voyage Sybil persuaded Lewis to have breakfast in bed quite often and for the first time in his life, he acquiesced without feeling guilty about it. Lewis's sight was now very bad, and it was at this time that Sybil began the habit of reading aloud to him. This reading was to become one of their happiest activities in the coming years and they saw to it that somehow it happened every day.

They had a spectacular welcome when they reached London from Ian, Mary, Diana, Anthony, Penny, Jane and various other Thorndike and Casson relations. Sybil has always been a kind of clearing-house for the distribution of family news and she sent us pages of letters telling us what even our second and third cousins were doing. It is just as well, I suppose, that there should be one member of a large family that keeps in touch with all the others, and in Sybil's case it is one of the reasons, one among very, very many, why she became quite early on the Mat-riarch – owing allegiance to all, but fealty to only one – the Patriarch.

Within a matter of days of their arrival home they were settled in a cottage at Fishbourne, near Chichester, and began rehearsals for *Uncle Vanya* with Larry Olivier, Joan Plowright, Michael Redgrave and a lot of other old friends. Our Jane was with them at the cottage. Having missed out on getting a place in the company, she got a job as an usherette in the theatre and so was able to take on a lot of the domestic chores. She was also able to spend time every day with Lewis reading poetry and plays, with a fair number of good old barneys with Sybil, who cannot see any of her relations as other than babies to be controlled and directed. The only time she never tried to control or direct her own four was when they *were* babies. But it didn't always help her relationship with her very independent-minded and energetic grand-daughter. Jane's time spent reading aloud to Lewis was invaluable, because he was able to pass on to her so much of his knowledge of the rhythms, the phrasings, the sensitivity to sound and the projecting of thought and emotion to listeners. He told me during his last year that he felt that she would be able to take up the torch of making people think of speech as an art in itself, when he had to drop it.

One of Sybil's letters at this time is of particular interest. The Chichester Theatre has an open-thrust stage like its forerunners and counterparts in Stratford, Ontario and Minneapolis. Lewis and Sybil were thrilled with it as they always have been with anything that is breaking out into new fields. But they were not so thrilled with the way many of the company were using it – especially, of course, in the matter of speech in audibility and effectiveness:

. . . we love our cottage but the theatre work depresses us a bit. It is being done like film acting – everything thrown away and honestly I can only hear a quarter of what anyone is saying! I can't bear this over-intimate acting. Everything underplayed. It's a lovely theatre. Michael Redgrave beautiful as Vanya – and I hear about half of what he says. The rest are *so* good – and I hear only about a quarter of it – that is if I'm fairly near!!

But they were enjoying playing with each other even though Lewis was having a very bad attack of eczema and shingles on his legs and body, and her rheumatism (which was found to be arthritis) and sciatica were giving her constant pain. The show went well, too, despite their forebodings about the speech, and Lewis's Telyegin was as exquisite as her Marina.

In the autumn Sybil went into her first musical, the ill-fated *Vanity Fair*, directed by Lionel Harris again. Jane auditioned for it and got herself one or two small parts in it. I can't say why it didn't go in London after an apparently enthusiastic tour of the provinces, but go it did not. Sybil as usual had another ball and acted everybody else off the stage – or so I was told – and wrote to tell us that the appalling cold 'kept everybody at their TV and they wouldn't go out in case they got pneumonia.' By now Sybil had celebrated her eightieth birthday (and Lewis his eighty-seventh), which is not a bad age to make a start in musical comedy, and as ever the audience adored her.

Lewis was writing fewer and fewer letters as his eyes got worse, but he wrote about *Vanity Fair*. Having done the whole tour with Sybil he was now in London feeling once again rather left out. This letter was dated 5th December, 1962:

At last since the tour and the chaos of opening *Vanity Fair* I am attempting to write another letter. Most nights so far I have spent the evening in Sybil's dressing-room, living on the pocket radio the Godfreys gave me when they went back to Tasmania. [They had lived at 98.] To-night (the third consecutive thick fog!) I have spent the evening at home. We still don't know the fate of *Vanity Fair*. It started off well, and considering the fog it is keeping up fairly well, and seems to go splendidly with the audiences, but I'm still not sure. The notices were putrid and rude, and many people seem not to care for the Becky Sharp. It's a very clever performance and she has plenty of vitality, but not enough charm. We still hope for the best. I am finding it rather hard to keep boredom at bay. By myself mostly, and reading, and writing mostly impossible. I don't get much out of going to the theatre when we do go. You will have heard that some friends of mine have given me a new tape recorder and have done literary tapes for me – such a formidable collection, and I got a lot of pleasure from them. But alas I look the gift horse in the mouth by criticising the quality of the speech.

The criticising of tape recorded speech also prevented his recording letters instead of writing them. He told me that he couldn't talk freely and casually while doing it because he couldn't bear the thought of a badly spoken speech of his being on record. It had, too, a certain amount of inhibiting effect on our sending recordings to him. All the same, during the summer of this year they were both preparing to play in Judy Guthrie's play *Queen Bee*. Lewis could not of course read his script, and so Sybil read the words aloud and recorded them on tape, from which Lewis learned.

Earlier in February he had given a lecture on the work of his guide and mentor, William Poel. He had nearly refused the invitation, but with the help of a friend of the whole family, the actress Freda Gaye, and the tape recorder he put it all together. When he came to the lecture Freda followed the script and became in effect a live set of notes that he could not only refer to but also have as a highly sensitive partner to support him. The recording of the lecture, which we still have, provides not only a fascinating study of Poel's work on the technique of stage speech but presents a most moving picture of Lewis's successful struggle to rise above his near-blindness.

Just after Easter Ian and Mary, after much skilful and tactful planning, took them off by car for a holiday in the Lake District. They all four stayed at a little farmhouse by the Langdales which Ian had known from boyhood. As was to be expected Sybil's enthusiastic description of it beats any words I could have written:

Darlings, Oh we're in heaven! Drove up here on Tuesday and when we got to the Lake District we nearly passed out at the beauty – it was raining but it looked glorious. This old farmhouse is just under Langdale Pikes, Bowfell, etc., all hills around. Yesterday it poured but we drove to Grasmere – all along Thirlmere to Derwentwater where we did a lovely rainy walk along the shore and had a picnic. Then up to Watendlath in pelting rain. Lewis and I turned back after two miles – a bit too stiff it was – and sat in the car and read till Ian and Mary came back soaked! To-day it was raining hard when we got up so we left at 9.45 to go to Seathwaite and find the family graves all along the Duddon Valley. The river was a raging torrent, waterfalls and rocks and all. We found Wonderful Walker's grave and the stone by the church where he sheared the sheep. The churchyard was full of Casson graves all over 80 and 90!! We were thrilled. Lewis signed the visitors' book in the church 'great-great-great-grandson of Wonderful Walker'. We all signed but Lewis was the important one. Then the weather had cleared so we went on a glorious drive to Wastdale, so quirky – great cliffs overhanging – lunched by the side of the lake then went for a walk, Lewis and I up the slopes of Great Gable – just a nice, stiff walk – but Mary and Ian went up by a marvellous route – we came back and sat in the car. Lewis can't do *very* long walks – nor really can I – but we did far more than we expected. We sat and watched the clouds and sun over Great Gable and over Scafell. How glorious this country is, isn't it? I'm too sleepy to write more, I'll write a long letter later. Oh I *do* like a hill holiday. Lewis is fine and happy, and so am I.

They played *Uncle Vanya* again at Chichester that summer and in the autumn went off on tour with *Queen Bee*. Sad to say it never got to London and towards the end of the year Sybil was offered the part of the Dowager Countess of Lister in William Douglas Home's *The Reluctant Peer*.

Some time in December I had a long 'business' letter from Lewis about family finances in general and their finances in particular. He and

Sybil had distributed already to the four of us the proceeds of a life endowment policy in 1950 and on two later occasions disbursed some of their capital to us 'to save death duties'. But it helped us to buy our respective houses; Douglas and Ann in Canada, Kiff and Kay in Dublin, Ian and Mary in London and ourselves in Australia, without having to crush ourselves with gigantic mortgages. Indirectly, I suppose it also helped to give each of us that degree of security which comes from a home of one's own.

But Lewis still worried about all our security and did endless sums and got endless different answers – all in his head because he couldn't see well enough to do sums on paper – and the figures went round and round in his mind. His letter about it had cost him a great deal of effort to write because he could only see the blurred outline of the words. Furthermore, if he was interrupted at all he found it impossible to pick up his train of thought again because he couldn't read what he had written. The details of the letter are of no great interest outside the family, but the opening paragraph by a man of 88 is worthy of record:

'I think this is the third attempt to write this letter, which is mainly financial and about the future. I feel the end of 1963 is rather a milestone as I don't suppose I shall earn my living any more. And this moves me to look ahead a bit and get your views on the facts.' As it turned out we were going to be able to thrash it all out in London.

In Australia Patricia and I had been saving hard for a trip to Europe. I had not been outside Australasia for nearly ten years and we had not been away together for about twelve. By September of 1964 we at last had enough money and time to make the trip. Anthony had returned to Australia as a computer man in 1962, and Jane at the end of 1963. Sybil, I don't think, had been altogether a help with Jane's career as an actress. Her very enthusiasm to all theatrical authorities had firstly made Jane unhappy about herself, and secondly caused the managers to regard her rather as 'Grannie's pet'. She had got a job this year as small part actress and assistant stage-manager at the Newcastle Repertory, which called forth even more enthusiasm from Sybil as if she had won the lead in a major Hollywood epic. There was a bit of tension all round with everyone giving advice and all talking much too much about it. Jane has what is mostly the disadvantage of looking very like her grandmother, the same disadvantage that Ann has had to suffer. For example, when either of them has ever given a good performance someone has almost invariably come up afterwards and said, 'Has anyone ever told you how like your grandmother (or mother in Ann's case) you are?' It can make one feel that one has no identity of one's own and is something of a cross to bear. That's why Jane came back to Australia and two years later went off on her own to Canada to be, as she put it, 'where I am not always seen as my grandmother's granddaughter.' There were no harsh feelings about it either way. It was just one of the harsh facts of life.

Sybil found herself in quite a success in *The Reluctant Peer* which ran from February to July that year. Because the play was based on Douglas Home's brother, Sir Alec, and Sybil played his mother she got to know the family and had one or two Conservative/Socialist sallies with the then Prime Minister.

In August Anthony became the first of their ten grandchildren to become engaged. His fiancée was Janneke van Holst Pellekaan, the daughter of a Dutch-Australian family all of whom had been our friends from our first year in Australia. Her parents had already set off on a trip to Europe and met Lewis and Sybil in London exactly as my future in-laws had met them thirty years before.

Meanwhile we had booked our flights for a three months' holiday (a part-working one for me) and we landed at London airport on 17th December. As we came through into the Customs Hall we saw through the glass door the faces of two beaming mothers, Sybil and Betty Chester Master, arm-in-arm waiting to greet their offspring. An hour later we were all at 98 with Lewis. What a reunion it was and the other residents of Swan Court must have had a hard time making themselves heard for the next few days.

But there was still more excitement than our reunion. On our flight home we had stopped for three days in Rome. Waiting for us at our hotel had been a cable from Anthony saying, 'Flying London end January. Wedding February 4th. Please arrange.'

Her parents were somewhere in Europe in a caravan. We were staying in the tiny spare bedroom at 98 with Lewis and Sybil and so it all got rather Cassonly hectic within days of our arrival. Add to this the onslaught of Christmas, two cocktail parties for all our long lost friends, with Lewis and Sybil at both, of course, given at the flat Penny shared with two other girls and our completely childish excitement

at being back in London over Christmas and you have all the ingredients for pandemonium to reign supreme.

Living in 98 we found that Lewis was very down first thing every
morning. Anything that caused the slightest change in his routine
seemed to upset him until he had had a bath and got dressed by around
10 a.m. Even carrying the breakfast tray to the kitchen for the washing-
up was not allowed to be done by anyone else because it was 'his job' –
important because it was one of the things he could do despite his
blindness. We soon learnt to be very careful to keep off contentious
subjects till lunchtime and then he would join in the argument with
gusto.

On the morning of Churchill's funeral he had stayed in bed listening
to the ceremony on his little radio while the rest of us in another room
watched it all on television. Something that he heard in the service, or
maybe the whole emotional impact of it all, suddenly triggered off what
was very nearly a brainstorm of depression in Lewis. He was in an
agony of some strange remorse and for a quarter of an hour no one
could comfort him. Eventually Sybil and Patricia calmed him down and
got him to relax, but it was our first experience of the melancholy
that gripped him like a fever more and more frequently during these
last few years.

On the day of Anthony's wedding, however, he was in tremendous
form, as was everybody else. Jane's godfather, Mike Turner, had given
her the lovely present of a return air ticket from Australia, and the
Dutch community in Melbourne had given Janneke's grandmother
another, and so it was a huge family gathering. There were in fact four
grandparents present whose total ages came to 340 years – old Mrs
Hart, Betty Chester Master and Lewis and Sybil. But of course grandparents don't have major rôles at weddings and so there was a certain
amount of jostling for limelight among the three grandmothers, both
at the church and the reception. It was very much a family affair but
not all that quiet a wedding. A cousin of Patricia, Nan Spite and her
husband Frank, both of New Zealand, happened to be in London on
holiday and very kindly allowed their house to be used for the reception
and so the generations below the grandparents all held the centre of the
stage. Lewis and Sybil, however, were thrilled that their only male
Casson grandchild had married a wife that the whole family adored,

and delighted to feel that perhaps before long they were going to play the new rôle of great-grandparents.

The bridal pair had a short honeymoon in Britain and Europe and then went off via America back to Australia. I met them again in New York on my way back at the end of February. By then Sybil had just opened in a not very good play called *Return Ticket* at Eastbourne, and the first night there was on my last evening in England.

Patricia, who was staying on for another month, and I went down to Eastbourne for the night and saw the play, which we didn't like at all, and nor quite clearly did Lewis. This time it seemed to us that the producer had either been completely overawed, or over-ruled, by Sybil (and almost certainly the former). Sybil had in fact been given her head. Furthermore the rest of the cast were on an entirely different level so that Sybil was clearly working on the theory that she had to double her attack to make up for the lack of it in the others. When Sybil doubles her attack you don't see anything else but her, and I fear it is usually much too much unless the producer controls it firmly. This one didn't.

I was flying off next day which meant driving off from Eastbourne at a little after 4 a.m. The two of them had insisted that we wake them to say good-bye and we all four had tea together in their bedroom before we left. It was snowing heavily and I shall always see in my memory the picture of the two of them standing at the first-floor window in their dressing-gowns while we waved up at them from under the street lamp. When we drove off the falling snowflakes seemed to make a gentle slow curtain to yet another act.

Such a curtain, dramatically speaking, should have been for a long, long separation. The scene demanded it. But it didn't get it. We were back within the year. Penny had now been with BOAC for just over four years. Just before we left Australia for this trip she had told us that she could now nominate one of us for one of those wonderful staff concession flights at only ten per cent of the fare. This time Patricia used it and I paid for mine. But if we waited one day over the year from Patricia's arrival back in Australia we could both have another trip. I can't help feeling that there was something anti-climactic about our arrival back in London again at the end of the following March.

Before we got there, however, Lewis celebrated his ninetieth birthday. From October 1875 to October 1965 is quite a span of years and I wrote him a special letter:

What in the world can an eldest son say to his father for his father's ninetieth birthday? Many happy returns? Yes, of course. Happy birthday? Yes, of course. But both these are ludicrously inadequate for such a day. One can't make memorable moments by saying 'Let's make this a memorable moment!' You can in a play because the future is already written. But in life a moment can't be memorable till it is part of the memory. What matters to you and me is the total of those moments when we were both much too busy to think about them as memorable moments. Mending punctures in Brittany, walks along the sea-wall after supper at Dymchurch, your meeting me at Tilbury when I got back from China, working on Macbeth at Ayr, hearing you do the Elgar speech in *The Linden Tree* (one of my favourites), all these and hundreds more are the undesigned, unpremeditated, unforeseen and, at the time, unnoticed memorable moments.

We have arranged to have sent to you for your ninetieth a bottle of *very* good whisky because of Glasgow and Scotland (do you remember our walks along the river at Perth when I was trying to learn Sir Robert Bowes in *Jamie the Saxt*?) and a bottle of *very* good Armagnac like Marion gave to Professor Linden in *The Linden Tree* for his sixty-fifth birthday. They are not meant for dispensing unlimited largesse. They are for *you* to enjoy with *a* friend or perhaps two! Have a nip or two of one or the other or both *every* evening so that you can have a really luxurious taste daily. This particular whisky should be taken strong because it's lovely, and the Armagnac *only* as a liqueur because it's gorgeous. We want a report on the drinking of them.

Bless you and we'll be thinking of you on 26th.

We got a scrawled answer from him which was short and almost illegible but when we got back to England five months later he had kept enough in one of the bottles for him and me to be able to have a tot together.

Just before we got there they had opened with a revival of *Arsenic and Old Lace*. Sybil and Athene Seyler were the two charming ladies who took pity on lonely old gentlemen by poisoning them with their special brew of elderberry wine, and Lewis played the Superintendent of the Mental Home, who comes at the end to take them away and gets poisoned himself. Despite his gloomy predictions about 'not earning his living any more' here was Lewis at 90 very vigorously alive and earning an excellent income. His age was mentioned in a programme note, and the audience's knowledge of this added greatly to their tension when on stage he bounded up a flight of stairs. He then had to

descend them again a moment later carrying half a dozen large parcels
and a tennis racket. You could feel the audience willing him to be
careful. They both loved performing in it and the whole production
was hilarious.

Our visit this time was short and rushed, and we had to be away
again by the middle of May. But just before we left a letter arrived
addressed to them both from Anthony. It began:

'We are thrilled to be able to tell you that Janneke is now three
months pregnant. . . .'

The post had come just before breakfast and Lewis was still in bed.
Sybil had read the first sentence and had gone in to Lewis calling us to
go in too. We all sat on the bed while she read the whole letter aloud
holding Lewis's hand all the time. Here was the beginning of yet
another generation and they were so happy and so deeply moved.

We flew off ten days later back to Australia via Canada to see Jane
and on across the Pacific to Melbourne. On 8th November Anthony
cabled them, 'Your great-grandson Randal Lewis Casson arrived to-day.
Both well,' and we sent, 'Congratulations on becoming great-
grandparents.' Anthony and Janneke had kept the proposed Christian
names a complete secret, and we were all so touched that they had
chosen two which belonged so much to the family. A son had been
born to the 'last of the Cassons' in Anthony's generation and the
Casson line would go on.

In June they had been jointly honoured by being made honorary
doctors of literature at Oxford. We had sent them a cable for the
occasion in a quote from *Treasure Island*. It read, 'Doctors is all swabs.'
A few days later we had a wonderful letter from Sybil telling us all
about the day.

23rd June '66. Darlings, Thank you for your cable. We roared when we
read it. Where did it come from? You do think up killing telegrams. Sweet of
you to remember the day. And *what* a day! The night before I'd have given
anything not to have had to go through it. I was worried about Lewis who felt
agitato and nervy about not being able to stand it all. But prayer does a lot!
We woke at 6.30 a.m. both feeling O.K. I got our early breakfast, and then
dressed. I wore a white dress with yellow, grey and black floweries on it and a
large white hat. Lewis in his dark suit (cleaned for the purpose, and I only
found out the afternoon before that all the lining had run amok so me
mending and cursing and strengthening buttons – he just wouldn't get a new
suit, though he needs one!!). When we were dressed we both took a pill – the

A study in exasperation after a performance in Wellington N.Z.

On the way to receiving honorary doctorates at Oxford

green and whites which make you feel you don't give a damn! Hire car came at 8.40 and I explained the whole drill to our dear driver Yvonne – and as we drove a calm descended, 'then a new and wondrous light dawned on her wondering mind' – see Matilda Bligh – the Victorian recitation. As the pouring rain got less and less we felt better and better. Arrived in Oxford – drove down the Broad, when a policeman stopped us. 'Hey! I'm looking for you – they're all waiting,' *so* friendly. In then to Exeter College to the Rector's Lodge (photographers everywhere). There the Vice-Chancellor himself, Sir Something Wheare, came out and greeted us like old pals, and his wife Lady Wheare. He is a Melbourne boy – got a Rhodes Scholarship from Scotch College and has ended up with the biggest plum in the university world, Vice-Chancellor of Oxford – a perfect darling. Then 'ticket-office' [Casson word for Loo] and then we went to a lovely drawing-room to try on our robes. Scarlet and grey (exactly matching the colour of the flowers on my dress). Lewis had a mortar-board hat and mine was *killing* – a mortar-board, only soft. I looked awful. Then in came Sir Geoffrey Gibbs who's head of your Australia Bank (we liked him awfully). Then came the Rt. Hon. Harold Macmillan who is Chancellor of the University. He looked very sad as he's just lost his dear wife. Then the other five Honorands joined us and we all went to the Big Hall for champagne. It was a picture – all oak-panelled and everyone in scarlet robes, about 200 of them. Much talk with old friends and new friends etc. *and* Peggy Ashcroft who had a degree last year – her first (it was my 4th!!!). Then the procession formed, all 200 of them in scarlet with black-garbed figures with rods preceding and we seven bringing up the rear. Sir G. G. leading alone, then Lewis and me together – then John Piper the painter, two foreign professors and Dr Cartwright – the woman head of Girton who got the degree of Doctor of Science – she's one of the first mathematicians in England (and Diana's boss at Girton). We proceeded through crowds (who clapped Lewis and me and called out our names – *our* public!) right up the Broad we went at funeral pace – but all scarlet and looking fine – then turned into the Sheldonian – through lovely gateways and up and down steps – put there to trip one up – and into this glorious Sheldonian Theatre where great ceremonies are held. Mr Macmillan had a black robe with gold (worth £1,100 the VC told us, all real gold). He was on a sort of throne high up and we seven stood in the aisle – and one by one called up by the Public Orator to stand beside him while he read out a long bit about us in Latin (I was cheered to hear Sybillianus Thorndike and Ludovicos Casson). Then we went up six awful steps and were shaken by the hand by the Chancellor and told we were now Doctors of Letters – all in Latin. Then we sat down on high seats near him. Mary and Ian, Diana and Pen were in the front row behind us. The ceremony *all* in Latin lasted till one o'clock when we all, to bells and trumpets and a lovely march, filed out and proceeded to All Souls where we had drinks on the lovely lawn (all sunshine now – lovely) and Mary and Co. arrived and drank and I introduced them, especially Pen, to the VC as she'd been a Melbourne gal, and Diana to her Head from Girton, and Mary and Ian were full of life and beans. We all went in to lunch – the Chancellor looked very old and tired and he went home. But I sat on the VC's right with a Danish professor on my right. The VC is a darling and we had a huge talk about Australia, which he still hankers after, and has a warm Australian accent. When I said 'We're going back to the theatre Sarvo' [Australian for 'This afternoon'] he nearly passed out and said he felt at home and I was 'a beaut'!! We left amid cheers after lunch and everyone was so *kind* to us – and Mary and Ian *loved* it so did the girls, who stayed on for the Big Garden Party. No more, I'll write again. It's been the Crown of our Life, and Swabs or not we feel at the Top. Lewis was in marvellous form and looked about 50!

But as time went on Sybil's letters spoke more and more of the effort they were having to keep going, to keep going not just as two old people, of course, but as two people of twenty years younger. She wrote in September in answer to some question from Patricia about England.

We have got to remember that the world is in a state of change and the people who want England to be strong very often are the ones that feel we should call out troops in Rhodesia, etc. The Government here hasn't got any great men (but neither has the Opposition) and they are trying to do their best in very difficult changing conditions (if only some of them would put England before party!) It's almost like birth-pains going on all over the world. The black Africans would love us to bring out armies and bash UDI and Mr Smith but that's not the adult way. The country's got badly into difficulties over finance but it's been piling up since the war, and the victors in war always suffer the worst! I think people are all right here. There's crime but there always will be and we are trying to deal with it in a decent way. I think prayer helps more than anything – it is helping *me* more than cod liver oil. I am getting better. Lewis's illness – if one can call it illness – is a depressive one. He's all right with heart, blood pressure, blood tests, lungs, etc., but depths of depression in the mornings. We are very close to each other and do help each other.

And then a few weeks later soon after Randal's birth:

Lewis and I are both very tired and when this Duras play is over I'll make Lewis come on a trip. We very much want to see Ann and Douglas and family as they are getting so grown-up. I think a good trip will do us a lot of good. I feel so tired to-day. I've been doing *Jane Clegg* BBC, for three days. We recorded this morning. It's one of the plays in what they call 'The Sybil Thorndike Festival'. I do a play a month of my own choosing. I've done *The Foolish Gentlewoman*, I'm doing an hour of *St Joan* scenes, *The Potting Shed*, *The Lion* and the Unicorn, Captain Brassbound and The Distaff Side, The Corn is Green and Passage to India. All good grist to the Tour by Sea to Australia! Lewis is feeling he wants to stop, and after Golders Green next week we'll be off to stay with Kiff and Kay in Dublin, and rest there for two weeks. But if you do come home next year we can return to Australia with you for we must see Randal – and Mathoura Road again. Lewis is wonderful if feeble. I am feeble but not wonderful!!

The 'Duras play' was *The Viaduct* translated from the French. It began in Guildford and got terrible notices from all the critics except Harold Hobson and after a short tour it came off without going to London. But once again Sybil found it thrilling, deeply symbolic and rewarding:

It has been a real disappointment to us that the notices put an end to a possible run in London, but I think it's understandable. It's a play on 3 levels: 1) the naturalistic one of a very horrible murder by 2 quite respectable people, 2) the expression from the woman of the need to expiate in a dramatic and public way her whole unfulfilled life, and 3) the wider thing of a soul having to expiate all the sins and deficiencies of past life or lives – and paying for it being a sort of redemption. This to me has been a rewarding experience. I've been able to 'cast off' something in this play, and have had some very wonderful letters expressing the same thing, such letters of depth that I've never had before. I think it would have been better if Lewis could have played it with me. Max Adrian was *very* good, but Lewis would have been true *and* symbolic and we'd have played as one. (Max is a darling and I've loved playing with him).

In July they went off to Minneapolis to stay with the Campbells (but it couldn't be the pure indulgence of a holiday, so Sybil did a very full programme of lectures to the University of Minnesota).

We are having a most happy time here. The jet-plane was wonderful and we enjoyed it. But Lewis can't stand very much and I don't want to *over* do him. I want to keep him as long as possible. He rests a lot here and if he takes a pill he enjoys the theatre. He gets very weak and curiously frightened of dying and leaving us. The family very lively, tall and clever – and such darlings – so very kind to us. Jane is coming over from Canada on Sunday and we're living for it. The Mississippi is terrific.

After our 1966 trip to London Patricia and I were going to have to wait a couple of years before we could get another joint concession flight from Penny and BOAC. Towards the end of 1967, however, I was invited by the firm I worked for to come to the headquarters in

London for a year or so. Accordingly we made our plans to leave Melbourne early in May, 1968, fly to Vancouver, have a three weeks' holiday in Canada and get to London at the beginning of June.

Appropriately and dramatically, as a young Australian, at noon on Anzac Day, 25th April, 1968, Lewis and Sybil's second great-grandson was born to Anthony and Janneke in Melbourne. Sybil had just finished another short tour of another play which didn't get to London, *Call Me Jackie* by Enid Bagnold, and they were about to start on another project. Her letter, however, began with great enthusiasm for the arrival of the baby.

Darlings. We are all *thrilled* about Thomas Walter, and so glad it's another boy, aren't you? The thrills are *too* much. We long for details and how Randal takes to Thomas Walter. Lewis is so bucked, another Thomas Casson (*his* father).

I'm a bit worried over this next play. Emlyn Williams wants us both in *Night Must Fall* with the TV star Adam Faith in Emlyn's part. It will be his first straight part and a bit of an experiment, but he's enormously popular as a TV and pantomime actor and is a *darling* fellow – but I'm scared of doing another tour with Lewis. He gets so worried with quite absurd phobias. The contract is very good and Lewis is the Judge at the beginning – just one speech – and they say they could tape that so he would only have to *show* himself in this prologue. But he gets in such a 'tiz' over it, though deeply I think he wants to do it. Oh dear, old age problems of long ago are very worrying. I think he'll talk to you about it. He makes mountains out of small things in the past. He's such a darling, and I love him always and the difficulties have only seemed to make our real love greater. But marriage isn't always easy especially with violent people like Lewis and me. So much to be thankful for, and so much to be sorry for!! But more to be glad about.

We hadn't the faintest idea when they were starting off because Sybil rarely mentions any other dates but birthdays (*none* of which she ever forgets). We landed at Heathrow on 2nd June with no one to meet us as Penny was away on a BOAC job in another quarter of the globe. We telephoned Swan Court from the airport and there was no reply. So we telephoned Mary. 'Mummy and Daddy are on tour,' she told us after we'd got through our greetings. 'They're in Bristol this week, I think.'

And it was in their bedroom at the Grand Hotel in Bristol that we ran them to earth the next morning and all fell into each other's arms after our two-year parting. Lewis was now only a few months short of

92 and after a joyful lunch he took me aside and said, 'I'm afraid you'll find I'm getting dreadfully old these days,' in an apologetic voice as though I might be expecting him to climb Snowdon with me.

We saw the show that night and I'm afraid secretly hoped that it wouldn't get as far as London. We felt that it was reasonably good middle-level repertory standard with two stars to give it a boost, and two stars who should never have been asked to give such a show a boost, because everyone knows that if they are asked they will always try to give any show a boost. And Sybil thought Adam Faith was a most charming young man, which he is. But for her it seemed to follow that he was a very good actor, whereas to me at any rate he was not much more than a competent actor. I got the feeling that Lewis saw all this but thought that the best thing to do was to play along with it and earn a bob or two while playing. None of us were really surprised that it didn't go into London. After we saw them in Bristol they went on for another week in Southsea and that was the end of it. Thereafter we were all together in London.

Penny had given us the spare room in her small flat at Earl's Court, and I was working in Knightsbridge. So it was easy of an evening for me to walk round the back of Harrods and through Chelsea Green to Swan Court when I had finished at the office. I usually found them in the flat with Sybil reading to Lewis. They used to enjoy this reading immensely and they tackled works of great philosophical difficulty. As Lewis explained it: 'You can have tremendous discussions like this without arguing *against* the other person. One of you has stated a case in words out loud, but is not responsible for the ideas themselves – only for reading them aloud. And so the one who's listening can argue against the ideas without attacking the person who stated them. It's far the best way of discussing anything.'

We had a mad whirl of theatres and dinners and visits that summer and autumn. Lewis was usually in good fettle and Sybil even more so despite the crippling and almost constant pain from arthritis and sciatica.

In November our friends the Carlisle Taylors went off on a trip to Australia and at their invitation we moved into their large and blissfully comfortable flat in Holland Park. Furthermore it was on the ground floor, so it was easy for Lewis and Sybil to come and have meals with us without the trouble of climbing a lot of stairs, and they came often.

Jane came over from Canada early in December to spend Christmas with us for one thing, but more importantly to be with us on 22nd December for their Diamond Wedding. Kiff and Kay arrived from Dublin a few days before. There was a steadily growing excitement as the great day drew near and the 'clan' began to assemble in London.

Two or three days before the celebration we took Lewis and Sybil with Jane to see the film *2001*, the space epic. Whatever the merits or demerits of the film as a whole, nobody could be unmoved by the shots of a spaceship manoeuvring into the space-dock, with the huge curve of the earth filling one side of the screen with the moon and the stars wheeling around as the ship turned in to land. Jane was sitting next to Lewis and at this moment happened to look round at him. He sat with his head to one side so as to make the best of his limited peripheral vision, and tears were streaming down his face. 'Why are you crying, Grandaddy?' whispered Jane, and he answered, 'I was alive when they invented the motor car.'

On Sunday 22nd December, 1968, we gave a party to celebrate their Diamond Wedding. But then I've already said that. And although there is so much more that could, and I expect will, be said about these two splendid and astonishing people, there is not very much more for me to say.

Chapter 15

EPILOGUE

ON Sunday 29th December, 1968, a week after their Diamond Wedding, we celebrated their Diamond Wedding again. This time it was 'Family Only' at the home in Hampton of Owen and Paddy Reed, and without much difficulty we managed to assemble nearly as many relations as there had been friends at the first party. For us who had been so long in Australia it was a revelation to discover that we had so many unknown nephews, nieces, cousins and even children of cousins, whom we had only heard of vaguely as babies. But Lewis and Sybil needed no introductions. They knew every single one of them and all about them. This time it was Owen, as the host, who proposed their health and said all the things and more that we were all thinking. They stood hand in hand, the patriarch and matriarch of this large, eccentric, very energetic, very clannish and on the whole mutually admiring family.

Among the guests was my second cousin, Tom Pocock. Sybil's episcopal Uncle Jack Bowers had two children, Basil and Dorothy, who were therefore her first cousins. Dorothy had married Guy Pocock and they had one child Tom whom I had not seen since he was ten years old, over thirty years before. On our return from Australia, Sybil had said, 'You must meet Tom Pocock again. He's your – what is it? – second cousin, and such a nice boy. He's a journalist and writes awfully well. We loved his book on Nelson, didn't we Lewis?'

And so of course we asked him to dinner and put him next to Penny. This was in the previous November. In the middle of a night in February Penny came round to our flat with Tom to announce that they had become engaged.

The two of us and Penny had already arranged to have drinks at 98 the next evening and so we all decided that Tom should come too and break the news. Patricia and I got there first with a bottle of champagne that I managed to hide in a cupboard. When the bell rang I opened the door and let them in. Sybil said, 'Penny darling, how nice to see you,

327

oh! and Tom! What a lovely surprise!' Penny then said, 'Can I introduce you to my fiancé?' Sybil looked rather shocked and thought, as she told us later, 'Penny shouldn't joke about things like that,' and said, 'Yes dear, yes.' We then put our oar in and said, 'But it's true. They're engaged!' Lewis not trusting his hearing said, 'What? What's this?' and Sybil said, 'I don't believe it. Oh! I'm going to cry. How lovely. You darlings!' and burst into tears followed by Lewis. Then out came the champagne. For nearly ten years Penny had been the member of the family who had lived near them, had kept an eye on them, had helped them and generally provided such cosseting as had been required. They were overjoyed that she was going to marry Tom. 'Wouldn't Dorothy have been delighted,' she cried, while Lewis made sort of humming noises of affection, which he always did when his delight bereft him of speech.

They were married at Lewis and Sybil's church, Christ Church, Chelsea, on 26th April. As I led Penny up the aisle Lewis seized Patricia's hand and never let go of it till the service was over. He couldn't see or hear much, but Penny had said, 'We are going to speak loud enough to be sure that Grandaddy Lewis can hear it all,' and they did. At the reception in the Holland Park flat, Lewis said to me, his face brimming with happiness, 'Listen to Penny's voice. It resounds with joy.' He really adored Penny, and seeing her so happy on her wedding day was a crowning moment of his life.

On 4th May at the suggestion of the energetic and unflagging secretary of the Apollo Society, John Carroll, I partnered Sybil in a poetry recital at Ken Wood. We had run through our poems together a night or two earlier under Lewis's 'watchful' ear. So watchful was he of me that I had to beg him to remember that I was not a highly skilled professional like him and Sybil. Would he please not pull it all to bits, but just help me not to let Sybil down. I remember he took a great shuddering breath just like the time when I dropped the spring-gadget from the car engine into the long grass, and then said, 'Sorry, I was forgetting we're not in the theatre. I mustn't be too perfectionist.' And then he laughed in that very special way that somehow apologised and said, 'Let's get on with it and enjoy it,' all at the same time. We got on with it and by the end of the evening he was, I hope, 'pleased – but *never* satisfied.'

That evening of early summer in the lovely Ken Wood house, he sat with Patricia while I took the place with Sybil that should have been his. Sybil recited Hecuba, I remember, and spoke it as though it were specially for him, which perhaps it was. I watched him while she was speaking and there was a look of faraway smiling contentment on his face as his lips moved in unison with Sybil's words.

When it was over he told us both how much he had enjoyed it. I had done the long narrative poem of Kipling, 'The Mary Gloster', and we had had a lot of difficulty at our rehearsal about my inability to characterise it to his satisfaction. In the little dressing-room he said, 'Lovely John, especially in the first part.' 'What about "The Mary Gloster"?' I asked (it had been in the second part). 'It's a very difficult one to do, isn't it? But I think to-night you were nearer to it. We must have another go at it.' But I'm afraid we were never going to read together again.

A week later Sybil had to go to Rochester, the city where she had been brought up, and of which she is a Freeman, for an evening civic function. We had all been a little worried about Lewis, who didn't appear at all well, and so Sybil went to Rochester on her own. To keep Lewis company Patricia spent the evening at Swan Court. He went to bed early. At about 11 p.m. he rushed into the room wild-eyed and in the grip of some sort of nightmare. 'Where's Sybil?' he kept saying. Patricia calmed him down and waited with him till Sybil returned. The next morning she telephoned the doctor despite protests from both Sybil and Lewis. After his examination the doctor said Lewis should spend a few days in the Nuffield Hospital for a number of tests as he was not at all easy about him.

They both knew the Nuffield because Sybil had twice had deep injections into her shoulder there during the past year and each time they had arranged a double ward so that Lewis could be with her. On Tuesday 13th May, Lewis was taken to hospital, and although we were all concerned, as one is with anyone of 93, we were not unduly worried. But on Wednesday afternoon John Janvrin, our doctor, telephoned me and said that Lewis was much more seriously ill than we had all thought. He was gravely concerned and not optimistic about his recovery. That evening Patricia and I had to tell Sybil this news at Swan Court.

She hadn't really considered the possibility of Lewis dying, even though they had often talked about 'our not having all that much time

329

left to be together'. Or rather she had considered the possibility but hadn't really admitted it to herself. We didn't use the awful word 'terminal' that the doctor had said to me, but we had to say that Lewis was very seriously ill. She took the news bravely and of course half of her believed that it wasn't true.

On Thursday evening we went with the car to pick Sybil up at the hospital and to spend a few minutes with Lewis. But when we got there we found Sybil waiting in the vestibule.

'He was very tired,' she said, 'so I tucked him up and he's going off to sleep. He looked so sweet. He sent his good night and will see you to-morrow.'

Early on Friday morning Sybil was driven to the Nuffield by Patricia. Lewis was to see a specialist first thing and she wanted to be with him directly afterwards. But by some rather wonderful trick of fate the rush-hour traffic seemed to open up before them, almost as if it had been arranged for her, and she was able to see Lewis before the doctors came.

She found him much calmer and more peaceful than the night before and they talked cheerfully together for ten precious unexpected minutes. A cable had arrived that morning from Jane in Canada saying, 'Darling Grandaddy I love you very much. Get well soon,' and when Sybil read it to him he smiled happily.

A little while later after he had seen his doctors and with Sybil beside him holding his hand he quietly slipped away from her.

Sybil and he had been together for more than sixty years and suddenly he wasn't there any more to be her husband, her companion and her strength and stay. We took her home and she talked incessantly about him. Her own strength was wonderful to behold as she held on, talked to friends and relations and insisted on making all arrangements herself for whatever had to be done. On the day before the funeral she asked Patricia to take her to Harrods to order flowers. It was so like her that she ordered not only flowers from herself but from all those relations who wouldn't be able to afford much themselves. She ordered masses of flowers. And then wiping away her tears, she looked up at the ceiling and said, 'I've spent an absolute fortune. Lewis will be simply furious, and he can't do anything about it.'

Over the next week flowers, telegrams and letters poured into the flat from people all over the world. The very first message came before

Epilogue

she got home from the hospital. It was from Larry Olivier, who had gone to Swan Court in person at once as soon as he heard the news. She had something like fifteen hundred messages of one sort or another and she answered every single one herself with a short personal note. She told us that it was this that kept her going during those first few achingly empty weeks.

She was greatly moved when the Dean of Westminster wrote to her to say that he and the Chapter would deem it a great honour if Lewis's memorial service could be held in Westminster Abbey. And she was even more deeply touched when a few days later he told her that some of their friends who wished to remain anonymous had made themselves responsible for all the expenses of the Abbey Service as a token of their affection for Lewis.

At the Dean's suggestion it was not to be called a Memorial Service but 'A Service of Thanksgiving for the Life of Sir Lewis Casson', and it was held at midday on 3rd June. The service was beautifully conducted by the Dean and the Precentor, and the Abbey was packed with what seemed to be half the population of London.

Sybil sat between Mary and me, her head held high and her whole personality dominating the crowded Abbey, and wanting so much that Lewis would be proud of her. I'm sure he was. She was superb.

She had asked me to read his favourite poem, Henley's 'Margaritae Sorori', during the service. I had heard Lewis himself read it so very many times, and his voice was in every line of it. It seemed to me that he took over my reading in the Abbey.

> A late lark twitters from the quiet sky
> And from the West,
> Where the sun, his day's work ended,
> Lingers as in content,
> There falls on the old, gray city
> An influence luminous and serene,
> A shining peace.
>
> The smoke ascends
> In a rosy and golden haze. The spires
> Shine and are changed. In the valley
> Shadows rise. The lark sings on. The sun,
> Closing his benediction,
> Sinks, and the darkening air

331

Thrills with a sense of the triumphing night –
Night with her train of stars
And her great gift of sleep.

So be my passing!
My task accomplish'd and the long day done,
My wages taken, and in my heart
Some late lark singing,
Let me be gather'd to the quiet West,
The sundown splendid and serene,
Death.

And later John Gielgud spoke Prospero's speech from *The Tempest*:

Our revels now are ended. These our actors,
As I foretold you, were all spirits, and
Are melted into air, into thin air . . .

When the moment came in the Service for what would have been the Address there was a long silence and then suddenly the organ burst forth with the glorious opening chords of Bach's 'Toccata and Fugue', of which Lewis had once said when asked why he had put it first of his 'Desert Island Discs', 'I think it's the finest music I've ever heard and I'm ever likely to hear.' In the middle of the Service old Basil Dean, one of his earliest colleagues in the theatre, whispered to his companion, 'How Lewis would have loved this superb stage-management.' It ended in the Casson tradition of us all singing 'Now thank we all our God'.

In the months that followed Sybil never flagged. She broadcast, gave recitals and appeared on TV. She was at the opening of the Thorndike Theatre with Princess Margaret and Lord Snowdon on 17th September. She and I travelled to Leatherhead with Larry Olivier in his car, and at the party afterwards no one doubted who was the leading lady of the evening. In early October she played the funny ragged and homeless old creature in *There Was an Old Woman* at the Thorndike Theatre. I don't think it was a very good play and on the opening night hardly anyone of the very distinguished audience took their eyes off Sybil. It wasn't really so much a play as an opportunity for Dame Sybil Thorndike to make a personal appearance in a kind of charade. It was memorable only for her achievement in rising magnificently above and beyond her personal appearance. For myself I remember very little about the play except the sight of Sybil sitting very still at the side of the stage remembering. I wish the play had been a better one, for the character would have made a beautiful swan song for what was almost sure to be, not by any means her last appearance on a stage, but her last performance in a play.

That autumn Patricia and I went back to Australia to sell our house and pack up all our goods and chattels for passage to England. I'm glad that we had made our decision to come back to live in London before the end of 1968. Lewis had been delighted about it and we had talked of plans and organisings. On the day after the auction we wandered through the house soon to be emptied of familiar Casson belongings. In that corner was the armchair where Lewis had held forth about everything under the sun. Over there was the piano that Sybil had played to us. Outside the window was 'Lewis's shed'. Here was the bedroom where Sybil had found Donalbain. Before we left it the two of us once again sang 'Now thank we all our God'.

In London Penny and Tom had found us a house in the same street as themselves in our beloved Chelsea, only a little more than five minutes walk from Sybil in Swan Court. When we got back to London we bought it with the proceeds of the sale of the house that Lewis had helped us to buy in Melbourne. In renovating it we made the ground floor into a little flat with access into the garden. It is there for Sybil if for any reason she ever has to leave Swan Court. We moved into it at the end of the year, and somehow managed to squeeze fourteen of us, including Sybil, into the tiny dining-room for Christmas dinner. And for once, to Sybil's delight, Patricia's and my family were complete. Anthony and Janneke were and are living in Twickenham and early in December had added one more male Casson to the clan in the person of Owen John. Penny and Tom came across the road from their house, Jane had once again flown over from Canada. While we toasted 'All old friends round Walla Burra Crag' Sybil's three great-grandsons slumbered away upstairs in our large double bed.

To all our several and respective joys and delights in June of that year Sybil had been made a Companion of Honour. She went off to Buckingham Palace on her own, and joined forces when she got there with Sir Frederick Ashton and together they received their Companionates from Her Majesty. She didn't tell us very much about it when she got home except to say how kind everybody had been and 'the Queen's an absolute darling, isn't she?'

On Lewis's birthday 1971, we all went to St Paul's Covent Garden, the actors' church, for the unveiling of a memorial plaque to Lewis. The plaque itself is a solid piece of slate that was taken from the slate mines of Blaenau-Festiniog, the place where Thomas Casson the First had taken his bride, Esther, the granddaughter of Wonderful Walker, in 1800, and where she had set up soup-kitchens for her quarriers during the Napoleonic Wars.

The words on the plaque, simply and exquisitely carved by Madge Whiteman, who had acted with Sybil in the early days of the Old Vic, read:

In loving memory of
LEWIS CASSON
Kt., M.C., LL.D., D.Litt.
Actor, Director and Manager
Born 26 October 1875
Died 16 May 1969

What else is Wisdom . . .
To stand from fear set free,
To breathe and wait.
Euripedes

At the head of the plaque is the Casson crest, a bird perched on the battlements of a castle with our motto, *Prosequor alis* – 'I follow on wings', which is what they have both done so splendidly for so long, followed their grail on wings.

I wonder what their grail has been, and whether any of us can discover a hint of it. Years ago Rosemary Leather, Hugh Casson's sister, asked Lewis what to him was the most important thing in life. 'The search for beauty,' he answered. He might have added, though he didn't say it in exactly these words, 'It is the search for beauty that is at once the justification and the motivating force in all our lives.' From this, I believe, came his almost frighteningly high sense of duty. Because nothing is ever as beautiful as it could be, and as it therefore ought to be, there is no time that can be spared for wasting. At times his feeling of the need to hurry amounted almost to a panic. His very walk demonstrated urgency, head slightly bent over to the left and forward, short rapid strides and his right arm, hard and tense, swinging like a piston rod.

But this didn't mean that the sense of urgency entirely dominated his life. When the problems were other people's rather than his own, there was nobody kinder, gentler or more understanding.

Like most sensitive people he didn't laugh prodigally, but when he did he either chuckled unrestrainedly as a gay-hearted boy, or threw back his head and bellowed like a man. I never saw him laugh at anybody or laugh nervously. He gave one the feeling that he believed laughter to be divine and that it was almost blasphemous to use it as a weapon for attack or defence.

Unhappily he never came to terms with old age. The frustration of his deafness, his semi-blindness and his increasing inability to walk during his last years meant that his search had to slow down. He never learnt to sit back and savour the achievements of his life, but was for-ever striving onwards because he didn't think he had achieved any-thing, and there wasn't much time left for real achievement. He felt, with Cecil Rhodes, 'so much to do, so little done.'

Sybil has always had the same sense of urgency, but she has never had the same urge to reform as Lewis. Where Lewis was impatient with himself to the point of feeling guilty, Sybil was astonished that people didn't all feel the excitement of being alive. Her goal has been not to improve them but to help them find excitement and joy in their own lives. Her greatest gift, which she uses assiduously in her profession and out of it, is her ability to be aware of how other people see them-selves, to be aware of each individual's self-image. On the stage she uses it to become and to project the character she is playing, and it is this that has made her a great actress. Off the stage she uses it to play up to the images people have of themselves. She plays instinctively the rôle of the appreciative audience of one, and the one whom the in-dividual wants to play to. She never tries to impress anybody but rather makes each one feel more impressive. If she speaks to a typist then she makes the typist feel that typing is the one activity above all others that keeps the world going. No one has ever been made to feel afraid or insecure by Sybil. Whatever you do, ten minutes with Sybil will make you feel dedicated to it and able to do it better. You always leave her presence feeling more useful, more capable and more enthusiastic than when you came into it.

She is not a saint, as perhaps some people believe, but rather some-one who knows what sainthood would be like (perhaps a little too much influenced by her view of her early ecclesiastical 'heroes' in Rochester). Her endeavour is to model herself on this view and to arrange her life to fulfil it. This is perhaps what makes her love every single person she meets and of course makes her very lovable. Her own self-image, it seems to me, is of a vigorous rebel striving towards a higher image of sainthood, not a rebel saint, but a saint-inspired rebel. She was able actually to live this image in both *Saint Joan* and *Saint Teresa*.

In fact she has been able to satisfy nearly all her needs on the stage – which is a much safer way of doing it than in real life. In a play you are not finally committed to anything, but you can feel and live through every kind of emotion on the grandest scale without having to worry about the dangerous and discordant consequences. And in the last resort isn't that what art is all about – to take the apparently discordant and unrelated bits of life and then to mould and resolve them into a harmonious pattern?

She has never lost any of her childlike enthusiasm and has in this sense remained a child – except in music. Music is something quite apart for her. With music she achieves maturity on a level which most people never reach, and her whole personality seems to take on the wisdom of the ages when she is at the piano. The enthusiasm is still there but it is balanced and controlled by a first-class intellect, which is devoted to music before everything else.

Music is a love that she shared with Lewis. As he said at the beginning of his 'Desert Island Discs', 'Yes (music) has always been part of my life. I've no instrument that I can play, except a very simple one. But music has always been a hobby and an inspiration.' To Sybil it was a profession, which she had to abandon, and also an inspiration.

They shared something else – an arrogance almost amounting to conceit about their health. Because in their youth they had never been ill, it never occurred to them to look after their physical bodies, as Lewis always did with his motor-cars. Bodies were there to drive and to use, and if anything went wrong with them that was something rather shameful that must be ignored. It also meant that there was nearly always an impatience with anybody who suffered from minor ailments. If you were conscious you played your part. If not then, 'How stupid to be ill.' It's a wonderful doctrine if you are fit, as they were, but it meant and means feelings of guilt once more when the tribulations of old age began to afflict them.

Undiminished zest

Reading to Lewis after his sight had begun to fail

By the plaque in the Actors' Church with her great-grandson,
Randal Lewis Casson

When they are considered as a pair, however, which was always how they preferred to be considered, it becomes immediately apparent how they complemented each other. Where Sybil's genuine imaginative appreciation of people tends quite often to make them uncritical of themselves, Lewis tended to make them much too critical of themselves. Sybil makes people believe life is gorgeous, and Lewis urged them to make life gorgeous. Both of them used acting as a tool to bring more people to a state of grace. As a vicar's daughter Sybil used the tool as a means of doing good, and her radiance comes from making people feel good. Lewis was an artisan who used his tools of speech and acting to help people to see the good for themselves. He had a radiance which shone like a beacon when he was in full creative flood and opening doors for people to see the good more clearly.

They had tremendous arguments and rows, but the rows usually happened when one of them had a splendid idea at a time unsuitable to the other. Way back in 1935 when they were going off to Bron y Garth for a quiet holiday together, just after the run of *Henry IV* and Sybil's return from America, Sybil was furious when she found Lewis had asked John Drinkwater to go with them. It had not occurred to him that she would mind, and it so happened she minded very much. 'He seemed rather lonely,' Lewis had said, 'and I thought we could help him.' Another one came, and this was a humdinger, when Jessie Street, the wife of an eminent Australian judge and very left-wing, called on them in London after a trip to Russia in 1961. Patricia was at Swan Court and told me that Sybil was enthralled to learn how utterly and unreservedly wonderful everything was in Russia. Lewis, however, was at his most wicked, and pricked every enthusiastic balloon that was flown with down-to-earth, and for Mrs Street awkward, questions. He did, in fact, wreck the enthusiasm of the evening. As Sybil finally shut the door on Mrs Street, she swung round and kicked the umbrella stand very hard. It was made of glass and shattered into a thousand pieces. Sybil then threw a vase at the wall. Lewis turned to Patricia and said quietly, 'Go and shut the kitchen door or we shan't have any crockery for breakfast!' That really exploded it all, but it ended as all their rows ended, and as most good marital rows do, with Sybil bursting into tears and Lewis putting his arms round her while he made soothing and comforting noises.

Their joint motto, which consciously or unconsciously they spent their lives following, could have been taken from Tennyson's *Ulysses*

> . . . that which we are, we are;
> One equal temper of heroic hearts,
> Made weak by time and fate, but strong in will
> To strive, to seek, to find, and not to yield.

Neither of them has ever yielded and ever since Lewis's death Sybil has continued not to yield. John Carroll has seen to it that the British public continues to have opportunities of seeing and hearing her reciting poetry in various parts of the land. She gave a reading in Westminster Abbey only a few months after Lewis's memorial service there (and when she found in the first few moments that a peculiar echo made her words almost inaudible, she changed her pitch and her phrasing with such subtlety that almost no one noticed it and she got rid of the echo). She has played drums with pop-singers, recited with an orchestra and given a reading at a recital of the West Indian pianist Ian Hall. Rarely, even now, does a month go by without her being heard or seen on radio and television. She is indefatigable and indomitable, and the wicked look in her eye can be conjured forth as quickly as ever to make fun of pomposity and self-importance wherever she meets it.

But few people know that she is seldom free of pain, which she describes as 'like a lot of nagging teeth', from arthritis and sciatica, because she sees to it that people don't find out about it. And somehow, to the astonishment and admiration of us all, she has learnt to live with it, with a courage and forbearance that puts most of us to shame.

In the summer of 1970 while staying with Kiff and Kay she was suddenly taken ill and spent three weeks in the intensive care unit of the Dublin Hospital. Nearly a month later she was put into an ambulance where she remained during the ferry crossing and the drive from Liverpool to London. She was in it from 7 a.m. until 10 p.m. Twenty miles out of London on the M.1 she was met by a police car to escort her in. The ambulance was overdue at Swan Court and we were worried. So I telephoned Scotland Yard Traffic Control – 'There's an ambulance just gone past the patrol without stopping and the boys are after it. I'll phone you back, sir,' said the officer. Five minutes later he came through to me, 'All's well, sir. It's the Dame.' And when they had caught up she had insisted on the convoy's stopping so that the two police officers could be presented to her.

When she reached us she was very tired, very sick and very old, we thought, and we were deeply concerned about her. She was put to bed in Swan Court with a nurse attending night and day. She got rid of the nurse three weeks later and at the end of the month was up and about and trying to organise and arrange not only her own life but everyone else's in the vicinity.

On what would have been Dame Gladys Cooper's eighty-second birthday, Patricia and I took Sybil, now in her ninetieth year, once more to the 'Actors' Church' for the thanksgiving service for Gladys's life. It was a happy service with everyone feeling that Gladys was present, delighted to see all her friends, all the actors and actresses. When it was over, we put Sybil in the car, but couldn't get away because of the crowd. So we opened the window of the car and Sybil, as it were, held court sitting in the car in the churchyard. She saw all her and Gladys's friends and was enchanted. As we finally drove out she turned to us and said, 'What a lovely party! And how much Gladys must have enjoyed it. When's the next Memorial Service?'

Back in December of 1968 Sybil had been asked to talk about Ellen Terry in the series arranged by John Carroll at the National Portrait Gallery. The record of this talk was, I believe, last year's best-selling spoken recording. Patricia, Jane, Lewis and I had sat together in the gallery and listened to her. At one point she quoted Graham Robertson's description of Ellen Terry's arrival at a party, 'She was saying "Now don't you bother about me. I'll just slip in without being noticed and sit down somewhere," a feat which might have been performed with equal ease by the sun at noonday!'

There could have been no better description of Sybil herself. Towards the end with Lewis smiling his delight we heard her speak of a meeting she had had in 1909 with Ellen Terry, who had said, 'And I hear you've married that nice boy Lewis Casson. I'm so glad.'

And so are we.

INDEX OF PLACES, THEATRES
AND SHIPS

Index

INDEX OF PERSONS

345

Index

INDEX OF PLAYS
AND FILMS